BLOOD ORANGES

CONNECTING THE GREATER WEST SERIES

Sterling Evans, Series Editor

Blood Oranges

COLONIALISM AND AGRICULTURE
IN THE SOUTH TEXAS
BORDERLANDS

Timothy Paul Bowman
Foreword by Sterling Evans

TEXAS A&M UNIVERSITY PRESS
College Station

This paper meets the requirements of ANSI/NISO Z39.48–1992
(Permanence of Paper).
Binding materials have been chosen for durability.
Manufactured in the United States of America

∞ ♻

LIBRARY OF CONGRESS CATALOGING-IN-PUBLICATION DATA

Names: Bowman, Timothy Paul, 1978– author.
Title: Blood oranges : colonialism and agriculture in the South Texas
  borderlands / Timothy Paul Bowman ; foreword by Sterling Evans.
Other titles: Connecting the greater west series.
Description: First edition. | College Station : Texas A&M University Press,
  [2016] | Series: Connecting the greater west series | Includes
  bibliographical references and index.
Identifiers: LCCN 2015044744| ISBN 9781623494148 (cloth : alk. paper) |
  ISBN 9781623494155 (ebook)
Subjects: LCSH: Foreign workers, Mexican—Texas, South—History—20th
  century. | Migrant agricultural laborers—Texas, South—History—20th
  century. | Mexican American agricultural laborers—Texas,
  South—History—20th century. | Unfair labor practices—Texas,
  South—History—20th century. | Mexico—Emigration and
  immigration—Economic aspects—History—20th century. | United
  States—Emigration and immigration—Economic aspects—History—20th
  century. | Mexican-American Border Region—Ethnic relations. | Texas,
  South—Ethnic relations.
Classification: LCC HD8081.M6 B69 2016 | DDC 338.1/7431097644—dc23 LC record
  available at http://lccn.loc.gov/2015044744

FOR MY PARENTS, LOIS AND PAUL BOWMAN

CONTENTS

FOREWORD

Before you is an important new book on a fascinating angle of the agricultural history of the bordered region between Texas and northeastern Mexico. *Blood Oranges: Colonialism and Agriculture in the South Texas Borderlands*, by historian Tim Bowman, narrates several stories all under one cover. First, it deals with the history of the citrus industry in the Lower Rio Grande Valley of South Texas, with emphasis on the development of grapefruit and orange orchards there. Thus, the book, as an agricultural and commodities history, contributes significantly to a larger Texas historical literature. That the industry developed in that bordered area of South Texas and the Mexican state of Tamaulipas, and that it was dependent upon a Mexican labor force for its success, however, makes this book an essential addition to the ever-expanding historiography of North American borderlands as well. But it goes geographically further than that, as we learn herein that the developers lured farmers and investors from other parts of the United States, and especially from Midwestern states such as Iowa—by advertising the area's mild climate and year-round growing climate, the proximity to inexpensive Mexican labor, and the cultural exoticness of being next-door to "Old Mexico"—to relocate to the Lower Rio Grande Valley to try their hands at citrus growing on land that very certainly used to be Mexican and more recently had been owned by Mexican Americans. In many ways, then, the orange and grapefruit orchards became a connective force throughout the American West, linking agricultural development in the Valley to a Mexican migrant labor regime, to Midwestern farmers, to markets for citrus throughout the United States, and to competition for those markets with other citrus regions such as Florida and California.

And connections are what this series of books is all about. Bowman's *Blood Oranges* fits to a T as number five in the Connecting the Greater West Series. These books explore new ways in which historians and other scholars are coming to view the North American West, a region that must include the western United States, northern Mexico, western Canada, and the borderlands between the regions. Along with other books in the series, *Blood Oranges* deals with transnational history, immigration, the importance of borders (as permeable in many ways, but intractably cultural and political in others), and how agriculture developed in this natural and political environment. Readers will quickly discern the importance of Bowman's borderlands thesis and analysis as it applies to this bordered region of the Greater West.

Not all of the borders here are between nation-states. There is a very important dimension of interior separation between ethnicities that Bowman explores here, framed and analyzed via the theory of internal colonialism. One of the book's many strengths, this methodology of seeking to explain racial dynamics between Anglo-Americans, Mexican Americans, and ethnic Mexicans goes far in helping us see just how difficult race relations were at this time and place and how they played out through citrus development in the Valley. As Bowman calls it, citrus was none other than a "colonial crop." The result for many years was yet another example of how the Jim Crow South had permeated Texas and crossed the color line from injustices against blacks to those against Mexicans and Mexican Americans. *Blood Oranges* shows very clearly that industrial citriculture development in Texas was only possible through the internal colonization of a subjected people, a people whose history needs to be told and is told here.

To accomplish these goals, Bowman relied on a wide array of archival and other primary sources to research the many dimensions of the history of oranges and grapefruit in the Lower Rio Grande Valley. Combined with a thorough exploration of secondary sources, this book reflects the author's knowledge of his craft. And as such, the book not only represents fine agricultural and borderlands history, but also is an important contribution to American labor history, race relations history, Texas history, and the greater history of the American West—a region so inherently characterized by the many types of layered themes presented in *Blood Oranges*.

—STERLING EVANS
University of Oklahoma

ACKNOWLEDGMENTS

I first became interested in the history of the Lower Rio Grande Valley and greater South Texas many years ago when I was a graduate student at the University of Texas at Arlington. One day, while spending a few hours digging through the university's magnificent Texas Labor Archives, my naive younger self became sincerely shocked when I discovered the level of abject poverty under which ethnic Mexican migrant laborers in deep South Texas toiled during the 1960s and '70s. Some of these people lived in the most rundown shanties that I had ever seen. What was even more shocking to me was that large corporate agribusinesses, many of which could undoubtedly have afforded to pay a fair living wage, employed the vast majority of these impoverished people. After taking in all of this, I next proceeded to write a master's thesis about labor organizing along the Texas-Mexico border during the mid-twentieth century. When I finished, however, I was left with one important question: How did such a society, where wealthy corporate agribusinesses could get away with employing a totally impoverished and almost entirely ethnic Mexican labor force, come to exist in the modern United States? To put it more directly: What had happened in the South Texas borderlands to make such a situation possible? The book that you hold in your hands is my answer to this important question.

Many wonderful people have provided me invaluable assistance along the way. My dissertation advisor at Southern Methodist University (SMU), Ben Johnson, has provided years of encouragement, help, and support and a great sense of humor. Ben's expertise in the history of South Texas, as well as the greater US-Mexico borderlands, is unmatched, and it has been my great pleasure to study with him. Ben has devoted countless hours of his personal time even beyond graduate school in helping me launch my career. I owe him an immense debt of gratitude for his guidance and friendship.

I am also deeply indebted to my other mentors from graduate school. John Chávez has been a friendly supporter of mine since I first arrived at SMU. His intellectual influence on me, which includes his vast expertise on Mexican

American history and internal colonial theory, will be apparent to anyone who reads this monograph. Sherry Smith has also been a constant source of knowledge, friendliness, and support, and my years of study under her at SMU have helped me realize that I can be a historian equally of the US-Mexico borderlands and the US West at the same time. Finally, I am forever indebted to the late David Weber, the world-class historian of the Spanish borderlands in North America, who taught at SMU. Dr. Weber always took time out to have lunches with me, informal chats about research and being a historian, as well as just life in general, despite the fact that I was not one of his dissertation advisees. I will forever be in debt to Dr. Weber for his gentle guidance, for the consistent example that he set of how to be an excellent scholar while maintaining a sense of deep personal humility, and finally, for the confidence that he placed in me at a time when I had precious little confidence in myself.

My good friend Sterling Evans at the University of Oklahoma has been a supporter of mine since my early days as a PhD student at SMU. When Sterling offered me the opportunity to publish this book in the Connecting the Greater Wests Series at Texas A&M University Press, for which he is series editor, I jumped at the chance. I owe Sterling a very large debt for the positive impact that he has had on my career. I would also like to thank Mary Lenn Dixon and Shannon Davies, both of Texas A&M University Press, for giving me the opportunity to publish my book. I have also benefited tremendously from the help of Jay Dew, who took over at Texas A&M University Press upon Mary Lenn's retirement.

Several scholars at other institutions have also taken time out of their busy schedules to talk to me about history, answer emails from me, collaborate on conference panels and projects, or simply give me their genuine enthusiasm and support. I am grateful to Miguel Ángel González Quiroga at the Universidad Autónoma de Nuevo León, José Ángel Gutiérrez at the University of Texas at Arlington, Rob Johnson at the University of Texas–Pan American, Karen-Beth Scholthof at Texas A&M University, John Weber at Old Dominion University, and Robert Hutchings at Carnegie Mellon University. I give special thanks also to Roberto Treviño, recently retired from the University of Texas at Arlington, for first introducing me to South Texas history many years ago.

I have been fortunate enough to be a part of the goings-on at SMU's Clements Center for Southwest Studies for a number of years. I am deeply indebted to Ruth Ann Elmore as well as now-retired Andrea Boardman. I worked particularly closely with Andrea and Ruth Ann during my final year at SMU, when I was fortunate enough to be named the William P. Clements Dissertation Fellow for the 2010–11 academic year. Andrea and Ruth Ann went above and beyond in helping me have a productive fellowship year, and I will always appreciate their willingness to help and accommodate me with everything that I needed.

I would also like to thank the anonymous donor who established the William P. Clements Dissertation Fellowship. The generous financial support that came with that fellowship gave me an entire year for further research, writing, and thinking about and honing my arguments. My dissertation and the resulting book became immeasurably better thanks to the donor's generosity. I would also like to thank the Clements Center for providing me with a research travel grant during the spring of 2008 that helped kick-start my dissertation research.

A number of wonderful archivists lent me their help and expertise. I would like to thank the following people: Joan Gosnell, Russell Martin, and Cynthia Franco at the DeGolyer Library at SMU; George Gause, Virginia Gause, and Janette García at Special Collections at the University of Texas–Pan American; Sandra Rexroat at the Jernigan Library at Texas A&M University–Kingsville; Adán Benavides at the Nettie Lee Benson Latin American Collection at the University of Texas at Austin; the staff at the Dolph Briscoe Center for American History at the University of Texas at Austin; the staff at the Bancroft Library on the campus of the University of California, Berkeley; and the staff at Special Collections at the University of Texas at Arlington.

I presented portions of this book at numerous conferences and public forums, where I received invaluable feedback that helped shaped my thinking about the history of South Texas and the nearby border. I would like to thank all of my session chairs, copanelists, and session attendees at meetings of the following organizations that I have attended since 2008: the Texas State Historical Association, the Rocky Mountain Council for Latin American Studies, the Western History Association, the Agricultural History Society, the Newberry Library Seminar series for Borderlands and Latina/o Studies, and SMU's Graduate Humanities Research Day.

My friends and colleagues at West Texas A&M University have played an integral role in helping me turn my dissertation into a book. Not only did my colleagues in the history department take a big chance in hiring an unknown borderlands historian like myself, but they have also provided encouragement, support, and a wonderfully collegial atmosphere along the way. I would like to thank Byron Pearson, Jean Stuntz, Chris Johnson, Steve Bogener, Marty Kuhlman, Bryan Vizzini, Paul Clark, Elizabeth Clark, Bruce Brasington, Matt Reardon, Wade Shaffer, Jessica Mallard, Brian Ingrassia, Kris Drumheller, Krista Troy, Ashley Eller, and Carmen Terrell, all of whom have made the WTAMU history department a truly wonderful place to work. It is an honor to be able to call all of them my friends and colleagues. I would also like to thank the many wonderful and intellectually engaged students in the WTAMU history department who have kept me on my toes as I finished this book.

I made a number of wonderful friends in graduate school whose friendship and support made dissertating and starting an academic career all the more enjoyable. I would like to thank Christy McPherson, Todd Meyers, George Díaz, David Rex Galindo, Gabriel Martínez-Serna, Alicia Dewey, John Gram, Matt Alexander, Luis García, Jenny Seman, Matt Babcock, Houston Mount, Paul Santa Cruz, Scott Cassingham, Carla Mendiola, Anne Allbright, Anna Banhegyi, and Paul Nelson.

No historian can engage in any long-term project without the loving support of friends and family. My mom and dad, Lois and Paul Bowman, have been unendingly supportive and encouraging of me as I chased my dream of getting a PhD in history and becoming a professor. Aside from their emotional support, my parents provided occasional financial assistance along the way as well. My parents also instilled in me, from a young age, a passion for thinking and speaking for myself. I love my mom and dad dearly. Thanks also to Jenny, Beth, Shaun, Celeste, Matt, Josh, Robbie, Meagan, Sarah, Aiden, and Jackson for putting up with my history talk and bad jokes over the years.

NOTE ON TERMINOLOGY

Readers will find a number of words and phrases in the following pages that might at first glance be confusing, so I provide this note on my admittedly imperfect adoption of certain terms. I use the appellations *ethnic Mexican* and *South Texas Mexican* somewhat interchangeably to refer to anyone of Mexican descent, regardless of nationality. Similarly, *Mexican* and *Mexican national* refer to someone born in Mexico or claiming Mexican citizenship. Mexican American refers to anyone of Mexican descent born in the United States, while *Tejano* is also occasionally used in reference to someone of Mexican descent born in Texas or having lived for an extended period of time in the state. I utilize the overly simplistic and admittedly problematic words *Anglo, Anglo American*, and white in reference to people who might more accurately be referred to as having European or Euro-American heritage in the region; I do this not to over-generalize, but simply because these terms were commonly used in post-1848 South Texas in reference to Caucasian and European-descended Americans in the region. I differentiate between *grower* and *farmer* in order to distinguish individuals who grew citrus (the growers) from people who grew other types of crops. Finally, for the purposes of this book, *South Texas* refers to the regions between the Nueces River and the Rio Grande, stretching north and west to Zavala County (including several subregions such as the Lower Rio Grande Valley and the Winter Garden District).

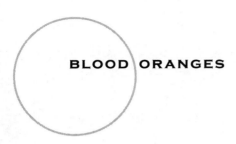

BLOOD ORANGES

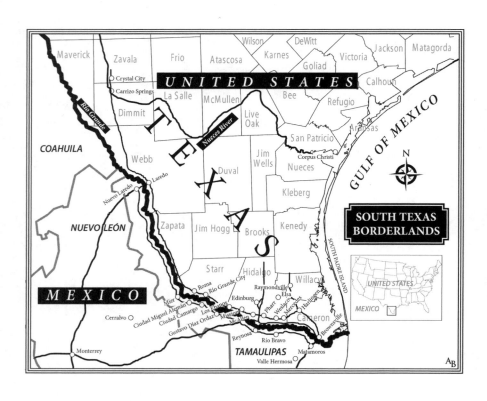

Introduction

The story of agriculture in the Lower Rio Grande Valley
is principally a story of great expectations, which at best
came to moderate realization and at worst were dismally
unsuccessful.[1]

Carrol Norquest recalled feeling as if he had arrived in "a
new world" when he stepped off the train in Edinburg, Texas, in 1922. He had
come from Kansas following his parents, who had bought a farm from a local
land development company. Norquest arrived feeling "hungry, filthy, [and]
unshaven" when two uniformed men in a Model T Ford motioned him over as
soon as he hit the streets. The following exchange took place:

"Where you from, boy?"
"I'm from Kansas."
The officer seemed surprised. He took a closer look at me. He hadn't
expected me to speak English, I decided later.
"Where're you going?"
I pointed. "Over there to get something to eat. Why?"
"We just wanted to know." He shoved in the clutch and the jitney started
to move.
"Are you Texas Rangers?" I asked quickly.
"Yeah, we're Rangers." He pulled down the throttle, gunned the old con-
traption, and left.[2]

After discussing the incident with some friends, Norquest came to realize
that the two men were not Rangers at all. His friends also explained that the
men had indeed mistakenly thought that he was a Mexican.[3] What the two
men would have done with Norquest had he been a Mexican remains a mystery. What is beyond any doubt is that Norquest—himself a future *patrón*-style
boss of Mexican migrant workers in Texas's Lower Rio Grande Valley—little
understood the legacy of Anglo–Mexican relations in the area. His parents, who
had preceded him to the Valley, might already have been told by other Anglo
Americans, however, that Mexicans were a reliable, simplistic, yet unevolved

race of people whom they could employ on their new farm in the South Texas borderlands.

The following is a book about how Mexicans and Mexican Americans in the South Texas borderlands became marginalized and increasingly discriminated against over the course of the twentieth century. My thesis is a simple one: twentieth-century South Texas history unfolded the way it did because Anglo-Americans colonized the region after 1848. As such, *Blood Oranges* is a work of conceptual history: it conceptualizes South Texas as an internal colony of the United States and argues that this was the primary driving force behind Anglo–Mexican interchange, farming, and economics and what I call the negotiated conquest of the region's ethnic Mexican inhabitants, whereby the people native to the South Texas borderlands actively asserted themselves against colonialism and the changes that Anglo-American colonization brought with it to the region. Ultimately, as in the typical story of colonialism throughout world history, the post-1848 colonizers of the South Texas borderlands sought to extract one valuable resource from the region: the labor of human capital. All other considerations remained secondary.[4]

Blood Oranges is thus different from studies of the South Texas borderlands that came before it, perhaps most notably David Montejano's classic *Anglos and Mexicans in the Making of Texas*, in that *Blood Oranges* conceptualizes the region's history through one specific paradigm—that of internal colonialism. I do not necessarily intend to argue that the internal colonial model should be resurrected as applicable to the experiences of all ethnic Mexicans in the US Southwest or all minorities throughout US history, as some previous scholars have attempted to argue. Likewise, this book does not emphasize racism or the overcoming of Anglo colonialism and racial oppression simply for their own sakes. *Blood Oranges* rather quite simply emphasizes that the driving force behind economics, politics, social ills, conflict, and compromise in the region was South Texas's colonization by Anglo-American farmers. As such, the South Texas borderlands region shares much in common with other parts of the American Empire during the Gilded Age and Progressive Era. Furthermore, the conquest that ethnic Mexicans asserted themselves against bears striking resemblance to formal settings of settler colonialism in which many people throughout the world during the nineteenth and twentieth centuries found themselves. The advancement of the US-Mexican border south and west into the former Mexican North is thus a crucially important chapter in the larger history of colonialism in the modern world.

Indeed, *Blood Oranges* argues that the marginalization of ethnic Mexicans in the twentieth-century South Texas borderlands occurred because white

Americans, mostly from the US Midwest, colonized the region in the early twentieth century. The typical story of colonialism—one in which Western nations colonize spaces inhabited by racial or cultural Others and subsequently marginalize those groups within their own homelands—thus took place, but this time just within the contiguous borders of the United States.

Perhaps the greatest historical significance of South Texas's colonization is the intellectual construct of the notion of South Texas as the Tejano homeland. For the reconstruction of notions of homeland, particularly in this book's final chapter, I employ the framework of scholar Anthony Smith, who argues that "the 'territorialization of memory' . . . turns particular territory into ancestral homeland." I also employ the framework of geographer Alexander Diener, who argues "that territorial belonging is not a simple relational juncture between ethnicity (or any other identity) and place—but a daily performance of history, economics, politics, and socio-cultural behaviors that is affected by and in turn affects the border." As such, the Chicano Movement's flourishing during the late 1960s was the fundamental act in constructing South Texas as the Tejano homeland, and it came at least partially in response to the regional history that unfolded previously. Furthermore, South Texas's colonization by Anglo-Americans after 1848 can best be understood as a larger part of the territorialization of this borderlands space. As Anssi Passi writes, territorialization can best be described as "an ideological practice and discourse that transforms national spaces and histories, cultures, economic success and resources into bounded spaces" while in the process, in the case of post-1848 South Texas, marginalizing the region's native inhabitants. As such, it makes sense that groups facing such marginalization—in this case South Texas Mexicans—would eventually emphasize the reclamation of homeland. As will be seen in later pages, ethnic Mexicans in the region reimagined South Texas as the Tejano homeland—a subsection of the larger Chicano homeland of Aztlán, the so-called lost land of the Aztecs—while forcefully emphasizing civil rights and belonging inside of the South Texas internal colony. Significantly, this story adds colonialism as an important mechanism in the lived experiences of South Texas borderlanders. Americans' participation in colonialism or empire building in the western United States is a part of the hidden history of colonialism that cannot be ignored.[5]

Generally, the South Texas borderlands story goes something like this: Anglo-American farmers and land developers transformed much of South Texas from its past as a Mexican ranchland into a commercial citrus and agricultural sector. These people, in turn, who brought commercial agriculture to the border also brought with them prescribed roles that they forced onto the region's native inhabitants. Despite the fact that ethnic Mexicans had controlled the region for over a century, the region's natives found themselves forced into the roles of workers and servants for new Anglo farmers and power brokers. Just like ethnic majorities in colonial Africa, South America, the Middle East, and Asia, ethnic Mexicans in the twentieth-century South Texas borderlands were a colonized people, oppressed by a foreign power that knew and cared little for them or their history of leading independent lives in their homeland. Colonization, then, explains the well-documented and high degree of racism that South Texas Mexicans toiled against for the majority of the twentieth century. The rise of South Texas commercial agriculture—perhaps most notably Texas's newly founded citrus industry—came at a steep cost for ethnic Mexicans throughout the region.

The South Texas borderlands have been noted as the Texas-Mexican homeland by several scholars who are cited within the pages of this book. As such, *Blood Oranges* essentially tells the story of that homeland's modern rebirth in the minds of many of its inhabitants. One scholar notes that "a stronghold of seventeen counties, which were part of a thirty-two county South Texas Mexican homeland in 1990, constituted a nearly contiguous territory from Del Rio to Brownsville along the Rio Grande, with interior points at Frio, Jim Wells, and Kenedy Counties." Colonialism made no distinctions with regard to class. As historian Cynthia Orozco notes, the small but well-documented Tejano middle class in early-twentieth-century South Texas was colonized along with the much larger ethnic Mexican working class. The establishment of Anglo-American enclaves on top of Mexican spaces was not lost on locals. Brownsville, for example, which became one of the major cities in the region, was founded by a wealthy Anglo merchant named Charles Stillman, who angered locals by placing the town on disputed land claimed by people from Matamoros, the city across the river in Mexico.[6] The Mexican-born population of the larger region tended to congregate around specific areas, such as Brownsville, McAllen, and Laredo. Anglos, this book will show, became attracted to this foreign space on American soil specifically because this concentration of racial Others living in an area outside of the first-world economy begged for exploitation by profit-minded farmers and business owners. The concentration of Mexican immigrants in Brownsville and McAllen, combined with those areas' potential for commercial agriculture, also made them particularly attractive destinations for Anglo colonists in the first part of the twentieth century.

Blood Oranges thus places ethnic Mexican–Anglo relations at the border within the larger context of a colonization movement that happened inside the borders of the modern United States (though, clearly, just barely inside them). In doing so, this book reorients the marginalization of ethnic Mexicans away from a simple narrative of white American racial hierarchy and toward a more complicated story of how whites benefited from marginalizing a group that was native to a borderlands space politically belonging to the United States. Historical actors who advocated for the better treatment of South Texas Mexicans throughout the latter part of the twentieth century, such as J. T. Canales, José Ángel Gutiérrez, and United Farm Workers officials who worked in the Lower Rio Grande Valley —worked in direct response to the changes brought about by white Americans who colonized the region, mostly in the early twentieth century. *Blood Oranges* will also show that the actual international borderline itself played an indispensible role in helping these colonizers accomplish their objectives.

I should again note that it is not my intent for *Blood Oranges* to prove or defend any specific theoretical models for understanding racial difference; however, the efficacy of the internal colonial model in allowing understanding of what happened in South Texas during the twentieth century is quite clearly apparent in the narrative I relate in this book. Because of this, *Blood Oranges* does not fit neatly within current trends in borderlands or Chicana/o historiography, where internal colonialism finds admittedly few adherents. The story that follows, then, is a narrative history of white Americans' colonizing of a large chunk of what historically constituted a Mexican space, which happened to be on the Texas side of the modern US-Mexico border.

Internal colonialism is an intellectual model for understanding the history of racism in modern nations. One theorist writes that internal colonialism "seeks to explain the subordinate status of a racial or ethnic group in its own homeland within the boundaries of a larger state dominated by a different people." This theoretical model first became popular during the 1960s, although numerous scholars later dismissed the concept during the 1970s and 1980s. The research for *Blood Oranges*, however, clearly shows that white Americans knowingly came to South Texas in the early twentieth century as colonizers and in many cases formulated new identities based on such self-perceptions. Internal colonialism's better-known counterpart, overseas colonialism, had simultaneously influenced Americans at the time to support colonizing far-flung places such as the Philippines. The Philippines would serve as a stepping-stone, it was thought, to tap into the vast sums of wealth that Chinese consumers could bring to US manufacturers. Imperialists at the turn of the twentieth century were more than happy to exploit Filipinos, whom many Americans considered biologically inferior to themselves. Internal colonialism thus has a clear relationship to the better-explored phenomenon of settler colonialism, which contributed to the rise of the United States and England as premiere world powers during the late nineteenth and early twentieth centuries.[7]

Even beyond comparisons between internal colonialism and overseas colonialism, similarities between experiences of world powers as they colonized stateless people inside of international borders abound throughout world history. Historian Steven Sabol argues, for example, that the processes whereby the Americans colonized the Great Plains and the Russians colonized the Kazakh Steppe during the nineteenth century are remarkably similar, not to mention the outcomes of said colonization for the Kazakhs and the Sioux. Land developers' and farmers' desires to make money and exploit the allegedly uncivilized ethnic Mexicans in South Texas demonstrate, then, a clear link between popular ideas about international relations and internal social relations during the dawn of the age of US imperialism.[8]

At least one proponent of internal colonialism argues that the theoretical model is applicable to understanding the history of South Texas and the US Southwest after the US-Mexico War of 1846–48. Historian John Chávez writes that the "displacement and outnumbering" of South Texas Mexicans by Anglo colonists during the early twentieth century "had all the makings of the larger internal colony" of the US Southwest. Furthermore, the establishment of commercial farming in South Texas, as well as the armed rebellion of some Mexican Americans against Anglo-American dominance in the region during the irredentist Plan de San Diego uprising of 1915–16, Chávez argues, parallels the larger experience of colonialism and armed resistance against colonizing powers throughout world history. In addition, ethnic Mexicans on both sides of the border have held the proposition that the US Southwest after 1848 was Mexico's lost northern borderland, with the borderline itself representing something that became "immoral and irrelevant." Furthermore, Chávez argues that internal colonialism's "emphasis on conquest and incorporation" challenges borderlands historians to resolve the situations of indigenous or hybrid populations who were colonized inside of the contiguous bounds of modern nation-states. Notably, this model also includes Mexican citizens whose lives became affected by the borderline after 1848.[9] *Blood Oranges* shows, then, that borderlands history and the creation of internal colonies contiguous to modern first-world nations are inextricably intertwined.

Another immediate link between South Texas and the larger colonial paradigm can be seen in the experiences of Anglos and Mexicans in Mexico itself during the same time period. One historian argues that Americans lauded the progress and modernization of Mexico that apparently came at the hands of British and American capitalists, who considered themselves biologically and culturally superior to Mexicans. Similarly, white Americans in the South Texas borderlands saw themselves as more progressive and advanced than ethnic

Mexicans and thus considered the latter to be both exploitable and "improv-able," which explains the numerous commentaries by colonizers about their presence in the region being a source of uplift for the "Mexican race." Land developers' self-conscious marketing of the South Texas borderlands as a col-onized space, as well as new growers' attempts to realize the vision of colonial-ism, will be explored throughout *Blood Oranges.*[10]

Despite some scholars' call for a revival of internal colonial theory, a num-ber of theorists have raised heavy criticism of the model.[11] Nevertheless, this book will display the model's utility for understanding South Texas through-out the twentieth century. Historians and social theorists, I argue, dismissed the model's utility before it could be fully tested in various settings throughout world history. *Blood Oranges* will also show how colonialism affected the lives of ethnic Mexicans and Anglos in South Texas.

South Texas's colonization happened in several distinct stages. After the region's military and political conquest at the end of the US-Mexico War in 1848, Anglo-Americans slowly began to use the US political and legal systems to consolidate control over the area's most valuable asset: its land. Still, how-ever, some natives did retain political and economic power. Although Anglos came to dominate most of South Texas, ethnic Mexicans did maintain politi-cal, social, and economic power in some enclaves. The wave of white Ameri-can demographic and economic dominance of the region, which began with the arrival of the railroad in 1904, tapered off in the middle of the 1930s when local small farmers could no longer compete in large numbers in the commer-cial agricultural marketplace. Nevertheless, ethnic Mexicans in South Texas remained among the most impoverished people in the United States at the end of the twentieth century, even with the increased educational and job opportu-nities for later generations that began to accrue over time by virtue of living in a developing part of the United States.[12]

Although South Texas's physical colonization ended with the movement of thousands of farmers into the region in the 1910s and 1920s, oppressive race relations and extreme poverty persisted over the course of the twentieth cen-tury. In more traditional settings of settler colonialism, whole populations relocated to foreign lands for the purpose of making money; similarly, in the wake of the railroad's arrival in 1904 thousands of Anglo farmers from the US Midwest relocated to South Texas in order to become commercial farmers and live in communities that development companies intended to support the region's burgeoning commercial farming industries, most notably its cit-rus industry. These new Anglo arrivals also perceived the South Texas border-lands as a wholly foreign space on a wild frontier. They consistently referred to themselves as Americans and all Hispanics as "Mexicans," denoting the perceived foreignness of the region's native inhabitants whether they were actually born in Texas or not. Aside from being separated geographically into segregated communities that met for the most part only in South Texas's agricultural fields, Anglos and ethnic Mexicans in the region were also separated by an ocean of language, culture, and customs that, in the beginning, few people dared to cross. Such has been the case in numerous colonized societies, in the traditional sense of the phenomenon, the world over.[13]

The importance of all of this, of course, is that colonization shaped the very lives and identities of both Anglos and ethnic Mexicans in the South Texas borderlands over the course of the twentieth century. Not only did Anglos self-consciously negotiate wholly new identities as colonizers by relocating to the region, but colonization also forced responses to the oppression of ethnic Mexicans inside of a space that had been only nominally inhabited by Anglos since the middle of the nineteenth century. Thus, not only did South Texas's internal colonization shape relations between Anglos and ethnic Mexicans long after the colonial movement ended at mid-century, but also certain aspects of colonial relations—namely, the relationship between Anglo agricultural growers and Mexican migrant workers—survived. By subtracting the narrative of colonization from a narrative of the South Texas borderlands' twentieth-century history we not only lose an understanding of how Anglo–Mexican relations functioned in one of the Chicano Movement's epicenters, but we also lose the origins of modern agricultural relations between white growers and ethnic Mexican migrant workers.[14]

As mentioned previously, the looming presence of the US-Mexico border undergirded colonial-style relations. Numerous aspects of South Texas's colonial system depended on the border and its ability to create a huge reserve labor force across the river in northern Mexico. It comes as little surprise, then, that this particular iteration of internal colonialism existed just miles within the borders of the United States. South Texas had indeed previously been a thoroughly Mexican space before the influx of Anglo-Americans, but the history of the border as a lawless and contested space in the nineteenth century after the US-Mexico War also gave boosters an inroad into selling the vision of colonialism to US farmers. As will be described later, lawlessness also allowed the Anglo newcomers to identify as part of a legacy of Anglo imperialism and adventurism in the US West that made colonizing South Texas an exciting prospect, one in which Anglos could follow in the footsteps of the ubiquitous nineteenth-century "pioneers."

The border is also important to the story of commercial citrus and agriculture in deep South Texas for several reasons. First, the geography of commercial agriculture relied heavily on the border and the Rio Grande. Not only did the river provide near-perfect conditions for the large-scale implantation of irrigated agriculture, but, like other local agricultural enterprises, the citrus industry's very existence relied on the large pool of cheap laborers who could easily cross the border to escape the poor conditions inside Mexico. Second, the border's perceived exoticism helped lend to the colonial project an aura of other-worldliness that made the entire commercial citriculture and agricultural enterprises more of a pioneering undertaking than they might otherwise have been. Some borderlands scholars have characterized the US-Mexico border as having magnetic qualities that have attracted people from both sides of the divide; such was clearly the case with the role of the border in developing South Texas's citrus and other agricultural industries, for Anglos and Mexicans alike.[15]

Land developers and growers in South Texas also manipulated the border for their own purposes. For ethnic Mexicans in the region, the border had not mattered much prior to the twentieth century. Historical geographer D. W. Meinig argues that the Lower Rio Grande Valley was "essentially an extension of Mexico," being linked to the south bank of the river by economic relationships, labor commuting, schools, newspapers, and familial and social life. It was for this reason, aside from Anglos' racist characterizations of ethnic minorities in the United States, that Anglo newcomers to the region were essentially able to ascribe to all Mexicans and Mexican Americans in the region the all-inclusive identity of "Mexican." Despite the existence of numerous transborder commuters and field laborers, Anglos rarely acknowledged the existence of a Mexican American population in the region—unless it suited their own particular needs to do so. Ethnic Mexicans were, in almost all cases, simply referred to as Mexicans, thus being considered natives in this foreign region, until growers realized that recognizing the "wetback" status of undocumented immigrants made them in particular even more exploitable than local workers. Thus, the border served the important purpose of allowing Anglo farmers to control their labor forces while the colonists themselves still enjoyed the advantages of technically living inside the United States. The region's variation of colonialism, then, while technically existing inside the United States, was both domestic *and* international at the same time. The US-Mexico border, in South Texas, at least, cut straight through a previously Mexican space—a fact that Anglo-American colonizers consciously exploited.[16]

The irony of colonialism in South Texas is that, for small growers, it became self-defeating. Although the mostly Anglo growers and Anglo-owned agribusinesses began pushing many of the original colonists out of business by midcentury, the seeds of discontent that the colonial system had sown among Mexicans and Mexican Americans in the region had contributed directly to the rise of activism from the late 1920s through the 1960s and '70s, thus making it more difficult for Anglo growers to exploit Mexicans and Mexican Americans without people in the rest of the United States taking notice. Nevertheless, the brutal reality of the colonial structure would remain for countless people in the region, who, into the twenty-first century, still struggled against institutional racism and discrimination as well as the persistent commercial agricultural structure that continued to depend on farmers' ability to pay their workers subsistence wages and keep them in a constant state of poverty. Later generations of ethnic Mexicans in the region undoubtedly benefited from exposure to better job and educational opportunities as the area became more fully economically incorporated into the United States. But the colonial relationship set in place in the early twentieth century led ethnic Mexicans in South Texas to rank among the poorest, least educated, most unhealthy, and most exploited people in the United States by the middle of the twentieth century. Clearly, the legacy of colonization in the South Texas borderlands was a brutal one.[17]

Blood Oranges is informed by several interrelated historiographies. Numerous historians have documented anti-Mexican treatment in places such as South Texas. One important work on Anglo–Mexican relations that addresses the US-Mexico border and the larger US Southwest is Rodolfo Acuña's *Occupied America: A History of Chicanos*, a survey-style text inspired by the Chicano Movement that addresses Anglo maltreatment of Mexicans and Mexican Americans. Acuña argues that Chicanos suffered under occupation of the border region at the hands of the US government, and Anglo treatment of Mexicans "ranged from paternalism to racism." Arnoldo de León also published two groundbreaking studies on Anglo racism and the mistreatment of Mexicans and Mexican Americans in Texas in particular. Social historians' focus on Mexican and Mexican American histories came as a much-needed response to the earlier Anglo-dominated histories of the US Southwest that ruled the region's historiography up to the 1960s and '70s. These Anglocentric works typified the earliest Anglo-dominated histories of Texas that were common during the first half of the twentieth century, characterizing Anglo-Americans as heroes and leading pioneers in the vast western wilderness.[18]

Blood Oranges marks a departure from the other leading studies of the South Texas borderlands region. The most influential study of the region is arguably David Montejano's classic *Anglos and Mexicans in the Making of Texas, 1836–1986*. Montejano, a historical sociologist, examines conflict but also the overwhelming sense of compromise that developed between Anglos and ethnic Mexicans in what he would describe as the "nation building" project of twentieth-century Texas. As such, *Blood Oranges* challenges Montejano's work by arguing that the imposition of colonial power was indispensably prominent in shaping the modern South Texas borderlands. *Blood Oranges* also makes Anglo-American historical actors in the borderlands (mainly boosters, agrarian colonists, and politicians) come alive, whereas Montejano relies more on structural changes in South Texas to drive his narrative. My study also adds a layer to the story of Anglo–Mexican interaction in the borderlands by examining, in part, Anglo identity development and linking it to popular notions about race, imperialism, and the US West during the first half of the twentieth century.[19]

Still other historians have analyzed the social conditions that led to Anglo–Hispanic violence in early-twentieth-century South Texas borderlands. James Sandos and Benjamin H. Johnson are notable among those who have studied Mexican and Mexican American resistance to Anglo racism, violence, and general maltreatment. Johnson's book, a pioneering study of racial politics in the South Texas borderlands, explores how the region's native inhabitants transformed from asserting themselves as the armed protectors of Mexican rights into Mexican Americans who emphasized the channels of legal protest to defend their rights as American citizens. By focusing on the conflict and oppression in the region that survived well past the 1920s, *Blood Oranges* places Mexican American politics (as well as its later, more militant iteration during the Chicano Movement of the late 1960s and early 1970s) into a larger temporal context—that of Mexican American politics as a direct response to South Texas's early colonization during the 1910s and '20s.[20]

Finally, this book will also address current developments in the historiography of agriculture and particularly commercial citrus. A number of recent books have been published on the history of citrus in California. Noteworthy among these is Douglas C. Sackman's *Orange Empire*. Sackman's study of the California orange industry, however, is an industrial history of orange growing in California at the turn of the twentieth century. *Blood Oranges* builds on the scholarship of Sackman and others by providing the first major study of citrus in the South Texas borderlands, which rank among the most prominent citrus-growing regions in the United States. Although I do not focus solely on citriculture throughout the book, *Blood Oranges* identifies the Texas citrus industry, which rose to prominence in the 1920s, as the perfect entry point into studying broader issues of racial difference and colonization in a modern borderlands setting.[21] My study builds on this and the larger historiography of citrus by taking the study of citrus outside the bounds of California. Surprisingly, no major studies of Florida or Texas citrus have been undertaken in recent years, making the citrus-related concerns raised by the above-mentioned historians transferable to the growing regions of these two under-studied agricultural sectors. This historiographical trend leaves open the possibility that understanding different regions might lead to the illumination of different historical experiences that happened in separate but similar regions.

What follows revises previous histories of South Texas while questioning the basic functions of Anglo–Mexican relations in the region throughout most of the twentieth century. Put simply, this book answers several fundamental questions: Where did the well-documented anti-Mexican racism of South Texas come from? What identities developed in the region? How did the process of Anglo-American colonization cause misery and toil for countless ethnic Mexicans during the twentieth century? Consequently, *Blood Oranges* will show that South Texas Mexicans shared much in common with colonized people the world over during the twentieth century. By reorienting the discussion of Anglos in South Texas away from their previous characterizations as simple racists and recasting them as colonists in a once Mexican space inside of the borders of the United States, this study emphasizes the importance of understanding borders and borderlands to historians of imperialism and race relations.

Blood Oranges is divided into six chronological chapters that examine the Anglo-American takeover of South Texas and its effect on Anglo–Mexican relations over time. Chapter 1 examines the larger context of South Texas's history as a contested space between peoples and nations. Essentially, the region has been a space over which different groups, empires, and nation-states have competed and laid contesting claims as far back as the early Spanish colonial period. Chapter 2 examines land boosterism during the early twentieth century, when Anglo-Americans began moving to the South Texas borderlands en masse. I argue that examining booster literature reveals the larger vision that Anglo-Americans had for their new farming society on Mexico's doorstep. Anglos' attempts to grapple with this vision and make it a fundamental social and cultural reality are key components to understanding the complex discriminatory relations that developed between Anglos and ethnic Mexicans on the Texas side of the border for the remainder of the twentieth century.

The next two chapters examine various aspects of life in the new white South Texas farming communities. Chapter 3 examines the nascent citrus industry as a lens into the new Anglo South Texas of the 1920s. A distinct Anglo-American culture in the South Texas borderlands manifested itself around commercial citrus. This chapter argues that growers' implementation of their new industry helped reinforce their identities as rulers at the top of the local racial hierarchy. Chapter 4 delves specifically into the functions of white supremacy in the new South Texas, and in it I extensively use some of the original research of the famous agricultural economist Paul Schuster Taylor, who conducted numerous oral interviews with Anglo growers and farmers in South Texas communities during the late 1920s. Unbeknownst to Taylor, the ideas about race that whites expressed to him were the results of the region's colonization.

Chapter 5 argues that it was during the Great Depression that Anglo South Texans began to see the first major cracks develop in their new borderlands society. Nevertheless, Anglos suffered from the Great Depression less than ethnic Mexicans, who themselves became the unwitting targets of a crisis in confidence among Anglos at the local level. Finally, chapter 6 explores the ways in which growers began to see the original vision of their internal colony face previously unforeseen challenges. During the middle of the century, corporate agribusiness came increasingly to push small growers in South Texas out of business. Additionally, Mexicans and Mexican Americans more forcefully rejected colonialism; negotiating control over parts of the region came in the articulation of a sense of belonging in the South Texas homeland. Ultimately, labor and Chicano Movement activism came as a localized response to the particularly harsh conditions under which Mexicans and Mexican Americans had lived in South Texas for decades.

Although the attempt to re-create something resembling mainstream white America along the Texas-Mexico border quickly fell apart at midcentury, the legacies of colonial marginalization continued to influence Anglo–Mexican interaction in the South Texas borderlands through the end of the twentieth century. Anglo-Americans at the beginning of the twentieth century learned of the potential benefits that marginalizing ethnic Mexicans could bring to themselves. Understanding the colonization of the South Texas borderlands in the modern period will help Americans learn from the mistakes of the past and overcome the acute racism and national exceptionalism that still exist within the United States today. With the current wrangling and debates over undocumented immigration and the wholly negative ways in which many Americans conceptualize the southern border, it is quite clear that we still have much to learn.

CHAPTER ONE

Border Colonies

Mexicans, Anglos, and the South Texas Borderlands from Ranchland to Commercial Agriculture

My advice to anyone who wants to close the border and get them Messkins out is this: *don't dare start counting how many of your words are Latin, Baby.*

—LUIS ALBERTO URREA[1]

The South Texas borderlands have long been a contested space, a place in between peoples, empires, nations, and cultures. While the boom in citrus growing during the 1920s as well as the subsequent rise in Mexican and Mexican American activism mark the region's transformation from a rural US-Mexican hinterland into an increasingly modernizing space, a brief look at the region's history prior to the 1900s helps explain the origins of the colonialism that overwhelmed the area throughout the twentieth century.

Beginning with the arrival of Spaniards into Indian-controlled territory in the sixteenth century and ending with American political and economic incorporation of the region, South Texas—again, the area extending from the Rio Grande, from the river's mouth to about Laredo, north to the Nueces River—is a landscape over which people have clashed, struggled, and competed for centuries. In an article in the *American Historical Review*, historians Jeremy Adelman and Stephen Aron argue that once Euro-American empires ceased competing over certain North American lands and gave way to nation-states establishing modern borderlines, the "peoples in between" subsequently lost the ability to play competing imperial powers against one another for their own benefit. When the US-Mexico War ended in 1848, the people of South Texas—primarily, Mexican Americans and Mexican nationals—still wrestled with competing power claims. Eventually, but not until the early twentieth century, an Anglo-American colonization movement took hold throughout much of the region. That movement of white Americans to the South Texas borderlands and its implications for Mexican–Anglo relations just north of the border throughout the twentieth century are the primary focus of this book.

But the movement of Anglo Americans to South Texas in the early 1900s was only the latest in a long history of local power struggles. People have been mixing, cooperating, and clashing over the region for centuries.[2]

The Spanish Frontier and the Making of the Texas-Mexico Borderlands

The first glimmers of European colonialism arrived in what would later become South Texas during the sixteenth century. The earliest written record of the area comes from the famous Spaniard Álvar Núñez Cabeza de Vaca. Stranded in North America after getting lost in Florida and wandering through what would become the US Southeast, Cabeza de Vaca and his small band of explorers set off southward toward the Rio Grande and New Spain early in the summer of 1535. The Spaniards faced many days of fleeing from bands of Gulf Coast Indians who had the reputation of being unwelcoming. The South Texas landscape in those days was "a lush tapestry of brush lands and prairies, graced with thickets of mesquite, prickly pear, and creosote." Cabeza de Vaca himself later complained of the difficulty of traveling near what became the Rio Grande: "The land is so rugged and impassable, that many times when we gathered firewood in the dense thickets, when we finished taking it out we were bleeding in many places from the thorns and brambles that we encountered, for wherever they ensnarled us they broke our skin."[3]

Some local Indians helped the Spaniards procure food. Natives of the region subsisted on the fruits and boiled pads of the prickly pear cactus. Cabeza de Vaca also wrote that local natives—two groups of whom the Spaniards referred to as the "Maliacones" and the "Arbadaos"—were warlike and cunning. Other scholars have noted, however, that the groups Cabeza de Vaca and his men encountered mostly consisted of detribalized fragments defeated in wars with more powerful groups to the north and west. Cabeza de Vaca reported living among these people at one point for two weeks in a large settlement of forty or fifty dwellings.[4]

The Indians in the area did not have dense population numbers, as did the Aztecs or Mayas. The whole region also remained an afterthought to the Spaniards for some time, as the Indians of the northern frontier posed little threat to central New Spain to the south. While the Spaniards made several forays into New Mexico in the seventeenth century, the more eastern part of their northern frontier in Texas remained a provincial backwater until much later. The Spaniards became interested in colonizing Texas during the latter part of the seventeenth century, when French traders and explorers made inroads into the territory from the east and along the Texas Gulf Coast. The spike of Spanish interest in colonizing Texas, then, mostly came as defensive posturing against perceived French interest in the region. Still, the colonial Spanish population throughout Texas remained small. By 1760 about 580 people lived in San Antonio, 350 at Los Adaes in eastern Texas, and 260 at La Bahía along the coast. These figures do not include mission Indians. Most of the Spaniards living in Texas were either soldiers or civilians who depended on the military in order to subsist. Numerous presidios (military forts) as well as mission outposts were intended to fortify the region and convert local Indians to Catholicism. In short, Texas as a whole remained more of a military outpost during this early period than a place where Spanish colonists thrived in any significant numbers. Spanish missions focused more on converting Indians and less on promoting civilian population or economic growth. Few Spanish settlers enjoyed a stable or profitable existence in Texas during the eighteenth century.[5]

The same reason that the Spaniards began to populate Texas—defense against outside imperialism—brought them to settle the future Texas-Mexico borderlands during the mid-eighteenth century. Spaniards founded the colony of Nuevo Santander, a region along the coast of the Gulf of Mexico that included parts of the modern Mexican state of Tamaulipas, the Lower Rio Grande Valley, and up the coast to the Nueces River, to thwart the English from seizing unpopulated stretches of the coastline. Unlike the earlier colonization of Texas, for which the Spaniards relied primarily on missionaries and soldiers, Nuevo Santander was settled with mestizo or mixed-race families and some converted Indians. Between 1749 and 1755, head colonist José de Escandón settled six thousand people in Nuevo Santander, founding twenty-three towns and fifteen missions.

Like Cabeza de Vaca and his men before them, these settlers encountered numerous Indian groups. Exact demographic statistics are difficult to establish. Escandón estimated a population of roughly twenty-five hundred Indians in the Lower Rio Grande Valley in the middle of the eighteenth century. Unlike many other Spanish leaders who advanced onto New Spain's northern frontier, Escandón reportedly dealt respectfully and fairly with local Indians, who, in turn, appear to have reacted favorably to him and the Spanish colonists. In truth, Escandón and his colonists posed little threat to the local natives. Many of the largest towns on both sides of the modern border, such as Laredo, Camargo, and Reynosa, were all founded during this period of relatively peaceful colonization. The original Spanish settlers began grazing cattle, sheep, and goats. The crown also granted to many of the original settlers *labores*, or agricultural fields, adjacent to the towns proper as well as the grazing fields. Livestock, nevertheless, especially cattle, would remain the primary economic staple for roughly the next 150 years until white Americans began converting the lower Valley and other parts of South Texas into a commercial agriculture sector. Foreign commerce, particularly in the towns on the south side of the river, also played an important role in establishing the region's economy and would remain a permanent cog in the region's economic machine.[6]

Over time the crown struggled to bring new settlers into Nuevo Santander as well as the rest of Texas, relying instead upon natural increase to buoy population numbers. Some local Indians undoubtedly assimilated into the population, too, which helped sustain the towns. But in the early 1800s colonial officials began to worry anew about foreign designs on their northern frontier, this time from the rapidly expanding United States. After Mexico gained its independence in 1821, Anglo Americans swept into East Texas and the Gulf Coast, establishing legal settlements under the invitation of the Mexican government. In retrospect, it seems counterintuitive of the Mexican government to invite white Americans to settle in the state in order to maintain control over Texas, but with no significant numbers of Mexican citizens willing to move north into Texas, in large part because of the nearly constant threat of raids from the marauding Comanches and their allies, there was little else that the government of the fledgling nation could do. For a time the plan worked. But by 1835 the white American population of Texas was far greater than the state's Mexican population.[7]

Time would soon reveal the disastrous consequences of the Mexican government's inviting the then expansion-minded Americans into the province. An alliance between Anglo Americans and Cherokee Indians in East Texas led to an uprising called the Fredonia Rebellion in 1826, which the Mexican military successfully quashed in the town of Nacogdoches later that year. Trouble again stirred in Texas nine years later. What began as the Texas colonists' participation in what can most aptly be called a "states' rights" revolt against the increasing centralization of governmental power in Mexico City, during which the American transplants received some crucial Tejano support, ended with the Texans declaring and gaining their independence in the spring of 1836, whereby the rebels established a federal republic.[8]

The Texas Revolution led directly to some of the first widespread anti-Mexican sentiment among white Texans; many looked back to the famous battle of the Alamo and the subsequent massacre at Goliad as evidence of a treacherous nature that they argued was common among Mexicans. Threats and rumors that Mexico would retake Texas in the 1840s only served to further inflame anti-Mexican sentiment throughout the Texas Republic. Relations between the two groups, in fact, would sour considerably by the mid-1840s. In print literature and letters home to relatives, Texans wrote of their state as a wild place where vigilante rule and deceitful Mexicans reigned supreme. White Americans who came to Texas later in the nineteenth century, then, came with preconceived notions of what life in Texas was like. Racial stereotypes against dark-skinned people that were common in the nineteenth-century United States became blended with preexisting racist stereotypes against ethnic Mexicans that dated as far back as the 1830s.[9] Whatever relative racial harmony under which Anglos and Mexicans coexisted in Texas during the 1820s was fast eroding.

In the meantime, Mexican nationals squabbled among themselves over who should control the region between the Rio Grande and the Nueces River. Both the Mexican and Texas governments laid claim to the area. A rebellion among ethnic Mexicans broke out against the Mexican government along the Rio Grande in December 1838. This rebellion, which was partly motivated by the success of the Texas Revolution, served not only to interrupt trade and commerce in the region, but also to embolden the Comanches of western Texas to swoop down into the region and raid towns on both sides of the river. Thus, members of "la Comanchería" represented a foreign power invading what was now a series of long-established mestizo lands, adding yet another level to the overlapping claims to this frontier hinterland. The uprising would eventually be put down by federal troops in the fall of 1840. Both the Mexican government and the Texas Republic kept their claims to the Trans-Nueces intact (Mexico claimed the Nueces River as its northern boundary, while Texas claimed the Rio Grande as its southern boundary), although the white Texan presence south of the Nueces River was practically nonexistent during that period.[10]

The importance of Texas independence for the history of conflict over the border region cannot be understated.[11] This squabbling over the disputed boundary lasted through Texas's republic period and after its annexation by the United States in 1845. The US government immediately took up the cause of the Rio Grande as the southern border of Texas, invading Mexico in 1846 and using the subsequent treaty of Guadalupe Hidalgo in 1848 to permanently affix the river as the border between the two nations. The fact that this war took place under the watch of US President James K. Polk, who was an ardent expansionist, is too much of a coincidence to be ignored. Polk clearly provoked the war in order to protect Texas and gain a large chunk of Mexico for the United States.

It is important to note that throughout the period of Texas independence and during and after the US-Mexico War, South Texas remained populated almost entirely by ethnic Mexicans and a few Indians. South Texas was still very much a Mexican space, despite American geopolitical claims to it. The coming wave of Anglo-American sentiment after 1900 is best understood as people from one particular nation colonizing what was literally a conquered foreign territory. The few Anglo-Americans who did come to the region between the Nueces and the Rio Grande during the mid-nineteenth century, however, were a mix of soldiers, war veterans, criminals, and merchants looking for economic opportunities as well as some southern planters. Descendants of the original Mexican settlers of the region would eventually find themselves caught up in a transnational tug-of-war. When the dust settled from the US-Mexico War and the inked dried on the Treaty of Guadalupe Hidalgo, the Mexicans of deep South Texas, as in the greater part of what became the US Southwest, became "foreigners in their native land."[12] A complicated series of economic, political, and cultural conflicts and exchanges ensued in these borderlands after 1848.

The newly established borderline affected the lives of Anglos and Mexicans in South Texas alike. Numerous historians have commented on the border's tendency to disrupt the lives of nearby inhabitants. Now, for example, Mexicans who had spent their lives crisscrossing the Rio Grande and establishing social, cultural, and economic networks on both sides of the river found themselves caught in between two modern nation-states. Certainly, Mexicans and Indians found it increasingly difficult as time passed, particularly during the twentieth century, to lead transborder lives, especially when the US federal government intruded with increased immigration restrictions during the 1910s and 1920s. But the border also lent itself to the creation of a new colonial layer in South Texas in two distinct ways. First, the border cut a geographic line on the map that forced Mexicans to choose between citizenship in the United States or in Mexico. If they chose the United States, they chose to join a nation in which they would be exposed to relations with an ethnic majority that considered them racially inferior. White Americans could now take advantage of economic opportunities in a previously foreign space in which the American legal and political system directly applied. Also, because of the border's creation, Anglo-Americans gained the ability to see the region's future in new ways. This vision of the wild, untamed frontier was based largely on white American imagination: a fact that would become increasingly apparent after commercial agriculturalists began employing Mexican labor and shutting ethnic Mexicans out of the modernizing South Texas society a few decades later.[13] Establishing farms close to the border allowed white Americans the unique ability to be able to exploit both ethnic minorities in the United States and foreign nationals in another country.

Not only were ideas about internal social relations with ethnic Mexicans and international relations with non-Western nations similar in the minds of

Anglo-Americans, but the new white colonists in South Texas were also at the cutting edge of the US colonial experience by virtue of living along the border. A colonial structure with international reach that was based on a static racial hierarchy slowly came into being on Mexico's doorstep. Historian Gilbert G. González argues that during European powers' colonization of Africa, Asia, and India during the late nineteenth and early twentieth centuries, the United States initiated its own colonial venture in Mexico, establishing an economic empire and social hierarchy with white American businessmen and politicians at the top and Mexicans in a subordinate position. The implications of this structure for race relations, migratory labor, and class mobility inside the United States during the remainder of the twentieth century are profound and cannot be understood without taking into account Americans' views of nonwhites the world over at the dawn of the twentieth century. This spreading of negative racial stereotypes can be seen from the late nineteenth century through the World War I era, when the United States began expanding overseas to become a commercial and military world power. Not coincidentally, then, it was during that same time period when white farmers colonized deep South Texas, took advantage of the nearby border as a source of cheap labor, and pushed the region's native inhabitants to the margins of the new local society, run mostly by and for the benefit of Anglos.[14]

The population south of the Nueces River immediately following the US-Mexico War remained mostly ethnic Mexican. Though establishing exact population figures is difficult, one historian reports that in 1850 there were approximately twenty-five hundred Anglo-Americans and eighteen thousand ethnic Mexicans living between the Rio Grande and the Nueces River.[15] As the nineteenth century progressed, however, competing cultures and economic systems increasingly met and clashed in the new political reality that was Anglo-American South Texas. As with traditional westward movement earlier in the nineteenth century, white Americans sought for themselves and their families new opportunities that, overwhelmingly, were economic. A preoccupation with economic success, strengthening racial segregation, and notions of western pioneering combined to create a larger self-conceptualization of white Americans' collective mission on Mexico's doorstep.

The initially small number of Anglos in the region meant that land generally remained in the hands of Mexican Americans for several decades after 1848. In Hidalgo County, for example, in the Lower Rio Grande Valley where the South Texas citrus industry would eventually be concentrated, Mexican American ranchers were the primary landholders until about 1870. In order to gain influence in the region, the mostly male Anglo newcomers during the

second half of the nineteenth century required a certain degree of accultura-
tion into local Mexican society. Simply learning Spanish and how to behave
properly in polite society was not enough. Some converted to Catholicism,
became godparents to Mexican children, or married into prominent local
families. Many children born during that period in the border's history could
claim a Mexican mother and an American or European father, but they also
spoke Spanish and considered themselves Texas Mexicans culturally. Still,
wealthy ranchers would have retained far more influence in the new South
Texas than landless Anglo laborers during this early period of Anglo-American movement into the region.[16]

Early anti-Mexican racism in South Texas, in the words of one scholar, generally "accommodated the rich." Anglos seeking to make a life in the borderlands needed to maintain positive relations with local Mexican power brokers.
Thus, anti-Mexican sentiment was at first somewhat muted. White American
newcomers treated the Mexican upper classes well because they needed local
connections in order to establish themselves in business and political ventures.
This phenomenon was not unique to the Texas-Mexico borderlands; in places
such as southern Arizona, for example, the earliest white entrants often inter-
married into elite families when the relationship was mutually beneficial (aside
from, of course, simply a loving union). As in the case of South Texas, mar-
riages between white men and Mexican American women eventually plummeted in southern Arizona once increased numbers of more marriageable
white women moved into the region. For the South Texas borderlands, the
increasing scarcity of intermarriage in the early twentieth century could serve
as a barometer for the deterioration of Anglo–Mexican relations throughout
the region more generally. A sustained Mexican–Anglo "middle ground" simply had no way of surviving in South Texas.[17] As this book will later show, white
American farmers had an economic incentive to increase the marginalization
of Mexicans to new heights once farming became economically viable. Finding
common ground with ethnic Mexicans simply brought little reward to Anglos
in borderlands spaces as the 1900s wore on.

Despite the tendency of early anti-Mexican racism to be muted, white
Americans in the region did not necessarily treat ethnic Mexicans well immediately following the US-Mexico War. Frederick Law Olmsted, during his trav-
els through Texas in the 1850s, observed that "the Mexicans were treated for a
while after annexation like a conquered people." Their problems were many:

> Ignorant of their rights, and of [English], they allowed themselves to be
> imposed upon by the new comers, who seized their lands and their property

without shadow of claim, and drove hundreds of them homeless across the
Rio Grande. They now, as they get gradually better informed, come strag-
gling back, and often their claims give rise to litigation, usually settled by a
compromise.

Most adult Mexicans are voters by the organic law; but few take measures
to make use of the right. Should they do so, they might probably, in San Antonio, have elected a government of their own. Such a step would be followed,
however, by a summary revolution.[18]

The situation for ethnic Mexicans in the South Texas borderlands was
clearly similar to that of conquered or colonized people in other situations.
Marginalized in almost every sense from the end of the war until after the turn
of the twentieth century, the future for the region's native inhabitants looked
increasingly bleak after 1848.

This incipient anti-Mexican racism in the region grew more intense as the
nineteenth century wore on. Most of the white Americans coming into Texas
during the late nineteenth century had never before had any contact with Mexicans. As historian Arnoldo de León notes, Anglo attitudes toward ethnic Mexicans remained overwhelmingly negative, often pathologically racist, into the
twentieth century.[19] Such racism grew worse and became endemic over time.
Original sources from the border region during the period support De León's
contention. Rev. Daniel D. Baker, who was probably the first Protestant missionary to reach the Lower Rio Grande Valley, traveled northwest from the
mouth of the river to Roma, recording his impressions of the region along with
his vehemently racist views of the locals whom he encountered during his trip.
In a letter to his daughter in 1849, he wrote:

> You never saw such a country in all your life! Not a single forest tree between
> this and the "mouth," nor for hundreds of miles around, except what is called
> the mesquit [sic], the ebony, and the marmosa, which in general are about the
> size of ordinary peach trees—and no houses—not even log-cabins! Here
> and there at great distances, you find a ranche [sic], a kind of shanty or hovel,
> made of cane, and thatched with a kind of grass, or rush; a miserable shelter.
> These wretched hovels are filled with lazy Mexicans, who lounge about from
> one year's end to another, doing almost literally nothing at all, except gam-
> bling. . . . I did not like to mingle with such a crowd of Mexicans.[20]

Melinda Rankin, an Eastern missionary who came to Brownsville in
1852 in part at Baker's suggestion to establish a school and convert Mexican

Catholics to Protestantism, reflected on her own views as well as those of her contemporaries:

> A new sensation seized me when I saw, for the first time, a *Mexican*, a representative of the nation for which I had entertained such profound interest. I did not feel, as many others have expressed, that the *sight* of a Mexican was enough to disgust one with the whole nation. A heartfelt sympathy was revived, not by the prepossessing exterior, surely, but because a priceless soul was incased in it for whom the Savior had died.

Rankin's ethnocentrism thus appeared less severe than what was common among her contemporaries. She continued, commenting on her young Mexican students in Brownsville:

> My school prospered, and I was encouraged in finding the Mexican children susceptible of moral and mental improvement. Many of them I found addicted to the vices peculiar to their race; but, by proper instruction, I soon observed a decided change. I was told by an American gentleman, who had considerable acquaintance with Mexican character, that stealing was inherent among these people, and could not be eradicated. My experience entirely disproved this assertion, as after a few months, children, who would take things which did not belong to them, became convinced of the error, and entirely abandoned the practice.[21]

The anti-Mexican views of Rankin and her early contemporaries were clearly quite pronounced. As American missionaries and teachers crossed the border into places such as Matamoros and Monterrey in the late 1860s and 1870s, such anti-Mexican sentiment and cultural imperialism became increasingly common. Cross-cultural violence also occurred further south on Mexican soil, such as a massacre of Anglo and Mexican Protestants by Mexican Catholics in Acapulco in the mid-1870s. Such violence did not sit well with the Mexican government, either. Recent scholarship has shown that Mexico sought to secure its northern border through the development of the region with repatriates from the United States after 1848, which, in theory, would also stem the tide of Mexican migration north of the border into the United States.[22]

Anglo American maltreatment of Mexicans and Mexican Americans on the Texas side of the border led to a number of violent outbreaks. In July 1859, Juan N. Cortina, witness to the pistol-whipping of a defenseless friend by a

Brownsville city marshal, shot the marshal and began an anti-American rebellion. Cortina's rebellion grew in popularity among local Mexicans and Mexican Americans who hoped to curb Anglo racism in the region as well as the loss of Mexican-owned lands. Support for Cortina also came from Mexican merchants on the south side of the river who were frustrated with American merchants' competition and tendency to participate in illegal smuggling. Deeper than surface issues about land, this and other conflicts also centered on important phenomena such as citizenship and belonging in the transborder region. Although US forces drove Cortina into Mexico in the early 1860s, *Cortinistas* participated in numerous raids across the border throughout the 1860s and '70s.[23]

A cycle of excessive violence and reprisal killings ensued over the following decades. Many ethnic Mexicans resisted the new racial dominance, viewing Anglo-Americans as ruthless colonizers and land-grabbers. De León argues that the Cortina rebellion led Anglos to further popularize among themselves images of Mexicans as cruel, lawless thieves. Throughout the 1870s and '80s the Texas Rangers terrorized Mexicans and Mexican Americans in the Lower Rio Grande Valley and other places, even crossing the border and committing untold depredations on Mexican soil. They operated, according to De León, "on the premise that the more fear they created, the easier would be their work of subduing the Mexican raiders." Historian Andrew Graybill directly correlates a "strong current of white racism" with the excessive violence of the Texas Rangers, who were "beholden only to the demands of a narrowly self-interested state government" and thus free to use lethal force to subjugate ethnic Mexicans across South Texas.[24]

But the region's violence was not only related to racial oppression. The entire area between the Rio Grande and the Nueces River had by the 1870s become internationally known as a place of excessive violence and lawlessness. An investigative committee sent by the Mexican government to assess the region's propensity for crime (primarily, in this case, transborder livestock theft), noted that some of the worst dregs of American society as well as Mexican criminals fleeing the long arm of justice had descended upon the area since the drawing of the borderline in 1848. Part of the reason for this stemmed from the widely held perception that South Texas was a frontier society in the iconic style of the Old West, where lawlessness was a valid path to gaining wealth. The "thirst for wealth" had become such a strong passion, the Mexican investigative committee argued, that once cattle theft became less common by the 1870s as a result of the depletion of the region's livestock, the unscrupulous elements of South Texas society set their sights on one another's land.[25] It was this same impulse—the desire to gain wealth based on acquiring valuable land—from which the later commercial agriculture would spring. Thus, the land colonization movement that would begin in the early 1900s rested heavily upon the earlier trajectories of brutal violence and land acquisition that had marred the region throughout the second half of the nineteenth century.

Even while boosters attempted to sell visions of South Texas as thoroughly peaceful and modern during the late nineteenth and early twentieth centuries, cross-cultural violence continued. Catarino Garza's rebellion in 1891 began as a movement to overthrow Mexico's Porfirian government from the northern borderlands; it transformed over time to include a protest movement against the mistreatment of ethnic Mexicans on US soil. The last major open rebellion in the South Texas borderlands was the irredentist Plan de San Diego uprising, which occurred from 1915 to 1916, several years after the upswing in Anglo-American movement to the region began. This final violent uprising of the borderlands Mexican population took place while development companies had just started to sell land in the area. A dissident group hoped to overthrow white American rule and break the Trans-Nueces region away from the United States. Some fighting between rebels and American troops did take place, but the real significance of the revolt was in the brutal response of the local power structure and the Texas Rangers, who wantonly killed and murdered perhaps thousands of ethnic Mexicans in the form of reprisal killings. Although most land boosters dismissed the rebellion (as well as the nearby Mexican Revolution) as an aberration, it clearly fit into a larger trend of ethnic Mexican resistance to white American dominance that dated back to the mid-nineteenth century. The real end result of the Plan de San Diego, however, was that it ushered in a new structure for Mexican–Anglo-American relations. Subsequently, according to one historian, "by the end of this period, almost half of the Mexicans living in Hidalgo and Cameron counties had fled northward or gone back to Mexico. Some never returned, and the invading Anglos consolidated their power in the region once and for all."[26] It was as if a decades-long war of conquest had finally ended.

One early 1900s land developer, railroad contractor J. L. Allhands, believed the Plan de San Diego rebellion actually had a positive effect on local life. Allhands noted that there was a "silver lining in the war cloud" in terms of bringing a railroad and, thus, modern life to South Texas. The railroad, which did not arrive in the region until 1904, "had been built before the country could support it, and prior to the movement of troops and supplies, it was starving. The rush of new business was, in reality, the renaissance of this property and put it on its own feet for the first time." Thus, the new era of agribusiness,

colonization, and settlement was born out of the bloodshed of the Plan de San
Diego revolt and the lives of perhaps thousands of South Texas Mexicans who
had been violently murdered by local law enforcement and the Texas Rangers.
"The bandits were thrown back," Allhands concluded, "and the Federal troops
soon liberated the border country."[27] Indeed, with South Texas now "liberated" of its troublesome native Mexican element, a new future awaited.

In all fairness there were of course some Anglo-Americans who lamented
the racist treatment of ethnic Mexicans. One of those was local lawyer Frank
C. Pierce, who in 1917 published a small book titled *A Brief History of the Lower
Rio Grande Valley*. Pierce had been a longtime resident of Brownsville, and
his book came at a time of the celebration of the Lower Rio Grande Valley's
settlement and development by Anglo-Americans. Pierce's main goal was to
inform the greater United States about the Valley: "The present generation of
Americans has known very little of that part of their country which lies along
the Rio Grande," he wrote, "and has had no realization of the ofttimes stirring
scenes which have been enacted along their southern border." But Pierce was
at least somewhat empathetic with the plights of native South Texans. After
discussing a series of conflicts between the Rangers and various outcasts and
lawbreakers, Pierce concluded: "The author cannot let pass this opportunity
to say that during the bandit raids of 1915 many evil influences were brought to
bear to clear the country of the Mexicans. To his knowledge more than one was
forced to flee and to convey his chattels before going." Pierce recognized that,
despite the Rangers' alleged heroism from the organization's inception in the
nineteenth century, the anti-Mexican reprisals during the Plan de San Diego
uprising were excessive.[28]

Pierce represented an older generation of white South Texans who, despite
the recorded elements of racism in the region, often attempted to live on something of an equivalent basis with the region's native inhabitants. But local whites
and ethnic Mexicans would be forced to deal with one another under different
terms after the end of the Plan de San Diego rebellion in 1916. Though common ground would occasionally be found, the two groups generally remained
at odds as the twentieth century wore on. Importantly, some level of cooperation in modernizing the region did take place: the colonization of South Texas
could not have taken place without the countless Mexicans and Mexican Americans who took low-paying jobs as laborers, primarily in the agricultural sector.
This hardly represented a truly cooperative effort in which all parties involved
benefited equally, but it is important to note that the Anglo colonizers could
not have achieved any level of success without Mexican and Mexican American
workers and power brokers. Even marginal cooperation, then, came at a steep

price. Nevertheless, whites and ethnic Mexicans remained deeply intertwined in one another's lives over the course of the twentieth century. Anglo-American newcomers sought to carve out an American farming empire in the region, and Mexicans and Mexican Americans, with few other opportunities remaining, provided the blood, sweat, and tears to make that vision a reality.

1904: The World Rushes In

The post-1848 colonization of South Texas essentially amounted to an invasion of a Mexican pastoral society by an American capitalist one. Although ranching continued to flourish in some areas—as well as the practice of *patronismo*, whereby Mexican laborers worked out of a sense of loyalty to their paternalistic employers—anti-Mexican sentiment dominated the parts of the region where the coming farming boom would take place. Ultimately, the newcomers hoped to carve a new society out of the South Texas brush, one in which small-scale commercial farming would become an economically viable undertaking. These Anglo newcomers conceived of themselves as modern colonizers and pioneers bringing American civilization into an allegedly wild and untamed region.

The modern period of the Valley's colonization can be divided into two distinct periods. The first, when Anglo-Americans migrated to the Lower Rio Grande Valley in increasingly large numbers, took place from 1904 until the end of World War I. The second period consisted of the region's agricultural boom, which lasted from the end of the war into the mid-1930s. Most of the newcomers were Anglo midwesterners, but several hundred thousand Mexicans also crossed the border to gain employment, mostly on local farms. These two primary groups collided in the South Texas borderlands during the first few decades of the twentieth century. Land speculators founded new "island communities" on the distended frontier that local growers and businessmen would work quickly to integrate into the mainstream US economy.[29] Toward that end, however, the new business and landowning elites needed to establish a region in which colonists and offsite investors could be assured of economic stability and comfortable living conditions. It was planned that farmers would take over the region; a large part of these "farmers," however, can actually be more aptly understood as commodities speculators who were part of a leisure class; some of them did not even live in the area. Newly established communities, in the vision of local town planners and land speculators, would include the creature comforts of modern society but also the familiarity of rural America. To build such a society, the area needed certain means for transportation but also places in which new settlers could live. An entirely new society needed to be formed.

The vision for a new society on the border would not be possible until the banner year of 1904. On July 4 of that year, no less, workers completed the extension of the first rail system to enter the Lower Rio Grande Valley— the St. Louis, Brownsville, and Mexico Railway. The line was an extension that connected Brownsville to the Corpus Christi terminal of the Missouri-Pacific railroad system. The railway, however, preceded the establishment of a strong regional economy as well as any sharp increase in population. One historian argues that "great expectations preceded the railroad everywhere" that it went in the nineteenth- and early-twentieth-century US West. As one Valley resident said at the time, the railroad "had to create its own traffic and commerce." Indeed, it would prove to be the defining moment in opening South Texas to the rest of the United States. The success of farming and the railroad in the Valley also spurred similar processes of colonization throughout other parts of South Texas, particularly in Zavala and Dimmit Counties.[30]

The railroad came at the vision of a handful of local Anglo ranchers and power brokers who had long thought that the Lower Rio Grande Valley's great potential still lay hidden under the vast ranching enterprises that they had established or taken over since the US-Mexico War. These men considered their own ingenuity and economic prowess vital to unlocking the modern potential of this historically Mexican space. This new vision and its implementation thus marked a turning point in the region's history. About 1900, businessman and railroad promoter Uriah Lott, along with Texas railroad magnate B. F. Yoakum, sought to connect the Valley by railroad to both the United States and Mexico. The group intended the new railway to extend from Chicago to Brownsville and then to Tampico in the Mexican state of Tamaulipas, which would be the end of the line. The later extension to Tampico after the track's arrival at Brownsville would have to be abandoned, however, because of political instability caused by the Mexican Revolution. Any setback in making a transborder rail system was not a concern in 1903, however, when the St. Louis, Brownsville, and Mexico Railway became chartered. A list of its original incorporators and board of directors reads like a "who's who" of powerful South Texas ranchers and land men. Among them were Robert J. Kleberg, head of the massive King Ranch; Robert Driscoll Jr., a wealthy banker, land speculator, and booster from the Corpus Christi area; the aforementioned Lott; John G. Kenedy, a powerful rancher and member of the King Ranch legacy; James B. Wells, a powerful local Democratic machine boss and politician; and finally, Caesar Kleberg, rancher and nephew of Robert J. Kleberg. Included with these well-known figures were several other less prominent local men. The company was to maintain the line and its Valley branch, which started about thirty miles north of Brownsville and extended through Hidalgo County and into the southeast corner of neighboring Starr County, constituting a total distance of about two hundred miles. Not coincidentally, the future farming empire of the region, including the citrus industry that would rise in the 1920s, would be concentrated in Hidalgo and Cameron Counties along the original branch of the rail line. Colonizing the Valley with Anglo-Americans was a conscious and deliberate effort. The railroad represented a direct connection from the core part of the American industrial metropolis into this "wild" borderlands space.[31]

Although it is true that the railroad was largely brought to the region at the behest of white American power brokers (only one of the incorporators of the railroad was an ethnic Mexican), it should be noted that a number of Mexican Americans were important in bringing the railroad to the region. South Texas was not awash with public land; as such, the railroad required a large amount of private donations of land for its completion. About one-third of the private land donated to the company came from Hispanic-surnamed individuals, including prominent local residents such as Francisco Yturria, the largest remaining Mexican American rancher in the region, and Brownsville merchant and banker J. H. Fernández. For their complicity in bringing the railroad (and, by proxy, their encouragement of the settlement of new Anglo-Americans steeped in the ideals of racial hierarchy), these prominent ethnic Mexican residents drew the violent wrath of the Plan de San Diego rebels in 1915 and 1916. The region's native population was unforgiving to their brethren who had allegedly contributed to the abject misery and marginalization of the poorer masses.[32]

New opportunities arose for the rich and powerful in the wake of the railroad's arrival. Some were philanthropies that undoubtedly benefited South Texas Mexicans. Henrietta Chamberlain King, widow of the powerful South Texas rancher Richard King, donated forty thousand dollars for the establishment of a school building for Mexican American children in the newly founded town of Kingsville and also gave generously to local religious establishments. According to J. L. Allhands, King exhibited an "eagerness to make the lot of the Mexicans better." This school, which was called the Texas-Mexico Institute and located five miles south of Kingsville, was a Presbyterian mission school whose primary purpose was to Americanize Mexican American boys. King's progressive vision for her town was one in which moral uplift as well as education were both paramount, although the education of local children was of course to remain a segregated enterprise. The Americanization of Mexican boys through education served to deepen Anglo-American domination of the region by placing upon Mexican Americans a subordinate social distinction and implying the necessity of their becoming like Anglo-Americans. Such race-based philanthropy was common in South Texas during the early twentieth century as well as in the greater United States during the Progressive Era.[33]

Other prominent locals began to act upon the attention that the railroad brought to the Lower Rio Grande Valley, hoping to join in the frenzied development. As the railroad wound its way south toward Brownsville in the spring of 1904, Robert J. Kleberg began cutting out parcels of his ranchland, anticipating that farmers would soon see the arability of the region and the profitability of having a nearby rail line. Kleberg hoped that land prices would rise enough that he could make a comfortable profit from unused portions of his ranch. According to Allhands, his prices ranged from fifteen to twenty-four dollars per acre.[34] In the end, Kleberg made few sales and eventually abandoned the enterprise. His problem was that he was simply ahead of his time. As time would show, other ranchers would follow his example, divvying up ranches and selling them off to farmers for large profits. Soon, land sales, not to mention commercial farming, would make small fortunes for many, furthering the economic prominence of American dollars in South Texas.

Property values shot up after 1904. Land companies and potential investors from throughout the country took notice. One of the executives of the St. Louis, Brownsville, and Mexico Railway responded to an inquiry on April 20, 1904, from a land company in Minnesota:

I have your inquiry of the 16th inst., and beg to advise that, at the present time we have the track of the St. Louis, Brownsville and Mexico Railroad laid 117 miles south of Robstown, which would be twenty-five miles from Brownsville. We expect to reach Brownsville on or about June 1st.

The parties who are managing the different land donations along the line are having some located and platted, and I believe in the near future it will be ready for the market. I understand that it is going to be put on the market at from ten dollars to twenty-five dollars per acre to start with and I am sure that some very valuable land can be secured at a very low figure if one grasps the opportunity soon enough.[35]

The land had to be physically redrawn and reconceptualized for potential buyers. Ranchlands would indeed be platted and divided into potential farms, but various moneyed interests also remade the countryside into a series of new towns and cities. The Valley's colonization carried more with it than economic distinction and racist characterizations of ethnic Mexicans; it also remade the countryside and established new physical spaces that would be inhabited by people who did not yet live there.

As the Valley's branch of the railroad pushed west along the river, new towns that would grow and prosper with the coming of commercial farming industries began to dot the countryside. Recounting the phenomenal growth that the Valley had undergone since the turn of the century, Frank C. Pierce commented in his book on the numerous towns. Table 1.1 profiles several towns in 1917 that would become or were then already hubs of local commercial farming. Over time, these communities would prove important to commercial farming, irrigation, and, in some instances, citriculture. Many of these towns will be discussed later in this book along with the land companies, promoters, farmers, and workers who were active in the citrus and vegetable industries. These new towns were outposts that promoters and land developers were clearly already having some success at populating.[36]

Sweeping physiographic changes also invaded the local landscape. Sectioning off land for use by farmers creates a phenomenon that naturalists refer to as habitat fragmentation, in which a region's native vegetation gives way as land is cleared for agricultural, commercial, or residential purposes. One scholar argues that the natural habitats in the Lower Rio Grande Valley virtually disappeared with the rise of commercial farming after the railroad's arrival. The Valley, which in reality is more of a river delta than a valley, was once "a wet oasis in the middle of a long stretch of scrub country." This fact explains why boosters spent at least some time convincing people that good

TABLE 1.1. New Anglo towns in the Lower Rio Grande Valley

Town	Date Founded	County	Population in 1917
Kingsville	1904	Kleberg	3,000
Raymondville	1904	Cameron	1,000
Harlingen	1905	Cameron	600
San Benito	1907	Cameron	2,500
La Feria	1908 (?)	Cameron	800
Mercedes	1905	Hidalgo	2,000
San Juan	1907	Hidalgo	500
Edinburg	1908 (?)	Hidalgo	900
Mission	1907	Hidalgo	2,500

agricultural land existed in what most people assumed was a dry, brushy part of the country. By the late 1930s, clearing of land for agriculture had caused the once extensive riparian woodlands and gallery forests to have receded massively. Between then and the 1920s farmers cleared 95 percent of the original native brush as well as 90 percent of the natural riparian habitat of the Valley. Clearly, the commercial farming boom was an immense undertaking. Once-dense stretches of local sabal palm forest became confined to an area bordering the river near Brownsville.[37]

Commercial agriculture's rise also threatened the existence of the Rio Grande itself. One watchdog group ranked it the seventh most endangered river in the United States at the end of the twentieth century, due entirely to diversions from the river for agricultural and municipal use, which claimed nearly 95 percent of the river's average annual flow. The sharp increase in irrigation from the river, so destructive to natural flora and fauna yet so rewarding to farmers, began during the initial commercial farming colonization movement in the early 1900s. During the 1910s, Hidalgo County experienced a 663 percent increase in irrigated lands, from 21,048 acres to 160,532 acres. Likewise, Cameron County experienced a 104 percent increase during those same years, from 29,439 acres to 60,008 acres. Access to water from irrigation, which was crucial for South Texas citrus and vegetable growers, proved one of the great challenges that the coming industries would face. These statistics also reflect the great need for river water by citrus plants, as almost all of the citrus fruits grown in South Texas would come out of Hidalgo County, in the heart of the Lower Rio Grande Valley.[38]

The town-founding boom had an immediate impact on the lives of local residents and newcomers alike; its legacy was one of great prosperity as well as violence and dispossession, some of which has already been mentioned. Between 1905 and 1910, land speculators and developers attracted so many new settlers that the region's population nearly doubled in size. Land selling for ten to twenty-five dollars per acre upon the railroad's arrival in 1904 sold for anywhere between one hundred and five hundred dollars per acre as early as 1912. Many Mexican American ranchers had insufficient capital to pay taxes on booming land values; one historian argues that sheriff's sales of tax-delinquent lands in Hidalgo County almost always went to Anglos, which meant that many Mexican American landowners lost their land. A mixture of these economic challenges, as well as the aforementioned practice of intimidation and outright theft of land, led to a large drop in Mexican American landownership in the region during the first decade of the century. Mexican Americans lost more than 187,000 acres in Hidalgo and Cameron Counties alone. In Hidalgo

County the percentage of Mexican American–owned lands fell from 28.6 percent to 16.8 percent; in Cameron County, 20 percent to 16.4 percent.[39]

White American newcomers also helped reinforce existing negative stereotypes of ethnic Mexicans. The development of commercial agriculture reinforced most Mexicans' standing at the bottom of a rural social order that included planters, farmers, shopkeepers, tenants, and laborers. Some ethnic Mexicans, however, did not fit so easily into the bipolarizing tendencies of South Texas's new race and class system. Mexican American shopkeepers, for example, maintained a role that required respect due to their status as the distributors of life's necessities for local residents. Nevertheless, a general anti-Mexican discrimination grew over time as the justification of the desire for cheap farm labor. Notions that Mexicans were lazy, treacherous, and unintelligent became part of the local Anglo lexicon as justification for hiring only ethnic Mexicans as low-wage farmworkers. Furthermore, historian José Pastrano argues that the primary blame for perpetuating the status of Mexicans as migrant laborers, which thus led to Anglos' widely held negative stereotypes of them, was the role that the state played in transforming Texas agriculture during the early part of the twentieth century. State researchers and experts, according to Pastrano, popularized the idea of seasonal agriculture, which in turn created growers' desires for seasonal migratory employment.[40]

Depictions of Mexicans by contemporary Valley-area writers reflected not only an anti-Mexican bias but also the difficult conditions that local Mexican Americans and Mexicans actually faced. In his 1931 volume on the arrival of the railroad in the Valley, J. L. Allhands wrote:

> Cheap labor was needed to develop this country and it was there in abundance. The supply was composed of swarthy poverty-stricken and half-starved Mexican peons, not one of whom could read, write, or speak a single word of English. They dressed in tight cotton breeches, and the cheapest shirts of the same material. They wore sandals, if they did not go barefoot, and the inevitable peaked straw hats with raveling gaudy blankets around them, that all showed much service, completed their costumes. They were plentiful and willing to work at sixty-two and one-half cents, Mex, per day, while the frowsy female hands or señoras were paid the small pittance of thirty-seven cents. But as "Los Americanos" continued to pour into the Valley and with the awakening of the land, these wages were steadily advanced.[41]

Advancement of wages for ethnic Mexican workers was clearly only a passing concern for men like Allhands, as well as others involved in founding the new

South Texas. Some of those same workers undoubtedly came from families who until recently had owned land and operated livestock ranches. But those days were now firmly in the past.

Although the Plan de San Diego of 1915 fit neatly into a preexisting cycle of violent rebellion in the South Texas borderlands, the impetus for the revolt also speaks to a general rise in violence in the region after the beginning of the commercial farming boom. It is no coincidence that this rebellion, which took place after farmers began moving to the region, was put down with more violence than the Garza or Cortina rebellions. With a collage of land speculators, land seekers, and dispossessed migrants living together in South Texas, violent outbursts and misunderstandings were bound to occur. The Texas Rangers were the preferred method of law enforcement—the summary executors of "justice" in land disputes. Locals referred to Harlingen, a particularly violent place where gunfights and murders were common, as Six-Shooter Junction. One scholar estimates that between 1907 and 1913 the Rangers killed sixteen ethnic Mexicans in Hidalgo and Cameron Counties, but based on the fragmentary evidence of murders and summary executions as well as the nefarious activities of the Rangers during the later Plan de San Diego revolt, the actual number of ethnic Mexicans killed by Rangers from 1904 to 1915 is likely much higher.[42]

Thus, in the early twentieth century a new era began in the history of the Lower Rio Grande Valley and the South Texas borderlands. In general terms, ownership of the land had changed hands—either through legal purchase, illegal theft, or intimidation—from Mexican Americans to Anglo-American ranchers, land speculators, and capitalists who in turn hoped to attract more American farmers. A modern economic infrastructure had begun to take shape, while discrimination, violence, and the ensuing resentment of white supremacy became systemic.

A Fruitful Harvest

Steep rises in commercial farming as well as population movement in the early twentieth century were of course not unique to the Lower Rio Grande Valley and South Texas. Throughout the US West, capitalistic farming ventures—even small-scale ones—reigned supreme. Industrial farming, by which farmers sought prosperity through large-scale ventures as well as the application of new technologies to growing crops, became the norm in places like South Texas, the Great Plains, and the Columbia River Plateau. Machines run by fossil fuels replaced human muscle as the primary drivers of crop cultivation.

Historian Richard White notes that during the first three decades of the twentieth century the size of the average farm increased exponentially. Statistically speaking, the reverse was true for most of South Texas, but this was directly due to the breakup of huge South Texas cattle ranches into farmland after the railroad's arrival. What happened in South Texas in the early 1900s, then, where Anglos and ethnic Mexicans interacted frequently, was not wholly unique. A similar reduction of Mexican American landowners into a rural workforce took place in northern New Mexico and Colorado in the early twentieth century, but White characterizes this change as "more gradual and less violent than the suppression of Mexican Texans." In other words, the rapid movement of Anglos into South Texas and the quick dispossession of Mexican American landowners helped create a cauldron of acute discontent in the Lower Rio Grande Valley. The reason the situation was worse in Texas, of course, was because the border offered South Texas farmers a way to suppress wages and working conditions.[43]

This foundation of commercial farms that White describes is part of a larger phenomenon in the US West known as homesteading. According to historian Walter Nugent, homesteading, in which people relocated within the bounds of the United States to purchase cheap lands, can be divided into two distinct periods: the first from 1862 to 1900 and the second from 1900 to 1913. Homesteading began in 1862 with the passage of the Homestead Act, which granted 160 acres of the public domain to any citizen or noncitizen who would occupy the land and farm it. Between 1862 and 1900, approximately 1,400,000 people applied for homestead lands. Many of these were small family farms. During the second period, from 1900 to 1913, another 1,000,000 applied, which amounted to twice as many per year than during the first period. Land rushes in places such as Kansas, Nebraska, and Oklahoma in the nineteenth century were only a prelude to what came later in the early twentieth century. Nugent argues that the first thirteen years of the twentieth century "were the true heyday of homesteading." From 1913 forward, land would be more difficult to obtain.[44]

South Texas was clearly an important part of this larger internal migration of farmers within the national borders of the United States. By about 1913, the year that Nugent argues homesteading declined, land companies and speculators owned most of the land in the Lower Rio Grande Valley, which they in turn parceled off and sold. In the Valley's case, then, Nugent's characterization that 1913 represented the fulfillment of Frederick Jackson Turner's 1893 thesis of the closed frontier is not quite correct.[45] In fact, people continued to relocate to new areas in the US West for several decades, just not under federal homesteading laws. This was certainly the case in South Texas, where no federal lands existed. Traditional homesteading, then, did not technically exist in Texas. Although the processes of population movement was similar, the ultimate goal in the Valley and greater South Texas was to create profitable enterprises for the numerous small farmers who moved into newly founded communities. What land buyers hoped for was to participate in a modern, capitalist-intensive and cohesive rural community rather than to establish an initial homestead on an independent family farm. Rural communities in the US Southwest would continue to develop and integrate the nation's hinterlands into the larger national economy. Capitalism and farming continued to pull people in different directions in the US West.

Who, then, came to South Texas? Three groups of people, whose interactions defined the social realities of the region during the twentieth century, collided during the commercial farming boom: land speculators, new farmers and growers, and migrant workers. At the turn of the century South Texas had a population of 79,934; that doubled by 1920 to 159,842 and doubled again by 1930 to 322,845. The majority of the 1930 population, or 216,822 people, were concentrated in the three counties that comprised the Lower Rio Grande Valley (Cameron, Hidalgo, and Willacy Counties) as well as Nueces County to the north—the four major farming counties in South Texas. Population figures indicate the high degree to which Anglo newcomers and Mexicans from south of the border overran the region. Three-quarters of the Valley's population lived in towns of over 2,500, which, by early-twentieth-century standards, meant that most people lived in urban spaces. Historian Cynthia Orozco explains that while ethnic Mexicans had once made up 98 percent of Hidalgo County's population, by 1929 that figure had fallen to 54 percent. Similarly, Cameron County, once 88 percent Mexican, had dropped to 50 percent.[46] For a short time Anglo immigration outpaced Mexican immigration to the region.

Given the mass deportations of Mexicans and Mexican Americans out of the US Southwest that began in the late 1920s, it is noteworthy that the Spanish-surnamed portion of the Lower Rio Grande Valley's population appears to have risen alongside that of the Anglo population for most of the decade. The high numbers of immigrants during the 1920s suggest that the Valley's commercial farming had become a serious pull factor for Mexican migrant workers from south of the border, aside from the hundreds of thousands of refugees who fled north across the Rio Grande to escape the violence of the Mexican Revolution. Still, the Anglo population in both counties combined had more than doubled.[47]

Several wealthy Anglo men played key roles in making Hidalgo, Cameron, and Willacy County lands available to newcomers. One of the first major developers who opened the region to commercial farming, and later citrus, was Benjamin F. Yoakum, a Texas-born businessman and one of the founders of the St. Louis, Brownsville and Mexico Railway. Recognizing, as did so many other local power brokers, the potential of the area's lands for agriculture, Yoakum in 1905 organized the American Rio Grande Land and Irrigation Company (ARGLIC) with $1.25 million in capital stock investments from Saint Louis–area investors. Yoakum purchased the company's lands from the heirs of the original owners of the Llano Grande and La Feria land grants, which were Spanish royal grants dating back to the late eighteenth century. The company not only promoted colonization and the railroad throughout its roughly quarter of a million acres, but it also founded Mercedes, a town that would become a major transportation hub for vegetable farmers and citrus growers. ARGLIC was also one of the earliest promoters of irrigation in the lower Valley.[48]

Yoakum wasted no time buying up portions of the land from original owners and turning it over to ARGLIC, which in turn sold plots to newcomers from the US Midwest. On December 5, 1905, Yoakum deeded the southwest portion of the Llano Grande tract, located in Hidalgo County, to the company, which was the first of many tracts that the company planned to parcel off and sell. Through the 1910s and '20s the company continued to add portions of land, which it would in turn prepare for farming and then sell to individuals or families. Most of the farm tracts were roughly twenty-acre lots. Individual growers or investors, however, purchased some larger tracts. For example, on January 1, 1914, John T. Beamer, an investor from Kansas City, Missouri, purchased 30,530 acres of land from the company. Another grower in the Llano Grande tract, W. T. Adams, owned roughly 11,000 acres of ARGLIC lands. These land purchasers, whether large or small, invested in land and either allowed land companies to grow crops and farm them on their behalf or relocated to live on their newly acquired properties. Some owners sublet or sold their lands to a third party, who then grew crops at either a fixed rate or a percentage of whatever crops came to harvest.[49]

Such a highly capitalized commercial farming situation in an arid climate required extensive irrigation. Although it is difficult to determine if the company's canals were the first to divert water from the Rio Grande to farmlands on its north bank, ARGLIC's irrigation prospect was certainly the largest in the Lower Rio Grande Valley to date. Work began on the company's concrete irrigation canals in 1905, and the canals were operational the following spring. State law required that any irrigation company apply for approval to divert water from state waterways for private usage, which ARGLIC did on May 25, 1906. The ARGLIC canals not only served as an example of how to establish an efficient irrigation system on Valley farmlands, but they proved a huge financial success as well, even attracting investment from other small local irrigation ventures. From that point forward, Valley-area farmers could rest assured that they would have adequate access to water for their crops.[50]

Another of the early founders of commercial farming in the region was John H. Shary. A native Nebraskan, Shary had developed and sold a quarter of a million acres in the Coastal Bend region of Texas, attracting farmers and businessmen alike. His major legacy, however, would later be established in Hidalgo County, to which he turned his attention in 1912. Noting the fertility of the soil as well as its promise for commercial farming, Shary first purchased twelve thousand acres in what became the San Juan–Pharr region, then known as one small part of the Judge Brooks estate. The following year he purchased six thousand acres in the McAllen area. Finally, in 1914, Shary purchased sixteen thousand acres of the Swift estate as well as twenty thousand acres from the Oblate Fathers of Mary Immaculate. This property became the heart of Sharyland, which, alongside Mission, emerged as a major center of the Valley's citrus and vegetable industries.[51]

Shary would later be dubbed the Father of the Texas Citrus Industry. Before he planted his first acreage to citrus, however, he had two main prospects: colonization and irrigation. One man, Joe Kilgore, whose family purchased land from Shary and relocated to the region in 1929, later remarked, to quantify Shary's impact, that "it's probably true that John Shary brought more people to Texas, more colonists to Texas, than Stephen F. Austin." Shary had scores of agents scattered throughout the US Midwest, recruiting people to visit his lands and purchase tracts.[52] His biographer, Zulema Silva-Bewley, speculates that Shary's success in permanently relocating families to the Lower Rio Grande Valley was somewhat modest compared to the successes of other promoters, since Mission's population increased only 33 percent during the 1920s. Silva-Bewley fails to note, however, that Mission's population grew from about 2,500 to 3,847 between 1917 and 1920 alone, an increase of about 54 percent in just three short years. If one considers the population increase in Shary's Mission lands alone—not including Sharyland itself—from 1917 to 1930, Mission's population increased from about 2,500 to 5,120, an increase of roughly 105 percent. These statistics, which consider neither the high number of absentee landowners in the Valley nor Shary's own personal investment in local citriculture, fit well into larger patterns of the growing Anglo American demographic dominance over the region. Indeed, by 1920 about two-thirds of the population in Hidalgo County were recent Anglo-American immigrants.[53] Shary may not have been the most successful land developer in the area in terms of sheer numbers, but he was, in fact, a colonizer extraordinaire.

Men such as Shary envisioned themselves to be like the colonizers of old. His initial legal agreement in 1913 with his land company, the International Land and Investment Company of Omaha, Nebraska, made Shary wealthy. Shary received a flat payment of thirty thousand dollars as well as vendors' lien notes of ten dollars per acre on all properties sold by the company. The language of the initial agreement reveals a project that envisioned the establishment of a fixed colony of farmers. Although the agreement implied a somewhat more benign use of the term *colonization* that simply referenced population movement to Shary's lands, still, it displays the self-consciousness of land development companies in creating colonies in a new or foreign space:

> Party of the first part will give it exclusive efforts in the colonization of these tracts of land during the term of this contract, with the exception of its liberty to colonize its present scattered holdings. . . . Party of the First Part agrees to stand all expenses in the colonizing of said lands, such as contracts with agencies, salaried contracts, office expenses, and all other expense incidental to the colonizing of these tracts, including any special improvements in the way of building or developing they may see it fit to do. . . . This includes all sales made on or after July 1, 1913.[54]

Developers clearly sought to bring about striking changes to the Lower Rio Grande Valley through their colonization efforts. It comes as no surprise that the best characterization of Anglo–Mexican relations in the region after 1904 can aptly be described as that of colonizers and colonized.

Developers and growers played important roles in coming together to make commercial farming a reality, but there were also key differences between the two groups. Notably, their motives for coming to the region were different. While developers' primary objectives were to sell land as quickly as possible and attract as many colonists as they could to the region, growers and farmers needed to make money from their crops. These interests of developers and agriculturists naturally dovetailed, but they could also occasionally work against one another. For example, although it became increasingly clear that the local economy functioned primarily on land sales rather than crop sales (a fact that will be addressed later in this book), developers and larger companies relied on crop growing and unusual crop returns as promotional tools for land sales. Thus, new recruits became increasingly frustrated when life in the region did not bring the fabulously wealthy returns that developers often described. Also, unscrupulous land-sales tactics left many new growers and farmers to fend for themselves after making their purchases. As time would show, Anglo colonizers in the Lower Rio Grande Valley by no means represented a completely unified or holistic group. The local leaders, who controlled land sales and communicated a vision for the future of local commercial farming, often found themselves addressing "knockers," which in the local vernacular meant landowners who felt that they had been swindled by the land companies. Although ethnic Mexicans clearly lost much when outsiders colonized their homeland, it would be mistaken to assume that all Anglo-Americans rode the tide of commercial farming and anti-Mexican racism to a bright future. Some of them gambled and lost everything.

Bitter Fruits

Building South Texas's irrigated farmlands took a backbreaking effort. Just as in the case of the future citrus-growing region around Mercedes, the Mission-Sharyland area required an irrigation system before its commercial farming project could be launched. In early 1916 Shary purchased the Mission Canal Company properties and established the United Irrigation Company. With this $850,000 investment Shary gained direct control over when and how his colonists would receive their water. This proved important for the budding citrus industry, as citrus trees require heavier irrigation than do most other commercial fruit plantings. The system consisted of over 240 miles of canals, which Shary planned to extend later with an additional 100 miles. At the time, the Sharyland tract was about two-thirds developed or sold, but the popularity of citrus as a cash crop on Shary's lands was still in its infancy.[55]

Clearing the land into small settlements for new farmers was an enormous undertaking. The intensive work offers a perfect snapshot of how ethnic Mexicans became marginalized in South Texas in the early 1900s. Four or five months of labor went into making a tract suitable for farming. Joseph Ebbers of Dodge, Nebraska, bought a farm in Mission in 1916, eventually setting five of his forty acres to grapefruit, oranges, and lemons. Work commenced the previous spring on clearing wild vegetation from Ebbers's property. On April 15 workers began tilling Ebbers's soil, putting in a total of 20 hours of work at $0.10 per hour. In May, workers built irrigation ditches and cut weeds, putting in a total of 170 hours of work at $17.60 total. As the summer months dawned, the intensity of the work increased. In June, workers cut weeds and built and cleaned irrigation ditches at a backbreaking total of 560 hours with a cost of only $56.00 to Ebbers. It is unclear how laborers divided their work, but multiple labor crews clearly put in long hours on Ebbers's land. July was the busiest month of all. Workers tilled, cut weeds, continued to irrigate, planted sugarcane, and planted and cultivated trees. Work crews put in 590 hours during July at a total cost of $59.00. This latest bout of work was the last and most difficult stretch. Ebbers's labor force appears to have taken the entire month off while the hot August sun beat down on South Texas, only to return in September to stack and cut hay, putting in 240 hours of work at a cost of $24.00.[56]

Ebbers did not pay the entire cost of clearing his land. The International Land and Investment Company, which had sold Ebbers his tract, likely shared some of the costs. Land companies, citrus cooperatives, and growers' associations often shared the burden of labor costs in all aspects of caring for citrus orchards and picking fruit. Ebbers, who stayed in Nebraska and remained an absentee grower until at least 1927, eventually had 412 citrus trees imported and planted by the company on his behalf.[57] This kind of situation, in which a company planted trees on behalf of an individual grower who did not live on his or her land, was fairly common.

Work crews on early commercial farms consisted almost entirely of ethnic Mexican workers. In the burgeoning citrus industry, all growers employed Mexican and Mexican American workers. Growers' associations and land companies hired most workers through labor contractors. For that reason small citrus growers in the 1910s had little contact with the people who actually worked their lands. Mexican laborers during the 1910s operated within the larger context of the commercial farming boom and changing demographic patterns. They had marketed themselves in the form of labor crews in Texas since at least the 1880s. Crews generally consisted of a *mayordomo* (foreman) and a *cuadrilla* (crew) of about twenty-five men. The labor companies usually paid their workers once a month, sometimes operating out of a supply headquarters or nearby office space. Labor contracting in South Texas could be a profitable enterprise, depending on the type of labor contract in which the company chose to engage or was lucky enough to acquire. Historian Gilbert González argues that "the major social consequences of" the US imperialist domination of Mexico since the late nineteenth century were "the mass uprooting of people from the countryside and the migration of that labor to the heart of the US economy." This system became normalized later in the twentieth century, he argues, through guest labor and contract labor programs. Thus, labor became one of the great commodities of the South Texas colonial enterprise, as well, and the labor contractor stood to benefit. Workers also often brought camping equipment alongside their work tools with them to various jobsites so their families could migrate with them.[58]

Employment for manual laborers was irregular. Early on, in 1887, farmers devoted less than fifteen thousand acres of land in Hidalgo and Cameron Counties to agriculture, of which the primary crops at the time were corn and cotton.

An unspecified pest destroyed nearly 90 percent of the cotton crop in Hidalgo County in 1887, driving most of the workers to nearby Cameron County to seek employment. Thus, as workers glutted the labor market in Cameron County, the average wage paid to farmworkers on the few operable farms in Hidalgo County in 1887 remained relatively high, at $9.05 per month, which was significantly more than the $6.76 monthly income of Cameron County workers that year. Workers just to the west in Starr County, where the only farms consisted of a mere 702 acres planted to corn, earned about $10.00 per month. Most of the workers in these three counties could expect steady employment on farms for only about six months out of the year.[59]

Population and wage statistics for other corn- and cotton-growing counties in Texas reveal that South Texas workers earned minuscule wages even before the railroad's arrival. For example, in 1887 in Tarrant County in North Texas, farmers grew mostly corn, cotton, and wheat. Farm laborers in Tarrant County earned on average $25.25 per month, which was two to four times as much as their South Texas counterparts. Of the 24,671 people in Tarrant County in 1880, only 27 were ethnic Mexicans.[60]

Only at the turn of the twentieth century did Anglos in South Texas normalize certain aspects of hiring ethnic Mexican workers. It was still not uncommon by 1900 for crop pickers to make as little as twenty-five cents per day, but the arrival of the railroad did appear to offer some significant changes to the structure of the wage scale for ethnic Mexicans. The company that built the St. Louis, Brownsville, and Mexico Railway, for example, paid its workers one dollar per day across the board and used nearly one thousand workers to lay its tracks. One likely reason for the relatively high wages was that the work was exceedingly difficult. Workers had to cut unending amounts of brush and natural vegetation out of the ground in order to make room for the new railroad tracks. Then they would have to pick everything up and set up new work camps farther down the lines. Perhaps because of the work that the railroad provided, the dollar-per-day wage became common in the Lower Rio Grande Valley after the railroad finished its trek through the area in 1904.[61]

Despite the rising wages, ethnic Mexican workers could not expect to live in any semblance of comfort on the dollar-per-day wage. The statistics cited above for Joseph Ebbers's land-clearing project indicate that the average unskilled ethnic Mexican worker earned about ten cents per hour, which, given a ten-hour day, suggests that Ebbers's workers received a relatively common wage. The average income for US workers in 1900 was between four hundred and five hundred dollars per year, while six hundred dollars per year was generally considered the necessary minimum for basic needs.[62] Although poverty was clearly rampant in the United States at the turn of the twentieth century, it was much worse among ethnic Mexicans in the new farming communities. If a worker was fortunate enough to maintain employment year-round at the ten cents per hour wage, he or she would have to work eighty hours per week each week to earn an annual income of about four hundred dollars. Given the irregularity of field-labor work in South Texas at the turn of the twentieth century, it becomes apparent that even the hardest-working and healthiest ethnic Mexican workers could not afford to feed, clothe, and shelter their families adequately on such paltry wages.

Capitalists from outside the region began to form their first impressions of Mexican and Mexican American workers during the railroad's building. One refrain that was common among employers, reminiscent of the American dialogue on overseas colonial expansion at the turn of the twentieth century, was that the arrival of white Americans would help to pull Mexicans out of their alleged barbarism and into a more civilized status. F. G. Jonah recalled a conversation that he had at the time with one of the railroad's founders, the previously mentioned Uriah Lott, about the conditions of Valley-area ethnic Mexicans prior to the railroad's arrival:

> Along the old military trail in the Rio Grande Valley the native population were living alongside the road in wretched hackals [sic], small dwellings made of sticks, mud and grass. A few goats, chickens, [and] small garden[s] comprised their earthly possessions. Cooking was done in a few pots and pans over a fire on the ground. Children ran around with scarcely any clothing. The family slept on the floor, and yet in and around the dwelling there would be a profusion of bright flowers, showing the native love for bright colors. The women could and did make beautiful drawn work, showing an innate artistic sense. I well recall a remark of Colonel Lott's as we were making one of these journeys and talking about the new era to follow the railroad. He said, "Jonah, we must get these people up off the ground."[63]

Lott's allegedly big heart for local Mexicans clearly resonated with his contemporaries. Nevertheless, growers found that they had a high turnover rate, as their workers seemed unaccustomed to gainful employment over extended periods of time and simply did not know how to handle making such high wages:

> Our axemen and teamsters were receiving what at that time was a fabulous wage for Mexicans in that section of the country, $1.00 per day and board. As

we reached the Mexican border we found difficulty in holding our men, they had received a pay day and were anxious to spend it among their friends in Matamores [*sic*]. We found that the more they made the less they worked. A couple of days a week sufficed for all their wants, but there was no trouble in recruiting others to take their places and they would follow the same routine. The provisions in our camp were plentiful and good, and when a new bunch of Mexicans came in they ate so much the first few days that they invariably made themselves sick, but we worked long hours and hard, and it was not long until the Mexicans could assimulate [*sic*] their strange dishes and thrive on it.[64]

Jonah closed his reminiscences by stating that he "formed a very favorable impression of these Mexicans as laborers. They have admirable traits, uncomplaining fortitude, obedience, and a painstaking desire to do their work well. They cannot be hurried to any sudden bursts of speed, but . . . the race has great capacity." Such notions of ethnic Mexicans as hardworking yet childish and backward became common among Anglos in South Texas throughout the coming commercial farming boom and served as an excuse for their exploitation during the area's development. "Getting these people off the ground" to fulfill their "great capacity" exhibited a sense of benevolent paternalism common to US overseas imperialists at the time. The prescribed foreignness of the native population lumped Mexicans into the same degraded racial status as that of the nonwhites encountered by the Anglo-Americans the world over, who needed the presence of white, Protestant Americans in order to be "lifted up" or "civilized."[65]

Ethnic Mexicans still dominated South Texas's population after the railroad's arrival. Mexican Americans also voted and held office, and some had become wealthy long before 1904. Records from the Texas State Department of Agriculture reveal that in 1887 in Hidalgo and Cameron Counties, where citriculture eventually took hold, the total population consisted of 3,082 Anglos as opposed to 17,327 ethnic Mexicans (the census of the Texas Department of Agriculture for that year made no differentiation between Mexican Americans and Mexican nationals). Considering that US authorities in the nineteenth century made no quantifiable efforts at controlling immigration along the border, the likely presence of numerous Mexican immigrants suggests that the number of ethnic Mexicans in those two counties was much higher than those counted for the census.

As stated, almost all manual laborers in South Texas were Mexicans or Mexican Americans. Again, statistics from 1887 help reconstruct early demographics. As a result of the previously mentioned failure of the cotton crop in Hidalgo

County that year, many people migrated to Cameron County, leaving a population of 1,892 Anglos and 2,098 ethnic Mexicans in Hidalgo County. Cameron County, where there was less demand for farmworkers due to healthy crops, had an Anglo population of only 1,190 but a high ethnic Mexican population of 15,229. Likewise, population statistics for Starr County, on the west side of Hidalgo County, reveal 166 Anglos and 8,074 ethnic Mexicans.[66] Clearly, the rough demographic parity between Anglos and Mexicans in Hidalgo County that year was highly unusual.

But again, the arrival of the railroad and commercial farming brought higher wages to local farmworkers and day laborers along with an increased Anglo-American demographic. In the 1900s Lon C. Hill, a lawyer from Beeville and the founder of Harlingen, arrived in Brownsville. Hill observed that the ninety or so ranchers in Cameron County who owned 95 percent of the county's farmland were becoming wealthy using the cheap Mexican workers. Hill concluded that these "willing workers" would work for any farmer who desired to invest time and money in South Texas agriculture; he himself became wildly successful growing rice and publishing stories of his financial success in local newspapers. Other growers thus began to follow his example of purchasing large tracts of land and employing cheap laborers. Others noticed that as individual growers became increasingly successful in the early twentieth century, they began implementing the practices of their more successful colleagues. The use of cheap ethnic Mexican workers thus spread quickly throughout the Lower Rio Grande Valley and the greater South Texas borderlands.[67]

Table 1.2 reveals wages that Spanish-surnamed farmworkers could expect to receive for work performed for a ten-hour workday on South Texas farms in 1915.[68] Although not allowing for inflation, the dollar-per-day wage was higher than what farmworkers had received in the area thirty years previously. The data from Table 1.2 indicates that skilled laborers might have enjoyed a higher level of mobility than their unskilled counterparts. Still, evidence from farmworkers employed in the Mission-Sharyland district suggests that wage discrimination was still endemic among day laborers. One ledger book, which reveals wages paid to one English-surnamed carpenter alongside his many Spanish-surnamed counterparts, reveals that this particular individual received one dollar per day more than his colleagues for what appears to have been the same work for the same duration of time. A dual-wage system, then, was prevalent among the working class. Notably, the same English-surnamed carpenter is the only person listed on the register as having been charged room and board. Typically, farmers expected Mexican and Mexican American workers to board themselves. Often, when the farmer's or land company's representative

TABLE 1.2. Daily wages for manual laborers, 1915

Work Performed	Daily Wage ($)
Carpentry	3.00–4.50
Hauling Materials	1.00
Mixing Cement	1.00
Harvesting	1.00
Stonemasonry	2.50

either did not know the workers' names or was unable to spell them intelligibly, the bookkeeper would simply use the abbreviation "Mex." or "3 Mex. Laborers" to represent workers and their corresponding wages on the ledger sheets. Conversely, the same English-surnamed individual mentioned above always received the dignity of at least having his initials listed.[69]

The building of commercial farms in South Texas marked a new chapter in the region's history, one in which Anglo-American farmers had colonized the region, broken down the old social orders, and replaced them with something foreign and new. Citrus was on the verge of emerging as the region's primary commercial crop. Why did midwestern growers, who previously had no experience with citrus, choose to invest so heavily in the crop? Why would the region rally around citrus, rather than cotton or corn, both of which predated citrus in the region and were grown widely?[70] The answers to these questions lay in the history of citrus in the larger world, the North American continent, and in the South Texas borderlands themselves.

Oranges in the Borderlands

If the nineteenth century was the age of ranching in deep South Texas, then early decades of the twentieth century can be called the age of citrus. Numerous contacts between Europeans, Arabs, and Moors during the first millennium of the common era helped bring citrus fruits, which originated in Central and Southeast Asia, to Europe. The long occupation of the Iberian Peninsula by the Moors helped make citrus growing a popular phenomenon across Spain, where farmers cultivated both oranges and citrons. Historian Pierre Laszlo writes that although the military clashes between the Muslims and Christians on the Iberian Peninsula are now long in the past, "a hybrid culture was their result—including citriculture." Although citrons predated oranges in Europe by at least several centuries, the sweet orange arrived in Europe sometime in the early fifteenth century, likely at the hands of Genoese traders, and it became exceptionally popular there. Citris was grown widely in Portugal, a small kingdom itself then on the verge of becoming a colonial superpower.[71]

Citrus spread far and wide during the age of exploration. At the turn of the sixteenth century Columbus himself brought oranges to the Americas, where they spread around the Caribbean and into Mexico. Citrus had not previously grown wild in the Western Hemisphere. The conquistador Francisco Pizarro took citrus seeds into Peru in the early sixteenth century. Although it is not recorded exactly how oranges came to Florida, historians date the crop's first appearance to sometime after Ponce de León's arrival on the peninsula in 1513, perhaps even with his initial exploration of the area. By the founding of Saint Augustine in 1565, orange trees grew wild in Florida. Indians reportedly took a quick liking to the fruit, spitting out the seeds while traveling and thus playing the primary role in helping orange trees spread. Grapefruits arrived in the Americas sometime later in the seventeenth century, while the citron arrived in Puerto Rico in 1640 and in Saint Augustine at a later date. Citrus growers in South Africa began harvesting crops as early as 1654, while citrus's earliest recorded appearance in California was in 1769.[72]

Comparatively speaking, citrus was a much younger colonial monocrop than other, better-known commodities. Sugar, coffee, and cotton, for example, had all played important roles during the age of European exploration and transatlantic colonialism that began in the sixteenth century. Commercial citrus growth appears to have begun in Florida in the 1760s and in California sometime in the early nineteenth century. By 1821 the still small citrus industry in Florida had begun expanding in the Saint Augustine region. A major freeze in 1835, however, killed all of the trees in the state used for commercial growing. The seeds from the grove of a single grower—William Dummitt, considered by many the founder of Florida citrus—provided the basis for the revived Florida industry after 1835. The Florida citrus industry fully recovered, experiencing a great boom during the 1870s. Florida's citrus production would overtake California's after the Great Depression, and Florida would become a leading world producer of orange juice alongside Brazil. Florida's citrus industry subsequently earned nine billion dollars annually through the end of the twentieth century.[73]

Citriculture got off to a later start in California, but the industry there actually boomed much earlier than it did in Florida. Commercial growth remained small until the 1870s, when orange growers in the state began to plant orchards on a larger scale and marshal the state's resources toward cultivating a vibrant industry. According to citrus historian Pierre Laszlo, the first decades of

California citrus saw the embodiment of the Jeffersonian agrarian dream for citrus growers, with a society of equally independent small growers earning wealth from lands that they privately owned. By the post–World War II era, however, sprawling urbanization and industrialization in the state served to drive growers from the heartland of California citrus in the Pasadena-Riverside area and into California's Central Valley. From that point forward the federal government stepped in, helping growers revive California citrus and procure the necessary water for their crops. But government assistance would soon recede as large corporations took over farms and groves in Florida and California, effectively spelling the end of the Jeffersonian dream for small citrus growers in those two states.[74]

Florida and California led the way in citrus production for the country just as the industry took off in Texas, helping the United States to become one of the leading producers of citrus in the world. From 1925 to 1930 the United States was the top producer of oranges, shipping on average 38,500,000 boxes annually. Spain was a close second, with 36,700,000 boxes, followed by Japan and Italy at a distant third and fourth, respectively. Brazil, Australia, Algeria, and South Africa rounded out most of the rest of the world's orange production in the late 1920s.[75]

Theoretically, Texas citrus growers should not have had a difficult time stepping in and making a contribution, since they could follow ready examples set by their successful counterparts in Florida and California. Only when the railroad opened South Texas lands to agricultural development in 1904 did local growers and land promoters begin to seek new ways that they could best promote profit and development from the land. Corn and cotton, already grown in South Texas by the time the railroad arrived, could not provide a differential advantage for development, since farmers already grew those two crops widely throughout Texas. The entrepreneurial spirit led several key Texas growers to set the first commercial citrus orchards in the Lower Rio Grande Valley, which would promote economic growth and stability in the region.

Innovative commercial capitalists noted the region's suitability to citrus. The alluvial soils on the north banks of the Rio Grande consist of highly alkaline and very sandy loam, resembling the soil found in the richest grapefruit-growing regions of Florida. Texas growers also realized that minor or even "impact" freezes, when the temperature falls below 28° Fahrenheit for an extended period of time, which can seriously threaten the life of a citrus tree, would be extremely rare. They also learned from their California counterparts how to use smudge pots to help trees survive such freezes. Lower Rio Grande Valley growers understood the benefits of studying citriculture from scientists in California's and Florida's university-backed experiment stations. Early investment in a citrus experiment station in Weslaco in 1931 is a testament to the powerful example set by growers in the two other states. Finally, Texas growers also experienced the benefits of cooperative marketing. By 1931 the American Institute for Cooperation had declared the California Fruit Growers' Exchange as the most successful cooperative organization in the United States and a perfect example for other cooperatives to follow. Growers' cooperatives in South Texas would play a key role in promoting and protecting profits for small growers until the Great Depression, mainly by promoting standardized canning, packing, pricing, and shipping methods.[76]

With the advantages of citrus growing becoming increasingly clear, all that the region needed was a prominent, adventurous, and entrepreneurial person to make the initial step by planting the crop. Locals would often credit John H. Shary with planting the first commercial citrus orchard in the Lower Rio Grande Valley, near Mission in 1915, and initiating the genesis of the industry that developed later in the 1920s. Shary enjoyed the distinction of shipping the first railroad car of citrus under standard packaging and grading out of South Texas, though in the early 1920s the conditions in which he shipped the fruit were somewhat crude. In this respect the Texas growers were far behind their counterparts in the California citrus industry, who often used imagery from the Spanish colonial era as well as other Spanish images on orange-crate shipping labels. This was done, in part, to create a sense of the exotic past of the colonial era for the average consumer. California growers clearly hoped to impress upon their consumers direct ties between orange growing and the state's Spanish, Mexican, and colonial pasts.[77]

What exactly prompted Shary to move into citrus remains a bit of a mystery. His biographer suggests that he had noted the Valley's potential as a citrus-growing region during his first visit to the area in 1912. Undoubtedly, a keen sense for the potential crop yields of the natural environments of the Valley must have given Shary the notion that citriculture could potentially be lucrative. Neither Shary nor any other Valley grower had yet visited any citrus operations in California or Florida and would not do so until the early 1920s, when Texas growers needed troubleshooting help with their nascent operation.[78]

Shary, however, was not the first person to grow citrus in South Texas. Citrus was undoubtedly introduced to Texas by the Spaniards, as had been the case in Florida and California. The original Anglo-Texas colonists in the 1830s cultivated citrus for home use, which indeed displays that trees existed in parts of the state since the Spanish period. Sources describe orange trees in the plaza of Matamoros, Mexico, in 1846, as well as orange trees in full bloom in

Brownsville's King Yard section in 1859. Future Confederate general Robert E. Lee noted numerous orange trees on the King Ranch during an 1850 visit. Other sources indicate that residents of the Gulf Coast region grew oranges and lemons as early as the 1860s. All of this early citrus cultivation was for private consumption.[79]

In reality, the first commercial citrus plantings in the Lower Rio Grande Valley predated Shary's by several decades. Celestin Jagou, a Frenchman living in Brownsville, sold lemons, limes, and oranges that he grew on trees imported from Florida and California as early as 1875. Jagou owned La Esperanza Ranch, where he operated a beer garden for the entertainment of soldiers from Fort Brown, to whom he sold his fruits. It was through this operation that Jagou inspired several fellow growers at the eastern end of the Valley to grow citrus as well. It was also during the 1890s that growers in Willacy County, as well as others further north in the Gulf Coast region, began planting oranges. Grapefruit did not appear in the region until 1904; some evidence places its first commercial planting near Mercedes in 1907. Prior to Shary's activities, other local prominent growers and land men, such as John J. Conway, James W. Hoit, A. P. Wright, and Virgil N. Lott, showed interest in growing citrus.[80]

Is referring to Shary as the father of the Texas citrus industry, then, a mistake? Not entirely, given that it was Shary who invested substantial amounts of money that led directly to the local industry's flourishing in the 1920s. Also, referring to a wealthy benefactor as the industry's father might have served as a mechanism to comfort potential colonists from the US Midwest, to assure them that if they moved to the region or invested in citrus they would be in good hands. Indeed, if no one purchased South Texas land, businessmen like Shary made no money. Farm colonization and land purchasing underpinned the entire commercial economy.

Mythical Origins and a Usable Past

If embellishments about a father of the Texas citrus industry could serve to calm potential colonists' nervousness about engaging in a brand new agricultural endeavor, outright mythology lent the nascent industry an aura of mystique that promoters and boosters used to draw people to South Texas, an area that would have been unfamiliar to most people in the United States. A founding myth did develop for Valley citrus. Although its origins are a mystery, its establishment and debunking can be traced through various sources. One can only speculate about the potential benefits that imparting a founding myth on the minds of colonists would bring for the boosters and landowners. The mythical founding origin lent mystique to citriculture and tied it directly into the region's past.

The story takes place on the Laguna Seca ranch, an old cattle ranch a few miles north of Edinburg in Hidalgo County. Sometime between 1865 and 1878, the story goes, Father Pierre Yves Keralum, a French-Catholic circuit rider and member of the local Oblates of Mary Immaculate, visited the proprietor of the ranch, Don Macedonio Vela, and his wife, Mercedes Vela, to administer the sacraments to their family. Upon readying to leave for the next ranch along his circuit, Keralum gave some orange seeds to one of the Vela children, who in turn planted the seeds, which produced seven trees. Keralum and his colleagues allegedly gave orange seeds to several ranch families in such a manner, usually during Christmastime visits. The Vela family expanded their orange plantings sometime around 1890, but a freeze in 1899 destroyed most of their crop. Several of the original trees, however, remained, and these surviving trees served as the genesis of the local industry. These trees were said to be the oldest citrus trees in South Texas.[81]

The fact that several subsequent investigators doubted this story suggests that more than a few people must have detected its lack of authenticity. G. C. Parrish, a graduate student from Kingsville, investigated the Laguna Seca myth in 1940, arguing that although its origins were unclear, what was clear to him was that the story began to circulate sometime after the industry rose to prominence during the 1920s. A discussion between Parrish and Carlota Vela, Don Macedonio's daughter, revealed that Mexicans and Mexican Americans in the Valley during the nineteenth century often gave gifts of oranges—then considered a delicacy—when visiting one another, and that such gifts were particularly common when Mexicans crossed the border and visited family and friends in Texas. The Velas in particular seemed to have commonly received gifts of oranges and other citrus fruits grown near Reynosa on the Mexican side of the border. Parrish also reported that Carlota remembered no priests bringing oranges to the ranch nor any pomp or circumstance surrounding their original tree plantings. Carlota did point out one tree that she claimed her mother had planted in 1880, but she made no claim that the tree was the oldest in the Valley; in fact, she seemed convinced that older trees could be found elsewhere. All of the trees that dated from the nineteenth century, she did reveal, came from the seeds of oranges grown south of the border.[82]

Virgil N. Lott, another early player in the local citrus industry, investigated the origins myth, noting that Don Macedonio Vela himself stated that he used to buy oranges and orange seeds in Cerralvo, Mexico, and that he planted a number of those trees beginning in 1893. Lott, who also argued that he himself deserved some of the credit for founding South Texas's citrus industry, claimed that it was only when John H. Shary and a few others came to the Valley that Mission became "the Home of the Grapefruit" and that Laguna Seca became the legendary birthplace of Valley citrus. Concerning the Laguna Seca myth, Lott wrote, "I know that two-thirds of our history is based upon just such legends as this one," doubting that the visit by the Oblate Fathers and the gift of the orange seeds had ever taken place.[83]

That history and myth played such an integral role in founding South Texas's citrus industry suggests the power that storytelling held in the minds of land men, growers, and colonists alike. Although it is unclear why the Laguna Seca myth emerged and not some other story, its placement as the mythical origins of citrus within the South Texas borderlands' Mexican past was clearly intended to evoke a sense of Old World exoticism on the part of the reader or listener. But it also evoked a connection to the land on the part of the newcomers. New recruits felt more attached to the land if their participation in the region fit neatly within the unbroken trajectory of the past.

The arrival of commercial citrus and agriculture was merely the latest attempt by one group to establish control over the South Texas borderlands and its inhabitants. Storytelling—or, at least, the printed word—was crucial not only in populating the region but also in helping new arrivals develop identities for themselves and ideas about the new, modern borderlands world in which they would live. If the Laguna Seca myth held sway in the minds of early citrus growers, what other kinds of stories and images did boosters portray to recruits, and what role did these images play in impressing upon the minds of some local citrus growers the type of society that they would help create in the region? Understanding the nature of the world that colonists set out to create is integral to understanding South Texas's subsequent history as a colonized space after the farmers arrived and began growing and selling their crops. Land had become widely available in the early twentieth century. Now, all that the land salesmen needed were people willing to relocate to the area. Boosting the region created an appealing opportunity in the minds of potential colonists; its significance would resonate not only within local citriculture, but also with all South Texans throughout the remainder of the twentieth century.

CHAPTER TWO

From Farmers to Colonizers

Boosterism and the Creation of Commercial
Farming Colonies

There was recognizable in the people they met in every
Valley town the spirit of the pioneer—the same that
conquered successively the bleak New England coast, the
prairies west of the Alleghanies [sic], the Western plains
and the land beyond the Rockies. These people have left
comfortable modern homes on the Atlantic seaboard,
ancestral mansions in Virginia, rich cornfields in Illinois
and Iowa, wheat fields in Minnesota, cotton plantations
in Mississippi—responding to the same urge that brought
their fathers to the Old World—and come here seeking
new homes and fortune. They have found both and are
content.[1]

Promoters and some land purchasers in the South Texas
borderlands saw their activity as merely the latest chapter in a much broader
American story of expansion, conquest, and colonization. Land sales advertising was common in the US West in the nineteenth and early twentieth centuries. Boosters, whom companies employed to promote land and real estate
ventures, sought to convince prospective buyers that the place they were
boosting was worthy of settlement. Whether through pamphlets, newspaper
articles, public advertisements, personal correspondence, or interpersonal
interaction, all commercial farmers and growers who invested in or relocated
to South Texas had been exposed to some form of boosterism.

The Lower Rio Grande Valley's citrus industry made up a large portion of
the regional South Texas economy beginning in the 1920s. Examining how
boosters recruited new colonists for the Valley's commercial citriculture project provides a lens into the types of communities that would be put in place
in the new, Anglicized South Texas borderlands. Boosters plied new recruits
with a veritable bombardment of images, constructing an imagined future for

the region's new inhabitants; they needed to convince others of the viability of this future before any fortunes could be made. The economies of the Valley and greater South Texas lived and died through land sales from about 1900 until the onset of the Great Depression.

Lower Rio Grande Valley boosterism flourished from the beginning of the commercial farming revolution in 1904 through the rise of the local citrus industry in the 1920s. Prospects for growing citrus, however, remained somewhat limited until the crop began producing sizable harvests in 1920. Although boosters' primary objective was to convince colonists of the profitability of commercial farming and citriculture in the Valley, images of local Mexicans as a racialized working class as well as romanticized depictions of Western pioneering and history also helped many farmers formulate new identities as patrón-style labor bosses. One must look deeper than the marketing of an imagined future in order to understand how Anglo land buyers negotiated their own identities as colonists. Notions of themselves as neopioneering farmers wringing profit from the backs of Mexican laborers in a modern agribusiness sector would inform Anglos' ideas of collective self-identity and race relations in the Valley and South Texas for decades. Much of the well-documented maltreatment of ethnic Mexicans in the region stemmed directly from and became systematized through the king-sized profit motives of early South Texas growers as sold to them by local boosters. Indeed, new colonists in the region's commercial citrus empire believed that fabulous wealth lay in their futures. As historian David Vaught argues for rural California growers at the turn of the twentieth century, South Texas citrus growers were more than simple industrialists or capitalists. Growers can better be understood as horticulturalists who exhibited multiple grower cultures of their own. Also, contemporary accounts of the Valley and its history show the degree to which the Anglo historical imagination differed markedly from what can be considered the empirical truth of the region's Mexican past.[2] In order to understand the origins of anti-Mexican sentiment in South Texas, then, historians need to carefully examine the cultures to which those growers belonged.

The human element involved in the process of farmers' negotiating new identities as colonizers should not be taken for granted. New colonists who bought into the boosters' vision of a new society at the border left everything behind in their hometowns—a sense of comfort, familiarity, knowledge of how farming operated in the US Midwest, and oftentimes even friends and families—to relocate to South Texas. It was a big gamble for all who came. Some became successful, while others lost everything. Others found themselves swindled by shady land salesmen. Thus, in re-creating the Valley's colonists it is important to keep in mind the hopes, dreams, and emotional tolls that pursuing new lives could engender in people.

Boosters presented the Lower Rio Grande Valley as a new adventure for the pragmatic, business-minded midwestern farmer. Rarely was the Valley described in paradisiacal terms. The images presented in the booster literature served as a blueprint for how to carve a new Anglo-American economic machine and society out of a rural Mexican space. Thus, though driven by money, the vision encompassed more than how a new settler could grow their bottom line. Boosters and developers wanted a specific type of person to inhabit the new South Texas borderlands, namely, white American farmers who were forward-thinking enough to perceive the benefits of living in a place that at first glance seemed wholly foreign to them. Colonists had to be convinced that relocating to the Valley was a once-in-a-lifetime opportunity that they could not afford to pass up. How colonists interacted with this vision in creating their new world, and how these ideas resonated throughout South Texas society over the course of the twentieth century, will be the primary concerns of the rest of this book.

Boosterism and the US West

Boosterism has a long history in the US West. As western lands opened up for new settlement in the middle of the nineteenth century, boosters acted as human magnets who had one goal in mind: making money. Boosters sought to make towns grow in order to increase property values, which in turn increased the wealth of landowners and businessmen. They attracted newcomers primarily through written literature and advertising. By the turn of the twentieth century, boosterism was commonly a joint project of municipal government and business leaders. As advertising became a highly structured and professional field, ad men joined the fray. Numerous advertisers launched legitimate careers promoting new towns that dotted the western landscape. Every new town and city in the US West was, to some extent, boosted.[3]

Historian David M. Wrobel has studied booster literature from the end of the Civil War through the 1920s. He argues that boosters captured a moment of anxiety in US history, one during which the United States transformed from a rural nation into an urban one. Boosters looked to the future during that period, often announcing the arrival of new urban spaces in the rural US West where they did not yet exist. Simultaneously, old-timers in the US West reminisced on a rural past slowly slipping between their fingers. Thus, according to Wrobel, "boosters literally tried to imagine western places through embellished and effusive descriptions."[4] Land buyers thus carried with them into those regions preconceived images of new spaces, laying the groundwork for what life in the new towns and cities would be like. South Texas's future was no different; it was, in accordance with Wrobel's larger thesis, an imagined one.

Another historian of the US West, Walter Nugent, has commented on the power of boosting and land promotion during the early twentieth century. "To read the promotional blurbs," Nugent writes, "one would think that women or men had to hardly work at all." He continues:

> A 1911 advertisement [for the San Luis Valley in Colorado] showed wheat that "threshed out 64 bushels to the acre." Artesian wells gushed water "soft and as pure as crystal." Problems? "We have no waste land. We have never had a failure. We have fine churches and schools. We have no cyclones or severe storms. We have the best artesian wells in the world. We have 350 days of sunshine during the year. We have a complete telephone system covering the entire valley. We have the best wagon roads and the cheapest fuel and the purest water in the world. . . . We hold the world's record on . . . potatoes, sugar beets, wheat, oats, barley, alfalfa, field peas, and onions. . . . We have the best irrigation and also the cheapest and best soil and climate in the world."[5]

Also, according to Nugent, a modern, profit-minded ideal that relied on cheap labor had replaced older notions of agrarianism (or pride in farming as a means to self-sufficiency, individualism, independence, and democracy) in the West: "Another effusion in 1915 insisted that millions of acres of first-class land remained open for homesteading and noted, not quite in the Jeffersonian spirit, that 'the easiest money a farmer can make is what he can make out of the increase in the value of his land. Every $10 per acre increase on 320 acres amounts to $3,200. Colorado's cheapest lands today will rapidly increase value as they are cultivated.' The old idea—get land almost free, work hard (or bet well), and end up a rich farmer—still beckoned in Colorado."[6] Farmers, then, in the early twentieth century, could still be independent producers, own valuable land, and live in pristine spaces suited perfectly to their needs. These images held strong sway in the minds of people who pushed west toward the Pacific and south toward Mexico.

Citriculture in California fit neatly into these larger patterns of boosterism, perhaps even exaggerating certain tendencies of the typical booster's embellishments. In his study of California citriculture, historian Douglas Sackman writes, "Guidebooks told would-be orange growers that fantasies could materialize in California, that the state was simply supernatural." As early as the 1880s, he continues, "Southern California was crowded with communities claiming to be [a] second Eden." Cities such as Pasadena were dubbed "an earthly paradise in every sense which the term implies," an attractive characterization for growers from the less-than-paradisiacal confines of the US Midwest. The image of an edenic landscape held such sway in the minds of growers that not only did it help build a successful new citrus industry in rural California, but growers also used it as part of a larger campaign to create markets of orange consumers throughout the country. Growers' associations such as Sunkist made millions of dollars, in part by presenting California as "an Eden in which fruits naturally materialized for the pleasure of the people."[7]

Images presented in western booster literature thus held powerful sway in the minds of commercial farmers as well as consumers of US-grown crops. Booster literature in South Texas fit into some of these larger trends. Geographer Terry G. Jordan correctly argues that boosters successfully created a "perceptual region" of the Lower Rio Grande Valley in the minds of Valley residents and visitors, popularizing the place as the "Magic Valley," a moniker that remained popular through the middle part of the twentieth century.[8]

Several questions about the area's "magic" remain. For instance, what was the Magic Valley, and what did this image mean to local farmers? How did the image rely on the nascent citrus industry, and what was the interrelationship between boosterism and citriculture? Twentieth-century Valley boosterism can be divided into two periods: precitrus boosterism, from 1900 to about 1915, and citrus-related boosterism, from about 1915 until the middle of the Great Depression. Each period exhibited distinct but interrelated characteristics crucial to understanding the role that boosterism played in kick-starting the citrus industry, modernizing the region through commercial farming, and ultimately creating a class of colonists who hoped to capitalize off the backs of a marginalized and supposedly premodern ethnic Mexican working class.

Magic for Sale

Boosterism got off to a slow start in the Lower Rio Grande Valley. Despite the fact that midwesterners came in smaller numbers during the first two decades of the twentieth century than they did during the 1920s, precitrus boosterism laid the groundwork for the citrus industry's founding and thus its promotion and expansion. The literature took on a number of forms, ranging from simple public advertisements to elaborate pamphlets. There was also a lot of face-to-face communication between boosters and potential colonists. While the mediums for communicating the boosters' vision never changed, the vision's substance transformed as the Valley become more successful and economically vibrant.

There is also a larger context worth mentioning that helps explain how land boosterism functioned. One commonality between Valley boosterism and formal colonial writing in other parts of the world is the idyllic literary flourishes used to describe colonized spaces. French writers in colonial Algeria in the 1840s, for example, depicted the Sahara Desert as falling "within the conventions of the pastoral and picturesque." Even while France expanded its empire through a bloody military conquest, writers "distinguished [the Sahara] by its visual beauty—drifting dunes, swaying palms, and bubbling oasis springs—bathed in a glorious luminosity that few regions could rival." This romantic image of the conquered Algerian Sahara persisted for about half a century, until the late 1800s. Lower Rio Grande Valley boosters and writers displayed a similarly long-enduring bipolarity of idealism amidst conquest, violence, and social inequality.[9]

But the imperial ethic in Valley boosterism appeared even before the military conquest of Mexico in 1848. Not long after the American occupation of South Texas, a group of newly arrived Anglo-Americans began publishing a newspaper titled *The American Flag*. According to one historian, the paper's editors "vociferously championed the glorious future of the Valley under American rule." Although their main goal might not have been to boost the Valley to potential settlers, the editors clearly sought to promote a vision for the future. The paper initially argued for the annexation of lands reaching all the way to the Sierra Madre (many Americans hoped to annex an even larger portion of Mexican territory than the United States eventually did). The popularity of this idea soon faded, but by November of 1846 *The American Flag* reported that a number of Americans had purchased land north of Camargo from Mexican landowners. Similarly, in the fall of 1847 the paper reported that a number of Mexicans had migrated north of the border, being so anxious to live under American governance that they had exchanged improved farmlands in Mexico for undeveloped tracts on the US side of the river. Americans, too, the paper reported, continued to buy up huge tracts of Valley lands. Some Mexican landowners had been eager to sell their lands on the north side of the river, even for drastically reduced prices, because they feared the end of the war would bring a loss of all Mexican claims to the Rio Grande's north banks. These visions for the Valley would not be realized for another fifty or sixty years, but the prospects in the Valley's future were clearly already taking shape.[10]

These early efforts at positive, future-oriented promotion aside, Valley boosterism prior to 1904 was relatively limited. After the railroad's arrival, and land became available for sale, the only way for land promoters and boosters to sell their lots successfully was to advertise. South Texas thus followed a common pattern with the rest of the US West. Once a railroad arrived, boosterism and land speculation began. But a railroad was needed for this whole process to begin.

About 1904, local newspapers—many of them run by land developers themselves—filled with advertisements for land. In an early edition of the *Missionite*, several companies published ads in the paper's classifieds section. La Lomita Company, run by prominent Valley boosters John H. Conway and James W. Hoit, boasted of having fifteen thousand acres of prime farming land in the Mission area *still* for sale, implying that they had already sold much of their initial holdings. The Mission Land Company also offered numerous acres for sale in the same issue of the *Missionite*. Finally, the paper included ads for neighboring counties. San Benito, a new community north of Brownsville in Cameron County, boasted a thirty-seven-mile-long canal for irrigation purposes as well as a population of about one thousand, which was high for South Texas agricultural towns at such an early date.[11]

Before long the traditional pamphlet-style boosterism kicked into full gear in the Lower Rio Grande Valley. One booklet, titled *The Lower Rio Grande Valley: Without a Rival*, published by the Lower Rio Grande Valley Commercial Club of Brownsville in 1909, is a perfect example of the use of photography in booster literature. The opening paragraphs of this pamphlet serve as a nice foray into local boosterism: "The object of this booklet is to portray by word and picture, as concisely as possible, and accurately, the natural advantages and the agricultural, industrial and commercial development of the Lower Rio Grande Valley. Because of the character of these conditions and the magnitude of the development, this Valley is, perhaps, attracting more attention than any other section of the United States. This booklet will answer most of the inquiries about this wonderland of horticulture and agriculture."[12] Although the images of an edenic "wonderland" were rare for the Valley in comparison with those of boosters of other Sunbelt regions such as California, this early piece highlighted a number of themes that would become common in early-twentieth-century Valley land promotion.

One of those themes is geography. An elaborate map early in the booklet shows the Valley—and, as importantly for the Commercial Club, Brownsville—inhabiting the twenty-fifth parallel, almost exactly in the center of North America. The Valley is shown to be 450 miles south of southern California, emphasizing the natural climatic advantages that the region would have in comparison with its well-known counterpart. The caption beneath the map also mentions the Valley's then nearly one-half million acres of untapped agricultural lands. The geographical advantages of the Valley were not only agricultural, but also commercial. The area was a short railroad trip to San Antonio, fifteen hundred miles by rail to San Francisco, and fourteen hundred miles by ship to the then-new Panama Canal, which was, in turn, two thousand miles from New York City. All of this implied that engaging in agricultural pursuits gave Valley-area farmers centrally located access to markets throughout the country. But there were natural advantages to the area for the farmer as well. The half-million available acres were all supposedly irrigable from the river. Also, the author correctly noted, the Valley was not really a Valley at all, but more of a river delta, or a place with rich soil gradually formed by the alluvial silt carried by the Rio Grande's waters—a fact conveniently attested to by a professor from the Agricultural and Mechanical College of Texas (today Texas A&M University). Truthfully, the Valley indeed lent itself to intensive agriculture. By implication, all that the area needed was a group of industrious farmers willing to seize its advantages.[13]

A second theme is that of personal testimony. Real-life examples from local growers could speak to any number of issues concerning farming, from profitability to crop bounty to leisure activity. Concerning the fertility of the soil, the author cited the Brulay Sugar Plantation near Brownsville, "where for thirty-eight years sugar cane has been grown continuously on the same land without one ounce of fertilizer other than that carried to it naturally in irrigating with the rich, silt-laden waters of the Rio Grande."[14] Real-world examples and personal testimonies from Valley growers would become increasingly common in South Texas booster literature over the years.

Another topic that appeared in the literature was that of irrigation, which would prove central to the burgeoning citrus industry. Nearly every Valley booster prior to and following the citrus boom discussed irrigation in at least some detail. Irrigation underpinned the entire commercial farming project. After providing a photograph of a modern irrigation pump, the author of *The Lower Rio Grande Valley* offered a long discourse on the topic. Because of the Valley's relative lack of rainfall, the pamphleteer explained, irrigation from the Rio Grande was an absolute necessity. Since 1905, thirty-two irrigation canals had been constructed in the Valley at a total cost of three million dollars. Some of those included the largest privately owned canals in the United States, with storage capacity for immense amounts of river floodwater. The author relied on the testimony of an expert, Professor Lucius M. Wilcox, who studied irrigation:

As a result of a five months' study of the water of the Rio Grande, a stream which carries excessive quantities of silt, it was estimated that in using one acre foot of muddy water in irrigating, nine hundred and fifty-five pounds of potassium sulphate, fifty-eight pounds of phosphoric acid and fifty-three pounds of nitrogen were added to each acre. A thirty-bushel crop of wheat usually removes twenty-eight pounds of potash, twenty-three pounds of phosphoric acid and forty-five pounds of nitrogen. It is also true that considerably more than one foot of water is generally applied to the land each year in irrigating. It would seem utterly impossible to exhaust the soil irrigated with such water.[15]

The promoters clearly hoped that such expert testimony would impress their potential colonists.

A fourth theme present in this early pamphlet and common to Valley boosterism is that of modernity and development. Like many others, the pamphleteer noted the arrival of the railroad in 1904 as the pivotal moment in local history that transformed the region from an allegedly backwards cattle range into a commercial farming region with all the modern amenities. The building of churches and schools, hotels, machine shops, mercantile establishments, and any enterprise involving large-scale capital investment constituted modernity's arrival in the region. Enjoyment of these modern amenities also hinged on a warm local environment in which midwesterners could escape from the cold winters, although later boosters often exaggerated the alleged mildness of the South Texas climate.

What underpinned this whole modern system, of course, was the ethnic Mexican farm laborer. The pamphlet's author claimed that "an abundance of Mexican farm labor at from 50 to 75 cents per day (they boarding and lodging themselves)" was available to the potential colonist. Farmers could rest easy and relax while cheap laborers harvested their crops. The workers allowed local farmers to become members of a new leisure class along the border. The linchpin of this new system was the relationship between the new growers and local ethnic Mexicans.[16]

Fitting with the notion of leisurely living, the author argued that the region exceeded both California and Florida in terms of opportunities for sporting and outdoor recreation. The Valley was perfect for fishing, hunting, and "bathing," which in the early twentieth century meant swimming on an oceanfront beach. "Automobilists" could also find better roads in the Valley than in Florida and California. Life in the Valley could be much easier and more relaxed than it was elsewhere, even more so than in the sunny climes of Florida and California.[17]

Could the Valley really offer more than what Florida and California could offer? Comparative analysis with other regions appeared time and again in the literature, but it is interesting that at this early stage, prior to the arrival of citrus in the region, boosters were already willing to compare the Valley to the two other primary citrus-growing regions in the United States. California especially evoked a leisurely, paradisiacal image in the minds of most Americans in the early twentieth century.[18] Not only were California and Florida competitors with the Valley for grower recruits from other areas, but also the three shared the distinction of being regions where commercial farming drove modern rural economies. All three shared similar warm climates. The later selection of citrus as the primary crop in the South Texas farming economy, then, was more than a simple consideration of environmental adaptability and agricultural economy: promoters and agricultural enthusiasts noted potential competitive advantages in learning from the successes and mistakes of citrus growers in those two other sections. From the beginning, then, the Valley shared much in common with Florida and California, including its coming status in the 1920s as another major member of the US citrus belt.

Another theme present in this early Brownsville pamphlet is an enumeration of the Valley's agricultural products. Even at this early stage in the area's commercial farming history, the region boasted a wide variety of crops, such as sugarcane, cotton, corn, broomcorn, alfalfa, winter vegetables, figs, grapes, dates, pineapples, papayas, bananas, guavas, pecans, English walnuts, almonds, and a small number of citrus fruits. The pamphlet also included expected yields for each crop, costs of planting, and crop prices. New farmers could thus expect to find in the Valley a diversified agricultural land with a number of potential crops that they could grow for profit. Such would be the case even after the region's large-scale shift to citrus during the 1920s.

The last theme was an invitation to the reader to visit the Valley in person and to explore its potential firsthand. In the case of the Lower Rio Grande Valley Commercial Club, people came down from all points north on the first and third Tuesdays of each month on cheap round-trip train excursions.[19] Visits on organized train excursions became common in the years to come, a form of in-person boosterism to which landowners and promoters devoted a significant amount of time, money, and salesmanship. Land salesmen would spin the vision of a "marvelous wonderland of agriculture and opportunity" in surprisingly similar ways. A consistent vision of what the Valley was and what it could become would be presented through the literature and the eventual in-person sales pitch in the coming years.

In sum, the vision for the new Anglo-American commercial farming colony prior to the arrival of citrus consisted of the following parts: the primacy of Valley geography, personal testimonies, the power of irrigation, modern development, leisurely living, an array of agricultural products, and finally, the invitation to potential colonists to come and visit the Valley. Mexicans and Mexican Americans, as time would show, had a unique marginal role; they were mentioned only as servants and manual laborers—when they were even mentioned at all. Ethnic Mexicans would have no other place in the modernized South Texas borderlands region.

All Lower Rio Grande Valley boosters followed the above-mentioned trends. In 1910 C. S. Fowler and Brother, a land development company near Alice, Texas, in the Texas Gulf Coast country bordering the Valley to the north, published a pamphlet advertising its lands. Purportedly written by "one who knows," the pamphlet laid out the general conditions for the reader of the growing season of 1910. The pamphlet's primary focus, however, within the context of the general trends set forth previously, was profit. All aspects of life in Alice in 1910 were secondary to profit. Since there was "practically no winter" in the Gulf Coast, growers could harvest two or three crops per year, which "naturally means two or three times as much profit as one crop." Furthermore, the author argued, "if crops are handled right you can have something growing and something to sell every week in the year." The author goes on to discuss building costs, livestock costs, as well as the farmers' ability to "secure good Mexican labor from 40c. to 75c per day . . . and they board themselves." The Fowler Brothers were part of a small cadre of growers promoting satsuma oranges and lemons prior to Texas citrus's shift to the Valley. Orchards commanded three hundred to four hundred dollars per acre when four years old. Most of the "cheap" and "very rich" fruit and vegetable land was on plots that were carved from a local ranch. Finally, the financial terms of buying a Fowler Brothers grove came at the end of the pamphlet, dangled there to encourage the reader to make a personal visit:

We have put the price of his land down to $40. per acre payable $1. per acre down and $1. per acre per month until paid for. No interest will be charged and we will pay all taxes until land is fully paid for. We also agree that in case of death before full payment, that we will cancel the balance due and make deed at once. Possession will be given as soon as first payment is made. Most anyone can buy a farm on these terms and this land is sure to increase very rapidly in value. Land that will grow Oranges, Figs, Lemons, etc., is not going to stay long at $40. per acre. We only have a limited amount of this land to sell on these terms.

The profitability and potential yield for satsuma oranges and other early citrus fruits of the region was such that promoters had hoped that a New California would take shape along the Gulf Coast.[20]

Again, that boosters referred to the state in such comparative terms comes as little surprise. Whether the "Magic Valley" or "New California," the nicknames thought up by boosters could be easily remembered and could impart some pizzazz in the minds of potential farmers. The Valley's "magic" was a marketing tool that in no way represented any widely held belief that its potential agricultural bounty was limitless. Many growers would learn this sad lesson only after having made their land purchases. The language of empire was also present. One booster, writing from Katy, Texas, on agriculture in the entire state, referred to Texas as an "agricultural empire," comparing Texas's geography and agricultural output to those of other US states but also to those of entire European nations. "Empire," in this case, augured a modern space filled with an agricultural output that relied on new settlers. This booster—who also boosted satsuma oranges in the Gulf Coast country—commented extensively on "northern home seekers in Texas," arguing that if "homeseekers and capital that are interested in irrigation projects only knew what is awaiting them in Texas, where millions of fertile acres of rich arid domain is untouched, there would soon be a rush to the State that would develop and populate the lands, build magnificent towns and cities, [and] new lines of railroads."[21] The author of the Katy pamphlet clearly meant to impress upon the minds of his readers a vision of colonization, settlement, and development that would never fail.

Lower Rio Grande Valley boosters incorporated the vision of colonization and settlement over time alongside the themes enumerated in earlier pamphlets, but again, the trend was to relegate all facets of living in the Valley's agricultural colonies to the ultimate goal of making a profit. One booster, writing for a land company based out of Kansas City, Missouri, wrote in 1913 that the Valley, "rich in historic romance and native resources . . . is being developed from *unprofitable* plains and jungles of cactus, mesquite and ebony into the *richest* agricultural and garden spot in the United States" (emphasis mine). The author relegated the common booster themes to list form, arguing that a great climate, rich alluvial soil, water for irrigation, cheap Mexican labor "without boarding or lodging"—noted again so growers could rest easy that they would not have to pay for ethnic Mexican workers to live near them—and a market for selling agricultural products could be found in the region. Again, however, we find these "natural resources" relegated to the gods of profit, as the author wrote: "Under such circumstances it is not surprising that millions of capital is being attracted and that prosperous farmers are flocking into this region and profiting by its development, besides enjoying comforts hitherto unknown to them."[22] Texas agricultural boosters and colonists in the early twentieth century were not solely profit-minded creatures, but they were clearly *primarily* concerned with profit.

The booster quoted above also devoted an entire paragraph to ethnic Mexican labor. After informing the reader that land plots in the Valley could be cleared at anywhere from eight dollars to sixteen dollars per acre, the author entered into a long description of Mexican and Mexican American workers. This description is worth quoting at length, since few boosters provided so detailed a snapshot into labor conditions in the Valley during the 1910s:

> The Mexicans are always available. The Mexican stays right on the farm in his own little bungalow of brush or of gunnysack over a mesquite bush ready on a day's notice to go to work at from 50 cents to one dollar per day and board himself, and prepared to lay off at a moment's notice. A great many Valley farmers are now providing their Mexicans with a one or two-room shed house, which is inexpensive. The Mexican laborer is not only a good worker, but he will neither steal you blind nor stab you in the back. He would protect your property or your family with his life. He is the best farmhand in America today, and there is an inexhaustible supply of these farm laborers just across the Rio Grande, ready to come at your call.[23]

The reader thus saw an elaboration of the image of workers presented in other pamphlets, which simply argued that Mexican and Mexican Americans worked cheaply and boarded themselves. Here, they are also loyal, compliant, and honest workers who treat the farmer and his family respectfully. The Mexican is neither slave nor equal to the farmer but quaintly stays "in his own little gunnysack" and does whatever the farmer commands. This image of the docile and pliant Mexican is important, as Anglo–Mexican relations in South Texas over the course of the twentieth century show that an overwhelming majority of newcomers in the early twentieth century bought into racist characterizations of their Mexican neighbors.

Notions that ethnic Mexicans in Texas were a violent, treacherous people were nearly a century old by this point. Many white Texans had written about ethnic Mexicans' alleged lack of morals, an idea originating, at least in part, from the famous cruelties that Santa Anna had shown the Texan soldiers during the Texas Revolution in the spring of 1836, as well as the growing distrust of ethnic Mexicans among white Texans in the decades that followed.[24] But now a benevolent paternalism, whereby new colonists came to consider

ethnic Mexicans as loyal subjects, was clearly rooted in the promotional literature. Boosters thus served to introduce Anglo-midwesterners to their new
neighbors. Also, the booster's Mexican could be either a person from across
the river or a foreigner who lived somewhere inside of South Texas itself, indicating to the reader that an unspecified permanent space would be maintained
between the new colonist and his workers. The racial border between whites
and Mexicans was intended to be a magnet for new farmers.

At least one historian has argued that the characterization of Mexicans as
surplus laborers dates back to Texas independence in the 1830s, meaning that
no natural market conditions led to the proletarianization of ethnic Mexicans
in South Texas. Rather, a culture of anti-Mexican racism predominated in
Anglo South Texas. New Anglo growers targeted by the boosters responded
by combining the arrogant excesses of Mexican *hacienda*-style feudalism with
modern capitalist exploitation to dominate the poor on the Texas side of the
border. Boosters thus relied on some preexisting ideas about race and class in
the South Texas borderlands that were already common among Anglo Texans,
arguing that farming in the region could be successful in large part because
ethnic Mexicans were exploitable and would work cheaply. Promoters, then,
built a preexistent racism into potential colonists' designs on the bottom line
of commercial farming. Ethnic Mexicans became an exploited underclass not
necessarily because small growers in the region needed cheap workers in order
to survive economically. Rather, land developers promoted ethnic Mexicans as
cheap, docile, and exploitable laborers in order to make local agriculture more
attractive to potential recruits from outside of the state and to sell them a plot
of land. Boosters clearly repackaged older strains of racism and sold them to
the region's new white colonists in an updated format.[25]

The La Feria Land Syndicate, a company based in Iowa and South Dakota
that boosted and sold land in Cameron County, released a pamphlet in 1914
that discussed ethnic Mexican workers. Alongside discussions of profitability,
crops, and the region's development, the author presented an image of pliant
Mexicans very similar to, if perhaps even more crude, than that of his previous
counterparts. Mexican workers were preferable to US farmhands, the booster
argued, "because they never heard of an eight-hour system or labor unions."
Furthermore, in Mexico the average wage for farmwork was twelve and one-
half cents US per day, so, with the fifty or seventy-five cents per day they could
make on the Texas side of the border, "they think they have struck it rich. Thus,
the opening of the Rio Grande Valley is a great blessing both to the people
buying the land who need help and the Mexican who needs the work."[26]

Growers, in the La Feria writer's characterization, were thus the benevolent employers of impoverished ethnic Mexicans, merely benefiting from the needy status of the latter. The notion that Mexican nationals lived much better in the Lower Rio Grande Valley than they would have otherwise south of the border was also a common apology among Anglos for Mexicans' marginalized status. Mexicans, in their view, should only be treated well enough to wring as much profit out of their labor as possible.

By 1914 the Mexican Revolution was in full swing, so the mid-1910s South Texas booster had the extra challenge of either ignoring the revolution or dismissing it as an aberration. The La Feria booster chose the latter and in doing so kept the image of docile Mexicans consistent with that of other boosters: "While the Mexicans have been having more or less gorilla [sic] warfare, yet this is due only to the oppression wrought upon them by a few who have been trying to control and rob the many. By nature they are quiet and peaceful, and while it has not been their ambition to progress in the accumulation of great wealth, yet they are exceedingly faithful in doing the work they agree to do. . . . In fact the Mexican labor is one of the biggest assets of the Rio Grande Valley."[27]

The Mexican laborer as great asset would become a familiar refrain in the Valley as well as greater South Texas after the rise of citriculture. Ironically, however, it would be only a year after the publication of this pamphlet that the Plan de San Diego rebellion erupted, wherein the Texas Rangers led a wave of reprisal killings against ethnic Mexicans in the region for allegedly planning to overthrow American rule. The revolt belied not only the image of ethnic Mexicans as pliant but also displayed the ability of Anglo-American racism to sow discontent. At the heart of this anti-colonial revolt against white Americans was resentment caused by the wide-ranging anti-Mexican sentiment that this piece of land promotion embodied. That violent Anglo reprisals took place during the rebellion only further emphasized the general lack of cross-cultural cooperation between Anglo-Americans and ethnic Mexicans in South Texas during the early part of the twentieth century.

Land tourists displayed a willingness to believe boosters' arguments that Mexicans were overwhelmingly peaceful. One group, in a private letter to the Southwestern Land Company in the mid-1910s, expressed excitement toward "the colonization and development of Sharyland" as well as their "unfaltering faith in its wonderful future." They also claimed that "the Mexican situation has been grossly exaggerated and from our talks with Valley residents and men who are in a position to know, we are satisfied that there is no reason whatever for apprehension and that what little trouble there has been, will soon be over."[28] The "Mexican situation" to which the writers referred was undoubtedly the Mexican Revolution, the Plan de San Diego uprising, or perhaps both. Any attempts by land promoters to assuage recruits' fears of violence undoubtedly downplayed the actual situation between white Americans and ethnic Mexicans in South Texas. Indeed, it is worth considering whether "the men who are in a position to know" purposefully misrepresented the situation or even received coaching from the company. With both the contemporary violence as well as the area's violent past shielded from the eyes of the growers, at least some new recruits considered the Valley's new agricultural regime as a peaceful entity that Mexicans and Mexican Americans would never attempt to challenge. It is little wonder that many Valley Anglos found Mexican Americans' assertion of civil rights later in the twentieth century so shocking. The legacy of racism and segregation continued into the twentieth century and fed directly off the naivety of new arrivals and investors from the US Midwest, whose perception of local society stemmed from boosters' duplicitous mischaracterizations of local history and contemporary life.

Deviations from the above-mentioned literary trends rarely occurred. Writers commonly characterized the Valley and South Texas as being part of a benevolent empire. John H. Shary's organization, one of the prime promoters of the citrus industry in the Valley, began publishing booster tracts sometime in late 1913 or early 1914. Shary's booster—it is unclear whether Shary himself was the actual author—presented Texas agriculture as an imperialist venture: "Texas is an empire within itself, 27 per cent larger than Germany, 28 per cent larger than France and 110 per cent larger than England. Yet its population is but a small fraction as compared with either country. If every man, woman and child in the United States lived in Texas it would not be as densely populated as Germany. If a wall were built entirely around Texas, shutting off intercourse with the outside world, it would be possible for Texas to furnish her people with all the necessaries of life."

Texas was a bounty in itself, set apart from the rest of the United States. Shary's writer also took the discussion of the Valley's climate one step further than his predecessors did, comparing the mean average high temperatures in Brownsville in July 1913 with those of four other US midwestern cities: Brownsville, 90.3 degrees; Omaha, Nebraska, 90.8; Kansas City, Missouri, 91.5; and Topeka, Kansas, 93.1.[29] The Valley's climate, by implication, was not that different from many places in the US Midwest. An empire of Anglo-American farmers could live comfortably on Mexico's doorstep.

One of the reasons that Shary became so successful was his promotional ability. A pamphlet published sometime about 1914 was a masterful stroke in using all of the previous themes seen in early-twentieth-century Valley booster literature plus a few new embellishments. The pamphlet used the past to appeal to potential colonists' sense of romanticism in the US West, helping to imbue a sense of belonging to a modern community of western pioneers. The author discussed the Valley's history from the end of the US-Mexico War in 1848 to the arrival of the railroad in the region in 1904. According to the author, the Valley might have been overlooked for development during that period because of events such as the 1849 gold rush in California. By discussing history, the tract laid a historical framework into which growers in the Valley could insert themselves. In doing so, growers could see themselves as inhabiting roles in a larger story of conflict and reclamation from the Valley's immediate past. The tale was, of course, one of Anglo-American success at the expense of ethnic Mexicans. A veritable bombardment of images from Anglos already familiar with the region helped inform newcomers who they were to become and how to interact with ethnic Mexicans. The latter, boosters implied, were the losers in the previous half-century of the Valley's history; if they had the modern capabilities to develop the region themselves, they would have done so.

One particularly interesting thing about the Shary tract, however, is its emphasis not only on the profitability of using Mexican and Mexican American workers, but also on the quality of the people, both Anglo and Hispanic, already living in the Valley. "The inhabitants of the Valley," the author wrote, "have come from nearly every state in the Union and every walk in life. As a class they are the very best and far different from the kind usually found in new countries." In other words, the writer self-consciously placed the Valley's colonization within the wider context of traditional settler colonialism. White Americans would have it easier in South Texas than in other parts of the world. Mexicans, allegedly

> prefer to live by themselves and do not try to mix up in other society. The most of them have been raised in this country and are above the average, very fine people. Some have brought their families out of Mexico during the recent trouble, as they prefer to live in peace and where they can secure steady employment, better pay, and send their children to superior schools. They quickly see the advantage of American methods and education, which they are not slow to assimilate. . . . A great many of the Mexican people speak some English and are quick to learn. They are peaceful, honest, polite and religious. The entire family works and are very handy, especially in picking

cotton and corn, transplanting vegetables and in harvesting and packing time. The women soon become fair domestic servants and the men will work day and night, rain or shine, in their own steady way and can plow a furrow much straighter than the average farmer.[30]

The society, then, that potential colonists saw themselves joining was a segregated one, not just one that relied on Mexican labor. But ethnic Mexicans also allegedly cared about assimilating into the coming Anglo-American society. Subsequently, since "Mexican contractors with Mexican labor" worked the growers' new lands, most colonists could be assured that their contact with workers could be kept at a minimum. That "the most of them [had] been raised in this country" speaks volumes to the coming development of the native-colonist relationship common to the colonial paradigm. Also, the prescribed roles of women as domestic servants displayed that boosters and promoters were more than willing to enforce normative American gender roles onto the Valley's native population. Overall, the depressed status of the worker only served to further reinforce any person of Mexican origin at the bottom of the Valley's social hierarchy.[31]

For the boosters, profit nevertheless remained king. One undated tract that appears to be from the mid-1910s opened with the exciting slogan, "Be your own master!" coupled with a drawing of a grapefruit tree with dollar signs sketched onto the fruits and the slogan, "Money grows," underneath. Although this tract promoted early citrus in the Gulf Coast region prior to its shift to the Valley during the early 1920s, it was one of the first to promote investment in farming in the region "as an old age pension and legacy for posterity," rather than simply an all-encompassing engagement or lifestyle. This would become an oft-used theme in later citrus-era boosterism.[32]

Boosterism prior to citrus's rise in the 1920s can thus be summed up as having two primary features. First, profit, above all, was the underlying concern, with every aspect of life in the Lower Rio Grande Valley farm colonies relegated to making money. Second, ethnic Mexicans remained at the bottom of the future social hierarchy, and when visible in the literature at all, they were an infantile people who would in no way challenge the new status quo. These elements remained in the booster literature throughout the following decades.[33] But growers also appealed to recruits' sense of history, implying that taking part in Valley agriculture would insert them into a larger story of pioneering and conquest.

Before discussing how growers attempted to realize their vision of the new order, one more important piece remains: the image of citriculture itself in

Valley boosterism. By the late 1920s, Valley citrus—consisting primarily of grapefruit and grown largely in the western portion of the Valley—was the most economically important crop in the region, with winter truck vegetables second and cotton third. When deciding what crops to plant, an observer noted that for small and large growers alike, "citrus orchards are given the first choice of land, and continue to grow at the expense of all other crops."[34] The image of citriculture in the booster literature became intertwined with profit and anti-Mexican racism, laying the blueprint for citrus growers to implement a new, albeit imagined, future in the Lower Rio Grande Valley.

Citrus Pioneers and "Sleepy Old Mexico"

Dreams of profit and Mexican workers were, however, only part of the boosters' vision. Immediately following World War I, boosters turned to the new focus of Valley agriculture: citrus fruits. Citriculture was the most vital component of Valley booster literature during the 1920s and '30s. On top of promoting profits, labor, and segregation, boosters promoted citriculture as the ultimate key to success. Writers not only introduced the ecology and marketability of the fruits to midwesterners—who, presumably, had no experience growing citrus—but they also wove citrus into the culture and history of the region itself, creating the image of a new farming world with exotic and exciting new crops. Ethnic Mexicans, however, also came to be relegated to relics of the past that were woven into this Anglicized, future-oriented citrus-growing space. As time passed, the resulting interaction of Valley growers with the vision of a society that consisted of commercial citrus farming led to the development of a modernized space fraught with the difficulties of intensive capital accumulation and race-based segregation.

Boosters flocked to citrus as it became increasingly apparent that it was the future of Valley agriculture. Writers provided important details and advice on citrus growing, marketing, and profitability, the latter being a difficult undertaking, since most citrus trees bear no fruit until three to five years after planting. Citrus-era boosters also built their vision for the new Valley on top of the conventions of pre–World War I Valley boosters, adding appeals to potential recruits' sense of history in an attempt to construct exciting new identities for Valley colonists.

One of the earliest and most prolific boosters of citriculture in the Lower Rio Grande Valley was Julia Cameron Montgomery, who wrote for *Monty's Monthly Magazine*, based out of Brownsville. The Lower Rio Grande Citrus Exchange, one of the first of many citrus growers' mutuals and co-ops in the

Valley, used Montgomery's magazine to publicize the nascent industry. Montgomery also published entire tracts devoted solely to the industry itself. Her first tract, *The Citrus Tree*, appeared as a supplement to *Monty's* in 1922. The tract included numerous photographs of large trees, testimonials, and advice for potential growers. Montgomery opened with grower A. J. McColl's "high five" of citrus growing in the Valley, which, if followed properly, could allegedly lead to fabulous wealth and prosperity:

1. Fertile soil without necessity of fertilization.
2. Inexhaustible supply of irrigation water with ditches on land.
3. A 12 month growing season to rush your orchard to maturity.
4. Cheap labor to do your work.
5. Good transportation facilities and ready markets for your crop.[35]

Aside from practicable advice, Montgomery's work is notable in that she remained one of the few boosters to promote Valley citrus as a whole rather than the vested interests of one land company over others. Montgomery thus presented a vision of society in which all growers enjoyed wealth and the benefits of citriculture. Many subsequent boosters would also show that citriculture was commercial agriculture on a grand scale.

Montgomery's publication provides a snapshot of the industry in its earliest stages. She described how in Mercedes, for example, residential homes whose yards had been beautified by citrus trees lay near the large-scale plantings of the Evergreen Farm, which had numerous rows devoted to grapefruit trees. There were already many noteworthy orchards, such as those of the Volz Ranch in Mission, which Montgomery argued gave Mission its slogan, "The Home of the Grapefruit." Montgomery also described orchards near Donna and McAllen as well as tracts in unincorporated areas between towns. Orange trees were so thick with fruits near Raymondville that one grower's tree had to have its branches propped up from the ground by long wooden poles. Finally, Montgomery included a photograph of the Shaw home, a residence with a grapefruit tree in the front yard said to bear over two thousand fruits at any given point during the year.[36]

What is notably absent from Montgomery's depiction is any flourish about the Lower Rio Grande Valley as an edenic paradise. Her focus on large tracts and plantings implied abundance and prosperity. Montgomery spent considerable time focusing on the great men of the local industry, the various citrus-growing districts, and the wealth that growers had accrued. Nowhere is the Valley a limitless paradise, but rather, it was an incredible financial and life-changing opportunity. A photograph of a "silvery sunset on the Rio Grande" at the pamphlet's end is coupled with the contention that "as old age insurance nothing compares with owning a citrus orchard in this incomparable subdivision of the United States."[37] Readers could not afford to pass up such a wise investment opportunity.

Growers, however, had to be practical, frugal, and smart. "It is fair enough to state that the Valley is no haven for a lazy, careless farmer," wrote Montgomery. It was only with hard work that the Valley's bounty would pay off. Despite the Magic Valley moniker, Montgomery continued, "everything grows with magic speed—weeds inclusive." Montgomery also showed that growers in the nascent citrus industry had quickly discovered that mutual accommodation best assured individual success. Marketing the citrus fruits, Montgomery wrote, would be done by the Texas Citrus Fruit Growers Exchange. The exchange was founded in 1923 to establish a marketing system and provide investment in packing plants and modern equipment. "Growers are coming more and more into the understanding that unity of purpose, principle, and action must be followed if there is to be an ultimate fulfillment of individual success and harmonious Valley-wide progress," Montgomery concluded.[38]

If the reader was to believe Montgomery, citrus farming was an engagement in which the Valley's natural resources, combined with hard work, paid off handsomely. Citrus was not an individualized pursuit, but one to which an entire stretch of the region would be devoted. The industry as a collective unit would only prosper if the individual grower succeeded and was cooperative with others. Although Montgomery spent the majority of her time discussing citrus above all, the ultimate goal of growing the fruits, in keeping with earlier trends in Valley boosterism, was of course profit. Montgomery also devoted a small amount of space to recreational activities, such as hunting and fishing, as well as the area's modern amenities. Unlike most of her predecessors, however, Montgomery made no mention of ethnic Mexican laborers, aside from her generalized comments about new growers needing laborers to work their lands.[39]

The vision of citriculture in the Valley thus began to build on top of the previous presentations of commercial farming prior to the industry's rise during the 1920s. It is also important to consider how other boosters articulated or added to the vision for citrus. Not all citrus-related boosters, for example, were as unwilling as Montgomery to discuss Mexican workers. A pamphlet published by ARGLIC to promote its irrigated citrus and vegetable lands around Mercedes declared, "Mexicans make ideal farm hands . . . [and] are industrious and law-abiding." The pamphlet reported accurately that wages for a twelve-hour day averaged one dollar, whereas "women and children work for from

50c to 75c per day." Furthermore, ARGLIC assured its readers that the racial stratification of Middle America would remain in place: "The Mexican women make excellent servants and many are good cooks. One of the pleasing features to the farmer and his wife is that there are no farm hands to board. Practically all labor on the American system is performed by Mexicans, there being few negro residents."[40] Ethnic Mexicans were obviously the preferred labor force, given the Valley's proximity to the international border. Segregation and labor exploitation, again, were clearly key selling points for the new industry.

Mercedes can aptly be characterized as a company town of ARGLIC. Other companies also promoted primary town sites, which were enterprises devoted entirely to citrus. The San Perlita Development Company, with its town site of the same name near Raymondville in Willacy County, grandly announced in 1925 that "the opening of the new townsite gives the public an opportunity to share in the profit from the development of San Perlita—a city in the center of a rich agricultural territory." Aside from land values that were sure to rise as a result of the Valley's rapid development, the writer continued,

> an appealing feature of this townsite is that the developers have arranged to plant budded citrus trees—either orange or grapefruit—on every homesite that is purchased. In other words, when San Perlita has been developed it will be in reality a beautiful grove of citrus trees within the city limits. These trees will be of commercial as well as ornamental value to owners of lots in San Perlita. Investigation has shown that the fruit grown in the Rio Grande Valley is of unequaled flavor and better than the California and Florida products. You as an owner of San Perlita property will have these fine trees in your yard. The purchase of lots in San Perlita not only places you in a position to share in its growth and prosperity—but to have a part in the citrus industry as well! The citrus trees will add materially to the value of the lots, no matter whether you intend building and growing up with San Perlita or make the purchase as an investment.[41]

If in the Valley growers could be brought together around citrus fruits, entire towns such as San Perlita were also to be devoted primarily to citri-culture. Citrus was to be woven everywhere into the new farming society at the border. According to one booster, Brownsville was where "Mexico meets Uncle Sam:" "A semi-tropical climate and an alluvial soil, assisted by irrigation, make the Brownsville country a veritable Paradise. Citrus fruits, namely, Oranges, Grapefruit, Limes, Lemons, Kumquats, Tangerines, etc., grow in abundance. Mature citrus orchards yield handsome returns for their owners, and citrus trees develop more rapidly here than in either Florida or California." In the Valley, then, Uncle Sam himself had combined with the Valley's natural advantages to make it a superior American citrus-growing sector.

Boosters rarely discussed Mexico itself alongside images of commercial citriculture, but when they did it always reverted to a place mired in passivity and Old-World splendor. Matamoros, for example, directly across the border from Brownsville, was "HEROIC" as well as "rich in romance and history. This interesting city of 10,000 people, in Old Mexico, holds many attractions for the tourist." Surrounding the booster's portrayal are drawings of a woman doing a traditional Mexican dance, a man in a sombrero playing a guitar, and a photo of a man riding a burro pulling a barrel next to a *jacal* (a thatched-roof hut). Similarly, this booster reported that "romantic night clubs in Mexico" were already a huge draw for Valley residents. One could also witness, "bullfights, horse racing, flower shows, fairs, fiestas, . . . Mexican celebrations . . . [and] colorful promenades by beautiful senoritas."[42] Mexicans became a quaint, exotic attraction for the interested Anglo-American. Mexicans' prescribed roles as local exotics separated out from the Anglo population indicated their lack of equality to the newcomers. Mexicans, in this characterization, remained alluringly backwards—misfits in the progressive and modern vision that Anglo Americans hoped to bring to the South Texas borderlands. They were to be gawked at and taken advantage of, but never taken seriously or treated as equals.

This constructed image of a sleepy and passive Mexican population dovetailed well with the typical booster's portrayal of the Valley's workers as accepting of their low wages and separated status. Even tacit recognition of the Mexican Revolution or of border uprisings on US soil would have belied this sense of passivity on the part of the local population. Additionally, recognizing border violence would have undermined any sense of safety that could be found in the Lower Rio Grande Valley. Uninformed readers would never have guessed from such portrayals that Mexico had recently concluded a decade-long bloody revolution. This slight-of-hand by the boosters is somewhat surprising given that a minimum of four hundred thousand Mexicans crossed the border and moved north into the United States during the Mexican Revolution. The social reality of the revolution contrasted markedly with the whitewashed image of Valley life.[43]

Describing Old Mexico, however, served purposes other than portraying to new recruits the passivity of the Valley's ethnic Mexican population. The aesthetic appeal to recruits' sense of the exotic was also meant to lure them to the Valley, where adventure and community intermixed and helped commercial farmers to live not only successful but also interesting lives. Citriculture and Mexicans shared, in a sense, depictions as the wild and exotic Other, which made them crucial parts of the Valley's cultural landscape. Valley boosters were not the only advertisers to construct images of the exotic Mexican Other to lure white Americans to a new place. Such was a common tactic in various parts of the US Southwest. For example, beginning in the 1880s, in order to attract tourists and new settlers, Los Angeles boosters promoted an image of a pastoral California that came to be known as "the mission myth." One historian argues that "by depicting the city's Latino heritage as a quaint, but altogether disappearing element in Los Angeles culture, city officials inflicted a particular kind of obscurity onto Mexican descendants of that [earlier] era by appropriating them and commercializing their history." Another historian argues that New Mexico boosters also relegated the Spanish and Mexican histories of that state to an alluring relic of the past, intent on "tidying up" New Mexico's messy social landscape and erasing from the minds of potential Anglo tourists and visitors the state's long history of racial miscegenation.[44]

Much of the above concerning California is functionally similar to what took place with boosterism in South Texas. Anglo-Americans who visited the region as early as the mid-nineteenth century had described the Lower Rio Grande Valley's inhabitants—both Mexican and Indian—as "uncivilized" and "savage." One historian writes that even as far back as the time of the US Civil War, Anglo-Americans' "confidence in the future prospects of the Southwest," including the Lower Rio Grande Valley, "derived from their singularly low estimation of the culture and capacities of those who inhabited it."[45] Anglo inhabitants of the Valley during the early twentieth century were no different; in fact, such views of the South Texas borderlands had remained unchanged for over half a century. By relegating the region's Mexican past to the dustbins of history, with sleepy "old" Mexico being its only remnant, boosters not only provided the necessary justifications for Anglo-American colonization and participation in the new citrus industry, but they also re-created Mexicans and local Mexican culture as a historicized relic that held some allure to modern Americans. Mexicans themselves were not only seen as native to the region, but they also became curiosities of the local experience. Valley boosterism not only helped Anglos reconstruct their own identities, but it also encouraged them to forge new identities for local ethnic Mexicans, without their knowledge or consent. The Valley's native population became passive members of the Old World who would give way to the dictates of modern, white America.

Valley residents who were "in the know"—a term appearing in several booster tracts that reflected simply having knowledge of life in the region through firsthand experience—often painted their own portrayals of the region through written commentary in newspapers. J. J. Morton, in John H. Shary's paper the *Mission Times*—hardly an objective source of information—published a series of articles in 1922 about life in the area. Writing that the people of the Valley score "higher in the standard of morality than probably any other place of its size and makeup in the world," Morton refuted notions that Valley life was dangerous, arguing that women and children could walk the streets alone and without fear of harm. Morton thus reemphasized the allegedly passive and law-abiding nature of Mexican men as described by previous boosters.

Alluding to the region's violent history, Morton also dismissed troubles related to past Mexican uprisings, claiming, "We here in the Valley are separated from the anarchistic element as much as if a sea occupied the place of the Sarita Range." Indeed, lessons of the past clearly displayed that the new growers had successfully implemented their vision for local society, which rested on the trials and often violent struggles of their Anglo-Texan forebears. Again, we see a booster cannibalizing history:

> The Great Southwest has many calls to the people of the nation, but one of its greatest appeals to the people who are coming here is the hand of friendship it is extending through the sons and daughters of the Texas pioneers who fought, not like in the wars in other states or countries, but a continuous war of bitter battles for the best part of an entire century, battles which only spared them enough time to put away their gun and saber and raise a crop for sustenance, to harvest the products and then to buckle on their armaments and begin to fight all over again. These people have won. Some people have asked why didn't the Texans develop this country and make the profits from it that are being made today. The answer is written into every acre of its soil. Every arroya, every Resaca, every clump of brush has a tale to tell of the days—and not so far away—when the pioneers of this Valley, the Texans who blazed the way of civilization, spilled their blood in keeping back those who disputed the existence of what is now the last Frontier, and the place itself is a monument to their pluck and chivalry in keeping it from being a "lost frontier."[46]

For Morton, the "tomorrow of the Valley" lay in the series of successes that past pioneers had accrued over time. These people, to him, were heroes who brought modern America to an untamed Mexican space. Morton made an interesting omission when he failed to name Mexicans or Mexico itself as the people against whom Anglo-Americans fought "a continuous war of bitter battles for the best part of an entire century." Morton thus ignored the violent phase in which white Americans conquered the region and dispossessed Mexican Americans. Historicizing the region's violent past like the boosters who came before him allowed Morton to place uprisings and rebellions in what for him was their proper context: that of the past Anglo incorporation of the area into the greater United States. It was, for him, the stuff of classic Western history. Acknowledging that at least to some degree the region could claim a violent past—though it may not have been the immediate "Mexican problem" of the mid-1910s—Morton asserted that a future of peace and prosperity lay in waiting. Social problems, to him, would no longer stand in the way of development.

The language of old-school pioneering appeared throughout Valley booster literature. Pioneers were also said to have reclaimed Harlingen from its early days as a Wild West hamlet:

> Shortly after the turn of the last century the eyes of hardy, ambitious pioneers, looking for new frontiers to conquer, turned to the Lower Valley of the Rio Grande—the sole remnant of the rough, raw, undeveloped Texas that was. Another group already was throwing the ribbons of steel into the last wilderness, but to the frontiersman there still remained the conquest of this wild region, the productiveness of which was doubted and which was at best a matter of conjecture.
>
> The pioneers came and conquered; and today the extremely fertile, highly productive Lower Rio Grande Valley of Texas is the result. And here, in the heart of this agricultural Golconda [a diamond-producing region in southern India] is Harlingen, the pivot city around which the tremendous development of the past decade which has amazed a nation has woven a web of industry and agriculture.[47]

This booster thus tied Harlingen's modern development into an unbroken past of pioneering and reclaiming valuable agricultural lands from what they considered to be the shortsightedness of the area's Mexican population. Clearly, then, the implication again was that Mexicans and Mexican Americans were fit only to be the new settlers' servants and laborers, due to their past failures at developing the region for themselves. Or they would simply be out of sight and out of mind altogether.

A sense of history occasionally showed up in legitimizing companies' land claims as well as their founders' own personal stories. John H. Shary, for example, in 1925 sought to legitimize himself through a discussion of history. The John H. Shary subdivision, located between Mission on the west and McAllen on the east, was a legal proposition whose ownership rights dated back to New Spain's control of the region. His grant "consists of three original Spanish porciones numbered 58, 59 and 60, having an area of approximately 20,000 acres. The water rights of the John H. Shary Subdivision are unexcelled." Conveniently, also, "the old Spanish grant of 1767 included, with the land, the express right to the use of the water of the Rio Grande River for irrigation purposes. This right passes with the title and the two are inseparable." Luckily for the potential new farmer, "the former owners of this land held it until they could sell it outright to a reliable and successful colonization specialist who had the means to take hold of it and make it the garden spot of the Valley." Fortunately, Shary himself was of course that "reliable specialist." The note ended by selling Shary himself as a colonizer: "Successful Colony Building: The cause for the great success which Mr. Shary has attained in the colonizing of vast tracts of land in South Texas and their development into flourishing agricultural communities cannot be attributed to luck." New Valley growers would clearly be in good hands.[48]

Potential "colonists," to use the booster's own terminology, could thus see that they were in good, competent hands, backed by legally sound claims. Again, both of these claims were made clear by appealing to readers' sense of legitimization coming from Shary's personal history as well as the history of the region itself. Shary knew that one of his greatest assets was something over which he had tight control: his business dealings and integrity. "Knockers," as they would come to be known, could complain about crops and harvests, but Shary strove to make sure they could not complain about his personal competence or his business acumen.

One of the seemingly most effective ways to promote Lower Rio Grande Valley citriculture was through the publication of stories about small growers. In June 1927 local writer Francis Miller published an article about citrus and vegetable culture to promote the area's growth and development. Despite appearing in a local newspaper, *The Rio Grande Valley Sun*, Miller's article has all of the informative and promotional tone of a standard booster tract. Miller began his article with the Shafer fruit and vegetable farm in San Benito. The Shafers, he reported, relocated to the Valley after working for years in Pennsylvania's steel mills: "'Father' Shafer, as he is known around San Benito, lives within 'hollerin'' distance of each of his sons and they'll tell you they wouldn't trade their farms for all the steel mills in Pennsylvania. A visit to the farm disclosed what energy, determination to succeed and economical management has done for that family. Acre upon acre of growing crops, orderly arranged, were seen. Mexicans were in the fields harvesting tomatoes. It was a scene of bustle and energy, and one that might be duplicated anywhere along the line at the various other farms."

Also, the Valley was a place in which enterprising young men could seek out a better future, much like the westward-minded young men of a generation or two before: "'Tell them to come to the Valley,' said L. E. Snavely, citrus and vegetable grower and operator of his own packing plant near Harlingen. 'That is the best word we can send farther up the state. That "Go West, young man" business was out of date a long time ago. There's more wealth and a bigger and surer future in this land skirting the Rio Grande than in the whole West, if a fellow has it in him to make good.'"[49]

Snavely's contemporary variant of "going West" was going south to the border. Instead of becoming a wealthy gold prospector in San Francisco or a rancher in the Texas Panhandle, one could travel from a great distance to the border in order to become a successful commercial farmer.

Snavely's narrative was remarkably similar to others. Expansionism and population movement, according to historian Matthew Frye Jacobson, included both domestic and overseas imperialism during the Gilded Age and Progressive Era. Americans at the time had new places in mind, including the US West, the Pacific, and Latin America. White Americans worked hard to dispossess darker-skinned peoples in all places. Just as gold prospectors and migrants pushed Indians and Mexicans off of their lands in California in the nineteenth century, for example, Valley Anglos worked feverishly to implement a new vision for South Texas's future on top of a much different Mexican past. This new vision involved re-creating the rural Midwest while substituting ethnic Mexicans for other minorities at the bottom of the social hierarchy. The Valley was a place of folksy charm, economic opportunity, and personal fulfillment. The *Sun's* readership is impossible to determine, but pro-Valley stories such as Francis Miller's likely reached a wider audience, a breakfast-table audience, than did standard booster tracts and pamphlets. South Texas had fast become an American colony inside of US borders.[50]

Oftentimes several local institutions would come together to promote whole towns or counties. Strategies for promoting specific towns, counties, or districts varied. In the January 1928 edition of *Monty's Monthly*, Julia Cameron Montgomery published a special issue on W. A. Harding, one of the original promoters of citriculture in Willacy County. Montgomery included a large piece on Harding's history, including his planting of a fifty-acre citrus tract on the Raymondville townsite some ten years previously. Montgomery also presented a lengthy discussion of Harding's plan to create a fifteen-thousand-acre citrus grove, including a thirty-one-mile-long "Citrus Boulevard" to run straight through the tract. Efforts such as Harding's, Montgomery concluded, helped "the Lower Valley of the Rio Grande . . . present a dazzling picture to one who reads by the light of VISION."[51]

Rather than promoting a vision, however, the primary purpose of the article was to publicize Harding's new venture under the auspices of his organization, the Delta Cities Company. Such a large commercial farming proposition required hundreds of thousands if not millions of dollars in investment. Interestingly, Harding appears to have been making his appeal to people already established in the Valley, instead of the typical appeals to people in other parts of the state or the nation. Harding explained in an advertisement at the end of the issue that his Citrus Boulevard proposition bordered his forty-thousand-acre Mesteñas Tract that spanned from Willacy to Hidalgo County. "If you want to investigate," Harding wrote, "drive north from San Carlos one and a quarter miles, then follow the continuous rows of orange and grapefruit trees already set, extending North and then East for a distance of four and a half miles."[52]

As the end of the 1920s approached, boosters increasingly focused on Valley citrus as a financial investment. They clearly hoped to appeal to readers as sound financial advisors, either during the increased popularity of stock trading that took hold of the nation during the 1920s or while the nation's stock market grew increasingly more volatile at the end of the decade. An Engelman Gardens booster proclaimed, "Every year you own [a citrus orchard], dollars and dollars will be added to your investment. *A splendid climate for health, a grapefruit orchard for wealth*" (emphasis in the original). The Nick Doffing Company, which owned a tract in Hidalgo County northwest of Mission, argued in a pamphlet *Golden Groves: Lower Rio Grande Valley* that the long-term financial security brought by investment in citriculture far outweighed the risks that one took when making traditional investments in stocks and bonds.[53]

At the dawn of the Great Depression profit still remained king in South Texas booster literature. Boosters never lost sight of the celebrated aspects of Valley life—modernity, recreation, community spirit—nor the simple aesthetics of citriculture. As one booster of Kingsville citrus reported, "These immense crops are harvested by Mexican farm hands, the most economical labor obtainable." Nevertheless, he continued, "the orange and citrus fruit groves are interesting and a fine place to spend an afternoon, especially if the fruit is ripening." Some boosters were better than others at integrating the many benefits of local life, including profit from citrus harvesting, into a cohesive vision. Boosters in the employ of John H. Shary presented Mission as a place driven by the economic success of citriculture: "The volume of business done by Mission merchants and farmers is best attested by the ever-mounting bank reports. No city can boast of less poverty, more progress and prosperity, higher degree of comparative educational facilities, fewer business failures, a better health record, or a higher standard of citizenship than does Mission."[54]

Boosters intended to show potential colonists that the benefits of South

Texas life flowed outward from the economic might of citriculture. One booster of Brownsville-based citrus reported that the four banks in that city held deposits totaling exactly $10,169,886.07. Furthermore, to promote the Lower Rio Grande Valley's growth, this same booster reported that in 1927 the thirty banks in the entire Valley held deposits of $22,000,000. That same year the community built $25,000,000 in new buildings. Finally, the booster projected Valley citriculture to reach a value of $25,000,000 by 1930.[55] Although it is unclear whether the booster produced the pamphlet before or after the stock market crash, the focus on bank valuation clearly meant to evoke a sense of economic stability in the minds of readers.

Some boosters reassured potential growers or investors that their money would be safe. One booster for John H. Shary laid out detailed plans for protecting a purchaser's investment. Marketing and profit, which the company would do on the growers' behalf, also required leadership and organization. Concerning the Texas Citrus Fruit Growers Exchange, one booster wrote, "More than one thousand citrus growers now belong to this grower organization, which has eight of the finest and largest packing plants serving the entire Valley, and which has built up a great selling organization through nine years of contact with the trade." None of this would matter, of course, without the "progressive, liberal, enterprising and thrifty people of a dozen middle western states" who took the Valley from being a series of "cluster jacals" to a modern and profit-minded agribusiness sector.[56]

Some promoters directly addressed their own profitability after the nation's economy had imploded. Charles F. C. Ladd reported on conditions in the Harlingen–La Feria area, stating that the income from all fruit shipped from the Valley between October 1929 and September 1930 amounted to $4,622,000. Owners of "good" citrus orchards allegedly realized a gross income per acre of from $600 to $700, and in several cases the returns were in excess of $1,000 an acre. Adams Gardens Nursery Corporation, the booster concluded, boasted a capital stock of $50,000.[57]

During times of economic distress boosters felt it necessary to reassure potential growers or investors that they were about to make a sound financial choice. Another Harlingen booster, after discussing an expensive civic beautification process undertaken in 1928, reported that of the 6,001,101 citrus trees present in the Valley, two-thirds would be producing by 1932. This was a far cry from Harlingen's once reputation as "Six-Shooter Junction," which the booster recognized but dismissed as a part of the city's distant past.[58]

Facts as reported by Valley boosters could be questionable at best. One Valleywide pamphlet published by the Missouri-Pacific Railroad Company argued that while only two thousand cars of citrus fruits left the Valley during the 1928–29 growing season, thirty thousand cars would soon be shipping out per year, once all of the 3,500,000 then-planted citrus trees came to bearing age. In addition, not only did Valley banks hold over $28,000,000 in total assets, but also Valley farmers had access to ample Mexican labor. On top of the usual booster refrain of ethnic Mexicans being "reliable, industrious, and capable workers" was the contention that "compared to many sections[,] farm labor in the Valley is unusually cheap and even at peak periods there is no labor shortage." While the previous booster reported 3,500,000 trees of bearing age, another writer, this one for the Valley-area publication *The Lower Rio Grande Valley Tourist*, reported in 1930 exactly 5,118,981 trees in orchards and over twenty-five thousand cars of fruits and vegetables shipped the previous season. Whereas the previous booster reported that thirty thousand cars of citrus would ship in 1930, this second writer reported that thirty thousand boxes of agricultural products would ship. Boosters clearly sought to manipulate data to whatever possible advantage they could gain.[59]

Walking and Talking Citrus

Promoters also found numerous ways to boost Lower Rio Grande Valley citriculture outside of the realm of print literature. Whether public speeches or excursions of home seekers to the Valley, the vision of citrus growing as presented in the booster literature reached wide audiences through nonprint sources.

Few forms of boosterism could be more convincing than face-to-face conversations or testimonies between boosters and prospective colonists. This type of promotion could take many forms: conversations between friends, personal testimonies of growers solicited by land companies, and finally, train excursion trips to the region. Conversation shaped people's expectations of life in the Valley as strongly and perhaps more directly than did print literature. Although many of these conversations are of course lost to historians, some can still be re-created. Cleo Dawson, from her novel about life in Mission during the early years of commercial agriculture that was based on her own family's experiences, re-created a booster's monologue that was probably not unlike the one that caught her own family's interest in the Valley:

"Scared to live close to Mexico!" Mr. Peterson slapped his knee in laughter. "My God, it's the safest country in the world. Old Porfirio Diaz is still President and will be till he dies. Thirty years of rule would fix any Government

on its feet. Revolution is a thing of the past down there. He hangs 'em on
the roadside when they don't do to suit him. Mexico's on the gold standard
just like us. Last year $800,000,000 of foreign capital went into that country.
Scared? No, folks, I feel safer livin' close to Mexico. As soon as the Missus gets
back on her feet we're headin' straight for the Valley. Wouldn't miss a chance
like that."

"What kind of business is goin' on down there?" Pat asked. "Is it land like
Oklahoma?"

"No man; it's agriculture. You can raise anything you plant. It's like the
delta of the Nile. Better not stand too long or you'll grow yourself."[60]

Dawson's booster goes on to discuss the various crops being grown in the region,
including some discussion of citriculture as well as the Laguna Seca myth.

This passage reflects some of the ubiquitous elements of Valley agriculture.
Mexico itself was safe, much like boosters' characterizations of violence in Valley
life. Concerns about the safety of living near Mexico and the Mexican Revolution, by implication, appear to have been common among the Americans that
land company agents sought to recruit. Also, the possibilities for Valley-based
agriculture allegedly knew no bounds. Later in the novel Dawson recounted how
the family patriarch overheard a conversation about the Valley in Laredo, Texas,
further north along the border, where people spoke as if "folks're pickin' money
off the trees down there. . . . Anything on earth will grow with the irrigation
system." The boosters' vision of unending wealth clearly resonated with people
everywhere, especially with farmers who, in Dawson's interpretation, were in
less desirable climes such as those found in the arid regions around Laredo.[61]

One of the most convincing arguments for becoming a commercial farmer
in the Valley was the persuasion of family or friends. Grower Carrol Norquest
recalled when, as a young man living in Kansas in the early 1920s, a group of
neighbors who had relocated to the Valley convinced his father to relocate. Not
only was the farming good, but also the warm climate, his friends reported,
would cure his father of rheumatism. They arranged a trade of his Kansas farm
for a prime piece of alluvial soil in the W. E. Stewart Irrigation Company District in the heart of Hidalgo County. Norquest's land was still "in the brush,"
although a bustling community (Edinburg) of five thousand had already developed nearby.[62]

Interestingly, the Norquest family made their decision to move to the Valley
despite hearing some tales of woe from people who had preceded them. The
elder Norquest appears to have not purchased any land on his first trip to the
Valley, but one relative did make a purchase and later went back on his own

to make another. Norquest noted that the relative—who poetically termed the Valley "la Gloria"—wound up paying his land company far and above the land's actual value. "He survived it," Norquest reported, "but a lot of people lost everything."[63]

Why, then, relocate to the Lower Rio Grande Valley at all? The Valley's climate appears to have been the primary selling point for the Norquests. Not only would the elder Norquest recover from his ailment, but also "the temperature [in Kansas] was nine below, and our gullible self-made rustics went readily." Norquest recalled the train excursion from Kansas to the Valley: "An old steam engine pushed our immigrant-car backward up the branch line from San Juan, piping her air whistle at animals on the tracks and stopping for us to chase off cows. Our former Kansas neighbors helped us unload. There was a large old house, dilapidated and paintless, on our land—relic of the Stewart debacle. We fixed it up and lived in it. Father got over his rheumatism in the first year. When he and mother died, I inherited the house and five acres."[64]

Though Norquest appears to have enjoyed some initial success as a cotton farmer in the 1920s and again some limited success during World War II, he recalled his farming experiences as mostly times of hardship and turmoil. Norquest, however, clearly accepted the vision of the Valley as a climatologically favorable place in which to pursue commercial agriculture, despite the fact that his sometimes difficult career as a cotton farmer may have contradicted his initial expectations.

Perhaps the most important interpersonal communication took place when the excursionists arrived in South Texas by train, because it was during such trips that land companies made their strongest sales pitches. Land agents proceeded to follow general guidelines when dealing with recruits. The vast majority, if not all of the recruits, originated from the agricultural sections of the US Midwest. Land company agents could be quite manipulative. During the train trips, when the cars rolled past particularly unsightly portions of South Texas where the population remained thoroughly impoverished and overwhelmingly Hispanic, agents would call for impromptu prayer and hymn-singing, leading the colonists in song and having the train's window blinds pulled down until they had passed by the unsightly environs. Sales tactics remained intense once the excursionists got off the trains. Agents used whatever perceived advantages they could to convince the visitors that the Valley was a worthy investment, such as the following: "This border country was just desert until man came along. It never rained much here until we cleared off the brush and put in growing crops. All these crops have made a radical change in the climate, and it will rain more and more as additional fields are cleared."[65]

Such was clearly untrue, although a midwestern farmer during the 1920s can hardly be expected to have been informed on the latest word in climatology research. Nor, of course, was the Anglo-American farmer the first man to enter the Valley. Nevertheless, such lies or embellishments did occur, and their later revelations undoubtedly helped sow some discontent among locals. Even when telling the truth, agents and developers often took on the tones of revivalist Southern preachers. Cleo Dawson provided a fictionalized account of one such incident in her novel, discussing a dinner at which a Mission-based developer hosted a group of excursionists:

> The people never settled down to eating—all they did was talk. Mr. Conlay led, and everybody dreamed and planned. They would build up a country in this delta valley of the Rio Grande that would top the world in the reclamation of the desert. They would pull the water from the river and give the land a drink. The land would yield its increase and make the people rich. They would be done with snow and winter, live here in the kingdom of the sun— rich, free, and easy—rid of industry's machine. They looked at the Allen patio and saw the country as it would be—oranges, lemons, jasmines, poinsettias, and castor beans.[66]

According to Dawson, men like the booster portrayed above "oozed salesmanship from every pore."[67] Boosters thus often whipped their potential clients into a frenzy and played on their emotions in order to make sales. Thus, it comes as little surprise that some growers bought wholesale into the boosters' vision for the Valley's future while others became disillusioned at their lofty goals after relocating to the area.

Establishing the frequency of such incidents is difficult. Nevertheless, the pitch that salesmen unveiled during these trips clearly worked. The seeds of the new South Texas border society had been planted in newcomers' minds, even if agents had to lie in order to get them to buy land. The excursion trips themselves fostered a certain sense of conformity through ritualized face-to-face sales practices. Agents often left the home seekers in the hands of trusted and successful local growers, who, acting as enthusiastic boosters, took them around by car and extolled to them the virtues of local life. Outside contact with parties loyal to other land companies, according to one source, was kept at a minimum in order to keep agents from competing companies from stealing one another's sales.[68]

Guides usually first took excursionists on sightseeing trips, pointing out sights around the Valley and its citrus orchards. Visitors always received a wide sampling of citrus fruits right off the trees. Irrigation ditches also served as essential stops on the tours. If possible, agents would show the homes of the megarich, such as Shary, who owned a large home surrounded by orchards in the Mission-Sharyland district. Agents would also talk up the Valley as the best place in the world in which to live, one with a romantic and interesting history. Predictably, the agents argued that the area provided modern progress, with schools, paved roads, and railroads. Agents would then discuss the possibility of growing grapefruit or oranges, which would not only prove profitable but also beautify a landscape that was well suited to outdoor recreation. In other words, the sales pitch was simply an in-person regurgitation of the booster literature. If all went according to plan, agents would close the deal before the excursionists returned home. Purchasers would then either relocate to the Valley at some point in the future or simply own a plot devoted to citrus, whose fruit organizations, such as the Texas Citrus Fruit Growers Exchange, would cultivate, pick, and sell on the owner's behalf.[69]

Positive reactions to the typical sales pitch appear to have been common. Negative publicity of the region during these early days was rare, but it could occasionally be found. In most instances, however, such criticism was nuanced. In an editorial in a local paper, a woman named Agnes McLaughlin perpetuated what was undoubtedly a common stereotype among Valleyites about ethnic Mexican laborers. Writing in November of 1926 that people in the Valley were "having trouble with their labor, as they do everywhere," McLaughlin claimed that "Mexicans can be had for one dollar and twenty-five cents per day, but judging by what I see and hear, it is dear at that, as they are not only ignorant but lazy—a trying combination." This, by insinuation, was something that the boosters did not advertise to prospective land buyers. Furthermore, she argued: "There's no doubt but that the 'Magic Valley' has a combination of soil, moisture, climate, labor (if you can boss it), and a coming market, so, as Arthur Brisbane said, 'There's just so much of this earth, better get some—in the right place—then hold onto it.' As many boosters think this is 'the right place' where God supplies the sunshine and man supplies the water. Now as to whether I am one of those boosters or not—but more of that later."[70]

Although it is somewhat difficult to generalize the attitudes of all Anglo farmers in the Valley toward ethnic Mexicans, the farmers clearly shared more in common with one another than they did with ethnic Mexicans. Keeping labor costs low, which in essence made dehumanizing and demeaning attitudes toward Mexican workers common, was a unifying bond that all small growers always shared.[71] The clearly manufactured image of a docile and tractable labor force that dated back to earlier print boosterism would ultimately become the most blatantly false image that boosters portrayed of the area. McLaughlin's claim of the inability to boss the allegedly slothful Mexican worker only reinforced the notion of a race-based hierarchy that was so common among local whites.

As one scholar noted, "The Midwestern farmers were, of course, far from stupid. . . . They were attracted by what seemed a dream that could not fail."[72] Part of the colonial project in the Valley, then, for the small grower, was to not allow that dream to fail. Boosters had their work cut out for them; constructing an image of local life as well as marketing that new vision to potential recruits and convincing them to buy into it were all difficult tasks. Whether the boosters told the truth or not, thousands of people bought what the boosters and land companies were selling. Scores of Anglo-midwesterners moved into the Valley during the 1910s and '20s. The boosters' new social vision of modernity, leisure, and subservient ethnic Mexicans would play out over the course of the next few decades—its ramifications for life in the twentieth-century South Texas borderlands would prove to be huge.

An early train depot in McAllen, Hidalgo County. The railroad's arrival signified a new era in South Texas history. (Courtesy of the DeGolyer Library, Southern Methodist University, Dallas, Texas.)

Promoters used the aesthetics of citrus to promote properties throughout the region. Here, orange trees beautified a trailer park. (Courtesy of the DeGolyer Library, Southern Methodist University, Dallas, Texas.)

A Model T Ford, a symbol of modernity during the 1910s and '20s, careens down a dirt road in rural South Texas. (Courtesy of the University of Texas–Pan American Libraries, Edinburg.)

John H. Shary in his Southwestern Land Company Office, ca. 1916. (Courtesy of the University of Texas–Pan American Libraries, Edinburg.)

A contestant, Elda Stovall, from Weslaco, during a 1923 event promoting South Texas citrus. Numerous people worked a total of 296 hours constructing the dress and jewelry, which are made entirely from citrus by-products. Stovall's dress consisted of tattered grapefruit membranes and peeled grapefruit seeds. (Courtesy of the Weslaco Museum, Weslaco, Texas.)

Groups of Mexican railroad workers were a common site in South Texas at the turn of the twentieth century. (Courtesy of the El Paso Public Library, El Paso, Texas.)

An excursion company that had arrived by railroad at the invitation of the Southwestern Land Company in Sharyland, 1923. Groups of excursionists were a common sight in the

A typical booster tract, entitled *In Rio Grande Valley Paradise*," ca. 1930. (Courtesy of the University of Texas–Pan American Libraries, Edinburg.)

Valley during the 1910s and '20s. (Courtesy of the University of Texas–Pan American Libraries, Edinburg.)

John H. Shary and Mrs A. Y. Baker, the King and Queen of Citrus, at a Valley-area citrus fiesta in 1923. Organizers meant this regal imagery to emphasize the power of citriculture in the region after the industry's founding. (Courtesy of the University of Texas–Pan American Libraries, Edinburg.)

A photograph of the alleged oldest forty-acre citrus orchard in the Lower Rio Grande Valley. (Courtesy of the University of Texas–Pan American Libraries, Edinburg.)

CHAPTER THREE

Making the Border Orange

*Citriculture and the Changing Landscape
of the South Texas Borderlands during the 1920s*

It is to be hoped that the aura of luxury surrounding citrus
fruits will not be lost.[1]

People bought land in the South Texas borderlands
because they believed in its future. The promise of tomorrow brought new
farmers down from the US Midwest by the thousands. The 1920s ushered in
the ascendancy of small commercial farming in South Texas. The new transplants came, primarily, because of land promotion. Boosters depicted the area
as one in which growers could engage in profitable agriculture, maintain segregation while relying on an ethic Mexican working class, and stand tall as modern pioneers who rested on the allegedly trailblazing work of those who came
before them. Many came immediately after World War I, but further immigration buoyed the South Texas borderlands population throughout the 1920s.

Growers strove to implement the boosters' vision upon their arrival in the
region. One of the easiest ways to measure the successes and failures of the
new South Texas borderlands is to examine one of its most promising new
industries. The Texas citrus industry, mostly located in the Lower Rio Grande
Valley, offers the perfect lens through which to view how new growers sought
to implement the ideas presented to them by land boosters as well as the ramifications of those changes.

If newcomers had colonized parts of the region, how successful were their
new financial endeavors? The citrus industry highlighted the activities of some
of South Texas's small growers and larger land companies, showing how they
attempted to realize the boosters' vision for a new commercial agriculture
haven. Although many of the new transplants succeeded, it would be a mistake
to argue that the system worked well for the entire white colonizing population.
Many growers and developers squabbled among themselves. Those who lost
faith in citriculture's initial promise still sought to reinforce their excitement
by emphasizing racial segregation and a triumphant Anglocentric narrative of
daily life. In the growers' own minds, South Texas was theirs, and their actions

and lifestyles during the 1920s reflected their domineering attitudes. An army of small growers—under the new regime of land developers and the emerging citrus agriculture—had come to power in the Lower Rio Grande Valley and greater South Texas.

A Slow Start

Despite their successes, a number of growers had significant problems getting their businesses off the ground during the 1910s. Consequently, there was a lag in the citrus industry's early development. Naturally, it took time for South Texas agriculture to become profitable.

Numerous early problems existed. Several land developers failed to deliver on their basic promises to the newcomers. For example, instability in irrigation costs in Cameron County put many growers out of business. Land developers who ran irrigation companies, one source argued, did not hire engineers or do proper research before establishing canals. Some unwittingly even tried to make water run uphill. This poor engineering contributed to an initially bad reputation for Brownsville-area agriculture, and it would take the commercial successes of the 1920s before the town's reputation recovered.[2]

Similar difficulties occurred in Hidalgo County, the future hub of the citrus industry and the exact place where by 1915 John H. Shary had envisioned the future citrus empire of the Lower Rio Grande Valley. Land companies around McAllen and Mission had developed, opened, and sold lands in those areas faster than they had constructed the necessary irrigation improvements to provide farmers with water. Some lands failed because of oversaturation with water from the Rio Grande, while others received precious little water at all. This, in turn, created widespread crop failures, which, coupled with the purchase of too much land by the new colonists, led to the repossession of numerous small growers' farms. This, of course, caused numerous ill feelings. One historian noted that Shary and A. Y. Baker—the widely unpopular and corrupt sheriff of Hidalgo County—had difficulty in keeping some small uprisings from becoming more serious. For example, in the fall of 1918 a group of Shary's growers sued him, alleging that the Mission Canal Company charged exorbitant rates for access to water. Shary dismissed the criticism as the product of "a certain clique of conspirators." Nevertheless, damage to the Valley's reputation was done. Although many small growers would buy into the vision for citriculture and the Valley's future in the coming decades, men like Shary already suffered from at least some unpopularity among the very growers to whom they had sold land.[3]

Access to water also led some small growers to have conflicts among themselves. In 1915 a man named G. Weiske of Mission received reprimands from the Mission Canal Company for closing the irrigation gates on his land and thus cutting off access to water for his neighbor, a man named Mr. Dew. The company threatened a lawsuit over the matter against Weiske, whose actions were in violation of his land contract. Such occurrences were common during that early period but also continued into the 1920s, as many growers had trouble paying the local irrigation companies' relatively high rates.[4]

Aside from issues with water, other problems included hasty purchases of land by people who could not really afford them, as well as buyer's remorse that was likely related to giving in to the high-pressure sales pitches by land salesmen. One man, John A. Levenhagen of Howard, South Dakota, in December 1914 made such a purchase from Shary, which he soon regretted. After writing Shary that there was "something wrong here" and asking the company to hold his check, Levenhagen begged Shary to be released from his contract. He later informed Shary that he wanted his money returned soon because his parents objected to his moving to the border. Levenhagen assured Shary that he would not become "a 'knocker' of that country because I still think the country a good one to make an investment in."[5] Sources do not reveal how Levenhagen's case ended, but problems of buyer's remorse or lack of good judgment on the part of new recruits—one or the other clearly an issue with Levenhagen—were undoubtedly common in the high-pressure sales situations created by land developers and agents.

Other deals went bad because some growers failed to make proper payments on their lands. Henry Mette, of Roswell, South Dakota, bought a tract in Sharyland that he could not afford, hoping to make money himself as a freelance agent for the Southwestern Land Company. Before making headway in the payments on his land, Mette inquired about the potential commissions he could get from bringing his friends and family to the Valley:

Roswell, S.D. Jan 18 1915

Mr. John H. Shary Dear sir I wish to rite you a fiew lines in Regard to take Down some ment to Shery Land Now these parties live in Iowa and are all Old friends of mine and they want me to go down With them and they say if it is like I told them they would like to By some land they are all Well to-do people Now I wish you would let me no What Commission there would Be for me and What it would Cost Each one and their Wifes to go down thee and would I have to Pay my way I can arang my Business to take them down there Now let me Now When the first Excursion goes Down in feBruary and

What Day we would start from Omaha Now Rite me all of the particulars as soon as Possible and I am purty sure they Will By if we go."
Yours truly
Henry Mette[6]

Mette, however, did not last longer than nine months in the Valley. Reporting that his wife had taken terminally ill, he informed the company that he was returning to South Dakota and recontracting with the company to sell his land. A series of delinquent payments and nasty communiqués followed. The entire relationship ended with a report from one of the company's land agents in South Dakota that Mette, once he returned to his home state, was "knocking and making it a business to see the people that expect to go to the Valley and tells them that John Shary is the crookedst man he ever saw and that people are starving in the Valley."[7] It is unclear what became of Mette's land, but presumably the Southwestern Land Company repossessed it for delinquency.

Such situations caused trouble for Shary, whose financial wealth hinged on the region's image and its desirability to outsiders. But developers had problems in every corner of the Valley during these early years. One offsite grower, Joseph Ebbers of Dodge, Nebraska, had come to agreement with the Southwestern Land Company that it would take care of his trees until he was ready to relocate from Nebraska. When a freeze damaged his trees, however, Ebbers refused to continue making payments on his land. The matter nearly ended up in a lawsuit, but after at least five years of negotiations, the dispute was finally resolved in the company's favor.[8] Nevertheless, another knocker had been created as struggles continued to consume small growers who either lived in the area or were financially invested in it.

Small growers and off-site investors sometimes sought relief from the burden of their investments through rather creative undertakings. Eunice Askew, an off-site investor from Donovan, Illinois, was having trouble paying for her lands, which were among some of the early citrus-related plots in the Mission-Sharyland area. Askew inquired of the Southwestern Land Company whether she could "build a farm or a small house for what price $150.00 or so suitable for a Mexican family to live in while tending the crop." The company responded, saying that "we do not lease land to the Mexicans but simply hire them for labor purposes," but that if Askew was willing to spend closer to $1,000 they could possibly find a white renter for that season's crop.[9] Thus, the company was not willing to risk the vision for the Valley's future—which hinged upon socioeconomic and racial stratification—in order to relieve the financial distress of one grower.

Oftentimes the developers got themselves into trouble. Developers and land agents were notorious for disparaging each other's propositions to potential buyers, creating a negative competitive atmosphere.[10] Other times, rich developers' egos could get the better of them, causing them to say the wrong things to their growers and come across as unfriendly or rude. For example, in the early days of the Mission-Sharyland area's development, Shary rebuked one of his growers with the following:

> With respect to the resale of your land and whether you got a bargain or not, would state that if I did not have a great deal of my own land to sell, I would be more than glad to relist your land for sale. You well know I have a very large proposition in Sharyland involving several million dollars worth of lands, which are up to me to sell out as rapidly as possible and I am not selling lands for the purpose of reselling them in a short while just because you think I should. If I were able to hold all these lands myself, I would never have given you a chance to buy them in the first place, especially in view of the fact that I gave exceptional terms, other than 99 percent of my customers. You have not yet, and it will soon be a year, even paid two-fifths payment on your land, which is supposed to be paid at the time of purchase.[11]

Chiding his customers was bad business for men like Shary, who relied so heavily on the ability to portray a positive image of their endeavors to potential colonists. Colonialism, of course, is an enterprise rife with salesmanship and putting positive spins on colonial enterprises. Leaders such as Shary shared much in common with colonizers during the age of exploration, all of whom needed funding for their efforts from either governments or private organizations. The entire effort required maintaining an image of the colonial enterprise as a worthwhile and assuredly productive endeavor.[12] Indeed, as time would show, the local economy relied more heavily on land sales than it did on fruit sales or any other locally grown crop. Developers' ability to portray Valley lands positively counted for everything.

The Lower Rio Grande Valley's image—and subsequently, the imagined reliability of local boosters in the eyes of their potential clients—often hinged upon the actual goings-on within the local agricultural industries as well as the early citrus industry. If the citrus industry suffered financially, potential land buyers would be less likely to fall for the land developers' sales tactics. Perhaps more importantly, however, if the growers were unhappy, they would "knock" the Valley, thus spreading a negative image of the developers with whom they had come into contact. These initial bad experiences and complaints about the companies and their enterprises would be quieted by the financial success of the citrus industry during the 1920s, although they undoubtedly did not disappear. Aside from the growers who succeeded and believed in the Valley's future during the subsequent decade, many of those who were unhappy still pushed for the brighter future initially promised by the region's developers and boosters.

The Orange Sunrise

All of the abovementioned experiences—problems with irrigation systems, inadequate access to water, crop failures, overpurchasing of land, or purchasers' inability to make timely payments on their land—marred Valley agriculture prior to World War I. After the war, however, things took a turn for the better. Part of the reason for this was that developers and growers finally began to work out the kinks in selling land and establishing working irrigated farms. Simply put, increasing numbers of people had begun to purchase land despite the fact that numerous people had already suffered setbacks and failures in the region.

Another important reason why the Valley's development took off after the war was the changing situation in which many small farmers found themselves throughout the nation. World War I was a period of prosperity for American farmers. Farmers during and immediately after the war thus had more money to spend on buying land and improving their farming capabilities. The United States also entered into a period of economic inflation after the war, which meant that farmers could sell land at prices never before thought possible. Many farmers, one historian argues, who probably had never written a check for more than a hundred dollars suddenly found themselves with thousands of dollars in their bank accounts. They began to see themselves as both businessmen and farmers, hoping to reinvest their newfound wealth. Thus, for Valley land developers there was a ready-made market of farmers who hoped to make money through land investment, among other things. Increased numbers of Americans came to regard farming as a means to financial wealth.[13]

Some of these investors formed their own corporations, as well, before investing in Lower Rio Grande Valley citrus and other forms of commercial agriculture. At the same time, however, because they were so eager to make money, many farmers could sometimes fall prey to unscrupulous land salesmen and still make purchases without realizing what they were getting themselves into. Movement to the Valley was rapid from 1917 to 1927, with a brief lull in 1920. The Valley's population doubled during the 1920s, indicating the strong pull that commercial farming held over both Anglo farmers from the

US. Midwest and Mexican immigrants.[14] So although a large portion of the area's newcomers were serious in their attempts to make money and bought wholesale into the Valley developers' vision for the area's future, a number still had falling-outs with the larger land developers. Either way, all still operated under the boosters' vision for a bountiful future on the border.

The year 1920, for a number of reasons, proved to be the turning point for South Texas citrus. First, as stated above, the region's population increased. Second, 1920 was the jumping-off point for Texas citrus itself. By 1939 citrus and vegetables combined to provide over 75 percent of the total farm revenue for the Lower Rio Grande Valley, meaning that in 1920 local citriculture was about to enter into an extended period of growth over the next two decades. Finally, by 1920 the Valley had surpassed all other areas of the state in terms of regional citrus production. The small area's 124,000 citrus trees in 1920 garnered much attention. The number of citrus trees in the Valley peaked at about 14,000,000 by 1949. After 1920 citrus became an important concern in all aspects of Valley life; no longer were Valley growers skeptical at the idea of growing citrus. Initially, when early promoters such as Shary and Virgil N. Lott saw the potential of the area for growing citrus fruits, many small growers scoffed at the idea. But, according to one historian, by 1920 these same cynics had learned from their mistakes. Not only did many newcomers engage primarily in citrus growing, but also numerous growers already in the Valley shifted to planting the fruits.[15]

Citrus instantly became the principal industry in the South Texas borderlands economy. By April 1922, forward-thinking farmers and development companies had planted about 1,500,000 citrus trees with more than $10,000,000 invested in the new industry. Commercial citrus had never even shipped a full carload's worth of fruit as late as 1918, but by the 1921–22 growing season that number had grown to about ten carloads. This may seem like a small amount, given the high dollar value of the overall investment, but only 12.5 percent of the trees in the Valley were of bearing age for that growing season (most citrus trees will not bear fruit until they are about five years old). Of those trees, about 60 percent were grapefruit and 35 percent were oranges, with the remainder divided among lemons, tangerines, kumquats, and limes. Half of all of the fruit trees planted in the Valley originated from nurseries in the vicinities of San Benito, Mercedes, and Mission, the balance being transplanted in from California and Florida. Initially, farmers had little to guide them in their choice of variety, so they wound up planting a wide array of citrus fruits. For example, although the principal orange in the Valley was the Washington Navel, there were ninety different varieties of oranges produced on the local level. Only about one-third of them, however, were found to be practical for the region.[16]

In response to this lack of knowledge by growers in selecting citrus varieties, as well as having few sources of information to turn to for guidance, the Texas State Department of Agriculture (DOA) published a guidebook in 1923 specifically for the use of Valley citrus farmers. In order to further support the farmers, the DOA used the guidebook to announce the coming foundation of a citrus experiment station that would promote citriculture throughout the region. The state's interest in publishing the guidebook, however, was not only to provide information to growers but also to promote the industry to outsiders and thus encourage the region's development. The publication is also important in that it provides one of the earliest snapshots of the industry outside of the accounts of growers and land developers.[17]

The authors of the DOA pamphlet first set out to explain how the Lower Rio Grande Valley differed from the other main points of commerce in the US citrus belt, Florida and California. First, the soil and climatic differences between the Valley, California, and Florida were vast. For this reason, the DOA informed farmers that following the examples or advice from the two other regions might not equal success in Texas. For example, scientists reported that sour orange was the best rootstock for all Valley citrus trees, and the best location for the trees was on high land made up mostly of sandy loam (a common soil type in the Valley). New trees should be planted in the spring after the potential for frost had passed, and artificial heat could be used to protect the trees in case of freezing temperatures later. Other points of emphasis included how to pick fruit as well as the necessary processes to ensure productive packing, shipping, and marketing. Finally, some of the advice that the DOA laid out seemed contradictory to the wishes of most local growers. The authors argued that too few oranges had been planted in the Valley during the previous growing season but that the market demand for Valley oranges would allow for more to be grown. "During the past season," the authors concluded, "we could have sold more oranges than grapefruit." Growers appeared to have ignored this advice, however, focusing on grapefruit primarily throughout the rest of the industry's existence, likely in part to differentiate themselves from the orange-dominated citrus industry in California. The many local orange varieties remained secondary to Valley grapefruit.[18]

The DOA sought other ways to promote the industry's well-being, which included ground-level research and analysis. In 1923 two of the bulletin's authors visited Mexico on a fact-finding trip. The two specialists inspected Mexican trees in order to ascertain what horticultural pathologies might exist that could potentially spread north across the border. Although there was little commercialized agriculture on Mexico's side of the Valley until the 1930s, there were enough citrus trees south of the border to make transborder horticultural health an overriding concern. The most pressing concern was insect infestation of citrus fruits. Thus, subsequent laws put in place allowed only for the importation of Mexican wild limes, outlawing the importation of any other Mexican citrus fruits. One goal of the report, which contained information on citrus canker, insects, and other diseases, was to establish an agreement between the governments of the two nations that Mexico would work to clean up its own orchards. Not only would the Valley's industry benefit, but also Mexican citrus growers stood to benefit from the research and agreements.[19]

Valley citriculture flourished in large part because of the proactive support of the state government as well as active scientific research. Although citrus contributed to the state's overall agricultural development, it is worth noting that citrus exports from the Valley were still only a small part of the total agricultural exports for the region at that early stage. Many growers still did not plant citrus. In fact, a number of local growers had become successful through crop diversification. One of Sharyland's early farmers, J. E. Meador, did not participate in citrus growing at all. In the early 1920s Meador became noteworthy for his lack of dedication to any single crop. For example, during one year he planted eighty acres to cotton, thirty acres to corn, ten acres to cabbage, ten acres to broomcorn, and ten acres to cane hay and milo maize. Meador also did well with livestock, raising sheep, cattle, and pigs. By differentiating his crops, Meador hoped to avoid the vagaries of market demand for one primary crop over the others. Meador was hedging his bets. Nonetheless, citrus would grow quickly in importance over the course of the decade. Farmers like Meador, if they had not already turned to citrus by the early 1920s, did so in increasing numbers as the decade wore on.[20]

Ebbs and flows in the labor supply no doubt affected employer-worker relations. Mexican Americans native to the region worked widely on Valley farms. With the prospect of an entire crew of undocumented workers being laid off or deported (especially at the end of the decade), many growers might have worried whether their lands would have been cleared at all or crops harvested in time to sell them on the market. Because of the reserve labor pool across the border as well as the reports of great wealth coming out of the new industry, growers and developers pushed workers as hard as they could for the lowest possible wages.

High-dollar investment in Valley lands also meant that new growers hoped to keep overhead costs as low as possible in order to regain the value of their initial investments. In early March 1924, Eltwood Pomeroy of Weslaco set a new record price for farming acreage in South Texas when he sold his twenty-acre tract to Barnett L. Hoffman, a Kansas City contractor, for one hundred thousand dollars, or five thousand dollars per acre. The tract was practically all set to citrus, with about twenty-five hundred trees. In the sale Pomeroy included a separate tract of six and one-half acres that sold for just under two thousand dollars per acre. He had come to the Valley about 1909 and purchased his farm at sixty-five dollars per acre.[21] Pomeroy had become fabulously wealthy, then, through citrus growing; or perhaps one could refer to it more accurately as citrus speculating.

Stories such as Pomeroy's had three main effects on local citriculture. First, they served positive ends in the realm of boosterism, advertising to potential growers the possibilities inherent in the new industry. Second, they served as an example to growers already in South Texas of the level of success that they could potentially achieve. With stories such as Pomeroy's circulating, a culture of wealth-seeking farmers who sought to wring high profits out of their lands grew in the region. Finally, and perhaps most important, the financial success of men such as Pomeroy could, ironically, work against the boosters' vision for Valley citriculture. By publishing Pomeroy's success and presenting it as an attainable goal, industry leaders and developers ran the risk that small growers would get frustrated when they were unable to attain Pomeroy's level of good fortune, which was clearly well above the average. The boosters' own vision and tactics, then, could potentially work against them and served to sow some seeds of discontent among small growers.

Valley media outlets were fond of publishing tales of otherworldly successes like Pomeroy's. In 1924 a local paper described the first bale of the 1924–25 cotton season, which brought in a whopping $1,405. Credit for the bale went to a John A. Cherry and an unnamed member of the not-yet-famous Bentsen family (later of Texas politics), which would become one of the most powerful families in Mission. Sixty-five pickers had been hired to pick the bale, which took two days. The owners took no part in the process but stood ready for a photo op after the bale had been sold. Interestingly, an article credited a man named Juan Diaz as having some involvement with raising the bale, although he was not included in the photograph and had his name misspelled as Diez. In the photo's caption, however, the author noted that "Diaz left the exchange before the sale was made."[22]

Much like the story of Eltwood Pomeroy's sale of his citrus orchard, accounts such as that of the Cherry cotton bale could be both productive and counterproductive. First, the unbelievable bounty of men like Pomeroy and Cherry in the early part of the 1920s served to reinforce the boosters' vision of

South Texas as a place of limitless possibility for the hardworking citrus or cot-ton grower. At the same time, however, what these stories failed to convey was that the success of these men was practically unparalleled. By presenting them as typical examples of Valley agriculture, media outlets conveyed that such success was possible for anyone, which was not true. That such heights were nearly impossible to attain, then, would have been of less concern to Valley farmers than the fact that one of their neighbors had enjoyed immense finan-cial success. Thus, despite the boosters' message, after some time the public celebration of a few growers' wealth and success would make most farmers feel like comparative failures.

Nevertheless, the region fast became one of the wealthiest agricultural sec-tions in the United States. One article noted that Hidalgo County, in particu-lar, was the single most valuable agricultural area in the country: "New farm-ers are pouring into the fertile valley which raises everything from citrus to feed crops twelve months in the year. Population and wealth are increasing rapidly as more acres are placed under cultivation."[23] The writer certainly did not embellish the facts. The 1930 populations of Hidalgo and Cameron Coun-ties each experienced a more than 100 percent increase over their 1920 census figures. Hidalgo County grew in ten years from a total population of 38,110 to 77,004, while Cameron County grew from a population of 36,662 to 77,540. Furthermore, the total amount of acreage under cultivation in the Valley would skyrocket from 486,487 acres in 1925 to 942,014 in 1930. A commercial farming boom was clearly in full swing. The Valley's population by 1925 had become roughly 50 percent Anglo; the overall number of Anglos, due to land sales and movement from the Midwest, would increase over the next decade. This sta-tistic is striking, given the region's proximity to Mexico. The Anglicization of the Valley, as well as its rapid transformation into an empire for commercial agriculture, was fast becoming reality.[24]

Aspects of the new grower culture began to take shape as the industry took flight. In the fall of 1924 the Valley Horticultural Society became popular among locals for its stand against the shipping of California citrus fruits with an infectious scale on them into the local marketplaces. If such scale were to spread to the Valley's orchards, the fallout for the local industry could prove disastrous. The committee sought legislative action against the importation of such fruits, showing new arrivals that Valley-area growers indeed sought to protect one another's investments by banding together to take collective action against threats to the region's well-being.[25]

One must consider who these small growers were and in what other ways they attempted to realize the boosters' vision for the Lower Rio Grande Valley.

While positive views of the region's potential abounded among its inhabitants, some growers had a far less optimistic (and less naive) take on life on the farms. Valley growers attempted to realize the possibility of citrus growing by being active in the marketplace. This was done, in part, by participating in organizations such as the Texas Citrus Grower's Exchange, which was the first farmer's cooperative in the region. Joining the organization in theory would not only protect the individual small farmer but also ensure the industry's overall success. Also, and perhaps most important, it is necessary to reconstruct what life was like on a daily basis in valley agricultural towns in order to recapture the essence of life in the region.

An undercurrent of negativity among small growers present from the early struggles during the 1910s was, in fact, still alive during the 1920s. Part of this can be seen in discussions that took place in the political sphere. In the congressional primary election in 1926, Sid Hardin, a businessman from Mission, ran against future vice president John Nance Garner for the latter's seat in the US House of Representatives. Garner was then a rising star in the Texas Democratic Party as well as a close friend of John H. Shary. Hardin sought to curry favor with the public by associating Garner with Shary in order to capitalize upon what he saw as Shary's general unpopularity. Hardin argued in a July speech that Shary was a big political boss who made five million dollars by bilking midwesterners into buying his land, that he did not mix with "commoners," and, finally, that Garner had pulled some strings in Washington to help Shary avoid paying some hefty taxes on his Hidalgo County lands. Hardin also dubbed Shary "the Mussolini of the Lower Rio Grande Valley," "King John," and "the Bohemian Czar" in order to drag Garner's political reputation through the mud. Shary responded to Hardin with an editorial in a local newspaper, noting that he intended "a courteous reply." Shary bemoaned the fact that he and Hardin were once friends who had now suffered a falling-out.[26]

Although Hardin failed to unseat Garner, the incident is noteworthy. The campaign shows that an ambitious politician sought to gain political advantage by capitalizing on Shary's perceived unpopularity with the general public. Shary, then, must not have enjoyed an entirely good reputation, despite the rising success of the new citrus industry. Why would Shary have been at least somewhat unpopular? One possible reason is that growers felt that either their experiences with their orchards or their participation in the citrus industry were not as successful as Shary or his land agents had claimed they would be. Second, it could be that the public fallout against Shary was simply a by-product of his alliance in local Democratic Party politics with the A. Y. Baker ring, which would be voted out of power in the 1928 municipal elections. Based on the growing unpopularity of politics-as-usual in the Valley, it would seem that the answer lies somewhere in between. Furthermore, it is important to note that even if some farmers had become cynical about the industry's leadership, they did not necessarily give up in their attempts to become successful small growers. Growers often worked in hope of a brighter future despite the stark realities of the more challenging present. Discontent with the industry did not necessarily mean the end or even a lack of belief in the Valley's future.

Local growers had many reasons to be optimistic as well. The industry gained in renown with each year and garnered increased financial investment. New money meant that farmers could plant more trees. The area had grown so much that by the end of the decade there were about five million orange and grapefruit trees in the Valley (it is important to remember that most of them would have been located in the relatively small confines of two counties: Hidalgo County, primarily, and also Cameron County). Also, the industry continued to hit various high-water marks. For the 1929–30 season the Valley shipped more than twenty-eight thousand carloads of citrus and vegetables, bringing in a total of over twenty million dollars to the local economy. Although only about five thousand of these carloads were citrus fruits, that number would increase to over eight thousand a few seasons later.[27]

Other statistics also reveal just how quickly the citrus craze had swept through the region. Cotton had previously been the primary cash crop grown in the area, but citrus, which had been practically nonexistent before 1920, had far outgrown cotton during the 1920s. For example, in 1930 in Hidalgo County there were 2,162 cotton farms, whereas the total number of fruit farms (many or most of which would have been citrus farms) was 924. Farmers then maintained a higher acreage of farms in cotton than in fruits: cotton acreage made up 246,855 acres in Hidalgo County farmland that year, whereas fruit accounted for 46,689 acres. The average cotton farm was 114 acres in size, nearly twice as big as the average fruit farm, at 51 acres. These statistics make it quite clear that cotton, which required more acreage to farm profitably than did citrus fruits, still dominated Hidalgo County's physical landscape.

Interestingly, however, the value of fruit farms in the Lower Rio Grande Valley had nearly equaled that of cotton farms, despite the greater number of cotton farmers who also happened to own higher acreages. In 1930 all cotton farms in Hidalgo County were worth a total of $28,210,356. Fruit farms were almost as valuable, as their grand total was $24,621,399. Citriculture, then, which was new to Hidalgo County in the early 1920s, had clearly made a major impact on the local farming economy. When excluding farmland and considering solely the value of homes or dwellings in the Valley by farm type, the homes of fruit growers in 1930 totaled \$1,510,085, while the value of cotton farmers' dwellings totaled \$1,099,893. Citrus growers thus appear to have been living more comfortably than their cotton-growing counterparts.[28]

Other developments brought promise to the new industry. By the middle of the decade Valley nurserymen grew their own trees. Although development companies still imported some trees from Florida and California, locally grown trees meant that growers would have more varieties at their immediate disposal and could be less reliant upon sources in the other two regions. Also, in 1929 A. E. Henninger of Mission discovered a strange cluster of grapefruit with a deep red pulp and a red rind growing on one of his trees. Thus, the Ruby Red was born, which later brought consumer interest and market attention to Valley citrus growers.[29]

Ruby Red grapefruits eventually became the icon of South Texas citriculture. A number of red varieties developed within the industry, so to simplify matters, South Texas growers patented the Ruby Red. After freezes in 1949, 1951, and 1962 decimated South Texas citrus groves (a phenomenon that will be explored further later in this book) South Texas growers eliminated the white and pink grapefruits in order to focus solely on the red varieties. Later mutations in the fruit produced varieties even redder than the original Ruby Red. Later research in the local Texas A&I Research Center produced in 1970 the deeply red Star Ruby, followed in 1984 by the Rio Red variety. To differentiate these varieties, Texas growers began marketing their grapefruit under two categories: the Ruby Sweet and the Rio Star. All of these icons of Texas citriculture, again, can trace their ultimate origins and the producers' obsession with redness and sweetness back to the industry's early history and the discovery of the Ruby Red during the 1920s. In sum, growers began innovating as the industry took off during its first decade.[30]

Other aspects of life for white Americans in the Lower Rio Grande Valley during the 1920s were not always positive. Success, in part, depended on whom one knew. Frank and Dorothy Anderson, new arrivals to the Valley late in the 1920s, had trouble finding jobs despite the Valley's great economic successes. Frank Anderson worked at a bank run by elements of the old-school Democratic machine that had controlled the Valley prior to 1928. Because of this, many of the newer arrivals in Valley agriculture considered Frank and his wife politically corrupt and thus wanted nothing to do with them. The post-1928 Republican political alliance, Dorothy Anderson alleged, blocked her from getting a teaching job. Interestingly, though, the Andersons seem not to have struggled during the Depression, which hit Valley growers hard during the middle part of the 1930s.[31]

What is perhaps most noteworthy about South Texas Anglos such as Dorothy and Frank Anderson is, however, not that they seemed to have faced political opposition from the new growers or that they weathered the economic storm of the 1930s. Like many others who commented on the region's race relations, Dorothy argued that there was no discrimination in the Lower Rio Grande Valley and that "everyone was one big family." Their own experiences with political factionalism clearly belied this naive claim, but this characterization also fit squarely into place with the promoters' depiction of Mexicans and Mexican Americans as willing workers who were happy to receive pittance wages and a segregated social status. There was also no discrimination further west in the Valley, the Andersons argued, because Rio Grande City had a Hispanic demographic majority. The couple moved to Rio Grande City in Starr County later in 1946, and Frank recalled that their children always dated and were friends with Mexican Americans. One of their grown children also had a Mexican American spouse, a union to which the Andersons gave their blessing.[32]

Even the Andersons, then, who did not outwardly exhibit any stark anti-Mexican prejudices, still fit into the Anglo boosters' line on race relations with Mexicans and Mexican Americans. This was true despite the fact that the Andersons themselves were targets of politically based discrimination from the small-grower class. The harsh racial discrimination of the South Texas borderlands—so well documented through the experiences of ethnic Mexicans in the region since the farming revolution—was something that most Anglos simply pretended did not exist. Even Anglos of opposing political stripes agreed on that point. People like the Andersons, who may have had numerous Mexican American friends, did not feel compelled to speak out against segregation.[33] The vision of segregation sold by the boosters was far-reaching and firmly entrenched throughout local society, existing sometimes as an unfortunate undercurrent that not all Anglos outwardly recognized. Many, also, would become shocked when labor and Chicano Movement activists asserted that ethnic Mexicans in South Texas deserved more rights than South Texas whites allowed them to exercise. The idea of a tractable and passive ethnic Mexican population held clear sway in the minds of Valley Anglos, although the level of anti-Mexican sentiment appeared in varying degrees among them. Occasionally one could find Anglos such as the Andersons, who did not appear to have exhibited any outward anti-Mexican prejudices. Above all, however, the stark racial hierarchy held sway.

Citrus growers and other people in the industry reinforced their "one big family" version of life in the Valley through other means. Industry leaders in Hidalgo County began holding the annual Texas Citrus Fiesta in Mission in

1932. The public celebration, which included four days of parades, exhibits, and numerous other attractions, took place in the middle of January during the high point of the citrus harvest season. Land development companies and railroads had organized agricultural fairs throughout Texas since at least the mid-nineteenth century for the purpose of attracting economic investment and home seekers, and the Texas Citrus Fiesta was no different. Organizers sought various ways to memorialize the industry. One of the more interesting celebrations in the Valley was a fashion show in which women's dress designs could include only by-products from local citrus fruits, vegetables, corn shucks, cornstalks, shell corn, corncobs, cactus, avocados and papayas. All accessories had to be made of those specific products native to the Valley. Alongside the fashion show was the Parade of Oranges, which featured Queen Citrianna and her court, riding floats decorated with citrus and vegetables grown locally. The Queen's Ball also featured a big dance and the crowning of Queen Citrianna, who ruled over the fiesta. Other attractions included numerous exhibits of the latest citrus and vegetables grown in the Valley, new technologies, and a golf tournament for men. Bright displays of citrus fruit also appeared in store windows for the town's passers-by to admire. The Citrus Fiesta was not just a celebration of the local industry—it was also a far-reaching community-building effort on the part of the developers and the major growers. The celebration served as marker for the industry's progress. It also helped inculcate a local culture centered on citrus.[34]

Citrus celebrations also took place at the Hidalgo County Fair, which was at the beginning of the winter harvest season in mid-November. At the fair organizers crowned a King and Queen of Grapefruit. Despite generally bad weather on the first day of the first Hidalgo County Fair, one reporter noted that "a slow, nasty drizzle . . . did not keep loyal subjects from coming to see their rulers honored." Congressman and future Vice President John Nance Garner served as Royal Grand Mufti, crowning John H. Shary the king and the wife of Sheriff A. Y. Baker the queen. Clearly, the most powerful citrus-related people in the Valley organized the ceremony. Each citrus-growing town also nominated a princess, a duchess, ladies in waiting, and numerous pages, who passed through the business section of Mission on floats.[35] The imperial imagery folded neatly into the larger structures of monocrop colonialism in South Texas.

Organizers hoped to create an event that would unify all citrus growers by having each of the towns send participants to the fair. Local unity, they hoped, would bring financial windfall and productivity to the whole industry. Developers only benefited if individual growers pushed themselves to their highest capacity. It is interesting that Shary, Garner, and the Bakers served as the self-proclaimed heads of the industry at the fair. Even though the growers were independent producers, it was clear who still inhabited the top of local hierarchy.

Such celebrations continued to be important events around which local boosters rallied throughout the rest of the twentieth century, reinforcing certain aspects of the Lower Rio Grande Valley's citrus crop to its overall success. In the 1932 Citrus Fiesta, promoters made much of the fact that ten thousand to twelve thousand people were expected to attend the event and that "Mission citizens, despite the depression, raised over $2,000 to finance the Fiesta, the sole object of which is to glorify citrus." Later Fiestas celebrated specific themes intended to bring local growers together; for example, the 1956 Fiesta was dedicated to the memory of early colonists in the Valley. The Citrus Fiesta proved to be a boon for local tourism for the Mission area and Hidalgo County for many years.[36]

In another cooperative effort, in order to ensure future successes, some of the industry's leaders developed a citrus growers' exchange. In 1923 Shary and a number of other local wealthy businessmen and developers founded the Texas Citrus Fruit Growers Exchange (TCX), which was the first organization of its kind in the area. The basic premise of the organization was that it would handle all of the marketing of subsidiary growers' cooperatives, charging twenty-five cents per box of fruit shipped to cover the cost of selling and advertising as well as all overhead expenses for the company. The cooperatives organized as community units. That is, growers from specific towns organized under a specific designation for that town. The organization hoped to enroll over 95 percent of the growers in each of its subsidiary districts.[37] In short, they designed the organization to enforce a standard uniformity by including as many growers as possible and making the entire region function as a recognizable economic unit.

The organization's founding was a big event. At its first Valley-wide meeting in Mercedes, the TCX adopted bylaws similar to those of a California citrus exchange, noting its potential to help growers dispose of their fruit at top prices. Shary himself visited the California exchange to discern how its Texas counterpart should function. TCX adopted standardized packing and shipping methods to increase the share of Valley fruits on the national market. Albert Kalbfleisch, the organization's president, argued that "the fact that the Valley can grow better citrus than California and produce it more economically will avail us nothing if we do not profit by the experience of California growers and form an exchange to handle our purchases and sales." Not only would stockholders and the growers prosper, but the TCX would also represent a fulfillment of a certain part of the Valley's original vision, that of bringing together growers from throughout the region into a single community of successful settlers inside of a borderlands space. Building a regional community based on shared ideals also served practicable economic purposes. Eliminating competition among marketers and shippers as well as establishing a uniform control of Valley-grown fruits would allegedly eliminate the negative influence of disagreement and infighting among Valley citrus interests.[38]

Initially, the TCX did seem to enjoy some financial success. Soon, however, cracks in this grand vision for the Valley's new industry would arise. One of the first signs of trouble came during the 1928–29 harvest, by which time the exchange's price for shipping Valley fruits had ballooned from its original twenty-five cents per box to somewhere around eighty or ninety cents per box. Also, it was that year that the TCX began an expansion campaign and added several new packing plants, much to the chagrin of some of the growers, who believed the new plants were unnecessary and required too much financial overhead. Finally, the exchange reported that a few of its growers had become impatient with its inability to move larger quantities of grapefruit that season and had thus sold the fruit to cash buyers themselves instead of selling through the exchange. "This is not cooperation," one officer noted, as the fruit had "gone out under cut prices to hurt the market and hurt their neighbors," which was anathema to the TCX's motto of "Pack-Market-Profit Together."[39]

Things took a turn for the worse when the exchange fell victim to the Great Depression. Squabbling over the exchange's leadership spilled over into the public sphere, calling into question the leadership and motivation of Shary and other high-profile managers. Indeed, the constraints placed upon small growers during the Depression led them to doubt the very men who had helped bring them to the Lower Rio Grande Valley in the first place as well as those who had sold them the vision of life in the Valley in general, which increasingly looked like a mirage for some. For the time being, however, during the 1920s the vitality of the exchange appeared to prove that the vision of a community of prosperous small citrus growers was essentially limitless. Growers sought specific ways to implement the boosters' vision at the ground level as the 1920s progressed.

Succeeding as a citrus grower had another, darker side to it. The industry's rise had stark consequences for the region's thousands of ethnic Mexicans. The difficulty of losing one's land and becoming an itinerant farmworker only scratches the surface of how bad the situation had become for ethnic Mexicans north of the Rio Grande. Not only did the new regime in South Texas bring with it an ideology that pushed ethnic Mexicans into the marginal roles of wage workers and servants, but ethnic Mexicans also found themselves at the whim of a new class of white Americans who, in many cases, considered them something less than human. The commercial farming boom and the Plan de San Diego uprising had swept in a new regime of Anglo-Americans who would not tolerate challenges to its authority. Notably, according to one historian, it was in the 1920s that South Texas Mexicans came no longer to view the region as lost, instead considering it American. South Texas was no longer a Mexican space. As such, emphasizing a certain Americanness became a strategy for emphasizing belonging in this new borderlands space.[40] Clearly, the colonization of South Texas was complete. Sadly, the next several decades, as this book will show, prove that Anglo-American power brokers in the region cared little for ethnic Mexicans' arguments about their own belonging in this American space; race alone became the defining factor of who could enjoy acceptance and mobility in the new Anglo-American borderlands and who could not. When conservative Mexican American strategies to combat oppression failed to achieve many widespread gains by the 1960s, Chicano activists turned to new strategies to emphasize belonging and demand their rights. Simply put, South Texas belonged to them—it was their home; they had been colonized. The establishment of commercial citrus during the 1920s came at a great cost for ethnic Mexicans in the South Texas borderlands—it cost them their homeland.

CHAPTER FOUR

"More Texan Than the Texans"

Colonialism and Race in the South Texas Borderlands, 1917–1930

They made us feel for the first time that we were Mexicans and that they considered themselves our superiors.

—UNKNOWN[1]

Citrus's rise was not the only change that swept through the South Texas borderlands during the 1920s. The spike in Anglo-American settlement coincided with some dramatic events in the history of the world. In 1917 the world was at war, and US President Woodrow Wilson hoped to keep the country out of what many Americans considered a European conflict. As it became apparent that the United States was slowly being dragged into the war on the side of the Allies, however, the Germans decided to act preemptively. Early that year, British officials intercepted a telegram from German foreign minister Arthur Zimmerman to the Mexican government in which the former promised the latter certain concessions if Mexico would agree to invade the United States, keeping its military busy and thus away from Europe. The so-called Zimmerman Telegram sent shock waves through the United States, whipping the nation into the fury that ultimately led to American entry into the war in April of 1917.[2]

Americans during the World War I era responded to increased fears of foreign radicals—be they Germans, Mexicans, or the left-leaning European immigrants whom many had blamed for the perceived excesses of American labor unionism since the late nineteenth century—with an increased level of nativism. The US Congress addressed these widespread fears of foreign radicals by enacting new immigration restriction laws. In 1921 Congress passed the first of what came to be known as two quota acts, which placed an annual limit on the number of immigrants by national origin whom the government would allow to enter the United States. Notably, the farm lobby in South Texas and other parts of the US Southwest successfully convinced lawmakers to omit Mexican immigrants from both the 1921 and 1924 quota acts. In 1926, Congressman John Box—a longtime judge, legislator, and Methodist minister from the Houston area—introduced a bill that would apply quotas to all Latin American immigrants, but the bill ultimately failed. The Box bill was, in effect, a way to placate the nativists in Texas who sought to restrict Mexican immigration despite the farm lobby's interests in keeping it open. Box became celebrated in the US House of Representatives as well as back in Texas for his efforts to keep the national origins quota system going, indicating the large-scale exclusionist bent that Box and many of his supporters had during the 1920s and '30s. In the words of one historian, it was during the 1920s when Mexican immigrants in Texas "found themselves positioned between hostile camps: on one side were the agriculturalists who wanted their long hours and low wages and on the other were resentful working-class Anglos." Either way they turned, then, Mexicans and Mexican Americans found themselves facing either people who wanted to exploit them or people who felt ethnic Mexicans had no place in the United States at all.[3]

Given this paradox of unbelonging, the era of the quota acts brought with it some of the most systemic anti-Mexican racism in South Texas borderlands history. The process of white American farmers' colonizing the region and imagining its new future during the 1910s and '20s, combined with the larger national narrative of nativism, explains the increasingly stringent level of racial oppression faced by ethnic Mexicans in the South Texas borderlands during the World War I era. In short, this chapter argues that the now well documented deepening of racism against ethnic Mexicans in South Texas would not have taken place without the region's colonization by Anglo outsiders. By the 1920s South Texas Mexicans became a colonized people in the Texas-Mexican homeland.[4] In a twist of bitter irony, then, the Mexican exception to federal immigration policy gained expression at the ground level in the South Texas borderlands with the creation of a racially oppressed and marginalized class of laborers that existed because of skin color regardless of the individual's actual national origin in either Mexico or the United States.

The New Order

As related earlier, citriculture exploded during the 1920s. Texas citrus had grown exponentially since its earliest days; initially, the industry concentrated in the Gulf Coast region, where oranges and satsumas grew on trees, many of which Texans had imported from Japan. But by 1925 the industry had shifted to the South Texas borderlands and consisted largely of grapefruits. Satsumas and Gulf Coast oranges dissipated strongly in the face of the borderlands citrus industry. By the end of the 1920s there were roughly seven million citrus trees in the state, most of them in the Lower Rio Grande Valley. Although the industry would suffer during the Great Depression, it would rebound to peak levels in the post–World War II era.[5]

Changes in the South Texas racial regime that arrived with the new citriculture did not go unnoticed by outside observers. Prominent agricultural economist Paul Schuster Taylor recognized significant differences between the small number of long-term Anglo residents in South Texas and the newcomers who had come down from the US Midwest to participate in the region's commercial agriculture boom. Taylor, who came to South Texas during the late 1920s to conduct oral interviews for a book about farming and Mexican labor, once wrote that the new South Texas colonists were "more Texan than the Texans," meaning that they became more ruthless in their racist attitudes toward ethnic Mexicans than the long-established Anglo residents ever had been. Taylor's work thus revealed an important component of the region's colonized status. A certain level of cross-cultural interaction had previously existed underneath the well-documented tension between whites and ethnic Mexicans in the region, but with the arrival of the new class of white farmers and growers in the 1910s and '20s, the region's native population found itself pushed even farther to the margins of the newer, whiter South Texas. One Wisconsin transplant related the following to Taylor: "Don't get to pitying the Mexican and depreciating the white people, holding him in subjection. He wouldn't have it any other way. The white man will cuss the Mexican, and then in the evening, on the cattle ranches, he's down by the fire with him, with the frying pan, and eating tortillas with his coffee. There never was a grander companionship between men. . . . Once [the Mexican is] attached to you, you never need worry; he'll defend you against all his kin."[6]

Other sources support the existence of these types of attitudes. Historian Mark Wyman notes that "many longtime residents [of Texas] were critical of newcomers from the North," as these long-established Anglo-Texans "had generally mixed amicably with Tejanos." Ethnic Mexicans in Texas also noticed some distinct differences between older Anglo-Texans and the new arrivals from the Midwest. One man commented, "Since the coming of the 'white trash' from the North and Middle West we felt the change. They made us feel for the first time that we were Mexicans and that they considered themselves our superiors."[7]

Taylor found such anti-Mexican attitudes prevalent throughout South Texas. One "professional man of distinguished southern ancestry" told Taylor that "the Mexicans are not equal and they know it. They're perfectly happy grouped together. . . . The Mexican is inferior, and not so intelligent, but no worse than any other [nonwhite] race." Several Anglos commented that Mexicans were preferable to other minorities because they knew to "stay in their place," with one man arguing that, "They stay in their place better than the nigger." Many of Taylor's interview subjects argued that Mexicans were a law-abiding and passive people, while one "town school authority" told Taylor, "The Mexican here is a servant class, a laborer, a peon, slave. The white child looks on the Mexican as on the Negro before the [Civil] war, to be cuffed about and used as an inferior people." Others reported that the Mexicans were "followers" and were "filthy and lousy." Still, whites usually characterized Mexicans as hardworking and law-abiding. "There is an inbred hatred in Texans against the Mexicans," one Anglo cotton picker reported to Taylor. He continued, "Do I like the Mexicans? No, did you ever see a Texan who did?"[8]

Social norms also helped Anglos to reinforce Jim Crow–style segregation in South Texas towns. Groups of Anglo men commonly attacked Mexicans who overstayed their welcome on the "whites only" side of the tracks. Lingering in "American Town" past sundown meant particularly bad trouble. In one incident, a Mexican man harmlessly laughed at a group of Anglos playing horseshoes when one of the players missed a throw. In response, the players abandoned their game, attacked the man, threw him in the back of a wagon, and dumped him on his family's doorstep.[9] Such incidents were common in South Texas farming communities.

Taylor's work showed that the ideal farmhand for South Texas Anglos during the 1920s was an undocumented Mexican immigrant. Farmers preferred undocumented workers because those who could read and entered the country legally were more apt to go north, while their undocumented counterparts would remain indefinitely and work for the pittance wage of one dollar per day.[10] For the worker, illegal entry was much easier than the alternative, as it allowed for the circumvention of some steep financial costs that the majority of Mexican immigrants simply could not pay. The following list outlines the subsequent costs for a US visa at the Nuevo León port of entry in late 1928:

One certificate of birth	1.50 pesos
Two copies of certificate of birth	1.00
One certificate of marriage	1.50
Two copies of certificate of marriage	1.00
One certificate of good conduct	.55
Two copies of certificate of good conduct	1.00
Four photographs	1.00
Total	7.55 pesos ($3.75 US)[11]

The problem, then, for most potential Mexican immigrants is clear: most were simply so poor that they could not afford to pay the necessary fees to enter the United States legally. South Texas farmers knew this, which makes the farming empire's proximity to the US-Mexico border so crucial to jump starting the process of migrant labor and illegal immigration into the United States. Still, whites had to justify their use of these undocumented workers in other ways aside from pointing to the cheapness of their labor. Thus, Mexicans became the "dirty," "filthy," "lousy," yet "hardworking" people described by Taylor's interviewees. Working cheaply on South Texas farms cost ethnic Mexicans much more than lost wages. Should undocumented workers not be available, then legal entrants and Mexican Americans, despite their likely higher rates of mobility and ability to move north, were the next best option.

The economic boom that had begun to take hold during the 1910s clearly did not trickle down to any great degree to Mexican American or Mexican workers by the 1920s. One land agent in Cameron County, Henry Allsmeyer, noted that before 1912 Mexican workers could make about three dollars per week, whereas afterwards that wage rose to about five dollars per week. (Wages appear to have remained at five to six dollars per week into the 1930s). Workers usually worked from 7:00 a.m. to 6:00 p.m., six days per week, and could usually find some kind of temporary farmwork. Given the fortunes made by some South Texas agribusinesses, as well as the crippling poverty that wracked the majority of ethnic Mexicans in South Texas throughout the twentieth century, it is clear that the small wages paid to undocumented workers were clearly not dictated by any real need on the part of the growers to keep costs low. Labor was, quite simply, a cost that white growers were determined to minimize in order enrich themselves. But racial marginalization did not stop in the fields and orchards. Ethnic Mexicans were also a people that white growers sought to keep segregated from all aspects of life in the new, white South Texas.[12]

Juan Crow on the Border

It was only during the 1920s that the maltreatment of ethnic Mexicans along the border transmogrified into something resembling the treatment of blacks in the Jim Crow US South. Taylor found white growers more than willing to explain the ins and outs of being a grower in South Texas. One grower, Felix Wirick, who had property north of Eagle Pass, had the following to say about his workers: "They were here before we were and they're working for us. They're durable and they keep their place better than negroes. We'll always need someone to do the menial work. They'll not be landowners. They don't save. Fifty percent draw money in advance of payday. They'll not rule our children. Our little boy bosses the Mexican children. Intermarry? Our children won't."[13]

Wirick also believed that Mexican workers were preferable to African Americans. His wife added that she "couldn't stay in a place alone" if there were blacks present, but that Mexicans were "ok." Also, Wirick's argument that Mexicans were preferable to blacks because they "don't seek to mix" clearly indicates the type of racially stratified class system that new white South Texans hoped to maintain.[14]

Blackness was not just a foil used to explain the marginalization of South Texas Mexicans. The labor system on South Texas farms was actually a close cousin to the plantation system of the pre–Civil War US South. Both systems were based on the same precepts: that the bottom line was all that mattered for the farmer, that the racialized laboring class often lived on the farm, and that white farmers defensively argued that ethnic Mexicans were content with their treatment as something less than a human being. Big farmers in South Texas usually built houses for their workers in order to immobilize them and, the farmers hoped, foster a sense of loyalty to the bosses. One farmer near Carrizo Springs told Taylor in late November of 1928 that ethnic Mexicans deserved to be discriminated against because they "are Indians—like niggers they're intended to be cleavers of wood and drawers of water." The farmer continued, "The Mexicans are fine laborers," because "you can tell them what to do and they'll do it."[15]

Successful growers and farmers in the new South Texas would never have existed without these laborers. The fact that the entire commercial agricultural system depended on these people for its success—as did the cotton empire of the antebellum South—is indicated by a number of sources. In Mercedes, in the Lower Rio Grande Valley, an official at the Agricultural Experiment Station informed Taylor that shutting off Mexican immigration to South Texas would be hardest on the large citrus growers. Smaller, younger growers who worked as tenant farmers often subleased their land to ethnic Mexican tenant farmers, but this was short of the white tenant's ultimate goal of becoming a wealthy large grower. Large growers tended to hold a monopoly over the available workers, leaving as few as possible to work for smaller growers or white tenants.[16]

Aside from black slavery, the South Texas farming system closely resembled yet another form of nearby labor exploitation: Mexican peonage or debt peonage. One farmer in Robstown in Nueces County recalled to Taylor a case during the World War I era when Mexicans were chained and guarded with guns. Even during the 1920s disputes over indebted Mexicans who abandoned their employers were common. Grower John Magee recalled the case of a Mexican who walked off the job in 1924 only later to be attacked by his former employer in a local store, where the grower beat the man mercilessly and confiscated $37.50 to pay for an alleged debt. Another grower, Clifford Gaudy, informed Taylor that many farmers would refuse to allow their workers to leave their farms until all debts were paid.[17]

Farmers and growers clearly enforced a system of unfair indebtedness. In early 1927 twelve men from Raymondville in Willacy County stood trial in the federal court at Corpus Christi on charges that they had participated in debt peonage, meaning that they had physically forced men to work in unfair conditions and forced debts on the men that could not possibly be repaid. The case made headlines, due at least in some part to the fact that two of the victims happened to be Anglos (which was an extremely rare occurrence and probably the only reason why the perpetrators faced any charges at all). As Taylor's interviewees would show, the trial and horrific crimes represented problems that were common to South Texas commercial agriculture.[18]

The Raymondville case publicized how farmers and law enforcement officers sometimes colluded to keep workers in debt and immobilized. Although all of the details of the case are too extensive to include in a short summary, some common practices came to light. Several cotton growers in Willacy County had men arrested after they deserted their employers with "unpaid debts." Growers often bought groceries and other provisions for workers on credit at local stores, which gave them a certain amount of leverage. If the worker was upset and left (for any reason), then the employer could have that person arrested for nonpayment of debts. Sometimes, too, the men involved in the peonage cases had not been field workers at all but had been arrested and convicted of innocuous crimes such as vagrancy. Whatever the charges against them, a local judge would tell the arrested men that they could work off their penance by picking cotton or working some other crop for a local grower. Often these convicted criminals toiled under the watch of security guards carrying guns in the field to guard the convicts from being hired away by other growers or to stop them from escaping. One grower brandished a revolver to Taylor, telling him that "if cotton pickers run off this usually brings them back." A laborer reported that his employer routinely confiscated his and his coworkers' clothes and shoes at night to prevent them from running away. One worker who had been summoned to appear before the grand jury reported that his employer, local cotton grower Carl Brandt, had promised him "a pass out of town and three dollars" if he would tell the jury that he had not "been working under a gun." Local officers used a pass system to prevent workers from leaving town. The witness against Brandt—one of the defendants in the case—furnished to the court the pass Brandt had given him, which simply read, "Frank, give these boys a pass to get out, Carl." The Raymondville case ended with the conviction of a county sheriff, justice of the peace, and three deputies (some of whom were also cotton growers) of peonage.[19]

Some growers and farmers in South Texas still practiced debt peonage as late as 1929, despite the well-established fact of its illegality stemming from the high-profile Raymondville case. Stokes Holmes, in the nearby town of Bishop in Nueces County, seemed unafraid of the antipeonage laws. "How do I know the Mexicans who are in debt won't leave?" he asked rhetorically to Taylor. Then he answered himself: "Have a regular Mexican to watch them. . . . If the cotton pickers to whom I advance started to move, one of my regular Mexicans would get my foreman out of bed and he would talk to them or threaten them or do anything else to keep them from moving off." Holmes left the clear impression that if threatening an indebted worker did not convince that person to stay on his farm, then perhaps actual physical force would be convincing enough.[20]

Competition for labor was clearly very fierce. Also, the implication in terms of the social status of ethic Mexicans in the local farming society is clear: "Those who get away from other farmers [to whom they are indebted] do so probably because the regular Mexicans know they haven't been treated quite right and sympathize with them," a Nueces County foreman told Taylor. Some coworkers clearly aided and abetted escaping workers. Growers and farmers thus in many cases did not practice basic human decency with regard to their workers.[21]

Although a number of growers and farmers told Taylor that the practice of debt peonage was by the late 1920s a thing of the past, there is plenty of evidence to conclude that it continued. One farmer noted that in the late 1910s Mexican workers had been "chained and guarded with guns . . . [but now there were] no cases like that." All of Taylor's interview subjects seemed to indicate that peonage was common before the Raymondville case. Nevertheless, even in 1929, a year after the highly public Raymondville case, a city marshal in nearby Robstown reported that incidents of peonage still took place: "You can't hold Mex for debt—peonage—it's a trust. Last year a negro came and told me a farmer was driving two negroes back with a blacksnake to the farm. I drove out and found the young farmer with a whip driving them up the road. I told the negroes to get in my car and drove away [and told] the young man that he was committing peonage."[22]

While the Raymondville case scared a number of the growers and farmers, some clearly remained undeterred. The high-profile nature of the case clearly did not dissuade many of them from keeping local ethnic Mexican workers in as close to a state of racial slavery as possible, even when those practices broke the law. Racial politics in the new South Texas in some cases clearly trumped the rule of law.

Taylor's interview subjects made it clear that the local Mexican population was expected to "remain in its place" across the new South Texas. "We admit them because we need them for labor, not from the point of view of citizens," reported A. O. Stubbs, president of the Chamber of Commerce of Robstown. "We would not want our schools full of them," he continued, "[and] that they don't advance is a protection to us in a way." Mexicans, according to most white South Texans, had to be controlled. "If we could not control the Mexicans and they could take this country it would be better to keep them out, but we can and do control them," Stubbs reported flatly.[23] The ways in which whites controlled ethnic Mexicans—segregating them, treating them as a laboring class—were too obvious for Stubbs to mention. Notably, although the border served as a gateway for labor controls in the region, the borderline did little in the way of determining who could make a legitimate claim to social belonging. "Foreign-ness" was determined by the racial border between white Americans and eth-nic Mexicans in the region, not the actual national origin of people of Mexican descent. Skin color equated working as a farm laborer in the new farming society. Cases of Mexicans who worked outside of this marginalized and proscribed role in the new, Anglicized South Texas were exceptions to the general rule. Through his interviews, then, Taylor had unwittingly recorded the arrival of a new racial regime in South Texas, one that rested on years of anti-Mexican sentiment but that had only recently come together to fully relegate all ethnic Mexicans to the margins of this modernizing borderlands society. This marginalization was clearly necessary in order for the colonization of South Texas by Anglo-Americans to work properly. Most of the Anglo grower class hoped these racial-ized labor practices in the South Texas borderlands would never change.

Aside from the clear divide in terms of labor, the social worlds of ethnic Mexicans and Anglo-Americans also became firmly divided soon after the farming revolution. In terms of the narrative of racial hierarchy, local ethnic Mexicans seemed to inhabit an in-between social space that was not quite the same as that of blacks. In Kingsville, for example, although there were no offi-cial deed restrictions that kept separate living spaces in the town for whites and ethnic Mexicans, the townsite company gave blacks, Mexicans, and whites each their own separate sections within the larger municipality. The county clerk for Kleberg County in Kingsville, a man named Bloodinorth, argued that such segregation was "the best way to handle the situation." Bloodinorth said that he felt "the same way towards the Negroes but I guess the community generally doesn't feel quite the same. The Mex will eat in the restaurants & at the tables in the drugstores, but the niggers wouldn't—and the Mexicans come to H.S. by the time they get that far they're usually cleaner and not objectionable. . . . [There is] very little intermarriage here."[24]

Bloodinorth recalled an incident when a local Anglo boy from a "good family" impregnated and married a local Mexican girl, which "knocked him out with the rest of the community."[25] Even though the local ethnic Mexican population seemed to enjoy somewhat more tolerance from whites than what was allowed the local black population (notably, Kingsville is at what could be described as the far north edge of South Texas), ethnic Mexicans clearly still suffered under a similar level of social segregation from Kingsville's white population.

When it came to voting, Anglo South Texans argued that neither Mexican Americans nor blacks should be given the franchise. One grower outside of Carrizo Springs noted that ethnic Mexicans used to be rounded up by political bosses to vote, but that such patronage practices had ended. According to that man, Mexican Americans knew that they were not "expected to vote [and they did not] care to vote. . . . No it's not legal, and they could if they insisted, but they know they're not supposed to." The implication as to how local Mexicans knew that voting was frowned upon was not left to the imagination: "To say 'Texas Ranger' to a Mexican is like saying 'Ku Klux Klan' to a nigger," noted one interviewee. The method of social intimidation clearly mirrored the ways in which white supremacy was maintained in the US South. Unlike in Kingsville, however, the ethnic Mexican population in Carrizo Springs did not generally mix with whites in public places such as restaurants. Segregation, the interviewee concluded to Taylor, was necessary because it kept whites and ethnic Mexicans from intermarrying, which was highly frowned upon.[26]

The Texas Rangers, who had become infamous among South Texas Mexicans by the time of the Plan de San Diego uprising (if not earlier), were not the only form of control that local Anglos employed. With the creation of the Border Patrol in 1924, growers had a new way to intimidate Mexican immigrants into doing their bidding. Farmers throughout South Texas used the Border Patrol to make their workers more pliant. One farmer in Raymondville noted that he called the Border Patrol when he had workers that he wanted "to discipline . . . , [which] scares the others, and they work better [because of it]." The threat of deportation not only served as a method of labor oppression, but it was also a constant reminder to all ethnic Mexicans that they were outsiders in a world dominated by white farmers.[27]

Even though ethnic Mexicans were differentiated from blacks by the new colonists, some of the attitudes of the white newcomers resembled the ways in which slave owners treated their chattel in the antebellum South. John Stone, an onion grower in Carrizo Springs, related to Taylor that most farmers favored Mexican workers over blacks, because even though "you can get more work out of a negro . . . a Mexican is a better citizen. You never heard of a case of rape by a Mexican; it happens all the time with negroes." Stone, however, showed an astoundingly hypocritical attitude about sexual relationships between white men and Mexican women:

> A Mexican respects a white man; you can do anything you want with their women; and their men won't attack you; of course some of these better edu-cated Texas-Mexicans would just as soon go after you. With the negro women you can do anything you want if you just get them off from the rest; the Mex-ican women will never say yes; you just have to go ahead, or you'll get left. Some of the Mexican men seem to feel it an honor that a white man will pay that much attention to their women. Infusion of white blood into the Mex-icans? Yes, I suppose that 25% of the Mexican babies born here have white fathers; boys will be boys wherever they are."[28]

Stone's cavalier attitude toward white men raping black and Mexican women is evidence that these attitudes were likely common. The implications for the social power structure are clear; white men "honored" Mexican men by "taking an interest" in their women, while ethnic Mexican men seemed to lack the ini-tiative or manliness to fight against the rape of their wives and daughters. One could imagine that Stone had stepped off an antebellum-era cotton plantation in the Mississippi Delta and into the South Texas borderlands of the 1920s. These parallels between the treatment of African Americans and ethnic Mexi-cans in South Texas were not lost on people during the early to middle decades of the twentieth century. In fact, historian Kelly Lytle Hernández argues that as late as the 1950s some elements in the Border Patrol recognized that the South Texas farming system bore a stark resemblance to antebellum-era black slavery and thus promoted an "abolitionist narrative" in their attempt to wrest undoc-umented immigrants from their employers.[29]

Several other men echoed Stone's sentiments. An onion grower near Car-rizo Springs reported to Taylor that a friend of his always hired Mexican fam-ilies, and if the family had a daughter he liked, he would inform the family's mother that he expected the daughter to "keep house" while the rest of them worked in the fields. If the mother expressed any kind of objection to such a situation, he would refuse the entire family work. The farmer, who was clearly raping young Mexican girls, had, according to Taylor's interview subject, "as nice a wife as you ever saw."[30]

Legitimate interracial relationships would never be considered socially acceptable by South Texas Anglos. As in the case of the young man from Kingsville who ruined his social standing with the white community by impregnating and marrying a young Mexican woman, such unions were shunned along the border. Intermarriage clearly did happen on occasion, as evidenced by one farmer outside of Carrizo Springs who mentioned to Taylor that "there should be a law against it, same as the negro." Anglo men who married Mexican women almost always lost their social standing with other whites, although one of Taylor's interview subjects exclaimed that he would not "blame the Mexican woman who marries a white man if she can," as it would advance her social status.[31] Intermarriage was clearly a point of contention.

Anglo women, of course, shared some of these same racist sensibilities with their male counterparts. One farmer's wife mentioned that Mexican children should attend separate schools from white children. When Taylor pressed the woman on this, she responded with an expected level of incredulity that stressed a perceived naturalness to segregation: "You wouldn't want your children to go to school with Mexicans, would you?" Avoiding intermingling with Mexican Americans and Mexican nationals so close to the border would have been difficult, but nevertheless, whites expected it. This same farmer's wife reported attending a Rotary Club meeting in Eagle Pass, which several Mexicans from Piedras Negras across the border also attended. Despite the fact that these fellow Rotarians were "lighter Mexicans," the farmer's wife reported telling her husband that she "didn't care how high class they were, they looked black to me and I didn't want to sit side of them. I don't care if they are rich and I have only fifty cents. And some of them have much better education than I'll ever have. I don't want to mix socially with them."[32]

Social segregation of course involved certain unspoken rules commonly practiced by households and in public places. Mexican workers always came to the back door of a white person's house. Two women near Carrizo Springs reported to Taylor that Mexicans came in only when there was work to be done and only stayed in the part of the house necessary for them to complete their work. "They know their place and you don't have to tell them," one wife told Taylor. She continued, "They are good domestic servants if you train them right. They're getting better . . . they can speak pretty good English, but they don't want to."[33]

Segregation was the common practice in everything from religious revival meetings to stores and businesses. A drugstore owner reported to Taylor that

Mexican customers could not be served at the soda fountains; the store would sell them bottles of Coca Cola or ice cream cones but refused to serve them where the majority of the clientele gathered. "We just tell them it's one of our rules," he said flatly. "Our white patrons wouldn't stand for it." Nevertheless, Mexican patrons were obviously indispensable to local businesses. "We sure do notice it when they go off to cotton," the store owner noted. The man also told Taylor that local Mexicans were "well educated" to the segregation, but that those from outside of the region were not used to it and could "get pretty hot about it when we don't serve them." But breaking the practice of segregation was a difficult one, since "it was a custom in the community before I came here," according to the store owner. He continued, "I've sometimes thought [that] if they made me serve them that I'd charge them so damn much they'd never come back—(.25 cents for Coca-Cola). I don't know whether I could do it or not." To complicate matters, however, the drugstore owner went along with the local custom of segregation only begrudgingly. Noting that the practice of not serving Mexican customers was "a problem, especially with those who come from other places," he longed for the end of the practice. "I wish they'd take a case up and force me to serve them," he argued, "then the white people here couldn't say anything to me for not doing it." Although a cynic would say that he simply feared alienating the most important component of his clientele, the fact that this unnamed drugstore owner longed for a challenge to the existing system speaks to the complexities of the Anglo–Mexican relations at the ground level in the new South Texas. Although most whites accepted custom as the prevailing practice in the farming communities, at least some clearly longed for the days when segregation could be challenged at the local level, even if such challenges came about only because of an individual's self-interest.[34]

Life in South Texas was clearly frustrating for ethnic Mexicans. Segregation in the 1920s indeed replicated itself on many levels throughout local society. White children, of course, picked up on their parents' attitudes about race. One man, Luis Perales of Valley Wells, reported that Anglo children commonly threw insults at Mexican schoolchildren in unsegregated schools, the pejorative "greaser" being the most commonly used one. The Anglo children, according to Perales, took a distinct pleasure in making their schoolmates miserable. After a whipping for whatever infraction the Perales children happened to commit at school, white children would "hoo-rah" them and tease them on the way home. Perales asked his children's teacher to let them out of school early so they could come home without being bullied, but the teacher responded that such was not possible and that the town also could not afford a separate school, which would theoretically have helped curb racial bullying.

Perales thus withdrew his children from school until he could "get a teacher with a better disposition towards the Mexicans."[35]

People affirmed such blatantly racist attitudes to Taylor time and again. Louis Bailey, a farmer near Agua Dulce in Nueces County, stated flatly that he had "hit only three Mexicans in eight years and I consider that a pretty good record." A school superintendent in Santa Cruz echoed these statements, saying that "if you have to cold-cock one out of 40 or 50 that isn't many . . . [but you only do it] if they get smart alecky." Bailey also said that there were deed restrictions in Robstown, the biggest local farming town, but that it did not really matter anyway, since "the Mexicans would rather have a quarter to live in." Bailey claimed that "respectful" whites did not mix socially with Mexicans and that "if you see a man who invites Mexicans to the front door of his house you will see a man the Mexicans and whites don't have anything to do with."[36]

The local racial hierarchy swept through the region in the early twentieth century and even reached as far north as Corpus Christi. A man named Miller at the Corpus Christi National Bank revealed his belief to Taylor that "Mexicans [were] not aggressive socially. They would rather be anything else than embarrassed." Even still, however, Miller also claimed, "Fifty percent of the whites are no better than the Mexicans," probably in reference to those whites mentioned by Louis Bailey who were lower class and mixed socially across racial lines. Miller himself could not help but casually wonder to Taylor if "it might be that we would be better off if we had not abolished slavery." Perhaps, for Miller, the enslavement of blacks would have eliminated whatever controversies had arisen with the "Mexican question" in South Texas. Despite this and the fact that Mexican labor was allegedly "more humble and gives you more for your money," Miller also noted that a "man has to watch out for the peonage law now."[37]

Work and Paternalism

Not only were poor relations between the growers and the workers sustained over time, but they also grew more strained and contentious. Although many instances of growers treating their workers poorly occurred, Anglo growers often argued that workers were at least treated better in Texas than they had been in Mexico, that Mexicans were childlike in nature and thus had to be treated like children, or, finally, that Mexican American labor contractors were the ones who treated the workers the worst. Even growers who claimed to treat their workers well, such as Carrol Norquest of Edinburg, served as apologists for South Texas's colonial racial system: "The worst offenders," Norquest once wrote, "were often of their own blood—labor contractors, overseers, bosses—Mexicans whose families had come to the United States a generation before, whose standards of living and education had risen." Norquest blamed this for South Texas's bad reputation of racism and oppressive labor relations. "It is an onus that the whole agricultural community has to bear in the eyes of the press and labor unions," he continued. Norquest concluded his diagnosis by arguing that "most wetbacks did not lose anything by coming, no more than did the earlier immigrants to the United States from Europe or Asia or Africa." Norquest clearly left little space for the maltreatment of ethnic Mexicans by whites. Instead, he gave the impression that Mexican labor contractors were the perpetrators of the most inhumane treatment of workers, most particularly those infractions committed against undocumented immigrants.[38]

Norquest was, however, correct in one respect: it would be too simplistic to consider the grower-worker relationship in wholly cruel or unkind terms. Although some growers treated ethnic Mexicans terribly across the board, others, like Norquest, enacted a kind of benevolent paternalism on their farms and treated local Mexicans and Mexican Americans as childlike, malleable, and deserving of some level of care. Nevertheless, outright cruelty was not a part of Norquest's character. Some workers undoubtedly benefited from the ill-inspired "kindnesses" of such self-identifying *patrones*. Norquest firmly believed that the use of Mexican workers, even when they crossed the border illegally, benefited all parties involved in commercial agriculture: "[The illegal worker's] trust in el patrón, if his patron was good to him, was complete. Life, liberty, health, welfare, money—he put them in the hands of el patrón. He gave in return the very best that was in him: good wishes, regard, loyalty, and labor."[39]

Norquest maintained that Mexican workers benefited equally with growers and consumers from South Texas's commercial farming operations. He also claimed to have been known among local migrant workers for his small acts of kindness, such as creating jobs to keep workers employed when he technically no longer had work for them. But small kindnesses only served to further highlight the dark side of farm life in 1920s South Texas. Two Hispanic sharecroppers in southern Hidalgo County reported having allowed a group of about 85 to 100 undocumented immigrants to raid their fields one particular year after the markets for their crops fell through, only to find their allegedly worthless harvest being sold in small fruit and vegetable stands on the Mexican side of the border. The two sharecroppers estimated that several tons of crops had been taken across the river by swimmers, none having been transported into Mexico by boat. The pittance wages paid to workers, in other words, clearly left many migrants desperate to eke out a living. Grower benevolence often allowed them these small opportunities, but the local structure of race and labor would not afford one grower to pay workers above the market's norm for their services.[40]

Norquest was so proud of his own record as a Lower Rio Grande Valley grower that he wrote a book about it. In 1972 he published *Rio Grande Wetbacks* with the University of New Mexico Press. Norquest's book is a reflection on his then nearly fifty years of hiring ethnic Mexican laborers to work his South Texas farm; the book also serves as a shameless apologia for the Valley's then already well-known history of depredations against its impoverished and racialized working class. Norquest describes himself as a *patrón* at numerous points throughout the book. His book thus provides a top-down account of relations between the ruling and *peón* classes in South Texas's new farming system.

Part of Norquest's purpose, seemingly, was to put on display some of the "backward" beliefs and practices in which many of his employees engaged in order to introduce Mexicans to his readership. In his first chapter, Norquest profiles a woman named Clementina who married one of Norquest's male workers, a man named Raul. Norquest wrote that "religiously, Clementina was mixed up. . . . She had a Mexican blend of Catholicism and superstition. She took her superstitions seriously and defended them with vigor, allowing no mirth on their account." Clementina eventually gave birth to a baby boy, but, much to Norquest's chagrin, she refused to cut the baby's hair. Norquest recalled the following exchange over the matter:

"Clementina, why no cut you that boy's hair?" I asked. "Are you trying to make a girl out of him?"

"I think he's muy hermoso, very handsome, no?" She laughed through her nose.

"No, I don't."

"Well, Carlos, I don't care if you don't." She laughed noisily again. "But Raul thinks it's alright."

It rocked along like that for some weeks. I'd twit her about her "girl." She'd come back with, "No es cosa tuya, it's none of your business." But the weather was getting hotter. The boy was suffering more. He cried a lot. I thought Clementina must be going loco, not to see it.[41]

After Norquest pressed Clementina on the subject one last time, however, her true intentions for not cutting the boy's hair are revealed:

"Carlos, to the Virgin de Guadalupe, I promised that if she would let him live, I would not for a year cut his hair. The year is now soon completed and my baby is still alive, no? Isn't that strong, that promise?"

"Yeah, I guess so." I subsided. Let the kid die, then, if she was so stubborn. I'd helped bury babies before.

But the boy instead survived, and Norquest praised Clementina for finally making "a macho, a male of him." She replied simply, "yes. . . I took him to the shrine of the Virgin of Guadalupe and prayed. Then I cut his hair."[42]

By ending the story with Clementina's simple declaration that she had cut her boy's hair, Norquest impresses upon his readers the implied fanaticism of Clementina's mystical beliefs. His characterization of the young woman, coupled with his practical response that the boy's long hair was making him too hot, is in keeping with displays of the allegedly exotic Mexican culture that South Texas boosters published in the 1910s and '20s. His juxtaposition of his own common sense with Clementina's "superstition" reveals the degree to which Norquest was informed by a colonial point of view when considering the cultural backgrounds of his workers.

Other snapshots of Norquest's infantilizing views of his workers are present throughout the book. Indeed, although Norquest admitted that the Anglo-Americans who came into the Lower Rio Grande Valley in the early twentieth century "pushed the native inhabitants to one side," he also argued that, for him, "the gap between the twentieth-century technology of this country and the primitive innocence of an untaught Mexican from the country was sometimes too difficult to grasp." Norquest included a subsection of his second chapter titled, "Curiosity." In this vignette he commented on the tendency that his Mexican workers had to look and sometimes stare through the windows of his house, despite the fact that most Anglo-Americans considered such behavior rude. "Our curious wetbacks," he commented, "believed that a window is made to look *in* through" and that all doors should be opened. Speaking to his point about doors and privacy, Norquest pointed to the example of his mailbox. Americans are "all taught that a mailbox is meant to be private . . . , but there was nothing like this in Mexico." So, due to the Mexican's alleged natural sense of curiosity, the workers who passed by his mailbox would open it every morning and look in: "The first one would open it, stoop, and look in. Empty! He'd slam it shut. The next one would open it, stoop, and look in to see why the first one had. Empty! Slam." This process, according to Norquest, would repeat itself over and over, every morning and every evening.[43]

Despite the relatively interesting tendency of his workers to peer inside his mailbox and windows, what is telling about Norquest's narrative on curiosity is how he ends the tale. This tendency of theirs, he implied, was a serious problem and a breach of natural social etiquette. "But how are we to teach them not to touch," he wrote, "without hurting their feelings?"[44] Norquest's question concerning teaching his workers US social mores is an interesting one on its own, but his worry about hurting their feelings again indicates the allegedly childlike innocence of his employees. Maintaining his workers' good spirits, Norquest would argue, was his problem, because he possessed the higher degree of emotional maturity. The balance of power, then, on Norquest's farm was far more uneven in his own mind than that of the typical employee-employer relationship throughout modern America.

Norquest also commented extensively on Mexicans' inability to grasp the modern technology that one could find in South Texas. In one incident Norquest described a man named Chico, an Indian from the mountains of Zacatecas who "must have been totally illiterate—a Stone Age character." While riding in a truck with another man, Chico stuck a cigarette in his mouth but soon realized that he could not light it since he was out of matches. The other man riding in the truck handed Chico the truck's cigarette lighter, but Chico could neither understand what the lighter was for nor how to use it. After staring at the red spot at the center of the lighter, Chico became intrigued, whereupon he decided to stick his finger on the heated spot. "All hell broke loose," Norquest wrote, as the red-hot lighter became stuck briefly to Chico's finger, burning his fingertip badly. Chico eventually learned how to use the lighter properly. "Chico was a very intelligent Mexican," Norquest continued, "but it's a great jump from Stone Age to modern technology. It's not really funny when you think about it."[45]

By characterizing Chico as a "stone age" but "very intelligent" Mexican, Norquest reemphasized Chico's foreignness as well as his alleged lack of modern sensibility. How could such a man, he implicitly asked, understand the workings of a modern society? As such, although Norquest considered himself a friend to Mexican migrants, he clearly reemphasized the gulf that many Anglo South Texans thought existed between themselves and their workers. In his chapter titled "Bandidos on Both Sides," Norquest describes how a Democratic official bribed two of his undocumented workers to take a day off from work and not to tell "el patrón" in order that the two could go into town and vote. Although Norquest said little of his own politics in the book, he intimated that this was during an election in the late 1920s when "we were trying to throw the old ring out, a corrupt white establishment that for many years had sucked white the living subsistence of the country." It is quite clear that the election in reference was one known in local lore as the 1928 Hidalgo County Rebellion, which occurred when the Republican Good Government League, backed by small farmers, eliminated the old-school Hidalgo County Democratic political machine. When Norquest asked how his two workers voted, one responded, "'Ah—we voted democrático, like the man told us to, derecho'—straight." Norquest's workers had clearly been bribed to vote for his own political rivals.

After explaining to Norquest how they did as they were told at the polls (ignoring the Republican candidates and voting only for the Democrats), one of Norquest's men explains that "it is easy, Carlos, to vote. Everyone should vote. It is very good that a man should vote."[46]

Norquest's inclusion of the story related how susceptible Mexicans were to being taken advantage of by the more nefarious elements in the Lower Rio Grande Valley. This story speaks back to the alleged childlike nature of his workers and their need to rely on people like him in order to learn how culture and society operated north of the border. His retelling of stories such as this clearly speaks to his views of Mexicans as generally ignorant and not capable of operating in the United States without the help of a patient patrón. As such, his characterizations of ethnic Mexicans in the Valley differ little from the conceptions of them presented by the earlier boosters as foreigners who did not understand or have a place in the society that they played such an integral role in keeping afloat.

But Norquest did make negative generalizations about Mexicans and Mexican Americans alike. Although he pitied and infantilized his Mexican workers, he displayed outright hostility to the region's Mexican Americans. Norquest thus left little room for outside observers to criticize the oppression of ethnic Mexican migrants within the Lower Rio Grande Valley's labor system, instead deflecting the blame of such mistreatment toward Mexican Americans. Norquest, in his book, introduced a man named Gómez whose parents or grandparents had fled Mexico during the Mexican Revolution. Norquest and Gómez had been employed to do survey work on some of the local farms for a government-run farm emergency program (assumedly during the Great Depression). During one particularly hot day, Gómez became thirsty and approached a ten-gallon water drum placed in a field by a group of nearby workers. A ten-year-old boy, who, because of his "scanty clothing and no shoes" was quite clearly the son of one of the workers, had been nearby getting a drink. Gómez passed the can in stride, failed to stop, and ordered the boy to give him a drink. The boy struggled to get the lid off the can but eventually did so, dipping a ladle in and carefully traversing back over the field with the water to where Gómez was standing. When the boy finally caught up to him, Gómez "took the cup, drank the water, and handed the cup back to the boy—still without looking at him. Without a word of thanks," Norquest continued, Gómez resumed his work, and the barefoot boy "trotted back to the watering can through the hot red dust." The one-word title to this vignette is "Haughty."[47]

Norquest never questions why Gómez behaved in such a manner. He simply implies that it was because Gómez and his kind were cruel. Perhaps

Norquest should have considered the degree to which Mexican American men such as Gómez sought inclusion into Anglo South Texas society and whether this capricious behavior was meant to impress a white man, whom Gómez naturally assumed would have approved of his "haughtiness." Still other Mexican Americans in the book are portrayed as behaving even more cruelly to workers. Norquest relates the tale of one grower, Arthur Thompson, who employed two Mexican Americans, Frederico and Alfredo, to run his farm and keep all of his account books. "By the amounts that Frederico and Alfredo always had available to spend on their families," Norquest claimed, "Arthur knew that the two were somehow cheating the men." Arthur eventually found that while he was paying the stated amount to his workers, Frederico and Alfredo were paying the men less, pocketing the difference and falsifying the account books. The two also charged each worker for their trips into town as well as a commission when the men bought groceries. But the whole thing kept going: "Arthur didn't like it, but he decided that he was free from guilt; *he* wasn't robbing the men. He was paying a fair, stipulated price. Frederico, with Alfredo's help, was doing the stealing. It was a 'family affair' (all Mexicans). Arthur told himself that as long as he was getting his work done, he had no complaint. It was no business of his what his American help was paying their cousins from across the river."[48]

Again, Norquest attacked Mexican Americans. Although he clearly did not let Thompson off the hook, his declaration of the scam being "a family affair" does draw a line of distinction between Anglos taking advantage of Mexicans on the one hand and Mexican Americans taking advantage of them on the other. Had Thompson not chosen to employ two corrupt Mexican Americans, the implication goes, his workers might have been paid their fair wage.

And so the story continues. In discussing *la Chota*—local slang used in reference to the Border Patrol—Norquest paints the patrolmen in a highly antagonistic light. In one story Norquest describes the captain of a patrol contingent, who, during two separate raids on a neighbor's farm, was both times bitten by the grower's dog. Norquest relates the tale in a comedic tone, leading the reader to believe that this particular patrolman was a buffoon who had not learned from his previous misfortunes with the animal. In another story, entitled "That Dumb Mexican," the author relates the tale of an undocumented immigrant who outwitted a Border Patrol officer by "playing dumb," taking him on a hundred-mile circuitous route to the farm of his patrón, confounding the officer with his feigned ignorance of the farm's location. Once they arrived back at the farm, the man escaped while pretending to be gathering his clothes inside the house.

This motif of Mexican worker as trickster continues later in the book. In another story related to the Border Patrol, the owner of a local coffee shop began charging double price for coffee to local patrolmen, ten cents per cup instead of his typical five cents per cup, when the frequent raids on his business kept his mostly ethnic Mexican clientele away.[49] Clearly, Norquest's implicit conclusion is that the Border Patrol was the enemy of both the grower *and* the undocumented immigrant, standing in the way not only of the Valley's agricultural development but also of the immigrants' ability to use the Valley's agricultural system for their own personal betterment. For Norquest, the Valley's widely practiced *patronismo* had to be defended in order to bring the highest level of benefit to growers, farmers, and workers. Anything that served to defend that system was, in Norquest's eyes, a good thing.

In the end, the new paternalism, segregation, and repression set in place during the 1920s would outlast the actual life span of small farming in South Texas. When larger corporate farms began to take over the region's agricultural economy during the worst dregs of the Great Depression, they adopted wholesale the system of racialized labor that was put in place by the smaller growers and land companies that came before them. This same structure of racial marginalization and labor oppression was what Chicano and farmworker activists would fight against later in the 1960s, emphasizing their own belonging in a place that was by all logical rights more their homeland than it was that of the Anglo farmers and growers who had only recently arrived in the borderlands. Indeed, the system of race that Taylor noted was the defining characteristic of Anglo–Mexican interaction in the South Texas borderlands for the better part of the twentieth century.

CHAPTER FIVE

Many Valleys

The Fates of Small Growers and Mexican Workers during the 1930s

To the Mexicotexan laborer, anybody who owned a truck was rich. He heard of some sharecropper families who had nothing to eat but bacon and flour. The Mexican laborer, who had subsisted on tortillas most of his life, wondered how people who could afford biscuits and bacon could be poor. He heard how people in the big cities were lining up to receive free soup and bread because of the Depression, and he would joke to his friends, "I wish what they call the Depression would come down here so we could get some of that." And in due time the Depression came.

—AMÉRICO PAREDES[1]

The great folklorist Américo Paredes used the term *la chilla* ("the squeal" or "the cry") in reference to the Great Depression in South Texas. La chilla actually referred to the great poverty suffered by Mexicans and Mexican Americans even before the Depression, but it also served as a mocking barb aimed at poor whites. As Paredes saw it, even after many Anglos became impoverished during the 1930s, they still had not reached the level of poverty under which the average ethnic Mexican toiled.

The Great Depression, however, did in fact worsen the lives of both Anglos and Hispanics throughout the South Texas borderlands. This chapter shows that the world of small commercial farming in South Texas was in a state of flux during the 1930s. Given that much has been written about the hardships Mexicans and Mexican Americans faced during the 1930s, this chapter addresses changes in the South Texas borderlands primarily from the perspective of small Anglo farmers. The Anglo vision of the future for small commercial citrus growers began to break down during the 1930s. Instead of ruining the region's economy outright, however, the Depression highlighted fundamental problems in South Texas's economic structure: namely, that the health of the local economy relied primarily on the vagaries of the land-sales machine that development companies had kicked into full gear during the 1910s and '20s. Rarely had the promise of financial security, let alone large-scale wealth, taken shape for small growers. The Depression, then, highlighted the truth for the small growers, which was that the local economic system was not built with their best interests in mind.

The Depression, if anything, revealed that not one South Texas existed, but many: different worlds for the rich, for the small grower, and, of course, for ethnic Mexican workers. Anglos found it increasingly difficult to bridge the economic divide between the rich and poor in their own communities. Many whites took their frustration out on Mexican and Mexican American workers. Even a growingly chaotic situation on the south banks of the Rio Grande reflected negative developments on the US side of the border. The vision for a racially stratified society based on wealth-chasing modern pioneers simply could not survive the horrors of the 1930s.

Rifts in the new Anglo colonizer identity also became apparent. Wealth and economic stability became impossible for most small growers to maintain. Not only did mistreatment of local Mexicans and Mexican Americans actually intensify, but also Anglos blamed one another for their shared woes. Small growers failed to understand what the Depression augured for the future of commercial farming in the region. Control of the area, or the ability to impose a vision for the region's future, began to slip from their hands.

Iowa on the Border

As in other parts of the country, the Depression did not hit South Texas immediately upon the stock market crash in October 1929. Notably, economic depression had hit many farming areas in the United States during the mid-1920s well before the crash.[2] The citrus and land boom during the 1920s, then, made the Lower Rio Grande Valley and greater South Texas something of an economically distinct place. In reality, the situation still appeared promising for local growers late in the 1920s and in the early 1930s. The grower vision and self-identification as the region's colonizers—which came to some fruition during the 1920s—was so compelling that many felt themselves immune to the larger economic crisis.

Aside from citrus' rising economic prominence during the 1920s, new growers had enjoyed other victories as well. The old boss political system in Hidalgo County received its deathblow in November 1928 in an incident that came to be known as the Hidalgo County Rebellion. Many new colonists had begun questioning the shady tactics of local Democratic political boss and

Hidalgo County sheriff A. Y. Baker. Baker had been in control of county politics since 1918, becoming a multimillionaire through a number of schemes of questionable legality. In essence, Baker operated in the tradition of old school South Texas political bossism. His wealth supported a lavish lifestyle for him and his wife, including a palatial mansion in Edinburg. The sheriff was indeed a ruthless and greedy boss. He had also served with the Texas Rangers earlier in the twentieth century and had gained a reputation for terrorizing ethnic Mexicans; a jury even acquitted him in a 1903 murder trial in which the evidence against him was overwhelming. Baker, an ardent supporter of segregated schools, had come to prominence largely through his patriarchal relationship with the local Mexican American populace, whose votes he wrangled in exchange for numerous petty favors. Baker was skilled at gaining votes either for measures that would benefit him or to get his cronies elected to public office.[3]

Many of the small landowners whom John Shary and others had induced to move to the Lower Rio Grande Valley distrusted Baker and coalesced into a political movement to remove him from office. After the November 6, 1928, county elections, the anti-Baker, Republican-run Good Government League (GGL) charged that Baker, County Judge A. W. Cameron, County Clerk Cam E. Hill, and a few others had dismissed votes from nearby Weslaco after alleging that the envelope containing the ballots had not been properly sealed and that the votes were thus subject to tampering. The GGL countercharged that the Baker ring simply wanted to throw out a portion of the vote that they knew did not favor their candidate for district judge. In response, the Bakerites intimated that the GGL had faked the vote in Weslaco and had intimidated hundreds of pro-Baker Mexican Americans into not voting. With the sharp increase in midwestern colonists during the 1920s, the GGL swept the county offices despite Baker's dubious tactics. In early 1930, adding insult to injury, a congressional investigative committee found overwhelming evidence against Baker in the scandal, convicting him and several other county officials of depriving citizens (the GGL supporters in Weslaco) of their right to vote. Later that year, Baker died unexpectedly of a stroke. Baker's death, the guilty verdict, and the Hidalgo County Rebellion all signaled an end to boss politics in Hidalgo County.[4] Local Mexican Americans and Mexicans, then, lost the support of their patriarchal political boss.

This incident just before the outset of the Great Depression held clear significance for the vision of the new Anglo growers in the Valley's citrus industry. First, it solidified the ascendancy of the new colonists into the political sphere. Growers allied with one another to defeat South Texas's old political bosses; their main point in opposing them was calling out the tendency of the old machines to corral the Mexican American vote. Concerns related specifically to small growers now would have larger expression in the political arena. Second, the incident displayed how the concerns of Mexican American voters were of absolutely no significance to the GGL and small growers. Baker's counterargument against the GGL—that they sought to suppress Mexican American voters—was at least partially true. South Texas's newcomers were vehement supporters of racial segregation and suppressing the Tejano vote. Mexican Americans thus found themselves even more shut out of the political process than they had been before. Although the new colonists distrusted the power-grabbing elements in the upper echelons of established Anglo South Texas society, neither side could rest easily without overwhelming access to their own version of patriarchal or colonial-style relations with local Mexicans and Mexican Americans. Labor relations remained the key element that drove the Valley's economy. The Anglo vision for the region's future had not changed, but a political battle had risen over who would control it.

Both the fallout from the Hidalgo County Rebellion as well as the alleged corrupting influence of Baker's ring on working-class Mexican Americans helped influence middle-class Mexican Americans to join the League of United Latin American Citizens (LULAC), a Mexican American civil rights advocacy group made up mostly of professional and middle-class men. LULAC formed in Corpus Christi in 1929.[5] Baker's fall left a vacuum in the area of Mexican American political activity in the South Texas borderlands, which LULAC hoped to fill. Notably, Baker, who considered himself the "Leader or Superior Chief" of ethnic Mexican Americans in Hidalgo County despite having murdered at least one person, was openly hostile to LULAC. Primarily, LULAC sought to advocate for Mexican American rights and encourage people to participate in a civil rights struggle that emphasized American citizenship and belonging. LULAC's goals, in this circumstance, emphasized the roles that the leaders or more successful people of the colonized class could play as intermediaries between the Anglo and ethnic Mexican populations of South Texas. This early manifestation of Mexican American political activism in the Valley appeared at just the time when the small farmers' vision for life and political ascendancy appeared to be all but assured. The high tide of the Mexican American outcry against the colonial system as well as their access to the benefits of mainstream American institutions, however, would not take place for another several decades.

The rise of LULAC and its emphasis on the politics of citizenship brings to light one important difference between the South Texas borderlands' internal colonialism and its counterpart, formal colonialism: a large percentage of ethnic Mexicans in South Texas did have legal access to citizenship rights. Repressing such civil and political rights helped Anglo South Texans perpetuate their racial dominance during the rise of commercial agriculture in the region. LULAC's appearance represented something of a shock to the system, but Mexican Americans' assertions of their citizenship rights would not take a large upswing until the 1960s, when activists began registering scores of new voters, many of whom had never participated in the political process. Only in the 1960s would Mexican Americans first be able to vote for their own political candidates with limited Anglo interference and engage in direct civil rights activism to counteract the widespread racial oppression endemic to Anglo South Texas. This nonviolent anticolonial revolt began slowly with the appearance of LULAC in 1929 but would thus continue in the coming decades. Still, the economic fallout of the Great Depression would be the first major event that shook the dominance of the Anglo-owned land development companies as well as their clients, the small commercial farmers.

Alongside the political victory for the farmers in the Hidalgo County Rebellion, the general economic situation for small citrus growers was not as dire as one might expect, given the larger national travails. Citrus agriculture catapulted a number of different interests to success. In August 1929 the *Lower Rio Grande Valley Magazine*, which had previously been devoted to general agricultural interests, changed its name to *Texas Citriculture* in order to promote continued growth in the industry and to provide a forum for agricultural issues. Expert predictions for the 1930s also looked promising. Although only a small percentage of the orange and grapefruit trees in the Lower Rio Grande Valley were of bearing age in the fall of 1929, local horticulturalists predicted that Texas would ship 5,000 carloads of citrus during that season (more than doubling the previous season's total), while the next year's harvest had the apparent potential to produce 30,000 carloads. The industry actually shipped 4,622 carloads of grapefruit alone that season, netting growers roughly $4,622,000 in total profit. The owners of top orchards could expect to receive a gross income of $600–$700 per acre for their citrus crops, occasionally exceeding $1,000 per acre. By the dawn of the Depression, Texas was the third-ranked citrus-producing state in the country, still far behind the top producer, California, and second-ranked Florida. Plantings and cultivation skyrocketed in South Texas throughout the early part of the Depression. While a *Citrograph* writer estimated the Valley's industry to have roughly 5,000,000 orange and grapefruit trees in the fall of 1929, another local source placed the number of trees just two years later in 1931 at 6,001,101, covering approximately ninety thousand acres.

As much as two-thirds of that acreage may have been producing by the 1932–33 harvest season. Despite that growth, though, growers in the well-established Florida and California industries had little to worry about in terms of competition from their Texas counterparts. Because of the promising projections in California, Florida, and Texas, the United States had become the world's leading producer of oranges by the mid-1920s.[6]

Land men continued to market the vision for the new agricultural communities, and newcomers continued to buy into it wholesale. Despite criticism of land buyers that became widespread during the height of the Depression, new colonists during the early 1930s still bought into an Anglocentric borderlands farming empire that would know few bounds. Part of the reason for the region's success in the early 1930s rests with farmers and land men of some means who escaped the effects of the Depression in the US Midwest and attempted to start their lives over in the South Texas borderlands. Recruits had begun writing thank-you letters to land companies as early as the late 1910s, presumably at the behest of the various companies that would then publish them and use the testimonials to sell the vision of local citriculture to other prospective colonists. Such practice appears to have become common as time wore on.

Many small growers were more than happy to help developers such as John H. Shary build a positive marketing image for endeavors such as Lower Rio Grande Valley citrus. According to private letters collected by Shary's Southwestern Land Company, some growers appear to have been quite happy as late as the fall of 1932. One grower, W. D. Toland of Mission, ran Blue Ribbon Groves, which grew citrus exclusively. Toland reported that his business was "very profitable" and that should the company choose to "use [my] letter in your campaign to seek new Sharylanders, bring them to see me and I will verify the statement here."[7] Another grower, B. N. Moore, an offsite investor based in Bayard, Nebraska, provided a lengthy discussion about why he chose to grow grapefruit in the Valley over other regions:

> As a member of the Sharyland family, I want to say a few words in regards to our investment and why I invested in the Lower Rio Grande Valley. First I visited all of the Florida grapefruit region, and the following fall my son and wife visited the Lower Rio Grande Valley or Sharyland and purchased ten acres. After arriving home telling me of their purchase I was not very well pleased, but they persuaded me to go down and look over their purchase. Well, the consequence was, I made another purchase adjoining them. So you see, my mind was thoroughly changed after visiting the other grapefruit states. We now have ten acres of grapefruit coming into bearing soon.[8]

Moore's tale, of a family member purchasing land prior to his own investigation, was common, since many others had made purchases after friends or family had preceded them on a train excursion. Other offsite investors, however, purchased their tracts as a sort of old-age insurance. L. E. Rosser of Dallas, Texas, had a tract devoted entirely to citrus. His mind constantly went to the "many fond dreams and anticipations in regard to my home there in my declining years. It seems an ideal place to 'slide down the hill.'" Rosser concluded his letter with the bold statement that "there is no reason why any one should suffer want in this part of the country." Genevieve Gowin, another offsite investor, agreed with Rosser, making the claim that "Sharyland has suffered less from the 'Depression' than any other place in the entire state and [I] would not hesitate to say the entire United States." Walter B. Ellis of Mission concurred: "Even now when people are talking depression and waiting for something to happen we are going right along planting and gathering good crops, and receiving fair returns considering the conditions elsewhere. I was out driving for an hour this morning and saw three new houses under construction."[9]

At least some small growers clearly felt that Shary's holdings had not yet been touched by the Depression and perhaps even thought that the economic downturn would never touch them at all. Land buying had continued to pump wealth into the local economy. Whether focusing on building wealth or retiring and enjoying one's "declining years," growers clearly maintained an overwhelming focus on future success. The vision of a positive future, even as companies collapsed and breadlines appeared in other parts of the country, was still very much alive and well.

Some people reported that their South Texas holdings enabled them to live "the good life." A. E. Bonnell, a dentist in Muskogee, Oklahoma, prized his citrus grove above all of his other investments, looking forward, like Rosser, to the day when his grove would "take care of me in my declining years." E. E. Russell of Mission bought his tract in 1929 and subsequently retired from his previous business, not only enjoying a "good, easy living" from his oranges and grapefruit but also reveling in the less extreme climes of South Texas compared to what he had experienced in the North. The northern escapism of the Valley even appealed to small growers as far away as Canada. J. Sherman Fox of Kelsey, Alberta, bought a citrus orchard in 1922 and returned there every winter to participate in the citrus harvest and escape the arctic Canadian air. "It is a pleasure," Fox wrote, "to breathe that fine Gulf air that eliminates head and throat colds, rheumatism and all such ills, where you are getting younger every day instead of stiff and old." Fox, and assumedly many others, relished the idea of the South Texas borderlands as a climatologically friendly place.[10]

Still other growers loved the western or exotic experiences of fruit growing in the early 1930s. Charles Richardson of Indianapolis, despite the dire economic straits of the country during the 1930s, found solace in "going west" to the Lower Rio Grande Valley to escape the challenges found in the US Midwest:

> Horace Greely was credited with saying, "Young Man Go West." Well, I have always felt about this quotation, that it was all right in its day, but that opportunity has gone now, there are no more chances as he had in mind at that time—the west like every other place is all filled up a long time ago; so why think about its advice any more—it's too old.
>
> Then after I visited Sharyland on one of your personally conducted tours I felt that as far as the west was concerned that I had traveled the limit, and I had, for I was right down near the end (Near the border of the United States and Mexico), in the Lower Rio Grande Valley—home of TexaSweet Grapefruit, and a place full of health and plenty of opportunities—so after all "Horace's" advice still holds good.[11]

C. A. Weego of Fort Wayne, Indiana, agreed, revealing that "the past two years of depression has demonstrated the soundness of my investment in Sharyland. . . . What America needs, is more investment opportunities of this kind." Finally, Dave Burgess of Waconda Springs, Kansas, could not pass up the allure of nearby Old Mexico. Although he was initially less than enthusiastic about the prospect of visiting the Valley, which he did only at the behest of his wife, Burgess fell in love with the foreignness of life at the border: "The only way they succeeded to get me to go on a vacation trip to the Rio Grande Valley was the prospect of seeing a BULL FIGHT in a Mexican border town. I fell for that."[12]

As disingenuous as the original vision for agricultural South Texas often came across in the 1910s and '20s, these testimonials show that numerous small growers believed in the image of a bright future as presented by boosters and land developers. Others, however, were far less optimistic. As the colonization movement continued into the late 1920s, some complained of the trials of citrus growing: land salesmen had pressured people into making purchases, the land was too expensive, or they (the midwesterner newcomers) could not possibly understand the technicalities and difficulties of citrus growing before making their land purchases. Despite the undying optimism of numerous small growers, there were other causes for concern by the early 1930s. The US Department of Agriculture released a bulletin during the summer stating that, because of the productivity of the Lower Rio Grande Valley's grapefruit industry, the stateside markets stood to become glutted in short time. The Harlingen Chamber of Commerce sought to combat this unfavorable publicity by lobbying Congressman John Nance Garner to promote the alleged superiority of Valley grapefruit, which growers thought would differentiate their product from those of other agricultural sectors. Growers hoped Garner would call attention to the fact that not only could they grow the fruit more cheaply than in other sectors, but they also had yet to institute any wide-ranging advertising, which meant that there was room for market growth.[13]

Land companies and large growers often took their economic worries out on their workers. Not surprisingly, growers were candid and matter-of-fact when it came to treating their workers poorly. Shary, in a letter to one of his own orchard managers, Carl Roetelle, complained of the costs of keeping on a large group for the citrus harvest. When finances became strained for one of Shary's orchards, he informed Roetelle that he "wanted one half of the men laid off this week, I do not care what happens. They should have been laid off all this week, and I want the balance of the men cut down to $1.26—I do not care if the whole thing blows up." Not only was Shary cutting his workforce, but also the men who stayed on his farm faced a drastic pay cut. Roetelle's idea was slightly more humane: he desired to lay off all of the labor crews for a week to ten days and hire them back at $1.25 per day instead of their usual $1.50. Naturally, ethnocentric men like Shary would rather see the ethnic Mexican laboring class suffer before they would willingly take a financial hit. Ethnic Mexican workers were their most valuable yet also most expendable assets.[14]

Despite some hardships, there was at least some hopefulness: a clear testament to the wide-ranging local identity of growers as forward-thinking, profit-minded people. By late December 1931, local pundits lauded that year's harvest, which thus far had increased the previous season's level of output by almost fifty percent. Also that month, the grower-supported GGL that had been ushered in with the 1928 election had begun delivering on numerous promises made to small growers in Hidalgo County. Despite an increase in local land valuation that totaled nearly $2,054,298, county taxes had dropped $912,452.66 from the previous year as a result of actions by GGL officeholders. Farmers could thus celebrate the benefits of their political victory that came with the fall of machine politics just a few years before.[15]

People, then, had real reasons to believe that South Texas agriculture was a bountiful financial windfall that even the economic ills of the greater United States could not touch. This sense of optimism continued into the early part of 1932 despite the numerous nationwide problems being addressed by the Roosevelt administration during the spring. J. W. Keefe, head of the

American Fruit Growers of Weslaco, stated that "the owner of a good Texas citrus orchard may look forward to the future with confidence. . . . Remember that only a few limited sections of the United States are suitable for growing of citrus fruits and that their consumption is increasing." A local newspaper article reported that, as a result of a recent upward spike in the stock market, cotton prices in Brownsville had gone up, and this should give immediate optimism to vegetable and citrus growers that their prices would soon jump as well. "The Lower Rio Grande Valley," the author wrote, "which was one of the last sections of the country to feel the depression, evidently will be one of the first to reap the benefits of the upturn in business." In fact, neither of these phenomena could be considered strong indicators of economic health. Little did the author understand how negatively the Depression would affect South Texas agriculture in the coming years.[16]

Local reporters published articles about small-scale growing to argue their point that South Texas remained largely unaffected during the early part of the financial downturn. One man argued that the key to success was not necessarily working your orchards on your own, but at least being on the job every single day. "In spite of the depression, I have been able to make a good living on my farm," the unnamed grower reported. The simple key was to live where one farmed and pursue a regular plan of planting. C. S. Gilkerson, an Oklahoma City–based judge, hoped to move to his citrus orchard in Mission as soon as possible: "We may be having a depression, but that hasn't stopped the growth of my citrus trees," stated the judge. "My place is looking so exceedingly good and I could hardly recognize my grove, it has grown so." Another writer dismissed the Depression's effect on the region by simply titling his article, "Depression Pooh."[17]

Continuing into 1932, quite a lot of public discussion of the economic situation remained optimistic. Because of the shrinking nationwide markets, shipping rates had begun to drop. The Texas Citrus Fruit Growers Exchange had also entered into the shipping business. Some nonexchange-affiliated shippers reduced their fees by as much as 70 percent from the previous season's prices. Although this may have signaled hard times for local shippers, growers reaped a clear benefit of the reduced prices in a market where consumers' buying power was marginal at best. Other experts continued to be quoted into 1932, such as the dean of the School of Agriculture at Texas A&M College, E. J. Kyle, who predicted a brilliant future for the Lower Rio Grande Valley during the 1930s and continued steady growth since the region's foray into commercial agriculture. In addition to Kyle, reporters tapped well-known capitalists to give their stamp of approval on the region's economy. Martin Insull, an investor from

Chicago who had over one million dollars tied up in South Texas businesses and properties, stated in a local publication that "not only is this section in full bloom physically but business conditions compare well with those anywhere else." Indeed, the movers and shakers in citrus and agriculture still hoped to impose the soundness of their vision for South Texas upon the small growers who read such publications, likely in an effort to combat whatever negative rumors may have begun to develop from the economic fallout.[18]

Signs of success in the citrus industry were numerous during the early part of the Depression. In one week during mid-March of 1932 rail shipments shattered all single-week records for the number of cars shipped out of the area, as thirteen hundred cars of citrus fruits and vegetables worth more than one million dollars left the region. Such information buoyed the hopes of many small growers and farmers. Prospects would look even better as the harvest season drew to a close the following month. Toward the end of the growing season the region had shipped twenty-five thousand carloads of citrus and vegetables worth twenty million dollars. Only twice during the heyday of the industry had it produced higher totals of shipments, the most being twenty-eight thousand carloads during the 1929–30 season. Never, however, during any previous season had the average prices of fruit been higher. Growers also benefited from lower land and water shipping rates between the Houston hub and the Atlantic seaboard, which meant that they could better compete in the larger markets with Florida and California growers. Texas growers were also able to ship to England for the first time, meaning that the local industry had a wider market share than ever before.[19]

Despite the general optimism of the region, numerous problems common to the rest of the country slowly crept into the South Texas borderlands. Although the average price of citrus had been higher than ever for the 1931–32 season, an unidentified grower wrote to a local newspaper strongly disagreeing. He argued that instead of fruit prices being higher, the strong season was simply a result of much better crop yields than ever before. This, to him, was a sign of trouble: growers might have been harvesting higher yields, but the increased income did not come from higher market value for the fruits. This unnamed man also noted that businesses not related to agriculture had already begun to fail. Much of this, he argued, was because of one large channel of income that was beginning to recede: the purchase of land by northern colonists.[20] The Depression made its greatest impact in South Texas when land sales began to dry up. Land sales drove the local economic machine as well as the marketability of the boosters' vision for the region. The new South Texas agriculture, it would appear, was for the first time facing serious trouble.

A Land-Based Economy

Numerous sources point toward the importance of land sales to the regional economy as well as its downturn during the early part of the Depression. Stories that land sales were beginning to drop circulated during the early 1930s; malcontented Anglo South Texans let their displeasure spread publicly. One anecdotal story had a Mission-based land firm driving a group of prospective buyers in front of a schoolhouse, whereupon some children on recess ran by, pelting the cars with pebbles and yelling, "Hello, land suckers, hello, land suckers!" The term *land sucker* was a pejorative that unhappy, struggling growers used to refer to northern home seekers who they thought were being "suckered" into buying South Texas land. The children in this example clearly had heard the term from their parents and undoubtedly dented what could have been a profitable excursion trip for the firm.[21]

Not all land seekers could aptly be characterized as suckers, although there are numerous cases of colonists being duped. Lloyd Bentsen Sr.—father of the Texas senator and 1988 Democratic vice presidential nominee of the same name—became fabulously wealthy in the Mission-Sharyland area. The senior Bentsen and his wife followed his parents to South Texas from South Dakota on a grueling 1,675-mile car trip that took nearly three weeks. The couple arrived penniless. Fortunately, Bentsen immediately found work as a land agent for Shary and also started a nursery-seedling business. The Bentsen family invested in and recruited so many growers that a large portion of the hundred-million-dollar citrus and vegetable crop in 1948 belonged to them. But despite the Bentsen family's seeming embodiment of success in Shary's colony, many colonists accused them of backwards dealings. One charge that kept surfacing was that the Bentsens sold land to growers without providing any water rights, which were obviously essential to growing crops. Needless to say, many of these purchasers would have felt duped, while Bentsen's long-standing relationship with John H. Shary certainly would not have helped popularize "the Father of the Texas Citrus Industry" among locals, either.[22]

In another incident, one promoter during the 1920s constructed a large lake and sold plots all around it, informing his potential buyers that "the lake will sub-irrigate your groves." After selling all of his land, the developer drained the lake and disappeared, leaving his buyers unable to irrigate their citrus groves.[23] Victims of such nefarious promoters, as well as those who had much smaller causes for complaint against other developers and companies, could hardly have been blamed if they self-identified as suckers. Growers caught in such circumstances found themselves pawns of the rich and powerful, unwittingly

falling prey to the more ruthless elements seeking to profit from the rapid
establishment of Anglo farming communities. Nevertheless, the sheer volume
and rapid growth of South Texas agriculture in the 1920s suggests that many
growers did quite well and did not become "land suckers." A wide variety of
experiences in the region's colonization clearly must be taken into account.

Land sales eventually plummeted during the 1930s. Some observers speculated that the tapering off in land sales was the first sign that the Depression
had arrived. The marketing pitch and vision for the region that so many land
companies had used to entice buyers from the north, then, ebbed in influence
along with land purchasing. There were five large land companies located in
the heart of the citrus industry in Mission, with others in Elsa, Port Isabel, Progreso, and Harlingen. These companies, until the early part of the Depression,
together earned roughly ten million dollars per year, about half of which went
into the pockets of employees, land agents, laborers, and local commodities
dealers. Those earnings, in turn, became funneled into the local economy. One
commentator speculated on the importance of the so-called land suckers, stating that he did not realize that they "contributed so much to our prosperity"
and "meant the difference between good times and bad times." Still, however,
"many of us did all within our power to discourage the 'land suckers' and to
hurt the development companies. We do not miss the water until the well goes
dry." When the Depression ended, he argued, all South Texans should "appreciate the development companies and . . . give them our enthusiastic support
because to a considerable extent they mean our own bread and butter." Land
buyers deserved everyone's support: "These 'land suckers' were not suckers
after all. They put their money into Valley real estate, and the Valley is the only
section in the United States where real estate values have been maintained,
instead of investing their capital in stocks that have gone down in value almost
to a whisper. These investors were putting their money into property that has
best withstood the depression and at the same time were assisting in the prosperity of all the men, women, and children, of the Lower Rio Grande Valley
of Texas."[24] Clearly, then, there was some local recognition that the backlash
by discontented growers against prospective buyers was destructive to the
regional economy. Those who contradicted the land companies' marketing of
a limitless abundance were thus singled out as being important contributors to
the Depression's arrival in South Texas.

Land company executives knew that the lack of tourism and land sales
during the early part of the 1930s had caused significant economic pangs.
Although the net cash income from harvested crops had been relatively high, if
prospective colonists did not buy any property, the Lower Rio Grande Valley's

net income from annual harvests was insufficient to cover the cash outgoing from the area for payment of public and private indebtedness.[25] Thus, land sales truly were the cog in the Valley's economic well-being, despite growers' successes or failures with their citrus harvests. Naturally, however, successful farmers were more likely to promote a positive image of farming, which in turn had the potential to convince newcomers to purchase property.

Twenty representatives from competing land and development companies met in September 1932 in Weslaco, hoping to prevail upon major railroads to provide special bargain rates in order to bring more excursionists to the area. Such a plan, it was thought, would boost the local economy and ensure that no more land companies would be put out of business because of the Depression-squeezed railroads' increased travel rates. The industry's heads recognized that the entire region lived and died by land sales and marketing, not what they had told potential colonists brought the region its greatest wealth: sales of its citrus fruits and other crops. Growers, then, had a logical reason to second-guess the original sales pitches that had brought them to the South Texas borderland in the first place.[26]

Meanwhile, company leaders disagreed on how to attract more people to the region. One developer, Charles F. C. Ladd, claimed that he enjoyed success with investors "of a higher class" who could enjoy peace and contentment in the Lower Rio Grande Valley and wait out the hard times of the Depression. Ladd also argued that discontented people needed to be resold on the boosters' vision itself in order to overcome the "knocking" that was taking place. John H. Shary, however, disagreed, arguing that instead of reselling the vision, local leaders needed to focus on economic recovery for local agriculture and business, and when that happened "then everybody will be boosting." In other words, the top land developers realized that people were beginning to lose faith in their vision for the future, if they had not already abandoned it entirely. The ramifications of this crisis of faith could prove catastrophic without quick action.[27]

Some locals promoted other stopgap measures. Journalist David Hinshaw argued that the only way the Lower Rio Grande Valley would shake off the effects of the Depression would be "if every satisfied property owner living in the Valley would spend a few hours of his time as an honest real estate salesman to the extent of trying to interest friends in his old home to come here and make the Valley his home." For Hinshaw, promoting further settlement through word-of-mouth would solve the Valley's financial problems: "If each satisfied resident in the Valley would undertake this fine service to his own investment in the Valley the development here would be unbelievably rapid and unquestioningly sound. Such work would stabilize land and property values, would increase bank deposits, improve commercial conditions generally and the additional force of good people with their new capital would make early solution of the Valley's transportation and other important problems which face it at this time."[28]

Interestingly, Hinshaw claimed that the reason California was comparatively better off than the Valley during the Depression was that California workers and growers boosted their home state heavily, which in turn attracted more settlement. If Valley growers were to survive they must once again mimic their more experienced California counterparts.

Even still, the leaders of the local industry continuously denied the effects of the Depression, despite the onset of the economic downturn. In an article written for a local paper, citrus scientist and local grower L. M. Olmsted claimed that South Texas would not feel many of the typical effects of the Depression because land and farm values would not follow stock values. Olmsted failed to recognize how important land sales to outsiders were to the local economy. Other members of the region's upper class naively tried to see the silver lining. John Shary circulated a newspaper clipping in the Southwestern Land Company offices that argued the Depression was actually a good thing because it forced people to stop spending money, spend more time with family, and get to know their neighbors. Of course, the average small growers who had few assets to begin with simply could never survive such a calamity like the wealthy Shary could. The divide between the rich, the small growers, and workers would become more apparent as the Depression worsened.[29]

The situation grew to near catastrophic proportions for small growers by 1933. Many needed money or homes built and required immediate financial assistance through charitable organizations. Simply put, the fallout of the Depression in other parts of the country had begun to drive down the number of people with money who were willing to purchase land in South Texas. This lack of money coming in reverberated through local businesses and farms. Numerous locals reported needing mortgage loans, in order to avoid foreclosure, as well as crop production loans.[30] These developments contributed to the clear mistrust that small growers were developing for their bosses and land developers.

Racism worsened. Some Anglos began to charge that workers were finding it more profitable to remain in the towns and accept government doles rather than work on orchards and pick crops. One writer charged that federal assistance given to the workers was greater than the meager wages local farmers paid, thus giving them no impetus to work: "It is a fact that these laborers have never received more than $1.50 per day and ordinarily would be glad to get $1 or less per day. But now the federal and state relief administration decrees made-work for them at not less than 30 cents per hour, six hours per day. This means $1.80 a day, which at three days a week gives the Mexican as much as the Valley farmer can afford to pay him in a week. The result is that the laborers remain in town, on charity."[31]

Government handouts blew the lid off of the inadequacies of the colonial order's ability to provide ethnic Mexican workers with humane wages. An industry in which laborers received pittance wages could little afford to compete with government assistance programs during times of stark economic crisis. This not only resulted in small growers' inability to pay workers to pick their crops, but it also drew the ire and resentment of the Valley's Anglo population toward the federal government as well as local ethnic Mexicans.[32]

Anglo growers allegedly had less luck than Mexican American workers in acquiring governmental assistance. Citrus growers had tried to attain federal loans in order to help them weather the financial storm, but the Federal Land Bank of Houston almost always denied their requests. Groves were too heavily burdened with bond taxes in irrigated districts and thus were not safe security for federal loans. Compounding the frustration felt by farmers was the fact that the federal government had urged local cotton growers to plow under a part of their crops, even providing them financial incentives to do so. The incentive for American farmers to plow under parts of their crops came under a 1933 federal program titled the Agricultural Adjustment Act (AAA), part of President Franklin Delano Roosevelt's New Deal. The goal for this piece of legislation was to improve the dire economic straits in which most American farmers found themselves. Subsequent infighting between growers concerning the relief-obstructing bond issue would flare up later in the decade. With no government assistance, small farming and citrus growing along the border was in danger of unraveling.[33]

What was already a bad situation for small growers in 1933 turned disastrous that September. On September 5, Hurricane No. 11 came ashore just north of Brownsville. The hurricane, which had formed off the coast of West Africa and had devastated Cuba in late August, hit Brownsville directly with sustained winds of 90–125 miles per hour. Residents of Brownsville and the greater Lower Rio Grande Valley had only about three days' warning before the storm made landfall; the hurricane eventually swallowed the majority of the region between the Nueces River and the Rio Grande. The storm surge reached thirteen feet in Brownsville, while about three feet of water flooded Corpus Christi to the north near Kingsville. Fortunately for the people of northern Mexico, the storm was far more devastating north of the border. The hurricane left nearly seventeen million dollars' worth of damage and killed about forty people, most of them in Cameron County. The storm also subsequently damaged about 90 percent of that year's citrus crop (a less severe hurricane a month earlier had severely damaged the region's cotton crop). Eventually, the hurricane proved to be one of the worst storms on record in the South Texas borderlands. Now, struggling growers had little hope of turning their finances around. Prospects for recouping most of that year's crop were lost. These snowballing struggles contributed to some contentious public squabbling and a crisis of confidence over the agricultural sector during the remaining part of the Depression.[34]

Realizing that the Depression could easily ruin the entire plan for commercial citriculture in the Lower Rio Grande Valley, John H. Shary decided to step in with a plan to help rectify the situation. Announcing the Shary Plan for Social Stabilization, the citrus impresario argued that if a proportion of the population could be distributed more evenly between the cities and the counties that the social destabilization caused by the Depression would not be so severe. People (in the Valley's case ethnic Mexican workers) in the cities allegedly became a strain on resources and the government. Shary's plan was to redistribute these people to the countryside, which would benefit not only the industry but also society and the state as well. This, he argued, was not a back-to-the-farm movement, but a way to regenerate idle and depressed men who were desperate from privation.[35]

Although it is unclear who Shary's target audience was, he clearly hoped to push Mexican American workers who were on federal relief back into the fields to work for small growers, whose morale and belief in the local industry were flagging. Such adjustments, he argued, could regenerate men and be a boon to agriculture as well as the inner workings of agricultural industry. This required moving people to good, workable lands (assumedly in Sharyland or Mission) and providing a sustainable family atmosphere on workable acreage. Farms and loans would have to be provided for these families, who would then have to pay off the acreage over a long period of time. In other words, everyone involved in the project would get some benefit, and the region would then be lifted out of its economic nadir. It comes as little surprise that Shary aimed his proposed relief efforts primarily at growers, however, and not for the benefit of Mexicans and Mexican Americans.[36]

The political powers that be nevertheless ignored Shary's self-interested plan, and the economy further unraveled. No other plan for fixing the region's economy appears to have been introduced. With the economic struggles, the hurricanes, and a frost that severely damaged the 1935 citrus crop, South Texas agriculture suffered from 1933 to 1935 despite a quick recovery in the amounts of fruits and vegetables shipped. The 1935 shipping season also found itself shortened because of a fruit fly infestation from south of the border.[37]

Frost and pests would serve to be environmental challenges to the Texas industry that growers would face for many years to come. A so-called impact freeze happens when temperatures fall below 28 degrees Fahrenheit for four hours or longer—a rarity given the warm South Texas climate but a potentially massive catastrophe when cold weather did strike the region multiple times later in the twentieth century. Such problems were generally avoided in Texas, Florida, and California by keeping the trees heated during cold weather. Citrus canker—a bacterial infection—would also rear its ugly head in the Texas citrus industry over the course of the twentieth century, as would numerous species of invasive pests, such as various aphid species and weevils.[38]

Regardless of the environmental dangers, it was in large part because of these many negative developments that 1935, the Depression's mid-point, can be seen as a turning point in the history of modern South Texas borderlands agriculture. Until 1935 the number of farm operators in the Lower Rio Grande Valley had increased while the average size of farms had decreased. This statistic reflected some basic facts about the history of agriculture in the region up to that point. At the beginning of commercial agriculture boom, large growers and land men had purchased huge tracts of land from which they grew and sold citrus and other crops. As the 1910s and '20s passed, increasing numbers of small growers had bought smaller plots of land that large landowners had marked off and sold. During the struggles of the 1930s, however, many of these same small growers had gone bankrupt, either selling their farms or having them foreclosed upon by banks. In 1935, then, this trend of high numbers of growers buying small farms began to reverse. As more growers went out of business, larger firms that found ways to survive the Depression bought up these smaller plots of land. In the key year of 1935, growers and farmers had still claimed only 65.3 percent of the Valley's arable land. From 1935 until 1954, the number of farm operators in the Valley—a previously steadily climbing number—dropped by nearly half, from 14,222 to 7,773. Likewise, average farm size, which had steadily decreased before 1935, skyrocketed. From 1935 to 1947 average farm size increased by 45 percent. Between 1945 and 1954 it increased a whopping 97 percent. Farm size increased by smaller increments thereafter, and the number of total farm operators in the Valley continued to drop even as late as the 1980s, when only 3,805 individual farm operators were left in the region. Also, between 1935 and 1940 about 4,906 farms ceased operating in the Valley, this after the area had experienced a growth of about 6,151 farms between 1930 and 1935. The Depression had indeed arrived in the Valley later than in most areas of the US economy; when it finally hit, though, small farmers and businessmen were its easy victims.[39]

Thus, the heyday of the small grower in South Texas agriculture passed away. Travails brought on by the Depression also signaled a turning point in the vision of what it meant to be a small grower in the region. While growers had bought into a colonial vision of a South Texas that consisted of small and successful independent farmers, what it meant to be a citrus, cotton, or vegetable grower changed drastically. Thus, class relations between rich and small growers changed, as well as interethnic relations between Anglos and ethnic Mexicans. Experiences during the rest of the 1930s are a testament to the changing identities of South Texas Anglos.

Despite these shifting relationships, the social and political structures of colonial South Texas remained intact. Ethnic Mexicans were still marginalized politically, economically, and socially; the power structure at the top of South Texas society simply shifted from small growers to increasingly larger and corporatized farming entities. In just the same way that commercial farmers, through the example of early Anglo-American colonists in the Lower Rio Grande Valley, learned from Lon Hill that exploiting cheap ethnic Mexican labor was profitable, so too did larger mid-twentieth-century South Texas farming interests adopt the exploitative labor practices of the small farmers who came before them. The more things changed, the more they stayed the same in the South Texas borderlands.

The Dominance That Once Was

Anglo farmers turned inward upon themselves as soon as economic instability set in. Conflict erupted around two key issues. The first of these was a disagreement among growers related to a bond-selling scheme in the Mission-Sharyland irrigation district of Hidalgo County. The problem began in the spring of 1935 with outcries over the collapse of bond prices related to the Hidalgo County Water District Number 7, the major supplier of water for citrus growers in the county. Twenty years earlier, in 1915, private irrigation companies had begun to enter bankruptcy (this was before the large upswing in immigration from the US Midwest after World War I), so the growers began to issue bonds to purchase the systems from men such as Shary, forming irrigation districts and taking control of almost all of the local irrigation companies by 1930. In the early 1930s, when Hidalgo County citrus land was selling for its highest prices (according to one source, five hundred dollars per acre in the brush and fifteen hundred dollars per acre for grapefruit orchards), the citizens of Mission voted to form their own water district in order to purchase the old irrigation canals instead of paying the allegedly high prices charged by Shary and his United Irrigation Company (UIC), which had been in operation for many years. The locals voted in favor of $2,750,000 to fund the irrigation project just before the county's bond system collapsed under the weight of the Great Depression.[40]

Economic hardship soon made it expedient to sell the bonds. Roughly one million dollars of the bonds went on the market, only to be purchased by a familiar figure, none other than John Shary himself. Rather than purchasing the bonds at their value, however, Shary bought the old irrigation system for less than its market value in bonds, which was roughly six hundred thousand dollars. A scathing editorial appeared in a local paper in which Shary was heavily criticized for repurchasing what was essentially his old irrigation system, which he had previously sold at a high price and now bought more cheaply. The editorialist referred to Shary as: "District overlord, who owned the U.I.C., a bank in Mission, and who controlled a citrus marketing agency to sell the fruit of the community, not to speak of a land company to sell the land, and a nursery company to sell the trees, a finance company to do the financing, with a few other linking and interlocking companies to throw in for good measure."[41]

Shary became widely and publicly questioned. To his critics, the bond financing scheme reeked of a rich man's attempt to hold on to power not only while many of his colonists went bankrupt, but also at the expense of the bonds that county taxpayers hoped to use to reduce their own water costs. The incident was a mess for Shary, who nevertheless emerged with his fortune largely intact.

Shary had made the purchase legally through a vote that allowed the bonds to be refinanced at under market value, but locals called the legality of the vote, which included other related bond issues, into question. Part of the money was to come from the Public Works Administration (PWA), a New Deal agency, which, at the behest of some locals initiated an investigation for voter fraud over the bond issue. The election had dictated that the district would sell $450,000 in bonds to the PWA, which would bring in a $107,000 grant in addition to the loans, making the total amount of federal dollars coming into the district $557,000. What further upset many of the locals was the refunding plan for the outstanding bonds that had not gone on the market when Shary repurchased the system. The plan was to issue $750,000 in refunding bonds to refinance the outstanding bonds still left after Shary's purchase, which totaled over $1,000,000 in value. Opponents of the plan had argued that the savings of about thirty cents on the dollar for the refunded bonds was not as great as the savings they possibly could have gotten through a different type of plan. Shary, of course, favored the plan, as he had sold the UIC to District 7 but had later purchased a large stake in the district through the depressed bond values. Some even charged that Shary had relied on old-school South Texas political bossism and rounded up numerous poor Mexican American voters, paying their poll taxes and obtaining their vote to pass the PWA funding, grant, and refunding plan. Any additional federal money pumped into the district would, of course, benefit Shary.[42]

Part of the conflict surrounding the bond deal can at least be attributed to clashes in personality. Shary had run afoul of the editor of his newspaper, the *Mission Times*, a man named Ralph Bray. Bray had been fired from his job in early 1934 over issues related to his job performance but also over an orchard he had purchased from Shary prior to his arrival in South Texas. Shary purportedly spoke to a mutual acquaintance of theirs about numerous articles Bray had written criticizing Shary over the bond issue prior to his dismissal from the *Times*, stating that the trouble they had "over District Number Seven . . . was mostly a personal matter and, in fact, that the whole situation was honeycombed with personalities."[43] Nevertheless, the squabbling clearly had the potential to spill over into a public forum—in this case, the local press—and influence the opinions of local growers. The bond issue represented a larger problem of citrus growers' flagging belief in not only the vision of agriculture that brought many of them to the region, but also the leadership of charismatic men such as Shary himself.

The other issue over which growers clashed during the 1930s was that of the growers' cooperatives, which were the primary form of marketing and selling citrus fruits. As one historian writes, "Farmers' efforts at market regulation collided with the efforts of wholesale agents and other middlemen to accomplish similar ends."[44] The existence of groups such as farmer's cooperatives proved that early-twentieth-century farmers and growers were, in large part, forward thinking and adaptable. The ensuing controversy over cooperatives—namely, the Texas Citrus Fruit Growers Exchange—proved that farmers focused first and overwhelmingly on economic success. The possibilities for such success became complicated by the Depression.

Since the vision for agriculture had emphasized community harmony and concerted action toward the future, it comes as no surprise that cooperative sales and marketing had their place locally. Agents for the Texas Citrus Fruit Growers Exchange publicly lauded "the value of its services to the citrus industry" and the advantage of "all the citrus fruit grown in the state [being] shipped through . . . one agency." The quality of the arguments laid out in favor of cooperatives in Shary's paper, the *Mission Times*, were reprinted in the *California Citrograph* in order to serve as an example of the necessity of cooperatives to growers in the much larger California industry. Competition between growers was allegedly destructive, and the citrus industry apparently bore witness to this fact. "For seven years," the article continued, "since we began the marketing of our citrus products, we have found that competition here in the marketing, lack of control of our product, would perhaps better express it, has cost us dearly." Discord abounded, as "we can see the destructive influence of fighting amongst ourselves for business. One shipper quotes at one price; and another, to get the business, quotes under. Both lose, and the grower always suffers." The proper response to this problem, of course, was to join the exchange.[45] Shary stood to benefit greatly from growers' buying into his argument in favor of the exchange. The evidence that small farmers would benefit from the shipping costs being dictated by one cooperative rather than having several competing cooperatives vying for their business, however, seems to contradict the traditional principles of market competition. Whether growers would be happy with the attempts of the Texas Citrus Fruit Growers Exchange to push other cooperatives out of business remained to be seen.

There existed numerous protests against the exchange that represented growers' lack of trust in the organization. Bray, after his split with Shary and the *Mission Times*, published an article in June 1934 arguing that the exchange was failing simply because growers did not believe in the idea. Many growers, he reported, did not want to join the exchange because Shary was too controlling and they felt their voices would not be heard. By the mid-1930s a number had, in fact, abandoned the organization. Projections of the number of citrus carloads to be shipped prior to the 1934–35 harvest season had indicated that the exchange would be glutted with fruit that it would be unable to ship. The organization proved incapable of planning or handling the bountiful harvest because of the large number of people who had recently joined. Thus, the exchange wasted much of the citrus harvest for the season. Another writer agreed with Bray, arguing that the exchange "outgrew its breeches" and that its sales team was not to blame for its inability to sell a large portion of the growers' fruit, insinuating that upper management was at fault. Distrust of Shary and the industry's leaders again seemed to be spreading.[46]

Also, no direct leadership had emerged from the ranks of the small growers. At a meeting in Weslaco in October 1934, which several hundred citrus growers attended, it was quite clear that there was no single spokesperson who would champion small growers' issues. Local shippers dominated the meeting and were much better organized than the growers. Bray argued that shippers and agents connected with the state and federal departments of agriculture should have been willing to speak for the growers, but that the growers still needed their own voices to be heard when problems vital to citrus growing occurred, since citrus was the wellspring of the region. The situation, in other words, was somewhat predatory: "Our history reflects the impotence of our producers to do anything about marketing problems or general policies vital to themselves. This does not mean that the shippers are guilty of any wrong, as shippers, but it does mean that the shipper's viewpoint comes first and molds the viewpoint of the farmer and or grower."[47] Clearly, then, in this view the growers needed an advocate whom they were not finding in any of the other Valley interests, be they Shary or the shippers. The situation seemed to be one in which no one had their best interests in mind; they would have to look out for themselves.

Bray oftentimes took it upon himself to speak out for the growers in the pages of his new position at the *McAllen Daily Monitor*. In June 1934 Bray wrote an open letter to Shary that was critical of the exchange, whose stockholders had completely failed to address any of the upcoming harvest season's problems. They knew he claimed that the organization did not have the capacity to handle the amount of fruit that would come in. Bray argued that, for years, growers had unselfishly given faith, loyalty, and money to the exchange and had followed Shary's leadership. They did this, he argued, "almost blindly, as our leader trusting in [your] judgment and sense of justice to bring us through[;] as each year adversity levied its toll, we told ourselves that the good day would come next season." Bray also stated that the exchange's members "were content to follow your policies and we were willing to give you the credit that was due in success," but that the members now

must hold you to the accounting that is due in failure. Our growers, although they may not have registered their protests with you, have taken stock of our situation. We realize that we have followed blind faith to the parting of the ways. Our membership, once dominant in the Valley and totaling nearly 1300 growers has almost vanished. Worse than that stockholders, who paid with the sweat of their brow for their stock, are leveling an accusing finger at us today and blame the Exchange for much of their misfortune. We are just a skeleton force of that once proud army of co-operation that had control of tonnage in this Valley in our grasp. And many are forced to remain under protest, when their better judgments tell them that theirs is a lost cause and that we are making sacrifices of ourselves upon the altar of domineering and unwise leadership.[48]

Bray continued his attack on Shary, arguing that he had "tried to protest before against policies that I felt were inimical to our organization, just as no doubt hundreds of others have and with probably the same result—nothing." Shary, he argued, simply did not listen: "There has been no spirit of true cooperation shown by you," Bray lamented. Bray also charged that Shary had "not consulted . . . your members, nor taken them into your confidence in the vital matters that have been determining factors in our decay." The exchange had fallen from thirteen hundred members, of the region's roughly ten thousand citrus growers, to, by 1934, "merely a handful."[49]

Shary not only ignored his growers, Bray argued, but also the policies that Shary set were unsound. One exchange plant at San Benito was operational less than two years out of its six in existence, while a plant at Harlingen handled no fruit at all. Another plant, this one at La Feria, handled very little product. Exchange members, however, were still paying for the excessive outlay of these operations. The company's stock was practically worthless. The farmers simply could not afford to shoulder the costs of these plants that were no longer operating properly.[50]

Another problem that Bray raised was the fact that the exchange sold its fruit at a price point that kept the organization afloat but did not allow the growers to see any profit. Nevertheless, Shary kept advertising the exchange in national publications, claiming that the organization returned more money to its growers than any other cooperative of which he was aware. This could not possibly have been the truth, Bray insisted. All in all, Bray registered his protests "not because I am one of the few growers who put hard cash into the exchange, but because I am still a believer in this Valley, in this citrus industry, and in true cooperation." In other words, he still hoped that the initial vision for the Lower Rio Grande Valley as laid forth by Shary and other men would hold true for the future. "Hundreds of stockholders of the TCX organization scattered all over the Valley," he continued, "not at [the] stockholders meeting because they had lost faith in our policies, and not our ideals, are protesting with me today against what you have done in arrogating to yourself the position of dictator of our affairs." One source reported that 30–35 percent of the citrus growers were in cooperatives, and many of them complained that Shary was a difficult man with whom to work. He concluded his note by protesting over Shary's "many mistakes, because you refused to heed our advice on matters, and because you did not respect the viewpoint of the average grower."[51] By the late 1930s the exchange had proven such a failure that, instead of carrying on its marketing and sales duties, its principal activities were confined to the operation of farms and orchards owned by the company. The exchange had

proven incapable of carrying out the best interests of small growers while facing economic calamity.[52]

No vision and hope for a better future was on trial, then, but instead the
allegedly failed leadership of Shary himself. This was particularly troubling,
as Shary and his assistants had been reelected to run the exchange just three
years previously in the summer of 1931, when the organization had undertaken
a reorganization to qualify for federal farm aid. Perhaps, if things could operate
differently and average growers could be involved in the decision-making process, the larger vision for a better future could be redeemed. The ultimate problem, Bray and others believed, was that a single, fundamental part of that vision
had been betrayed. At one point it had been axiomatic in the citrus industry
that the interests of both the rich and the small growers were one and the same,
but the struggles of the Depression had shown that this was clearly not the
case. Local leaders had started to look out primarily for themselves. But while
the rich saved their own finances, the true backbone of the industry, the small
grower, struggled and failed. This, in turn, advertised a struggling Texas citrus
industry to the rest of the country. With failing real estate values and a crum-
bling economic infrastructure, panic spread. The agricultural economy was too
singularly focused on selling land; dissension within the growers' ranks made
any kind of growth a difficult prospect.[53]

Perhaps one of the problems is that Shary, and men like him, who originally
set forth the vision for South Texas's future that so many of the land purchasers had bought into, still truly believed in that vision against the odds of the
Depression. One local writer for *Texas Citriculture* went so far as to say that perhaps all of the boosters during the 1910s and '20s had overestimated the region's
potential and naively believed that all people involved would accrue more
wealth than was humanly possible. In other words, the boosters had "simply
been too optimistic, rather than overly egotistical." Often, in order to induce
further colonization from the rest of the country, boosters cited hugely profitable groves in order to convince readers that they could achieve otherworldly
returns. Many newcomers, one writer reported, arrived with a sense of overin-
flated possibilities. "Perhaps *this* publication," the author wrote, "has painted
pictures of groves that are above average, and we do wish to state here that not
every grove is as good as the ones described in our pages. The groves we use
are more or less models" (emphasis in the original). Rather than painting a picture of fantastic wealth that could be accrued, *Texas Citriculture* hoped to show
that if one could remain pragmatic, citriculture could still be a very profitable
industry. Such a nuanced vision of the possibilities for Texas citriculture was
exceedingly rare.[54]

Any discussion of a complicated subject such as infighting and disagreement among small growers during the Great Depression deserves some nuance. Shary, for example, despite the widespread dislike of him among Lower Rio Grande Valley growers, still enjoyed a good reputation among some. Joe Kilgore, whose family went broke during the Depression, recalled fondly that Shary had allowed his father to make interest-only payments on the land he had purchased instead of forcing the family to deed him back their land. Another grower, W. W. Jones, told Shary's nemesis Ralph Bray that, despite Shary's many enemies, he had always found him a pleasant man and easygoing. Thus, the contention within the ranks of the small growers was not all-encompassing, and there were many who were still happy with the industry's leadership.[55]

Nevertheless, the divide between small farmers, big landowners, and shippers can be seen on numerous fronts. The United Irrigation Company had a dispute for more than six years with one of its citrus growers, a man named T. J. Walthall, over an irrigation tax rate on Walthall's land. The conflict appeared to have been heading for foreclosure and a court battle, but the events disappear at that point from the historical record. Nevertheless, such disputes between growers, developers, and companies undoubtedly became common during the Depression.[56]

Larger catastrophes abounded. Entire development companies often faced foreclosure, which spelled serious trouble for the futures of numerous growers and offsite investors. In early December 1937, for example, the Progreso Development Company was foreclosed upon by the federally run Reconstruction Finance Corporation (RFC). Like many of the land and citrus companies, Progreso had an entire town, of the same name, devoted to its efforts. When the RFC foreclosed upon the company for failure to pay its federally backed loans, the entire town went on the public auction block. The town's streets, sewers, undeveloped tracts, and unsold citrus orchards were all auctioned off, with only the property already bought and paid for by the company's growers remaining safe.[57]

One can plainly see why such an occurrence as the Progreso foreclosure would put a serious dent in growers' confidence throughout the entirety of the South Texas borderlands region. If the very company that had sold them their land and convinced them of South Texas's promise for unending bounty in the future had collapsed, no kind of bright future could await. It is worth noting, however, that although some companies collapsed, others survived. One of the largest development companies, the Port Isabel Company, survived the Depression primarily because of the business acumen and leadership of Lon C. Hill Jr. Hill, alongside his famous father, who had founded the city of Harlingen, was respected among South Texas growers. The younger Hill helped turn the company's finances around, saving the investments of growers and offsite investors who had hoped to retire on the earnings from their groves. The company, including its principal town of Bayview, remained a prominent shipper of South Texas citrus fruits into the 1940s.[58]

Also worth noting is that some citrus-related businesses suffered neither financial catastrophe nor even setbacks during the Depression. Perhaps lending validity to Ralph Bray's claim that shippers in South Texas were better organized than small growers, records from at least one shipping business, Cullen and Thompson Packers and Shippers in Harlingen, show that some businesses connected to the citrus industry did quite well during the Depression. Table 5.1 reflects how Cullen and Thompson's business grew during the middle of the decade, the time when the Depression had hit the region the hardest.[59]

Cullen and Thompson's net worth by October 1, 1942, was $30,009.13, a handsome sum for a business that came of age during the 1930s. Part of the reason for such success may have been because of disgruntled growers who left either the citrus exchange or other cooperatives in favor of independent shippers. Louis Cullen was also part owner of Elrod Ginco, a cotton-ginning business that he purchased after the success of his shipping and packing firm. Like Cullen and Thompson, Elrod Ginco seems to have done quite well during the Depression. Although small farmers may have suffered, Cullen, at least, not only weathered the storm but also enjoyed financial growth. The dependency of most small firms and growers on larger growers and land developers did not necessarily equate financial death for all small businesses in the region. Although economics drove the larger story of the South Texas internal colony, the capitalist marketplace also left room for advancement through personal ingenuity. This would have been more difficult, or perhaps impossible, had Cullen been an ethnic Mexican. Doubtless many growers in the 1930s would have chosen to ship with an Anglo-American over an ethnic Mexican shipper, had they been given the choice.[60]

TABLE 5.1. Cullen and Thompson financial data, 1930s

Year	Assets ($)	Liabilities ($)
1933	10,215.15	1,050.00
1935	13,253.06	1,363.33
1936	17,337.03	219.77
1937	19,779.73	442.17

Nevertheless, the typical small grower suffered greatly during the Depression. Fruit prices at mid-decade remained low. One possible explanation could have been market saturation and an oversupply of fruit, but several sources noted that the fault lay with poor marketing—again, a problem that fell squarely on the shoulders of the large developers and co-ops. By 1936, with the downturn of the TCX, there remained too many cooperatives and marketers fighting for business in the downturned markets. Naturally, in such a situation, instead of buyers bidding up the prices for the fruits, the sellers were bidding prices down, which meant that growers received less money in return.

Large growers also enjoyed economies of scale and better access to capital over their smaller counterparts. When large growers begged buyers to take greater quantities of fruits at lowered prices, this, in turn, set the prices for smaller growers, who were unable to survive at the depressed prices. This explains, in part, why smaller farms began to disappear in the mid-1930s and larger farms got bigger. Some of the larger growers also, who did not have to sell much fruit each season to survive, held their better crops off the market until all of their cut-price fruit was gone. The problem, one commentator noted, was that cooperatives had not conferred with one another to control their output and set prices on behalf of the smaller growers. (There was no federal law in place to block farmers from setting crop prices.) Growers would continue to struggle without such preemptive action made on their behalf.[61]

Labor, Race, and the Depression

If farmers struggled during the Depression, laborers were hit even harder. According to folklorist Américo Paredes, many of South Texas's poor ethnic Mexican workers scoffed at Anglos' difficulties during the Depression, as their own struggles—stemming from their long-term establishment at the fundamental periphery of the regional agricultural structure—were much more dire. Not only did ethnic Mexicans contend with a massive forced repatriation and deportation to Mexico that reinforced their status as unwanted in the United States—a deportation that may have involved as many as two million people, including many Mexican Americans—but those who remained in the United States had to contend with a strongly reinforced racial oppression on the part of the financially squeezed Anglos.[62]

Growers, before and after the Depression, had no problem acquiring "wetbacks" (a commonly used term for undocumented Mexican immigrants). One grower, speaking to an interviewer in 1950 about the "wetback problem," argued that in the Lower Rio Grande Valley a grower could get "a thousand [wetbacks] in a day. The only way to stop it is for there to be a depression. I worked at Mission during the last one and we set our quota of wetbacks at ten a month and it wasn't easy to get them."[63] Part of the reason that so few workers were available during the 1930s undoubtedly lies with the supply-demand relationship between low-paying jobs and undocumented immigration. With many growers going out of business, the industry needed fewer workers. Obviously, another part of the problem was the forced repatriation from the United States. A third contributing factor was the vehemence of the racial oppression that became reinforced during the Depression.

Numerous Mexicans and Mexican Americans remembered the 1930s as a particularly difficult time. Juan Castillo was born in Pharr and recalled life as a young boy during the Depression as being fraught with difficulties. Castillo missed many days of school in order to work in the fields. His father could not make enough money as a migrant worker to support his family, so Juan quit school at the age of twelve to go to work full time. According to him there were no government handouts available to Mexicans, so his family had to find work through whatever means possible. While his dad worked on building highways during the 1930s, Castillo worked as a shoeshine boy in order to help support his mother and six siblings. His family still could not afford electricity. After his shoeshine job, Castillo worked in the fields picking tomatoes. He received ten cents per hour while grown men like his father received fifteen cents per hour. After that, he and his father traveled north to pick sugar beets, tomatoes, and "pickles" (cucumbers) throughout the US Midwest and Colorado. Castillo worked from five o'clock in the morning until ten o'clock in the evening, leading an undeniably difficult life at such a young age. Most undocumented immigrants worked the same way, he claimed. Many immigrants did not even know that they needed to have a passport to travel in the United States.[64]

Castillo also recalled the horrendous discrimination that ethnic Mexicans faced in South Texas during the Depression. From time to time he and his father would pick cotton around Donna. In the evenings, after the day's work had ended, Castillo would sometimes attend nickelodeons shown in local tents. When he and his friends attended the movies, however, they were not allowed to use the restrooms on account of their ethnicity. He also remembered that Anglos treated African Americans in South Texas even worse, because their skin tone was usually darker than that of ethnic Mexicans. Generally, ethnic Mexicans used restrooms marked "colored" and sat with African Americans in public places. Castillo was also conscious of his differences from a young age. Anglo children constantly teased him and his friends for subsisting on tortillas, which were considered a "poor Mexican's food". Anglo parents clearly introduced racially insensitive behavior to their children from quite a young age.[65]

Other Mexican and Mexican American workers had similar experiences. José Infante was born in Harlingen in 1921. His family relocated to Lyford when he was a small boy, but they eventually moved back to Harlingen, where his father sought work. Infante attended school through the fifth grade until, like Castillo, he dropped out to work in the fields. He worked for a while in Adams Gardens, one of the larger land developments in the Harlingen area. After that he got a job working at a packing shed in Mission, where he made the almost unheard-of sum of fifty cents per hour. Infante knew he was lucky to have such a high-paying job. Nevertheless, he recalled that the packing-shed work was very demanding. Aside from working in a difficult environment, Infante remembered that it was all but impossible for a young boy who quit school to learn anything in those days. The racial discrimination in South Texas, he also noted, was particularly bad during the Depression. After his Mission job, he then worked for a while in a Civilian Conservation Corps camp in Wyoming, were he undoubtedly lived in much better circumstances than as a migrant worker in South Texas. After that he was drafted into the army and participated in World War II.[66]

Ethnic Mexican workers generally failed to make any great strides in terms of labor organizing during the Depression. Although a number of labor strikes had flared up in various South Texas towns, establishing inroads toward permanently organizing the workers was a nearly impossible task. The Valley was difficult for unionism, according to historian Rodolfo Acuña, for two primary reasons: first, local agriculture was not heavily industrialized, meaning that workers had few other opportunities to find employment if a strike persisted for a long period of time, since they had acquired few on-the-job skills; and second, and perhaps more important, growers had a huge reserve labor pool across the border in Mexico. Unionism was also generally weak throughout Texas, which was a conservative state. A concentrated effort did take place to organize skilled packing-shed workers in the Lower Rio Grande Valley during the latter stages of the Depression under the Fruit and Vegetable Workers Local 20603 of the American Federation of Labor (AFL), and in its heyday the local claimed between five hundred and six hundred members. But, as the economic fallout from the Depression worsened during the late 1930s, all organizing efforts stopped, and the workers were left to fend for themselves. Another union, the United Cannery, Agricultural, Packing and Allied Workers of America (UCAPAWA), which was affiliated with the more radical Congress of Industrial Organizations (CIO), was also active among Valley agricultural workers during the latter stages of the Great Depression.[67]

Strikes occurred in other areas of South Texas during the 1930s and early 1940s. Mexican and Mexican American agricultural workers struck in the fields surrounding Laredo, in the Winter Garden district just northwest of the Lower Rio Grande Valley, and in Mathis, Texas, northwest of Corpus Christi. These strikers all sought better wages and working conditions, and some of them achieved certain short-term goals. One historian reports a large resurgence of strikes in 1944. Unfortunately, however, these brought no long-term labor contracts, thus ensuring that unions would not have a permanent standing. According to one historian, even during the 1940s "Anglo farmers still ruled the Tejano homeland."[68]

Ethnic Mexicans in the Lower Rio Grande Valley and greater South Texas faced other forms of discrimination during the Depression. One Anglo woman, Pauline Dunham, who arrived in McAllen in 1940, noted that the prevailing attitudes of Anglos dictated that ethnic Mexicans were to be looked down upon and that their sole purpose was to work for Anglos and make the lives of the latter easier. This is the exact position that the Valley and greater South Texas's original land promoters intended ethnic Mexicans to inhabit. Most whites, Dunham recalled, considered all Hispanics inferior. Ethnic Mexicans and blacks were not allowed to enter many Anglo-run public establishments, most notably restaurants. Anglos also, she recalled, held most political offices in the Valley.[69]

As a schoolteacher, Dunham remembered that all lower-level schools were segregated and that the only integrated schools tended to be high schools. To her, the general prejudice against Mexicans was not the reason for the school segregation. Instead, Dunham argued that the schools were segregated simply because ethnic Mexican children could not speak English. Nevertheless, she could not recall a single instance of a child being punished for speaking Spanish while at school, which—given some of the activities that occurred during the Chicano Movement that are covered in the next chapter—one might assume was a misrepresentation of the truth. By junior high school the kids had allegedly learned enough English to enter integrated schools. Because the children were not allowed to speak Spanish, she argued, they learned English quickly. In her view, the children were unprejudiced against whites and wanted to become part of Anglo-American culture. Their parents wanted them to have an education in order to better their lives in the United States, despite the fact, she argued, that anti-Anglo prejudice was widespread among the adults. Parents, however, in her memory, never protested the English-only rule at the schools.[70]

Dunham exhibited strong racial prejudice in a 1987 interview, despite her claim that the predominate ethnic Mexican population numbers of the Lower

Rio Grande Valley had never bothered her. Dunham argued that there was an element of the "Latins" who just did not know how to work, but that others were acceptable people. She qualified this statement by stating that there were elements of all ethnicities, including whites, who did not work. More surprising than this, however, were some general conceptions she had of the more heavily Mexican-populated areas of the Valley. Before she and her husband moved into the Valley from North Texas at the tail end of the Depression, her husband had visited the area on a trip by himself. Upon his return home to report on local conditions, he told Pauline that one could "see little Latin boys running around naked." Dunham claimed that at the time of the interview she still encountered this problem. On the plus side, however, Dunham argued that Mexicans and Mexican Americans did not let their little girls run around naked. She ended by telling the interviewer that if he were to drive down to "Mexican Town" he could see for himself.[71]

Mexican and Mexican American citrus pickers also experienced the racist attitudes of Anglos who had been forced into migrant work out of necessity. Peggy Terry, from Oklahoma City, recalled working with her husband as migrants during the Depression. Their wandering brought them to the border, where they picked fruits in the citrus industry. Working with Mexicans, however, was a huge problem for her: "I didn't feel any identification with the Mexicans, either." Terry exhibited stark hostility toward her Mexican coworkers, who to her "were just spics and they should be sent back to Mexico." Terry also recalled feeling "very irritated because there were very few gringos in this little Texas town, where we lived. Hardly anybody spoke English. It never occurred to us that we should learn to speak Spanish."[72] Terry clearly fell into the typical pattern of anti-Mexican sentiment common among Anglos of the time. Interestingly, however, Terry's racist disposition softened later in her life. The Depression sometimes brought out the worst in people.

Somewhat paradoxically, recent scholarship has shown that Mexican repatriation and the Depression's effect on the Mexican side of the Lower Rio Grande Valley brought incremental improvements to the lives of growers and farmers and workers south of the border. Environmentally, however, these improvements fed off the river. Before the Depression life had been very difficult for Mexican farmers south of the border. The irrigation districts that farmers on the American side of the river had been forming since the mid-1910s made water from the river increasingly difficult for Mexican farmers to obtain, while the hurricanes in 1932 and 1933 severely crippled Mexican agriculture. Under the direction of Mexican President Lazaro Cárdenas, the federal government created the *Comisión Integral Decentralizada para el Desarrollo Integral del Bajo Rio Bravo* (Decentralized Commission for the Development of the Lower Rio Grande), whose primary objective was to develop a vibrant agricultural sector in the Mexican side of the Valley. The commission's founding was in direct response to the poor treatment of Mexicans north of the border as well as Mexican repatriation during the 1930s. Work began on the irrigation project in October 1935. The primary beneficiaries were impoverished farmers who planted on *ejidos*, which were communal plots of land devoted to subsistence farming. Their primary crops were corn and beans. By 1936, roughly 57 percent of all agriculture on the Mexican side of the river consisted of the *ejidos*, with some of them being *grandes propiedades* ("great properties") of more than 100 hectares, (about 250 acres).

The benefits of the ejidos to Mexican farmers cannot be overstated. Cárdenas saw the strengthening of the ejido system not only as a means for the economic improvement of Mexico, but also as a form of justice for Mexico's large class of poor laborers who had worked as virtual slaves for the country's hacienda system for centuries, or, more recently, for abusive and racist employers north of the border in Texas. Leaders from the Mexican Revolution who had supported the redistribution of land through the ejido system saw it as a more limited means toward land reform for Mexico's impoverished wage earners. Cárdenas, however, disagreed: "By the mere fact of requesting ejidos, the peasant breaks the economic tie to the landowner, and in these conditions the role of the ejido is not to produce the economic equivalent of a salary . . . but rather—by its extent, quality and the way it is used—it should suffice for the total economic liberation of the worker, creating a new economic-agricultural system . . . to replace the regimen of salaried field workers and eliminate agrarian capitalism in the republic."

Cárdenas's goal, then, was to replace the rigid class structures of the hacienda system with something that he considered far more democratic and humane. Without saying as much, Cárdenas sought to end the colonized status of rural Mexico's working class—on *both* sides of the border. The "economic liberation of the worker" essentially meant overturning a class system long entrenched throughout Mexico, including in the north. The Texas side of the Valley's colonial farming system functioned under similar dynamics as the oppressive hacienda system. Cárdenas thus showed that the Mexican federal government hoped to move its masses of poor away from the oppression of an agrarian class system, although he never explicitly addressed its younger cousin on the north banks of the river. Still, the federal government had finally addressed the rampant poverty of its agricultural workers and hoped to do something to curb its excessive tendencies.

The infrastructure of Mexican agriculture on the south side of the river had a surprisingly similar infrastructure to that of its American cousin: both relied on internal migration, both relied on federal intervention and support, and both consisted of towns that were essentially agricultural colonies. Transborder competitiveness between farmers and growers would last throughout the rest of the twentieth century. Also, many of the workers involved in establishing better agriculture on the south bank of the river—particularly those involved in planting cotton, which would become an increasingly important crop on the Mexican side of the border through the middle part of the century—found the work excruciatingly difficult and the working conditions on Mexican farms exceedingly poor. The preexistent force of US capital, commodities markets, and infrastructure that had already sped development in Mexican agriculture, mining, and industry in the Mexican north all made such development possible. This, combined with Mexican political expediency, made the Mexican side of the border increasingly resemble its counterpart north of the river. Although the situation on each side of the river would never fully sustain large populations of small growers, the similarities in all aspects of the commercial farming experience are striking. What preempted quick Mexican development, however, was the proximity of Anglo-American commercial farming to the borderline between the two nations.

Mexico's development of irrigation, however, had other ramifications for growers on the Texas side of the border. Not only would the river's natural habitats clearly suffer, which would affect people on both sides of the border, but transborder competition for the river's precious water would also accelerate. Construction of the Mexican irrigation system had proceeded so rapidly that growers on the Texas side began to panic during the late 1930s that they would run out of water from the river. Secretary of State Cordell Hull requested that Texas governor James V. Allred furnish the US government with a document outlining the desires of the state for a treaty with Mexico that would detail a statement about how much water each nation could divert from the Rio Grande and its tributaries. The Mexican side of the Valley had gained some parity with the Texas side in terms of the sophistication of irrigation plans for Mexican growers. Some would say that the Mexican irrigation system had actually surpassed its American counterpart, challenging Texas growers to upgrade what they feared was an outmoded system of canals and ditches, which had already depleted much of the river's natural flow.

In October 1938 Texas growers, the US government, and the State of Texas began planning a gravity irrigation canal to protect American water interests from Mexican diversions. During congressional hearings on the matter in April

1941, an American official of the International Boundary Commission noted that the proposed treaty and diversions should be "an international project. . . . This plan does for our side of the river just what the Mexican plan does for their side of the river." Although the American and Mexican governments agreed to the proposed treaty on February 3, 1944, the project continued to stall after the US Senate ratified the treaty in April 1945. Citizens in the Lower Rio Grande Valley's already established irrigation districts voted against construction in 1949 of a large diversion dam that the Bureau of Reclamation argued would protect Texas farmers if Mexico placed a dam anywhere on its side of the river. The government then tabled the project. Rampant overuse of the water would continue for the foreseeable future.

Vast decreases in the Rio Grande's water levels were more than just the simple product of some careless overdiversion for corporate, agricultural, or municipal irrigation needs during the late twentieth century. The establishment of the South Texas internal colony had completely reshaped the landscape on both sides of the border. Despite small growers' losses, the keys to the economic side of the South Texas internal colony became handed over to large growers. Marginalization remained intact. Concerning the Depression, the downturn appears to have hit Mexicans and Mexican Americans harder than it did some other groups, but it also brought about new opportunities. One writer argues that teenagers who entered into Civilian Conservation Corps work camps finally got their first chances to associate with other American young people and to develop better English and working skills. By 1940 this young generation had become less bound than its forebears to the drudgery of agricultural field work and the strict vagaries of South Texas colonialism. The outbreak of World War II brought about new opportunities for employment in the shipyards and airplane plants of California, for example, which in turn led to improved living conditions and better health for countless many. These developments predated the better educational opportunities that came for Mexican American veterans after World War II, which would give them further opportunities to challenge colonialism and racial discrimination in South Texas.[73] Still, the Depression served as a pivot point for the lives of Mexican Americans throughout the country. Living and working conditions worsened. Anti-Mexican discrimination became increasingly acute. For the people of South Texas, Anglo and Mexican alike, the world was in a state of flux. What they could not have known was that the middle of the twentieth century would bring about even deeper changes.

CHAPTER SIX

Toward a Homeland

The Chicano Movement and the Intellectual Creation of Homeland in South Texas

[Revolution] is radical in that it confronts and replaces
not only individuals occupying roles in undesirable social
institutions, but those institutions themselves. In a revolution new institutions are established to preserve and
promote the changes that have been effected and to insure
the capacity for change in the future.

—JOSÉ ÁNGEL GUTIÉRREZ[1]

South Texas's agriculture had begun to fail small growers
during the middle part of the Great Depression. As the small growers came
to be replaced by larger corporate agribusinesses, the nature of the internal
colony underwent drastic changes. While Anglo-American migration to the
region slowed, Mexican immigration continued. The South Texas of the 1960s
and '70s stood in opposition to the imagined future of the boosters and initial
Anglo colonists of nearly half a century earlier. The region's first generation of
outside settlers had begun to see their world unravel. Successes and failures
would be in store for both Anglos and ethnic Mexicans in South Texas.

As larger growers and agribusinesses became more powerful, labor continued to be in thrall to the region's richest and most powerful citizens. Meanwhile, however, young Mexican American activists challenged the established order. Building on the popularity of the African-American Civil Rights
Movement, organizers during the 1960s began challenging segregated school
systems and city councils, making never-before-seen inroads for South Texas
Mexicans. The structure of racial oppression built into the establishment of
the region's farming colonies slowly began to dismantle. Labor and civil rights
organizers in the South Texas borderlands were only the latest chapter in the
story of ethnic Mexicans' negotiation of greater futures within the South Texas
colonial regime, a part of the so-called negotiated conquest that I mentioned at
the beginning of this book. Previous work emphasizing ethnic Mexicans' rights
within the colonial South Texas regime included the irredentist Plan de San

Diego uprising in 1915–16 as well as the establishment of the far more moderate LULAC in 1929. But the labor organizing of the 1960s and the rise of the Chicano Movement were the latest chapter in negotiating a brighter future from inside the South Texas internal colony, one that would shape the social politics of the South Texas borderlands for the rest of the century.

Ultimately, the appearance of labor organizing in mid-1960s South Texas as well as the rise of the Chicano Movement helped intellectually cement the notion of South Texas as the Tejano homeland for the colonized natives of South Texas. Movement activists participated in "a daily performance of history, economics, politics, and socio-cultural behaviors" that emphasized notions of belonging in the South Texas borderlands. Emphasizing homeland became a centerpiece to the Chicano Movement; these ideas were not prominent during earlier civil rights efforts among Mexicans and Mexican Americans in the United States. Emphasizing homeland was the ultimate act of historical agency in face of the lived reality of negotiating the Anglo colonization of the region after 1848. As such, internal colonialism is a key component to understanding both the farmworkers' movement as well as the vibrancy of the Chicano Movement in the South Texas borderlands; the "territorialization of memory" helped carve out South Texas as an ancestral homeland. Chicano Movement activists, in essence, moved intellectually toward a homeland and away from a marginalized past.[2]

A Bitter Harvest

South Texas citriculture struggled coming out of the Great Depression. The citrus industry itself underwent successes and failures. Severe freezes in 1949, 1951, and 1962 led to substantial losses in acreage. Later leaders in the industry who survived the first two of these freezes came to view them as a benefit, as they eliminated several obsolete and unmarketable citrus varieties. Thus, the post-1951 plantings that replaced much of the lost acreage consisted of several new varieties, marking the beginning of what later industry leaders would call Texas's "Second Citrus Industry." But the 1962 freeze damaged much of the post-1951 plantings, so the industry once again suffered a crippling setback.[3]

Despite later leaders' proclamation of the great benefits of the Second Citrus Industry, the reality of South Texas citrus after World War II was bleak. The peak year of production for the industry was the 1944–45 season, when total production reached nearly twenty-nine million boxes. But production hit a nadir in the 1951–52 season, with a freeze-induced low of about one-half million boxes. Production continued at a low during the 1950s after the 1949 and

1951 freezes combined to destroy about 85 percent of the total citrus crop. Consequently, from 1951 to 1953, nearly three-quarters of the cropland in the Lower Rio Grande Valley became devoted to cotton, which served as a replacement for citrus. Numerous growers also turned to vegetables, which saturated the market and drove down prices for all South Texas vegetable growers. Although the citrus industry began a slow recovery, in 1956 it was still operating at less than 25 percent of its total production prior to the freeze in 1949. Since so many growers had planted only citrus and no other type of crop, their only choice was to plow under much of their citrus plantings. In the 1950s about four hundred thousand acres of cotton replaced citrus orchards, making cotton the top cash crop in the Lower Rio Grande Valley. Citrus was no longer king.[4]

These developments heaped further struggles onto those smaller growers who had somehow managed to survive the Great Depression. In this sense, South Texas was little different from other farming areas throughout the United States during the 1950s. One expert noted the rise of corporate agribusinesses across the country, arguing that larger operations would make small farming an untenable way to make a living. Small farms would require outside assistance from municipal, state, and local governments, and even then, nonintensive small operations would be suitable only for a part-time income. The farm population throughout the country declined by nearly one-third between 1940 and 1957, while the number of farm laborers also fell by nearly half. As stated in the previous chapter, statistics from the Lower Rio Grande Valley itself reflect this larger trend. While the total number of farm operators (large and small) in Hidalgo, Cameron, and Willacy Counties skyrocketed from 5,860 in 1925 to 14,222 in 1935, from that point forward their number went into a sharp decline. By 1940 there were 9,316 farm operators left in the Valley, and that number fell again to 7,773 by 1954. While all of this spelled trouble for small farmers and growers, the results for laborers were mixed. Increased wages due to the smaller labor pool remained a hopeful possibility. Also, the siphoning-off of farmworkers into the armed forces as well as the rising development of various industries boded well for second- and third-generation Mexican Americans as well as new Mexican immigrants. Increased employment opportunities in both agriculture- and nonagriculture-related industries created possibilities for higher wages and better education. Unsurprisingly, then, the most forceful challenges to the Anglo colonial order in South Texas were still just beginning to emerge by the middle of the twentieth century. Not only would more work be available for a greater number of workers, but also increased possibilities for farmwork meant greater demand for migrant labor. This last economic trend contributed to the founding of the Bracero

Program, which brought Mexican laborers and American growers together in greater numbers than ever before.[5]

Bracero South Texas

In the early 1940s the US and Mexican federal governments instituted what came to be known as the Bracero Program, which was the organized importation of Mexican workers to US farms to fill labor shortages during World War II. The agreement, known officially in 1942 as the Emergency Labor Program, gave both governments supervision over the recruitment of workers. The US government promoted the contract as an emergency measure to fill the vast farm labor shortages caused by the war. All aspects of the Bracero Program were regulated, including housing, working conditions, wages, transportation, and workers' rights. Under this agreement, about 220,000 braceros came to the United States from 1942 to 1947. The contract would be extended, however, until it was eventually allowed to lapse at the end of 1964.[6]

The Bracero Program's implementation highlighted the exploitative nature of labor relations between growers and migrant workers in South Texas. Many growers first opposed the new program. South Texas growers had all of the undocumented workers they needed, and many clamored against the program for its perceived deficiencies when compared to a smaller guest worker program that the federal government had initiated during World War I. Unlike the Bracero Program, the previous guest worker agreement had allowed growers to recruit workers in Mexico with no federal interference. Texas growers relented and requested braceros in 1943, but the Mexican government initially refused to allow any braceros to enter the state. Mexican officials were well aware of the widespread racial oppression and intolerable working conditions for migrants in South Texas and thus sought to protect their citizens from further transgressions. In response, Governor Coke Stevenson signed the Texas legislature's Caucasian Race Resolution, which affirmed the equal rights of all Caucasians in Texas mainly to appease the Mexican government. Since many white Texans considered Mexicans to be of a different race than themselves, however, the resolution was essentially meaningless. Stevenson next established the Good Neighbor Commission of Texas in September 1943 with the purpose of publicly stamping out racism. Still, the Mexican government remained unconvinced and opted not to remove Texas from its bracero blacklist.[7]

Texas officials continued to press for braceros for the next four years, but Mexico continuously refused, as racial oppression persisted relentlessly. Finally, however, in October of 1947 Mexico relented and began issuing bracero permits for Texas. Throughout the 1950s Texas would be the leading employer of braceros, accepting about 40 percent of all braceros entering the country. Bracero employment actually contributed to a vast labor surplus, driving down wages paid to nonbracero and undocumented workers. Mexican American laborers thus suffered from the shrinking job market in Texas, which sent thousands of people into the migrant stream across the country. Poor working and living conditions for migrants in turn spread to farms throughout the country along the migrant trail. Labor surpluses became common in other southwestern states, where the braceros represented a disproportionate number of the total seasonal workforce—even though braceros were ostensibly meant to fill labor shortages. The program's implementation in Texas, then, was a contributing factor to the perpetuation of the modern migrant stream across the United States.[8]

The Bracero Program revealed itself as a combination of blessings and frustrations for growers in the Lower Rio Grande Valley and greater South Texas. Whereas growers continued to hire illegal workers as unskilled laborers, braceros tended to be skilled workers. Growers could request workers with specific skill sets, such as driving tractors and working with machinery and irrigation, which did not require any of the time outlay normally spent in teaching undocumented workers how to do such tasks. One of the other benefits was that braceros could also do harvest work in addition to skilled work, making them valuable farmhands who often stayed on the farm year-round rather than migrating in for the harvest and leaving once the crops had been picked.[9]

Stringent regulations built into the Bracero Program, however, led many growers to continue to prefer hiring illegal workers. Braceros stayed in regulated housing on the grower's property and had minimum wages as well as certain other clauses built into their contracts. Border Patrol and Immigration and Naturalization Services (INS) officers would often inspect growers' farms to ensure that living conditions were up to contractual standards. Still, one grower later recalled that the housing provided to braceros was generally quite primitive. Law enforcement visits could often be problematic for growers, who used the bracero presence to hire undocumented workers even more cheaply than they had previously.[10]

While the Bracero Program co-opted certain aspects of the South Texas labor system and helped spread labor exploitation to the rest of the United States, it also offered Mexican workers certain never-before-enjoyed protections. Aside from contracts that growers were legally bound to follow, daily life was more regulated, although the work itself still offered challenges. The daily routine for braceros on one Lower Rio Grande Valley farm was 7:00 a.m. to 6:00 p.m. during the week with an hour off for lunch at noon. After about four hours of work on Saturday morning, the workers would get the rest of the weekend off, usually going into town on their own. Braceros often spent their time in bars or at organized baseball games, while some would attend Mass at local Catholic churches. Usually one worker, or a worker's wife, would be designated as a cook for the entire group in a specific grower's employ. Still, however, the growers tended to buy the workers their food and take care of medical expenses, much in the traditional *patrón* style of the Valley's colonial labor system. Braceros were still a colonized labor force since they were not free labor—not free to quit and get a better job in the United States. Spain had also regulated its colonial labor force through the *repartimiento*, a system whereby Spanish colonial authorities among other things distributed Indian laborers to landowners, oftentimes to little or no benefit to the worker. Clearly, then, with forced systems of racialized labor existing north and south of the modern US-Mexico border for centuries, there was precedent for the system of exploitive labor relations set in place by Anglo growers in South Texas during the twentieth century.[11]

Many people involved with the Bracero Program considered the system beneficial for the laborers. Carrol Norquest Jr. recalled that the braceros were hard workers. He argued that crews would work as hard as they could and earn as much money as possible due to the limited duration of their contracts. Jesse Treviño, at the behest of well-known Mexican American activist George I. Sánchez, took a job as a compliance officer for the Department of Labor, working in Harlingen and San Benito to mediate disputes between braceros and growers that the workers filed with the Mexican consulate. He argued that despite the numerous rackets that growers used to take advantage of the program, the system was still beneficial for farmers and workers alike. Growers were able to send undocumented workers whom they liked back to places such as Monterrey in northeastern Mexico, where the worker could then file for bracero status and reenter the country. Also, the grower and the worker both retained right of refusal, and the grower could pick workers whom he knew personally and wanted to continue to employ. Bracero workers thus had rights and some protection from the more exploitive growers, while undocumented workers were entirely at the mercy of growers and labor bosses. Although the men often suffered from mental and emotional stress due to separation from family and home life in Mexico, many workers expressed their appreciation for the opportunity to participate in the program, since it gave them opportunities to help their families.[12]

Still, South Texas's most rich and powerful growers continued to prefer hiring undocumented immigrants. Doing so allowed them to operate outside of the Bracero Program's web of labor controls. In June 1952 Congressman John

R. Rooney aroused great national opposition to Lower Rio Grande Valley agriculture by arguing that John Shary (who was now deceased), Lloyd Bentsen Sr., Allan Shivers—then governor of Texas and former associate of Shary—and seventy other prominent Valley farmers and growers had either currently or at some point in the past hired undocumented workers despite the availability of braceros. Rooney made these charges after personally visiting the region. Two of the worst offenders were Carl and Frank Schuster of Pharr and San Juan, respectively. These two men, who were community leaders and active in civic affairs, made open threats against Border Patrol agents and always worked hard to hamper the patrol's efforts. Border Patrol agents allegedly apprehended hundreds of undocumented workers on the Schuster farms weekly. Another grower, J. K. Bottinger, employed undocumented workers exclusively and, according to Rooney, "locked entrances to his farms to prevent the apprehension of aliens in his employment." Hidalgo County Judge Milton D. Richardson of Monte Alto "instructed county officers not to give the border patrol any assistance" in apprehending undocumented workers, including, it can be assumed, those in Richardson's own employ. Grower Jim Carpenter's father allegedly assaulted three police officers with a shotgun but was not charged later with a crime. Finally, a prominent local cotton grower, C. R. Parliamen, not only closed roads on his lands but also allegedly "placed boards with nails in them extending upward across his roads, [and] placed a chain fifteen inches high between two posts on another road." These booby traps were solely for the purpose of harassing Border Patrol agents looking for undocumented immigrants. Rooney named many other growers in Harlingen, Weslaco, Brownsville, and other areas in the Valley who engaged in similar activities. Rooney also claimed to have personally witnessed one undocumented worker receive five dollars for an entire week's work.[13]

The most prominent growers named by Rooney did not even bother to deny the charges. Shivers first claimed that the allegations were part of a smear campaign against him in Washington and Texas, but he later changed his story, stating that he did use undocumented workers but that he always treated them fairly, always paid them, and respected the Border Patrol. Milton Richardson responded with a contradiction by saying, "It's true that I've used them for years—everybody down there does, but I know the immigration laws and I respect them." Richardson went on to state that he never asked a man who was looking for work where he had originally come from. The Eisenhower administration itself supported Rooney's hard line against the use of undocumented workers. Secretary of Labor Maurice J. Tobin, in a speech in Fort Worth a few months before Rooney published his list, blasted Lower Rio Grande Valley

growers who employed undocumented migrants. Tobin also made the important distinction that such growers sabotaged their fellow farmers by threatening
the possibility of another bracero blacklist for the state, which would block all
growers from the possibility of securing legal workers.[14]

Growers' ability to manipulate the border for their own benefit thus became
more complicated. When commercial farming kick-started in South Texas, the
border was the linchpin to the success of the entire farming sector, due to its
status as a valve for the industry's reserve labor pool. Now, however, because
of wartime conditions and the popularity of the Bracero Program with farmers and growers elsewhere, South Texas growers found themselves having to
manipulate the border in previously unforeseen ways.

Federal officials during the 1950s considered Lower Rio Grande Valley
growers a particularly recalcitrant group who would fight the adoption of bracero labor tooth and nail. The new commissioner general of the INS, Joseph
Swing, thus developed a plan to force growers to participate in the hiring of
Mexican workers in accordance with federal law. During the late 1940s and
early 1950s, the INS made many arrests of undocumented workers, deported
them to Mexico, and then allowed them to return as legalized workers. Federal
officials referred to this process as "drying out wetbacks." In some instances,
apprehended workers would be allowed literally to place one foot on the Mexican side of the border and then come back into the United States through
legal processing. Many undocumented workers voluntarily participated in this
process. Swing, in March 1954, implemented these practices in the Valley. The
result was that while the number of bracero contracts dropped in the region,
growers could now contract with the INS for workers who had previously been
in the country illegally. The INS station in Hidalgo thus doubled as a recruitment station for local growers to reacquire deported workers without having to
go through the Bracero Program's usual recruitment procedures. The INS next
instituted Operation Wetback, a large-scale drive to apprehend undocumented
immigrants, in June 1954. The program, which led to the apprehension of hundreds of thousands of undocumented immigrants in 1954 and 1955, served the
dual purpose of attacking the problem of undocumented immigration while
also providing farmers with legal workers. One historian notes that the INS
counted 801,069 apprehensions between 1953 and 1955, while the number of
braceros admitted into the country doubled during the same period, from
148,449 admitted in 1954 to 298,012 in 1956. The program's clear intention was
to address the issue of undocumented immigration while maintaining a virtually uninterrupted flow of workers to the people who had been hiring most of
the undocumented workers in the first place.[15]

Both the "drying out" program and Operation Wetback complicated the relationship that South Texas growers had with the nearby border. While ethnic Mexican workers suffered under the forced deportations and militant tactics of the INS during the 1950s, growers benefited from the border's function of regulating their workers in the eyes of the federal government. The US public, in theory, would clamor less against the government's perceived deficiencies in dealing with the problem of laborers being able to cross the border relatively freely. Thus, although the Bracero Program and Operation Wetback complicated growers' ability to procure workers with the methods that they preferred, the US government had now legitimized the growers' system of colonial labor relations by turning undocumented workers into braceros, thus making the workers' presence more palatable to immigration restrictionists. The border, for growers, continued to function as a valve for a reserve labor force of ethnic Mexican workers.

The fact that so many Lower Rio Grande Valley growers essentially circumvented and changed the Bracero Program in order to keep hiring undocumented workers speaks to the far-reaching depth of the South Texans' commitment to an entrenched racialized labor system. Simply put, the Bracero Program challenged the South Texas labor system by instituting federal oversight and regulation. While many growers undoubtedly benefited from the specialized abilities of certain braceros that they chose to employ, the system of labor exploitation persisted despite the federal government's attempts to make acquiring Mexican workers easier. The burden of addressing the unethical qualities inherent in the relationship between ethnic Mexican workers and Anglo growers in South Texas would have to fall to someone other than the federal government. By the mid-1960s Mexican American labor and civil rights activists brought the strongest direct challenges to growers' power in the South Texas borderlands. South Texas's labor system would be cast more clearly into the national spotlight. There was simply nobody else left to take up the cause.

The Black Eagle Arrives

Labor organizing was an established fact of American life going back to the nineteenth century; as such, the arrival of labor organizers among the colonized laborers of South Texas farms thus augured the arrival of yet another American form of social protest for South Texas manual laborers. This one, however, was far more liberal or left-leaning than the previous efforts inaugurated under organizations such as LULAC more than a decade earlier. Needless to say, because the South Texas internal colony became established in order to extract cheap labor from the region, the possibilities for success among regional labor organizers were slim, at best, from the beginning. Clearly, however, an aggressive opposition to the South Texas colonial regime had once again, to Anglo South Texans, grown frighteningly more assertive.

Organized labor made few major inroads to speak of among South Texas migrant workers prior to the 1960s. Activists could make little headway against a South Texas power structure built on keeping ethic Mexicans subjugated under the dictates of Anglo colonialism. South Texas Mexicans had been so oppressed that by the 1960s most social activists and like-minded politicians had not been able to address many of their most basic needs. Two strains of the South Texas farming society needed redress: the colonial labor system and the oppressive racial segregation in South Texas towns. The spirit of the 1960s and the increasing educational levels of the younger Mexican American generation provided the necessary leadership to attack both of these issues.

The labor movement that arose among migrant farmworkers first in California would never have arrived in the South Texas borderlands had it not been for the tenor of the civil rights era. Historian Terry Anderson has noted "that the idea of 'Third World Liberation'" swept across the United States after the African American civil rights movement began. African American students, in particular, had a direct impact on the nation's next-largest minority: Hispanics. Thus, a direct link can be drawn between the black civil rights movement and the Chicano and farmworkers' movements of the mid- to late 1960s. The one man whose name became synonymous with the farmworkers' struggle— César Estrada Chávez—was also deeply "inspired by the [African American] civil rights struggle."[16]

The genesis of the farmworkers' movement had important repercussions for migrant workers in Texas. First, the national attention that the movement gained in California gave ethnic Mexicans in the United States an emotional leader in their hopes to overcome racial and labor oppression. Second, and perhaps more important, the movement spurred activism directly along the border in South Texas. Chávez garnered national attention by declaring the now-famous Delano Grape Strike and boycott in September 1965 in California as well as organizing in the following spring a three-hundred-mile march from Delano to Sacramento that culminated in a crowd of eight thousand demonstrators in front of the California state capitol. The march's purpose was mainly to publicize the grape strike and boycott. After that, various people within the ranks of the National Farm Workers Association (NFWA) began wondering where the union could potentially turn outside of California. One of the union's boycott captains turned his attention to the South Texas borderlands.[17]

In the spring of 1966 an organizer named Eugene Nelson broke from the NFWA and organized an independent labor union for South Texas workers based out of Houston. Nelson also organized an office in Mission—the heart of the South Texas citrus territory—but concentrated on enrolling workers to the immediate west in Starr County, where a large agribusiness corporation named La Casita grew melons. Two other organizers, Lucio Galván and Margio Sánchez, followed Chávez's example and began signing up workers for a new union. Nelson sought to foment their efforts into a larger farmworkers' strike throughout South Texas. By late May 1966, the newly christened Independent Workers' Association (IWA) claimed to have enrolled more than two hundred workers. Trouble appeared to be brewing for South Texas fruit and vegetable growers.[18]

The strike began on June 1 and soon picked up steam. Organizers hoped that the strike would achieve a minimum wage for all migrant workers in Texas. By June 2 the Produce Packers Local 78b, AFL-CIO, publicly backed the union, whose numbers had now reached more than five hundred members. Public pickets and marches occurred in and around Rio Grande City, the county seat of Starr County. But the local legal system responded quickly in the growers' favor. About June 2, a judge placed a ten-day restraining order on picketing, forcing the melon harvest to resume across Starr County. The following week, the San Antonio Express-News reported that an unnamed county official had allegedly given orders that county equipment be used to spray insecticide on a group of workers in order to break up a union meeting. The newspaper called this order a "Nazi-like deed." Local Anglos seemed befuddled by the union's activities. One, writing as "a loyal American" to the IWA headquarters, addressed Nelson and the small union's leadership: "Sir—Why don't you radicals go back where you came from and leave things be? The Mexicans have always been happy to work here and nobody asked you to butt in. 50 [cents] an hour is a lot to those people and without it they'd starve." Such characterizations of the union as outside radicals would become common throughout the duration of the strike. Finally, a reporter in Houston noted that the workers were on the "brink of revolt" and that unless their demands were soon met, "the strike could develop into a full-scale social revolution." Change was in the air, and long-standing resentments that workers had toward South Texas growers and the system that kept them in perpetual poverty finally appeared to be boiling over into the public sphere.[19]

But the small IWA clearly did not have the clout to take on South Texas's powerful agribusiness machine by itself. Because of Eugene Nelson's origins and the rising tide of Chávez's movement, an association with the better-known

California-based union made sense. Nelson wanted to keep an emphasis on the local character of the strike, but he knew that the IWA could get only so far on its own without help. So on June 8 Nelson called an election to determine if the IWA members would be willing to affiliate with the larger NFWA. The members voted 233 to 1 in favor of the motion, thus making their union Local 2 of the NFWA. The following week Nelson moved the union's headquarters from Mission to Rio Grande City in order to gain wider support for the movement within the Mexican American community in Starr County. The strike, which came to be known as the Starr County Strike, now had the NFWA's backing as well as that of its larger mother organization, the American Federation of Labor–Congress of Industrial Organizations (AFL-CIO).[20]

Events that took place over the duration of the strike, which lasted until the end of the summer of 1967, gave clear indication of what the union faced. In order to publicize their efforts, Nelson led the union on a 380-mile march from Rio Grande City to Austin. The 1966 march, which mirrored the NFWA's earlier march in California, lasted from July 11 until September 7 and ended with a demonstration outside the capitol. The march attracted national attention and brought support from various Catholic leaders in Texas, but it failed to gain the support of Democratic governor John Connally or any other prominent state politicians. The march's main purpose was to achieve a law that guaranteed all migrant workers a minimum wage of $1.25 per hour and an eight-hour workday, which would replace the more common practice in South Texas of $0.40 an hour and a fourteen-hour workday. Ultimately, the march failed to attain any of these objectives.[21]

Chávez worried that the Texas wing of the union was disorganized. Thus, he decided to send in the union's secretary-treasurer, Antonio Orendain, to take charge of organizing the strike. Orendain, who had grown up impoverished in Mexico, arrived in Rio Grande City on September 27 and instantly began changing the union's direction. First, since the Starr County Strike had now become publicized, a number of labor leaders had expressed support for the union. Orendain, however, considered those leaders to be quietly taking advantage of the union's media coverage in order to further their own personal causes. Orendain was also upset that the strike had become about attaining a minimum wage. To him, a minimum wage would not adequately address many of the workers' health, economic, and educational issues. Orendain instead changed the union's direction toward advocating for collective bargaining rights for all migrant workers in the state. He understood that this was a lofty goal in a conservative, right-to-work state such as Texas and that the union would probably fail. Still, he had the insight to realize that the union was not challenging simply the growers, but instead an entire region-wide system that took advantage of the workers' needy status. None of this is surprising: having grown up poor in Mexico, Orendain clearly recognized the systemic nature of rural poverty in both nations. The task of restructuring South Texas labor relations was a daunting one, but Orendain wanted to address the underlying structure of South Texas poverty: the region's very agricultural labor system itself.[22]

Subsequent events displayed the degree to which the strike represented a new organization's attempt to change South Texas's social structure. On October 21 a manager at La Casita farms declared publicly (in response to recent activities by the union) that he had more than 450 Mexican workers who were completely happy and satisfied with their jobs. In response, Orendain telephoned the local press, saying that he was "going to prove ... where [the manager] got all his good, happy workers." Orendain next led a group of sixteen union members to the international bridge at Roma, in Starr County, at 5:00 a.m. on October 24. His purpose was not only to prevent Mexican nationals from crossing the border to work on La Casita farms, but also to publicize the union and its cause. The ensuing events would go down as the most public display of proworker, antigrower sentiment in South Texas to that date.[23]

Orendain originally thought that the group would just play it by ear and that the American authorities would arrest them right away. When no arrests happened, however, Orendain decided to stop all traffic crossing into the United States from the Mexican side of the bridge. An employee from the US side warned the group that the bridge could potentially collapse under the weight of all the cars and large trucks that the protestors had stopped. After considering the potentially negative press that the union would receive if such a catastrophe occurred, Orendain decided to let the trucks go and only stop people who appeared to be potential strikebreakers. Texas law enforcement soon arrived; in response, Orendain led the group to the international line, where they stood. Not knowing what to do, the officers left them alone, and the protest continued for the next several hours. The group later claimed to have successfully stopped many strikebreakers from crossing the border.[24]

Texas police officers began arresting the demonstrators later in the morning, so Orendain and two of the other strikers crossed the border and stood on the Mexican side of the bridge. After some American officers told them that they had called the Mexican authorities, who were then en route, Orendain led the two strikers to the middle of the bridge, where they literally straddled the US-Mexico borderline, placing one foot on the US side and one foot on the Mexican side. At that point the US authorities ran out of patience, so they began knocking the demonstrators down and arresting them. In protest, Orendain led the group in a lay-in, whereupon they all lay down in the middle of the bridge, again blocking traffic. Starr County district attorney Randall Nye approached them in an attempt to lure some of the protestors away from the bridge, telling them that these "outside agitators" (Orendain and his two picket captains) were a corrupting influence. None from the group were convinced and instead began singing protest songs such as *Nosotros Venceremos* (We Shall Overcome) and *Solidaridad* (Solidarity), drowning out Nye's protests.[25]

The whole group, however, would eventually be dragged off to jail and the crowd dispersed. Authorities arrested them in a rough manner. According to Orendain, a few officers knocked Eugene Nelson down, "and they got him by the hand and were just dragging him along like a rag" about fifty feet to where the squad cars were parked. When they arrested Orendain, the officers allegedly "put [him] in an armlock," pulling him along and nearly breaking his arm while handcuffs dug into his skin and caused his wrists to bleed. The group spent the next few hours in the Rio Grande City jail. Orendain demanded that they be provided a lawyer, but county officials refused. Realizing that they were wasting their time and that the group had no money with which to pay their bail, the authorities released them without any charges. The incident became big news, making the front page of the local newspaper the next day.[26]

The Roma bridge demonstration was notable for two reasons. First, the incident was a public demonstration that showed locals that the union was serious in its demands for collective bargaining rights and better working conditions. Never before had such a highly dramatic show of support on behalf of South Texas migrant workers taken place. Nye's use of the term *outside agitators* is also telling. At a number of points during the subsequent strike, as well as during the Chicano Movement activism in greater South Texas that took place later in the 1960s, Anglos commonly used the term to dismiss the activists who sought to make improvements in South Texas. Nevertheless, it clearly took outside help to challenge a structure of ethnic relations that many locals had found themselves powerless to change over the past several decades.

The demonstration also highlights the significance of the US-Mexico border to the union's efforts to win greater concessions for the workers. Orendain understood that the largest obstacle to obtaining greater rights for migrant farmworkers was South Texas's supply of reserve labor. The US-Mexico border itself was the valve that regulated that labor source. If the union could somehow stop the flow of labor across the border, then the growers could be forced to negotiate collective bargaining agreements. This, however, was a nearly impossible task. As is clear from the authorities' quick response to the union's presence at

the bridge, the local power structure was in no way amenable to the union protests at such an important and visible juncture in the regional labor system.

Other aspects of the Starr County Strike demonstrate the degree to which
the union sought to challenge local growers and the endemic nature of the colonial power structure. On the evening of November 3, Antonio Orendain and
organizer Bill Chandler successfully convinced a train engineer in Rio Grande
City to stop his train, which carried five carloads of peppers, from leaving the
city. Strikebreakers had picked and packed the peppers, and the engineer, upon
hearing that the local union was AFL-CIO affiliated, decided to respect their
picket lines. Local law enforcement soon arrived and declared that the pickets
were in accordance with Texas law. Later that evening, however, a contingent
of Texas Rangers arrived from Corpus Christi brandishing machine guns and
semiautomatic weapons. Despite the pickets' legality, the Rangers successfully
got the train moving.[27]

No one knew who contacted the Rangers and asked for their involvement
in ending the train picket at Rio Grande City, but it was clear that progrower
forces had used the Rangers to circumvent not only local law enforcement
but also a legal labor protest. What happened next, however, made the union
infamous. As the train began rolling down the tracks, a rail trestle in its path
erupted in flames, again stopping the train. Reporters and local witnesses
instantly blamed the union, although Orendain denied the charges and no
proof could be found that any striker had set the blaze. The city made no arrests
at the scene, but locals began harassing the union, cutting its telephone lines
and scratching obscenities on the door of the union's headquarters. The trestle
was a part of the only railway leading out of Rio Grande City, so all rail service
had to be halted until a new one could be built. "Someone did this to make us
look bad and turn the public against us," one unionist opined. If this was true,
then the duplicitous tactic seemed to be working.[28]

Local police began arresting union members for burning the rail trestle
a few days later. Orendain later recalled his amazement at watching a judge
and several Texas Rangers type up his arrest warrant in the Rio Grande City
courthouse *after* his arrest. Fifteen strikers filled a cramped jail cell. One
Ranger threatened to beat Orendain. Another officer tried to bribe a young
union sympathizer, saying that he would release the young man and give him
fifteen hundred dollars if he would swear under oath that he saw Orendain
near the rail trestle just before it burned. A rumor circulated that a sheriff's
deputy had offered residents near where the fire occurred one hundred dollars apiece if they would blame the incident on the union. Realizing that the
authorities had hoped to pin the arson on them and effectively end the union's

presence in South Texas, the imprisoned men engaged in a six-day *huelga de hambre* (hunger strike), which eventually gained the attention of a Dallas attorney, who posted bond for them. The group spent a total of ten days in jail. The Missouri-Pacific Railroad, which was the railroad company whose service the fire interrupted, brought suit against the union a year later, but that effort also proved unsuccessful. No evidence could be found that directly implicated the union in the rail trestle's burning.[29]

Texas Rangers became more deeply involved in the Starr County Strike after the fire and arrests. Feuding between the union and law enforcement officials worsened. A local attorney supportive of La Casita and the growers began slamming the union, saying that they had started the bridge fire "and were a bunch of outsiders, liars, and ex-criminals." A spokesman for the union in California responded by saying that the "strikers in Texas have faced police-state tactics by the Texas Rangers" and that "opposition to the strikers is even more ignorant and brutal than in California." By casting the struggles of the Texas union in comparative terms, the progrower law enforcement displayed the particularly hard edge of South Texas's colonial labor system in terms of relations between growers and workers. Rangers might not be murdering ethnic Mexicans outright anymore in the South Texas borderlands, but the swift response of this paramilitary force to deal with the "outsiders" displayed the degree to which the regional power structure still oppressed ethnic Mexicans through force and intimidation. No challenge to the existing social order would be tolerated, especially one that was threatening to awaken a desire for social justice in the minds of impoverished crop pickers. Similar to the use of Rangers during the Plan de San Diego rebellion fifty years before, local and state-level law enforcement officers remained a tool for oppressing the poor and the marginalized.[30]

Orendain remained conscious of the problem that Mexican migrants created for the union. He was particularly wary of the border's status as the valve for South Texas's reserve labor supply. Nevertheless, it is important not to overlook the role that legal—as opposed to undocumented—Mexican immigrants played in South Texas farm labor and in breaking the union's strikes. A study published by the US Department of Labor revealed why the growers preferred undocumented laborers instead of Mexican Americans or documented immigrants. In November 1966, during the middle of the Starr County Strike, the average farmworker in the Lower Rio Grande Valley earned about seventy-five cents per hour, whereas the average farmworker in Texas earned about ninety-seven cents per hour. Somewhere between forty thousand and fifty thousand legal workers crossed the border daily. The presence of such workers clearly drove wages down. The problem, however, was that a substandard wage to American-born workers was much more adequate than what Mexican workers could earn in Mexico. The strategy for the union, then, had to change. Not only did Texas migrants require collective bargaining rights, but also the difficult problem of the border had to be addressed. One could not simply close the border when the region's most powerful elements wanted it to remain open.[31]

The Starr County Strike, however, achieved none of these goals. As the spring of 1967 passed, Chávez began to believe that organizing efforts in South Texas had been premature, so he decided to scale back the union's efforts, and he recalled Orendain to Delano, California, in early May. Chávez felt that Orendain's work as the union's secretary-treasurer would be more valuable than his engaging in fledgling efforts on the US-Mexico border. The Starr County Strike would eventually be defeated in the summer of 1967, as the union's efforts at winning concessions for the workers proved ultimately unsuccessful.[32]

Orendain had clearly empathized with workers along the border in South Texas, in particular, above those in California or other parts of the United States. He recognized something particularly egregious about the mistreatment of migrant workers in South Texas—something systemic and endemic that he recognized did not exist anywhere else that he had visited during his years as a migrant worker and activist since crossing the border from Mexico in 1950. The fact that the union failed to overturn the local social order should come as little surprise. A truly herculean effort would be needed to shut off the growers' most valuable asset: the nearby border and the reserve labor supply. The union understood that the wave of enthusiasm with which the strike had begun was not enough to overturn a long-established system of labor exploitation. With little enthusiasm for the strike coming from the larger union, the AFL-CIO had no real reason to open its coffers for any large-scale effort in South Texas. The silver lining in the Starr County Strike's failure was that more people had become aware of the workers' crippling poverty as well as the maltreatment that local companies like La Casita allegedly perpetrated. Still, the border was too strong a factor in the exploitation of cheap labor for profit. Even though the union had failed, it was also during the same time that ethnic Mexican organizers began to counterattack racism and segregation in South Texas on a general level.[33]

Death to Popeye

A six-foot-tall statue of Popeye stands in the center of Crystal City in Zavala County, Texas. The town is in the heart of Texas's Winter Garden district, northwest of the Lower Rio Grande Valley but still not far from the border. The homage to Popeye is meaningful to residents of the town. Crystal City has long dubbed itself the Spinach Capital of the World, just as Mission is the Home of the Grapefruit. Spinach—as well as other truck crops—was grown widely in Crystal City. Prominent companies such as Del Monte Foods, which moved to Crystal City after World War II, employed ethnic Mexican migrants. Ethnic Mexicans in Crystal City, as in the Lower Rio Grande Valley, have also ranked among some of the nation's poorest people. Unlike in the Valley, however, a large-scale revolt against the town's ruling elite took place, this one leading to lasting changes for the residents of this small South Texas farming community. The explosion of the Chicano Movement in South Texas society that emanated outward from Crystal City would come to represent the most forceful and radical challenge to South Texas elites since the Plan de San Diego uprising. Chicanos, however, would gain greater legitimacy with mainstream American society as civil rights organizers due in large part to the cultural tenor of liberalism in the United States during the 1960s and '70s. As such, the lasting changes made by Chicano organizers would fundamentally alter South Texas colonialism to a much greater degree than previous efforts had done.[34]

The city's early history is similar to that of other farming towns in South Texas. Crystal City was founded in 1907 out of a large nineteenth-century cattle ranch, and the area soon thereafter became populated by Anglo-American onion and spinach farmers. Land had been boosted and sold to farmers from outside of the region and the state. Also, like citriculture and vegetable growing in the Lower Rio Grande Valley, spinach farming in Crystal City boomed during the 1920s. Ethnic Mexicans, who came to Crystal City after the town's founding almost exclusively to work as stoop laborers for the town's new growers, inhabited a subordinate status. Mexican neighborhoods in Crystal City were shabby, while schools for ethnic Mexican children were dilapidated and inferior to Anglo schools. Also like Valley communities, Crystal City was run throughout the first half of the twentieth century by some of the same Anglos who had been involved in its founding. There was almost no Mexican American middle class in Crystal City during the early twentieth century. The city exhibited clear characteristics of being another pocket of colonialism in South Texas: "The Anglos own everything. They like to tell visitors about the decent, hardworking Mexicans they grew up with—Mexicans who would have been appalled at people who wanted something for nothing or at people who tried to create friction between the races. [They have] taken political as well as economic control more or less for granted."[35]

Although occupational stratification (with underpaid jobs that Anglos considered to be Mexican work) and a reserve labor force (migrants on both sides of the US-Mexico border) both existed, Crystal City's labor situation differed in one distinct way from that of the Lower Rio Grande Valley: Del Monte, which was the town's largest employer, allowed its employees to unionize. By 1956 a small Teamsters Union existed among the many hundreds of ethnic Mexican employees at the company's plant in Crystal City. Del Monte was a California-owned company that had long recognized its workers' right to collective bargaining. Additionally, Del Monte also paid its workers wages that were unusually high for South Texas agribusinesses. "The decision by Del Monte to move into Crystal City and establish a large plant," writes historian John Staples Shockley, "although it was welcomed by many in the city's agricultural and business establishment, ultimately weakened these local Anglos' ability to control the situation." The union angered some Anglo residents: "All this town was ever intended to be was a labor camp!" expressed one white resident during the 1970s. Nevertheless, with the entrance of the Teamsters in 1956, workers could expect to exert some level of control over their lives. This opening would be further exploited as the 1960s dawned and the younger generation of Mexican Americans became college educated. Life was little better for ethnic Mexicans in Crystal City than it had been for those of the Valley, but more opportunity for a better future existed.[36]

A modicum of change first came to Crystal City in 1963. What took place that year was so unusual that it drew national press coverage. Interestingly, however, the changes began with an Anglo man, Andrew Dickens, a former oil field worker who had retired to Crystal City and set up a donut shop in 1961. Dickens did not know, however, that his new shop was on a property that local authorities had wanted to use as a right-of-way for a new highway. Upon learning this, Dickens believed that he had been taken advantage of, so he turned to the city and county governments for help. Both entities agreed that the municipality could claim a legitimate right to his property, so Dickens got nowhere. In the process, however, he took a hard look at the local government, and what he found disturbed him: a small group of ruling families had been running the town and the county basically since Crystal City's inception. This, to him, was machine-style politics at its worst. From that point forward, Dickens vowed that he would oust the ruling elite and turn the town over to its majority ethnic Mexican residents.[37]

Dickens first contacted Juan Cornejo at the Del Monte plant in town. Cornejo was a Teamsters representative and also a political *jefe* in his own right whom Anglo politicians had often approached in order to corral Mexican American votes. Cornejo, Dickens, and several others talked about the possibility of organizing against the city government. Cornejo was interested in breaking away from the Anglo political machine and starting an organization of his own. These men, with the help of the larger Teamsters Union and the Political Association of Spanish-Speaking Organizations (PASSO)—an umbrella organization for Mexican American political groups that formed in 1961 from the remnants of the Viva Kennedy clubs, which had helped get John F. Kennedy elected—began a successful voter registration and poll-tax drive, registering thousands of Mexican Americans to vote by January 1962. The group eventually chose a slate of candidates whom locals referred to as *Los Cinco Candidatos* (the five candidates), led by Cornejo himself. None of these men were migrant workers, but nevertheless they were of basically the same social class: none had more than a high school education and all lived just above the poverty line.

Local Anglos attempted to stall the growing political sentiment within the town's Mexican American population, which had previously been politically apathetic. As the municipal elections approached, the local government tried numerous tactics, such as denying the presence of poll watchers during the elections and passing a bond package on the eve of the election that called for one-half million dollars to pave roads in the town's Mexican neighborhoods. Also, local growers announced that the then unheard-of wage of two dollars per hour would be paid on Election Day, while Del Monte announced that it was going into overtime production and that its workers would unfortunately not be able to vote. None of these tactics worked. On April 2, 1963, Los Cinco Candidatos swept the election and the incumbent Anglo administration was voted out. One commentator noted that it was not surprising that such an event could happen in a town such as Crystal City, given that its population was about 75 percent ethnic Mexican. What was surprising was that the electoral revolt *did* happen at all. This was the first time in the history of the region that the numerically dominant Mexican Americans had defeated a group of Anglo candidates in favor of their own office seekers. "Whatever the particular success or failure of this experiment in local government being carried out in Crystal City," one commentator noted, "the election signaled in rather dramatic fashion that things would never quite be the same again in Texas."[38]

The election was indeed only one step in ethnic Mexicans' assertion of their rights against one of the many oppressive municipal regimes in South Texas. The new government ran the city for two years, from 1963 to 1965, before itself being voted out of office. Cornejo turned out to be an ineffective and incompetent mayor. During his two-year reign, he became frustrated at his own lack of political power as well as his small salary. He also ran afoul of other city officials in his attempt to build a machine-style government in the tradition of South Texas politics. Cornejo had been an important political figure in the community before the election, but his inability to control the other council members as well as the city manager alienated him from his colleagues and the voters. Also, the general lack of education of the new slate made governing the city and corralling the public somewhat more difficult than it might otherwise have been. Most important, however, the local media and Anglo citizenry of Crystal City vociferously complained about and verbally lambasted Cornejo. With these factors working against it, the Teamsters-PASSO slate found itself not fully prepared to govern the town after its election in 1963.[39]

But politicized ethnic Mexicans would not remain quiet simply because the Crystal City government had failed in 1965. In 1967 activists formed the Mexican American Youth Organization (MAYO) at St. Mary's College in San Antonio. Among the group's organizers was a young man named José Ángel Gutiérrez of Crystal City, who would become the key leader in the Chicano Movement in South Texas. One of the things that made MAYO different from other organizations was the sizable number of young Mexican Americans attending college in Texas, which far outpaced the number of Mexican American college students in other states of the US Southwest. MAYO's organizers also conceived of a more direct and aggressive approach in forcing positive change for ethnic Mexicans in Texas. Organizers criticized other Chicano activists, whom they felt "had failed to engage in direct action projects" and more acute community organization. MAYO's founding would prove to be an important event in the fight against racial oppression in South Texas.[40]

MAYO's impact also immediately reached into the Lower Rio Grande Valley. The organization's message resonated with young Mexican Americans in that part of the South Texas borderlands, as leaders' concerns, "bringing out pride in Chicano youths as well as in grown-ups," seemed to strike a chord. The organization was the only one in the Valley for Mexican American youths, and it spread widely in local colleges, junior colleges, and high schools during the year after its founding. San Juan, Pharr, Edinburg, Weslaco, Mercedes, Mission, and other towns involved in Valley citriculture and commercial farming all established MAYO chapters. MAYO failed to reach some important areas in the Valley and South Texas, however, such as McAllen, where the school district had policies against students' joining outside organizations.[41]

MAYO immediately engaged in a number of activities intended to challenge some of the discriminatory tendencies common in South Texas schools and towns. Organizers struck hard at strictures prohibiting students from speaking Spanish on school grounds. One MAYO member spoke publicly on the subject: "Why Spanish? Here's the reason: Anglos. We are so closely related to Mexico and are in contact with its people everyday. We hear the language everyday and it's all around us. It's our native tongue and we're proud of it. So why doesn't the anglo learn it. I'll tell you why. Because he thinks it's dirty. And because it comes from the Mexican-American which they think are dirty and lazy. In other words we are not good enough for them. That is, according to them."[42]

MAYO also criticized school officials for having to be forced to make changes. The group protested against schools in the Pharr–San Juan–Alamo area over their handling of the unfortunate deaths of two Mexican American youths in a horrific train accident in 1968, asking: "Why did the school not provide a moment's silence in memory of these youths without having to be pressured by their fellow students?" The very attitudes of white South Texans were on trial. One cartoon in a local publication included a panel of four pictures of an Anglo cowboy with the following captions: "First we gave in and let them go to school with us, then we gave in and let them eat at the same place we do, then we gave in and let 'em run for office. Ptue! Next thing these lil Mexicans will want is to govern themselves, the ungrateful little wretches!" Indeed, complete self-determination was the goal. MAYO organizers knew that in order to change discrimination in South Texas, Anglo attitudes and behaviors had to be changed.[43]

MAYO also backed specific mass actions by students in South Texas schools. In the fall of 1968, MAYO supported a student boycott at the Edcouch-Elsa High School in the Lower Rio Grande Valley. Rumors of a school walkout had circulated for weeks during the early part of the fall semester. On November 15, about 150 students at the school walked out and refused to attend class. The students listed fifteen demands they wanted school administrators to address, which included: (1) that no disciplinary action be taken against MAYO members; (2) that no threats or intimidations against students in any clubs be made by teachers or administrators; (3) that the price of cafeteria lunches be lowered; (4) that students be allowed to speak Spanish at school without any penalties; (5) that courses on Mexicans and Mexican Americans be taught; and (6) that "blatant discrimination" against Mexican American students be stopped immediately. The school board met on November 18 but refused to take action on the students' demands. Instead, board members ordered the students to be expelled pending hearings before the board. Officials returned some of the students to class over the following weeks, but many remained expelled after November 18. Several weeks later, a judge ordered ninety-nine of them returned to class, and over the following month most of the rest of the expelled students reenrolled at Edcouch-Elsa High School or in other local school districts.[44]

The school board sought to head off the actions of these "outside agitators" from interfering with classes and school activities. A letter to students and parents outlined new policies that the board had passed, which not only included expulsion for the semester and loss of all credits, but also prohibited students from soliciting membership in organizations such as MAYO or others "bent on disrupting school."[45]

After the Edcouch-Elsa walkout, things heated up back in Crystal City. José Ángel Gutiérrez of MAYO had become a driving force in the new movement. He envisioned, from the centrality of Crystal City and Zavala County, a move to attack all of Anglo South Texas through civil rights organizing. "The institutions (of South Texas) exemplify elitism and authoritarianism," he wrote in November 1969. He also argued that "majority rule and democracy are not made operable concepts" in South Texas, while widespread ignorance of Anglo jurisprudence prevailed across the region. Gutiérrez had a number of good points. The median income of Spanish-surnamed people in Texas was $2,914 in 1960. Median education was 6.1 years of schooling. Forty-seven percent of Mexicans lived in overcrowded housing, while 12 percent lived in dilapidated conditions. In Zavala County in 1969, however, the situation was even worse. That year, median income for Spanish-surnamed individuals in the county was only $2,314 annually. Median education was a paltry 2.3 years of schooling. Of the 12,696 people in Zavala County in 1969, 11,415 were Mexican Americans. Many of these families lived on $1,200 to $2,000 per year, and the average family size in the county was five people. With such relatively large families and little income, most people spent all of their money on housing and food, which left little for other necessities, such as adequate clothing or footwear. Anglos still controlled Zavala County in the late 1960s, despite the 1963 electoral revolt. As late as 1977, twenty-six Anglos owned roughly 87 percent of the land in the county, as well as all major businesses and retail outlets.[46]

Before Gutiérrez and MAYO could focus on these larger issues, they decided to follow in the footsteps of the Edcouch-Elsa students and force changes in the local school system. What came to be known as the Crystal City School Walkout of 1969 served as another major step in the fight to overturn South Texas's colonial system after the earlier electoral revolt and the Starr County Strike of 1966–67. Even before the walkout, the US Commission on Civil Rights had already publicized the deficiencies of Crystal City's school system. Hearings in San Antonio in December 1968 validated a number of the complaints that MAYO and the students would soon raise. The commission found that the school district selected principals who did not understand the bicultural composition of the area. The district also made little effort to train teachers to deal with the special needs of impoverished families or the numerous migrant families who moved in and out of the county. Parents had often been excluded from PTA and board meetings because of language barriers. The commission also found that the school tolerated teachers who were insensitive to ethnic and cultural differences. One of the more common complaints was that the school district furnished textbooks that did not adequately represent the important roles that Mexican Americans had played in the history of Texas or the greater US Southwest. Interestingly, the board found that "the curriculum offered to Mexican American students by the school system of the state of Texas was deemed to be inadequate and more properly structured for children living in the Middle West." Other complaints also went on record, such as the schoolteachers' propensity to want to Anglicize Mexican American students, as well as the fact that most teacher-selected student awards went to Anglo students, despite Crystal City's student body being roughly 80 percent Mexican American.[47]

By late 1969 the students still believed that the school board had not adequately addressed their demands. On December 8 the MAYO-led group presented the predominantly Anglo school board with a petition and a list of demands, which the board subsequently ignored. Demands included providing bilingual and bicultural education, addressing inequities in certain types of testing, answering various charges of discrimination, and hiring a Mexican American counselor. The next morning, at 7:30 a.m., the students walked out of school; by 10:00 a.m. five hundred students had joined the protest. The students then held a march in downtown Crystal City, returning for a meeting with the school superintendent later that afternoon. After the superintendent refused to budge on any of the students' demands, the group's leader, a seventeen-year-old named Severita Lara, informed him that the students would stay away from school until their demands were met. Lara then walked back out to the demonstrators and spoke to the crowd, asking for unity and support. The Crystal City school walkout had begun in earnest.[48]

The walkout, which lasted for the next month, became a huge success. One of the reasons it was so effective was that Crystal City residents had been highly politicized since the 1963 electoral revolt. Parents tended to support their children. School administrators initially balked at numerous demands, saying that their budget was too limited to hire more Mexican American teachers and a new counselor. The administrators argued that the board had already taken certain steps, since the hearings a year earlier, offering a Mexican culture class and studying a proposal to instruct local teachers on how to deal with racial differences and prejudice.[49]

The Texas media made one important point: the poor conditions that Mexican Americans faced in Crystal City were not new, but what was new was "the involvement of young Chicanos, most of them still teenagers, demanding the changes they want." These young activists recognized the advantages that they would have in negotiating the changes as opposed to having their parents speak on their behalf. The school board majority wanted to negotiate with the parents only, but Lara adamantly refused. The students, in her words, were "not going to accept anything unless [the board talks] to us directly." She continued, "Our parents have language problems; they are at a psychological disadvantage before they ever sit down." A number of politicians had thrown their support behind the students, including Texas State Senator Joe Bernal of San Antonio, Bexar County Commissioner Albert Peña, and national figures such as Senators Edward Kennedy and Ralph Yarborough, the latter a liberal Democratic senator from East Texas. Most significant, however, was that the students had taken control of the situation. At various points during the nearly month-long walkout, about 1,600 of the district's 2,850 pupils took part in the demonstrations. "The students, like it or not, are in charge," said a Texas Education Agency representative. "It's been said that we can't let our students run the school. But who is running the school now?"[50]

Not only did the walkout shed light on the anti-Mexican elements of the South Texas school system—which were a symptom of the general anti-Mexican sentiment that had pervaded colonial South Texas since the early twentieth century—but it also gave ethnic Mexicans a clearer and more manageable objective in their attempts to enact change. The Starr County Strike, which preceded the Crystal City School Walkout by a few years, had shed light on the border's porous qualities and South Texas's unfair labor system, but it had ultimately proved unsuccessful in its direct challenges to growers and law enforcement officials. The Crystal City School Walkout not only brought state and national attention back to South Texas, but it also proved more successful in its core aims. On January 5, 1970, after numerous meetings between the administrators and the students and their parents, the two sides agreed to a compromise. The agreement met most of the students' demands, with only a few issues being ignored and some staying the same. Boycotters gained protection from scholastic penalties, earned grievance procedures to complain about discrimination, and set up three nights per week to use the school for study purposes. The school also agreed to special assemblies and speakers in recognition of Mexican Independence Day on September 16 and also agreed to hire Spanish-speaking teachers and provide bilingual education as well as a Spanish-speaking counselor. "We got what we wanted and we are satisfied with the outcome," stated sixteen-year-old Mario Treviño. "We're just hoping that the school board will keep its word. But if they don't, I guess they will suffer the consequences." The students returned to class on January 6, victorious. The balance of power had clearly shifted in Crystal City.[51]

Aside from the fact that the students had directly confronted long-established discriminatory practices in the Anglo-dominated South Texas school system and had won most of their demands, the boycott also gave South Texas ethnic Mexicans increased confidence in their ability to overcome racial oppression. First, the victory in Crystal City buoyed MAYO's hopes of making headway further to the south in the Lower Rio Grande Valley. MAYO held a conference in Mission from December 26–30, 1969, with the hope of encouraging local students to stand up and fight for their rights. The conference included workshops and panels on government, politics, culture, music, and folklore. MAYO employed strict security for the conference, with bearded security guards carrying nightsticks, using walkie-talkies, and wearing military fatigues. The conference undoubtedly gave the impression that a new era of radical political and social activism had dawned.[52]

MAYO's activities also brought increased attention to the colonial labor system. Bill Porterfield of the *Chicago Daily News* published a scathing report on Lower Rio Grande Valley growers' mistreatment of ethnic Mexican workers. Porterfield noted that cotton and citrus brought $125,000,000 annually to Valley growers, yet there were still "more peons down there than any other class." Despite the massive underclass in the region, Valley growers had gone to the Texas Employment Commission during the summer of 1969 and complained of a labor shortage. They wanted the commission to bring in workers, but the commission refused. More than four hundred thousand people lived in the Valley in 1969, but the previous year 14,533 families had received welfare checks. The total outlay for the welfare was $11,500,000, or $800 per family. To Porterfield, then, growers simply hoped to lure more workers to an area where unemployment was already high and wages were low in order to maintain the status quo. The growers were clearly directly responsible for the crippling poverty among the Valley's ethnic Mexican underclass.[53]

Citrus growers told a different story. H. J. Tanner of the Edinburg Citrus Association, which was the largest citrus cooperative in the Lower Rio Grande Valley, countered by saying, "We've had a critical labor shortage down here for years. A lot of these people would rather take welfare than work, and that's what they do." Tanner did not hide his feelings on the matter: "You know, these labor people, these do-gooders, and I'm including the church people in that category, they say these Mexicans down here are starving to death, but the truth is that a man willing to work can make from $1.50 to $2.50 an hour." He continued, "[Of] course, a loafer who sits in the shade eating his tortilla won't." Porterfield noticed in his investigation that Tanner's words reflected the views of most growers: "Lazy Mexicans [take] it easy on welfare doles." The similarities between these ideas and the themes of Mexican workers as slow-moving and unmotivated in booster literature from the early twentieth century are striking.[54]

Aside from spreading revolutionary sentiment and continuing to blow the lid off of racial discrimination, the Crystal City school boycott victory increased MAYO leaders' belief in the charged political awareness of Zavala County residents. Not long after the school victory, a group of students, parents, and MAYO organizers gathered together on January 17, 1970, in Campestre Hall just outside of town. The group formed the independent La Raza Unida Party (LRUP; the United Peoples Party), which sought to demolish the stranglehold that the Democratic Party had on South Texas politics. Gutiérrez in particular felt that now was the time to act in Crystal City, given the overwhelming success of the school walkout. The organizers had formed their own institution and sought to capture political self-determination in South Texas. The anticolonial revolt of South Texas Mexicans was now gaining in strength.[55]

First on the agenda for LRUP was the Crystal City school board. Gutiérrez, who was then only twenty-five years old, and two of his associates sought to fill three vacant seats on the board for the upcoming elections in the spring of 1970. The incumbent school board president, E. F. Mayer, noted that the election basically amounted to "whether MAYO is going to take over or whether they aren't." Gutiérrez explained that the group wanted new people on the board who were sympathetic to their cause. To support their hopes, MAYO launched a voter registration drive during the walkout in December. Several observers noted that public interest in Crystal City politics had not been so high since the 1963 election.[56]

The election campaign proved to be a bitter fight. LRUP held numerous rallies in the city during the following spring. Campaign tactics included dropping leaflets from planes to make sure that the candidates reached all of the potential voters. Gutiérrez called for federal regulators to oversee the elections. He charged that Zavala County had voting irregularities in just about every election since the town's inception. He also announced that LRUP was not just a one-shot political party, and that it would serve as a viable third party in Zavala County as well as greater South Texas for many years to come.[57]

Some members of Crystal City's Anglo community reacted with typical mixtures of shock and racist barbs. An anonymous note that made its way to Gutiérrez's office expressed the anti-Mexican views held by some Crystal City

Anglos: "ONCE AGAIN WE HAVE TO SHOW YOU STUPID 'MESKINS' THAT WE ARE SUPERIOR TO YOU. CAN'T YOU SEE THAT YOUR CANDIDATES CAN NEVER WIN? YOU WILL BE REASSURED OF THIS FACT WHEN 'OUR' MEXICAN FRIENDS WIN THE ELECTION. WHY DO YOU THINK THIS CITY HAS GOTTEN SO MUCH CRITICISM? IT'S BECAUSE THE MESKINS ARE RUNNING THE SCHOOLS, AND THEY KNOW THAT THEY CAN'T RUN IT AS GOOD AS AN ANGLO COULD. IF YOU WANT A SCHOOL THAT IS NOT COMMUNIST VOTE TED MUNOZ AND ALFREDO RAMON."[58]

By labeling LRUP "Communist," the author or authors labeled the threatening stance of the party as outside the typical Anglo–Mexican relationship in South Texas. Also, by challenging the dominant order, LRUP, in the minds of the note's author, had no place in Crystal City. The new political movement represented a serious threat to long-standing traditions in Anglo-dominated South Texas.

Nevertheless, the hope for positive change was enough to convince Crystal City's Mexican American population that the new candidates could be a part of creating a better future for them and their children. Gutiérrez and the two men running with him, Arturo González and Mike Pérez, easily won the three open spots on the school board. Many locals considered the election an issue of the "establishment versus young Mexican Americans seeking change."[59] The returns not only ensured control over the city's schools by the ethnic Mexican population in Crystal City, but they also further buoyed hopes that LRUP could enact its pro–Mexican American agenda throughout South Texas. The victory proved to ethnic Mexicans that forceful change against the long-established traditions of Anglo South Texas was possible.

LRUP followed this success with electoral victories in other parts of the region. The party fielded a total of sixteen candidates in April 1970, including the Crystal City candidates, all but one of whom won election. A week later, the party won two city council posts in Crystal City. Also, in nearby Carrizo Springs, LRUP candidates won and were the first Mexican Americans to sit on the city council in recent history. In Cotulla, also that April, LRUP defeated the Anglo mayor and won three seats on the city council. Finally, during the following November, LRUP conducted a write-in campaign and elected a county commissioner. The party had taken complete control of the city governments of Crystal City as well as San Juan in Hidalgo County, not to mention the board of education in Crystal City.[60]

Gutiérrez's own rhetoric gained him little favor with many Anglo South Texans. People began to take note of his radicalism during the 1970 election in particular. One of the things for which Gutiérrez became well known was his use of the term *gringo* to describe anti-Mexican, racist whites. Predictably, this got him into trouble on a number of fronts. After the victory in the Crystal City school board elections, Gutiérrez gave an interview to a San Antonio newspaper in which he commented that "'gringo' is an attitude. . . . It just means a foreigner. . . . It's also an institution . . . like the Democratic Party in Texas." When asked if there was any place for liberal Anglos in LRUP, Gutiérrez replied that there "certainly is. . . . I just think that liberal Anglos are not ready to accept our terms. When a Chicano sees a white he doesn't see a liberal Anglo, he sees a Gringo." Finally, when asked what percentages of Anglos in Crystal City and San Antonio were Gringos, Gutiérrez replied flatly, "Every last one of them." These people, to Gutiérrez, were a deep threat to ethnic Mexicans across the board and thus had to be attacked. "In elimination of the Gringos," Gutiérrez concluded, "we've got to do it in every way that is feasible."[61]

Nelson Wolff, a liberal Anglo who was the Democratic nominee for state representative from Bexar County (San Antonio), took offense at Gutiérrez's statements. Wolff privately stated that while he admired Gutiérrez for standing up for Mexican American rights, he also "despise[d] a man who uses this as a pretext to pit one race against the other." While he agreed that more needed to be done for Mexican Americans in South Texas, he also challenged Gutiérrez to "quit your loud abusive rhetoric which preaches hate and discord and try to work with Anglos who want to help the Mexican American better his life. . . . Don't threaten us with extinction." Wolff then challenged Gutiérrez to a public debate based on the content of his interview.[62]

At issue were differing strategies on how to fight the colonial power structure in South Texas. Gutiérrez employed rhetoric and tactics that incited South Texas Mexicans to action. Part of this involved describing Anglo–Mexican relations in antagonistic terms. Gutiérrez knew that the only way to enact forceful change was to strike a chord with the region's ethnic Mexican population and induce aggressive political activism. These tactics had worked well in Crystal City in 1969 and 1970. At the same time, his demonizing of Anglo Texans unnerved people such as Wolff. Wolff clearly empathized with MAYO and LRUP, but he little understood the context in which the members of such organizations lived and worked on a daily basis. Ironically, Wolff's accusation that Gutiérrez preached discord was accurate, but it was the kind of discord necessary to upset the power balance in a long-established racially oppressive system. Gutiérrez, along with Orendain before him, was among the new young leaders tipping the balance against white South Texans.

One reason why Gutiérrez so successfully led MAYO and LRUP is because he recognized the primary impediment to bettering the lives of South Texas

Mexicans: the fact that South Texas was a space now long colonized by white Americans. Anglo South Texans had identified themselves as colonists in the early twentieth century; now, ethnic Mexican activists, seeking to overturn the oppressive system that Anglo South Texans had set in place, began to recognize themselves as a colonized people. Gutiérrez spoke and wrote widely on the matter in a number of venues. After reading a privately funded political history of Zavala County by a historian named Sally Jones in the mid-1970s, Gutiérrez criticized the author for her portrayal of the failure of the 1963–65 City Council of Crystal City. Jones argued that the failure was due to a simple lack of experience on the part of the new government. "The applicable tool for viewing the Crystal struggle is that of a colonized people seeking to break with a society that seeks to dehumanize, dominate, and exploit Chicanos by a system of neo-colonialism," responded Gutiérrez. In making this argument, he contended that Jones was "not only blind to the underpinnings of gringo control and power, but [she] also erases Chicano history." By attributing the failure of the 1963 regime to inexperience and lack of organizational support "without even a passing reference to the vicious attack on these Chicano power pioneers by the media, the Texas Rangers, state and local authorities and Anglo citizenry," Jones, according to Gutiérrez, displayed her lack of understanding of the colonial nature of life in South Texas. Portrayals such as Jones's did little to encourage wider support outside of South Texas for the anticolonial struggles of MAYO and LRUP.[63]

Another reason why Gutiérrez and the activists in Zavala County were so successful was their emphasis on expanding the number of Mexican Americans in South Texas who voted. Through the efforts of groups like PASSO and MAYO in the 1960s, Mexican Americans had begun to vote for the candidates they favored, bucking the trend of their votes being corralled by South Texas political machines dominated overwhelmingly by Anglos. Thus, the widening of the vote was important not only because it was a practical way for Mexican Americans to force change, but also because an exponentially higher number of the local citizenry had begun to participate in the democratic process and exercise their legal rights as US citizens. Mexican Americans in South Texas, then, had begun to shake off one of the oldest vestiges of colonialism: the widespread inability by a colonized group of people to participate in self-government and to overthrow an oppressive political power. The Chicano Movement thus signaled a dramatic decline in the political structure of the South Texas internal colony.

Gutiérrez himself provided deep analyses of the colonial situation in South Texas. In an unpublished essay from the early 1970s titled, "La Raza and

Revolution," he stated flatly: "South Texas is a colonial situation. The middle and upper class is almost all white, Anglo, and Protestant. The lower-middle and lower class, economically speaking, are Chicanos. The middle class in South Texas will hardly raise a whisper in support of revolution. They have too much to lose. The Chicano, on the other hand, has little to lose and a great deal to gain."[64]

Gutiérrez was highly critical of the United States in general. He argued that America had tricked "minorities into believing that violence is acceptable and good depending on who employs it. For this reason, American violence in Southeast Asia is holy. Violence by Chicanos in the name of liberation is evil." He also blamed the American media for the general lack of empathy that the public had for the school walkouts and demonstrations. Media outlets had failed to do their jobs properly, which he saw in the fact that the long-standing oppressive conditions that ethnic Mexicans faced in numerous southwestern cities and towns almost never received any news coverage.[65]

"La Raza and Revolution" is a South Texas intellectual landmark. Notably, however, a literary tradition had existed in Texas since the 1930s in which Mexican American writers had begun challenging the colonial discourses that emerged in Texas history wherein the alleged racial inferiority of Mexicans justified the state's eventual conquest by Anglo Americans. Gutiérrez inherited this intellectual tradition and worked hard to explain the parallels between the lives of ethnic Mexicans in four South Texas counties (Bexar, Brooks, Zavala, and Kleberg) and those of people living under dictatorial rule in Latin American nations. In so doing he took the analysis of colonialism in South Texas one step further. In order to do this, Gutiérrez used a model by political theorist Seymour Martin Lipset that gave parameters for measuring democratic societies. For example, Lipset argues that between 6 percent and 40 percent of males in stable European democracies worked in agriculture, while from 46 percent to 87 percent of males in stable Latin American dictatorships worked in agriculture. By rate of comparison, 85 percent of males in Zavala County at the time Gutiérrez wrote his study worked in agriculture. Using this as an index, Zavala County (and, by implication, the rest of South Texas) could be ranked with stable Latin American dictatorships.[66]

But the comparisons went above and beyond the number of males working in agriculture. Barring per capita income, phones, and persons per motor vehicle, one could easily classify life in South Texas as equivalent to life under a Latin American dictatorship. "The statistics on South Texas would be even more similar to Latin American stable dictatorships," Gutiérrez argued, "if the data were broken into 'Chicano' and 'Anglo' categories. Among people twenty-five years old or older in South Texas in 1960, only 1.1 percent of Anglos had no formal education, while 5.5 percent of nonwhites and 22.9 percent of the Spanish-surnamed population had none. Gutiérrez reported that illiteracy rates among ethnic Mexicans were only 16 percent below those of stable Latin American dictatorships. In the four Texas counties under consideration, sixty-three Anglos each owned three hundred acres of land or more. Only five ethnic Mexicans owned that much land, and none of them lived in Zavala County. In Crystal City, 73 percent of the available workforce was qualified to perform only stoop labor, while only 35 percent of the city's workers made above the $1.60 per hour minimum wage. Also, numerous South Texas Mexicans were unable to vote because of their inability to pay the poll tax. A referendum on the poll tax in November 1949 showed that a vast majority favored its repeal, although the fact that it remained in place until a federal judge ruled it unconstitutional in 1966 speaks volumes to the then lack of political power among South Texas Mexicans. Because of the similarities between the economic development of South Texas and Latin American dictatorships, Gutiérrez argued, it is clear that political stability in both "is maintained through internal mechanisms like the political process or the military, rather than supported by social conditions such as education. These social conditions have never supported traditional democratic politics." As such, "the empirical conditions for revolution have been found to exist in the four counties in South Texas."[67]

Gutiérrez's focus on colonialism and revolution explains, in large part, why he was successful. He wrote widely on South Texas as a colonized space, sometimes explicitly, at other times implicitly. In one article outlining "the hopelessness of nonviolence" in ethnic Mexicans' quest for social justice, Gutiérrez commented on the irony that local schools taught Spanish as a foreign language, despite the fact that ethnic Mexicans made up a majority in South Texas and many claimed Spanish as their native tongue. He also noted that the "gringo" persona came about from a combination of colonialism and racism and dated back to western expansion and notions of Anglo-American manifest destiny during the nineteenth century. Colonialism was thus inseparable from the region's history.[68]

Nonetheless, the Chicano Movement continued to struggle in South Texas. Despite the fact that the Texas state legislature passed the once-sought $1.25 minimum wage for farmworkers a few years after the Starr County Strike ended (although the workers still did not receive the union's ultimate goal, which was collective bargaining rights), the LRUP-MAYO movement in Zavala County had not been able to add concessions for migrant workers to the list of its many victories. Nearly two years after the electoral victory, however, LRUP tried its hand at labor organizing in Zavala County.[69]

In late January 1972, forty workers employed by a man named Warren Wagner walked out of a spinach packing shed and declared a strike. The workers next met with eighty crop pickers in Wagner's employ, who also agreed to strike. At issue was a reduction in wages. The owner had reduced the wages of his packing-shed workers from $1.60 per hour to $1.30 per hour, while the field workers had their piece rates reduced from forty cents per basket of spinach picked to twenty cents. A week of picketing at the farm's entrances and packing shed followed, after which the county sheriff arrested sixty pickers, who subsequently refused to be driven to jail and instead marched to the Crystal City courthouse. When the strikers arrived, a large contingent of Mexican American youth from the nearby schools had gathered to witness the arrests. Many of these students were related to the workers. As a result of the crowd's size, the county police, state highway patrolmen, and three Texas Rangers who were on hand did not attempt to break up the demonstration. Of the sixty arrested workers, only five would be charged with obstructing traffic during the march.[70]

The next day, LRUP lawyers began negotiating with the struck grower. Support, financial and otherwise, began pouring into Crystal City from numerous sources. Organizers in Crystal City began to believe that the small strike would develop into a major regional strike against all growers and all crops. They had hoped that the strike would spread, particularly against prominent local commercial farmers such as John Connally, Dolph Briscoe, and Del Monte. Unexpectedly, however, the grower caved to the workers' demands, and the strike ended. "Victory . . . stopped our [planned] area wide program," Gutiérrez later lamented.[71]

After the short strike in Crystal City, Gutiérrez wrote to César Chávez asking for assistance. He told Chávez that LRUP stood to win several offices that year, including the offices of sheriffs, justices of the peace, county commissioners, county attorneys, and constables. Mexican American leaders in Zavala County had all supported the strike. Gutiérrez saw that while political offices did much to further the cause of all ethnic Mexicans in Texas, the heart of South Texas's anti-Mexican structure—the colonial agricultural labor relationship—remained intact. "We need to unionize our area and obtain better wages and working conditions for our Chicanos in the area," Gutiérrez implored. "Will you come in?"[72]

Chávez's direct response to Gutiérrez's plea for a reinvigorated UFW campaign in South Texas is not known. The fact that the Starr County Strike of 1966–67 remains the last major UFW-backed agricultural strike in South Texas to date indicates that Chávez refused Gutiérrez. Although the Starr County Strike was truly the only large-scale strike that had Chávez's backing, Orendain would later lead strikes against the Valley's citrus and vegetable growers from 1975 until about 1982. Orendain organized his own union, called the Texas Farm Workers' Union (TFW), specifically because of Chávez's continuing reluctance to declare a general strike in South Texas. The relationship between the UFW and the breakaway TFW remained highly contentious and bitter during the TFW strikes.[73]

One can only speculate about Chávez's reluctance to bring his union's efforts to bear in South Texas after the Starr County Strike of 1966–67, but logical conclusions can be drawn. Chávez, as well as perhaps other officials in the AFL-CIO, with whom the UFW was affiliated, probably considered striking in the South Texas untenable because of the area's proximity to the border. The reserve labor pool was the key resource that growers in South Texas used to keep wages down and, in times of labor disruption, break strikes. This one element of the labor system made union organizing time-consuming, costly, and virtually impossible. While Gutiérrez and LRUP had won some major victories against the Anglo-dominated order of South Texas, the heart of that order—migrant agricultural labor—remained untouchable.

The People's South Texas

What Gutiérrez, LRUP, and MAYO hoped to do was essentially to retake South Texas for the region's long-suffering poor. No history of the Chicano Movement would be complete, however, without adding some discussion of the people who might constitute the movement's rank and file. These people's lives demonstrate the same claim to homeland and response to colonization as the lives of the movement's leadership.

South Texas Mexicans tended to take similar paths to the Chicano Movement. José Mata was born in Crystal City on May 15, 1947. Like many others who came of age in South Texas during the mid-1960s, Mata remembered discrimination in the local school system, remarking that he and other ethnic Mexican students were pushed around by Anglo kids in the cafeteria and scolded by Anglo schoolteachers for not being able to speak proper English. Mata's parents, also, were illiterate farmworkers who dragged their children north with the harvest, meaning that Mata and his siblings attended school in Texas, North Dakota, Minnesota, and Wisconsin. Mata also recalled that Crystal City, like so many other places in South Texas, was divided by railroad tracks: the west side of the town was where Mexicans lived, and the east side

was Anglo. Clearly, Mata's was something of a typical experience for young ethnic Mexicans in colonial South Texas.[74]

Mata, who in his own words was "not a born politician," was present from
the beginning of the political uprising in Crystal City. The local forerunner to
LRUP was a group called *Ciudadanos Unidos* (United Citizens). Mata recalled
several decades later that the movement was truly community oriented; many
Chicanos sought active change for the betterment of the community, not for
personal gain, a perspective that he argued became lost after the high tide of
the movement. Furthermore, for Mata the people who sacrificed the most
were the families; lack of family time was the greatest cost that the movement
brought to him, his wife, and his children. Finally, and interestingly, Mata
opined in a 1998 interview that relations between Chicanos and Anglos in
Crystal City had improved significantly since the rise of the Chicano Movement. What Mata credited for the improvement in relations was not an enlight-
ening of the Anglo—he simply argued that there were fewer of them in the area
since the movement had started. Anglo South Texas had, since the movement's
inception, become increasingly "re-Mexicanized." As such, the Anglos who
remained in the region had no choice but to deal with the Chicano majority on
a fair and equal basis.[75]

Of course, not everyone in South Texas became involved in the movement
through the uprising in Crystal City. Ofelia Santos was for several years a member of the city council in Edinburg, Texas, in the Lower Rio Grande Valley.
Santos, a first-generation immigrant born to parents who migrated to Texas
from Nuevo León, remembered that her father was something of a civic organizer from the time that she was very young. Her father housed immigrants
from Mexico, helped them get their citizenship documents in order, and also
helped people find work and housing at the local level. Santos, when she herself
was only ten years old, helped her father learn English and American history in
preparation for his application for US citizenship. As such, by the time of the
Nixon-Kennedy presidential campaign, Santos was a high school student who
had already become politically aware several years before the Chicano Movement had even begun. Santos worked with Chicano Movement and farmworker organizers in South Texas during the 1970s; later, she went to college
while in her thirties and studied political science, including Mexican American
and Latin American politics. Santos eventually went into politics herself in the
Lower Rio Grande Valley.[76]

Still others came to *el movimiento* for different reasons. Rudy Espinosa
recalled growing up in Crystal City, where city officials forced his family out of
their home for an urban renewal project and failed to give the family enough

money to purchase a new home, forcing them to move into public housing projects. Thus, the family struggled to make ends meet during Espinosa's childhood. Like so many others, his family joined the migrant stream, but Espinosa recalled that his parents always prioritized his and his siblings' education (a priority that, according to Espinosa, was not shared by all ethnic Mexican migrants). Espinosa, in fact, was on the migrant stream in Wisconsin when the school walkouts began, but he remembered it as a watershed moment in his life: "It gave us some pride, because up until then all we saw was . . . the white little boys, the white teachers, the white cartoons. . . . In my personal life it woke me up."[77]

The colonial order's establishment along with the attendant racism that came with it all came clear to Espinosa in that moment. "Up until then," he remarked, "I didn't seem to see ourselves as a second class citizen and them treating us like that." Espinosa thought that mistreatment by Anglo-Americans was something that all ethnic Mexicans, like other ethnic minorities, simply had to deal with at the hands of the majority: "We are . . . and certainly can be . . . the masters of our destiny. We can have Mexicanos on . . . the school board, teachers, city councilmen, county judges, . . . set our own agenda. And [we can seek out] the American dream in . . . better housing, better education, better social services, things of that nature."

Espinosa became awakened to what life could be like if he and others pushed against the system that had been thrust upon them. He next became a member and eventual president of Ciudadanos Unidos, which according to him served in a number of capacities but was basically a steering committee for LRUP. Espinosa also ran for county commissioner and lost, but later he served as a city councilman and mayor of Crystal City.[78]

Espinosa and Santos both noted some kind of awakening that caused them to see the truth behind the South Texas social structure. Santos's awakening seemed to be when she had a political "coming of age," while Espinosa found direct inspiration from the advent of the movement itself. Espinosa's joining of the movement after it started was probably a common occurrence for many people in or from the South Texas borderlands. Clearly, the movement served as an example of what the future could be like for young people from the region.

Of course, the Chicano Movement was a young people's movement; many of the most active participants joined the movement while still in high school. Severita Lara, one of the leaders of the school walkout in Crystal City, was born to Tejano parents, and unlike many others in Crystal City, she and her family were not really migrant workers. Lara went north to pick sugar beets once when she was sixteen, mainly because many people around the city and in Zapata County used to talk about how great things were up north. Lara found when she went up to Minnesota that there was no glamour or glory to be found on the migrant stream, mainly because of the hard labor and the exceptionally poor living and working conditions.[79]

Lara was always one to challenge the rules, but she became incensed by some things that took place at her junior high school. Like many schools in South Texas, speaking Spanish was forbidden for Lara and her friends. After breaking the rule against speaking Spanish several times, Lara found herself hauled into the principal's office: "I was caught speaking Spanish in the halls and I think it was in eighth grade, Mr. Harbin [the school principal] called me in and says, 'you know the rules. You are not supposed to do this and you have been warned before.' And so I said, 'yes sir.' And so he called me in and he lifted my skirt, because I had petticoats on, you know, so he gave me two paddles or paddled me twice and I ran all the way home, crying and crying and so my dad came in, to the office."

Lara's father, who despite being born in Texas spoke no English, came to the school and accosted the principal, grabbing him by the neck and slamming him against the wall and screaming, "Este es mi lengua. Es lo que yo hablo en mi casa!" (This is my tongue. It is what I speak in my home!). The principal promised Lara's father that he would not punish her in such a demeaning way ever again, spanking her on her underclothes for speaking Spanish at school. Lara went on to excel in her studies, due in no small part to the fact that she attended school regularly as opposed to having to leave for weeks or months at a time to pick crops, as so many of her classmates had to do out of necessity.[80]

Interestingly, Lara seemed to become cynical about the state of things later in the twentieth century in South Texas. After a career in and out of politics, Lara decided to run for the city council in Crystal City during the 1990s. In her own words, she did this

because I felt that there was not enough things being done for, for the people. It was, our economy is shot; not enough programs for the people; Mexico Chico esta igual. No habido cambio. No hay cosas buenas. (Mexico Chico [a neighborhood] is the same. Nothing has changed. There are no good things.) And I wanted to impact at least that area and the whole community, but I wanted to do something for, for the youth too. I dreamed about that recreation center for the kids. You know, they don't have anything. You remember how we were promised one a long time ago? Nunca se hizo. (It was never done.) And I know now that it is not easy. Se hicieron muchas cosas pero eso no se hizo. (Many things were done, but that was not done.). I was not the mayor at that time. I was a member of the city council.[81]

Lara's words show that people who experienced the high tide of activism in 1960s and '70s South Texas later seemed skeptical that much of anything had been accomplished—or felt, at least, that there was still quite a lot of work left to do. Clearly, Mexicans and Mexican Americans in the region still had to contend with the mechanisms of marginalization that became institutionalized in the early twentieth century.

In fact, one could go as far as to say that there was a large-scale backlash in South Texas later in the twentieth century. Lara had much to say to that end and is worth quoting at length:

> There is a lot of negativism here, in Cristal [*sic*], and the Raza Unida. Their parents have told them, right, the Raza Unida was the worst thing for Crystal that Jose Angel Gutierrez . . . he came and changed everything. He made a revolution and then left, leaving us. . . . The Anglos left. The businesses left. Now, we have no business. We have nothing. And Crystal was ruined by Raza Unida Party. If there hadn't been the Raza Unida Party we would still have business. . . . Because of the Raza [Unida], . . . because of you, because of Jose Angel [Gutierrez] we have this mess here. People don't come. We need the white people to control here and fix everything here.[82]

Clearly, not only did some locals consider the Chicano Movement a failure, but also many argued that it had caused Crystal City and perhaps by implication South Texas to be retarded in its growth. By implication, then, the colonial order had brought a certain level of modernization, but the alleged general loss of Anglo interest in the region after the rise of the Chicano Movement had had a retrograde effect in terms of the region's social and economic development. As such, the region's economic marginalization might be said by some to be even worse than it was before South Texas Mexicans began more radically negotiating for themselves a stronger position within the South Texas colony. Indeed, any history of the Chicano Movement that casts it in wholly celebratory terms would be misleading at best; according to some of the movement's participants, either not enough had been done or the movement's members had been too forceful and had become too confrontational for Anglo power brokers in the region.

Perhaps one of the most important developments that came out of the Chicano Movement was a sense of gender equality for the movement's female participants. "We were, I guess, like an equal," Lara said. Women "participated in the decision making," she continued, and "men were supportive of women running for offices and [women] were seen as equals." Part of this change, it should be noted, came from a shift in generational attitudes. Lara's mother was more traditional, believing that women should neither work nor go to school and instead find a man who could support them financially. But Lara argued that La Raza Unida Party certainly opened up women's minds that there was a great deal more out there that they could do. Particularly, the party opened the door for women to gain education and become teachers: "We have so many teachers, *mujeres* (women) now, because of La Raza Unida." After the movement, Crystal City had an exceptionally high rate of women elected officials for any place in Texas or the United States.[83]

The movement's legacy is clearly a complex one that cannot be measured solely on the basis of economic improvement in the region or the general end of racism against ethnic Mexicans across the South Texas borderlands. Lara's point about women awakening to the possibilities for their lives speaks to the gendered element in the movement that shows the restrictions placed on women. Chicano activism thus birthed a gendered discourse about the contributions that women could make at the state and local level within the larger metadiscourses of colonialism and marginalization in South Texas societies. Clearly, despite the movement's limitations noted above, it was a central spark to the intellectual reawakening of countless women native to the borderlands.

Of course, one did not have to come of age in the South Texas borderlands to experience racial discrimination; in other places in Texas with high Hispanic populations migrants from South Texas found themselves discriminated against. Alma Canales and her family migrated north in the late 1950s to help with the massive cotton harvest in the Texas Panhandle. In fact, Canales remembered this being the first moment in her childhood when she became aware of segregation. Canales and her family lived in a little house on their employer's farm, going into town to purchase supplies on the weekends. There, she claimed, was where she noted her first "no Mexicans allowed" sign. When the family wanted to see a movie, they could go only on Tuesday nights, which the local theater dubbed Mexican night. Canales remembered it being more overt in the Panhandle; racism still existed in Edinburg, her hometown, but by the late 1950s, she argues, it had grown more subtle. "The numbers were starting to favor Mexicanos by then," she remembered. "We were starting to be a larger group of people." In her parents' generation, however, discrimination in the Valley was more blatant.[84]

For Canales, then, her formative moment in turning her into an activist was not exposure to segregation, it was the five years that she spent between the ages of twelve and seventeen as a migrant farmworker. Her family went as far north as Wisconsin. Canales remembered some of the important issues that farmworker movement activists would soon challenge during the 1960s and '70s: poor wages, lack of toilet facilities in the fields, and the necessity for the workers to eat their lunches in the open in the hot sun. Not long after, as a young adult, Canales began founding day care centers in migrant communities in Wisconsin. She hired a number of young people to run these centers, where, she remembered, they became cognizant of the possibilities of careers outside of migrant farm labor for the first time in their lives. Later, Canales dedicated herself to organizing for the workers as a part of César Chávez's activism.[85]

Canales thus sought to advocate on behalf of the working class. Her parents were not involved in organizations such as the Viva Kennedy Clubs, LULAC, or the GI Forum when Canales was in junior high and high school, in large part because those organizations had more provenance with the middle and upper classes. Canales got her first start with activism as an adult when she wrote for the school newspaper at Pan American College in Edinburg. The college president had transformed the basketball team from an all-white enterprise into an integrated one by recruiting African Americans from big cities throughout the state and country. Many Chicanos at the university were upset by this; Canales and many others believed that the university needed to put money into the baseball program—a popular sport at the local high schools—so Chicano baseball players could participate in college athletics. Upon the article's publication the president himself telephoned Canales's employer at a local media outlet. When the president threatened to expel Canales, her boss stood up for her and in turn threatened to cut off funding for a number of journalism scholarships that he supported at the school. "So that was my first inkling that, you know, money talks," Canales said. "That's power and you can bargain and you can have some kind of leverage."[86]

Canales was also in college when the Chicano Movement erupted in South Texas. Her perspective on the movement is fascinating, given the complicated contexts she later remembered in which the movement began. One night in 1967, a group of Chicano activists visited Pan American College to drum up support for the movement. Interestingly, the students who attended the gathering seemed rather split. One-half of the room argued that racism in the Lower Rio Grande Valley was not bad: "Oh, but I've never been discriminated against," they argued, "I've got some white friends and it's not that bad." The other half, however, agreed. They noted that discrimination did take place, while other systemic problems in the community—school dropout rates, teen pregnancy, crime, as well as other social ills—were the product of endemic racism and marginalization that did not affect the Anglo community to nearly the same degree. These two ways of thinking, Canales argued, had marked the Chicano Movement and continued to divide people in the same way.[87]

One can deduce from Canales's remembrances that the movement was thus never unified; a large chunk of society in South Texas, not including the Anglos, seemed completely against doing anything at all. Thus, the movement's many promises remained without full community involvement because of others who simply did not recognize that problems existed or felt threatened by the rising tide of activism sweeping the younger generation. Canales later went on to become a prominent Chicano activist and LRUP politician, serving as the party's nominee for the lieutenant governor's office in the 1972 Texas elections.[88]

Still others had different experiences in South Texas. Leo Montalvo became mayor of McAllen during the late 1990s, unseating long-term incumbent and pro-grower partisan Othal Brand, an old-school Anglo leader who used power politics and intimidation during his twenty-year stint as mayor. Montalvo was the first Hispanic mayor of the city; others also came into city politics in numerous important positions. According to Montalvo, Brand participated in patronage-style politics in the style of Anglo politicians in South Texas during the early twentieth century: "There were people in the community who, you know . . . Roberto Reyna, Fela Reyna, Lolo Gonzalez, Manuel Gonzalez that have M&T Motors, they were always strong supporters of [Brand]. And, you know, they practically worshipped the guy. And the Mexicano mentality of well, you know, we don't have any 'qualified Hispanics' to, to be mayor . . . es un complejo que tiene la raza de nosotros (it is a complex that our people have)."[89] Brand's practice of patronage politics clearly had some correlation to the old-school political bossism that Anglos had used to gain power in South Texas during the early 1900s.

Montalvo's path to politics was different from that of some of the others. Montalvo was born in a city called Caderrayta Jimenez, east of Monterrey in Nuevo León. He lived there until 1949. His father got a job working at the famous Cuahtemoc brewery in Monterrey until 1952. Eventually the family migrated north to the United States; Montalvo's sister had been born in Harlingen, which made moving across the border easier. Montalvo's father never learned to speak English; as a result, his hourly wage was only $1.25, whereas speaking English would allegedly have doubled his wage to $2.50 per hour. Like Severita Lara, though, Montalvo's family did not migrate to pick crops, which meant that he could stay in school year-round and have a better chance at excelling at academics than would his peers who were a part of migrant families.

Discrimination was a problem in the Lower Rio Grande Valley when Montalvo and his family arrived during the 1950s. For example, the Crystal Water Swimming Pool was located in the heart of a local Mexican neighborhood, but even still, ethnic Mexicans were not allowed to swim in it. McAllen had deed restrictions that determined where ethnic Mexicans could rent or buy homes. He also recalled other incidents such as being refused service at a restaurant later during the 1960s. Other problems were more systemic: Montalvo noted three Hispanic teachers in his entire high school. When he got to college at Texas A&M, Montalvo encountered a fellow student whom he was hired to tutor. The student—an Anglo from San Antonio—claimed that he was better than Montalvo because Montalvo "was a spic." The student later flunked out of college. Ironically, the subject in which Montalvo was supposed to tutor the student was English.[90]

Montalvo went on to have a political and legal career. Interestingly, running under the auspices of LRUP seemed to cost him votes during the 1970s, as many local people—Anglos and Mexican Americans alike—considered him a radical because of his association with the party. Also, locals had lost faith in the party after the arrest and incarceration of two-time gubernatorial candidate Ramsey Muñiz on drug conspiracy charges, an incident that effectively destroyed the party after 1978.[91]

Countless of the movement's participants went on to have successful careers in politics and public administration. Antonio Bill—not from South Texas but from Kerrville, in the Texas Hill Country—experienced the movement as a young man in his twenties and later went on to have a career that included being a school administrator in Alice, Texas. Unlike a number of the others, Bill became aware of discrimination as a young schoolboy, such as when Anglo children would call him derogatory names, such as "greaser," and challenge him to fights. One point of pride for Bill as a young man was enrolling at Texas A&I University in Kingsville. Upon arriving as a freshman, Bill noticed Chicanos everywhere: "Once I stepped on campus and . . . I went to registration . . . that is probably one of the, the proudest moments that I've, that I had as, as far as my academic life is concerned. Because I saw so many Mexicanos registering. . . . Out of a class of a hundred and forty-eight, there were fifteen of us that graduated and I was the only one that following semester that went to college, and yet there was a line that nearly curled around . . . that old administration building in Kingsville lleno de puros Mexicanos (full of Mexicans). It was mostly Chicanos."[92]

Bill became so enthusiastic and hopeful about his education that he finally found his voice and began to speak up in class. Thus, the college experience helped broaden his horizons. From there, he met José Ángel Gutiérrez, who helped get him involved with PASSO. What really inspired Bill, however, was moving to Alice. In 1970, roughly 68 percent of the students in the Alice school district were Chicanos; 13 percent of the teachers were also Chicanos. Bill then recognized certain systemic problems that needed fixing. Internalizing racial epithets and discrimination made no sense to him.

Bill also noticed that his experiences as a young man set him on a path toward activism—that it became a way of life. Nevertheless, for Bill, certain organizations that had been active previously were less effective during the late twentieth century than they had been before. LULAC and the GI Forum were no longer effective; these organizations, according to Bill, were sort of old school and no longer spoke to issues that were important to Hispanics during the late twentieth century. The Mexican American Legal Defense Fund (MALDEF) still sought to correct wrongs done to Chicanos through the legal system, which, to Bill, was one of the most effective approaches.[93]

Interestingly, Bill argued that there was little of a cooperative coexistence between Tejanos and Mexican immigrants. In fact, Bill argued that Mexican immigrants were "kicking our butts," meaning that they worked harder, did not live in public housing, and were more industrious than the native-born Chicano population in Alice. Problems, however, kept what might be termed the large Hispanic or Latin American community from working as a cohesive unit. Nevertheless, different issues and personality conflicts kept Mexicans, Chicanos, Central Americans, and people from the Caribbean from working together as a cohesive unit. Even when the unemployment level went up, Bill claimed, Mexican immigrants in South Texas always found a way to work: mowing yards, washing dishes, or cleaning houses. That willingness to work hard and do whatever it took to maximize one's experiences in the United States was something that definitely set Mexican immigrants apart from other groups, making an organized cohesion difficult.

People thus became dedicated to bettering their lives in South Texas in a more forceful way during the 1960s and '70s. Materially, little changed, as the regional economy remained marginalized or, in the case of Crystal City and the Winter Garden district, became worse after Anglo businessmen left following the Chicano uprising. Nevertheless, Chicanos had negotiated for themselves a more forceful presence in local society as well as a voice that Anglos in South Texas could no longer ignore. This intellectual and social victory came in response to years of marginalization and repression in colonized South Texas.

A paradigmatic shift occurred for the people, one that would influence the lives of countless numbers of people in the region for many years to come.

Had Chicanos retaken a key part of Aztlán, the mythical Aztec and Chicano homeland? In point of fact, they had. South Texas—long colonized by Anglo-Americans by the 1960s—had become forever changed with the rise of radical activism. Also, South Texas, with its own unique cultural traits, has been established by some scholars as the Tejano homeland. For better or worse, according to some Chicanos, Anglo power brokers—some of whom could trace their heritage back to the first Anglo entrants to the region in the late nineteenth and early twentieth centuries—no longer dominated society. A new day had dawned. Colonialism's legacy in the South Texas borderlands, however, lived on.[94]

Conclusion

Chicanos were an occupied people.

—RODOLFO ACUÑA[1]

Few things survived the middle of the twentieth century unchanged in South Texas. Labor and Chicano Movement activists of the 1960s and '70s left an indelible imprint on society. Many of the worst aspects of the racial regime put in place to grease the wheels of Anglo-dominated agricultural colonialism were finally rolled back: public segregation, discrimination, political oppression, and the lack of regard for Mexican culture, to name a few. All of this nefariousness, however, was the by-product of the primary element that attracted Anglo-American colonists in the first place—the US-Mexico border's wide-open maw of cheap and exploitable labor.

Texas citrus also declined in influence after the tumult of the mid-twentieth century in the South Texas borderlands. By 1959 there were about 5.5 million orange and grapefruit trees on over four thousand South Texas farms. For the vast majority of small South Texas citrus growers—many of whom could trace their roots in the region back to the initial colonization movement during the 1910s and '20s—the dream of a citrus empire was over. Massive fluctuations in the industry's ability to produce a viable crop further ensured that only the largest corporate producers could flourish; production and prices varied widely from harvest to harvest throughout the 1970s and '80s. Numerous freezes during the 1980s, like ones in the 1940s, practically destroyed the industry. In the 1991–92 season, growers produced a grand total of fewer than one hundred thousand boxes of oranges and grapefruits, a number far lower than the millions produced per season at the industry's peak during the mid-twentieth century. The industry's production would continue to be limited through the 1990s and early 2000s.[2]

But it was the growers and federal government themselves who, in the words of one scholar, kept the South Texas internal colony alive by recruiting migrant labor, which sustained the localized system of oppression and helped foster a "reactive solidarity among ethnic Mexicans." Poverty in the region worsened during the 1970s, the last decade that this study covers, to the point that by 1980 the poverty rates for ethnic Mexicans in the Lower Rio Grande Valley were twice as high as they were for ethnic Mexicans nationwide.[3]

The high tide of Anglo-American colonization in South Texas is now far in the past. Anglos had pockets of demographic majorities earlier in the century, as this study has shown. Demographically, the population has once again returned to a vast Hispanic majority, ranging from 87 percent to 95 percent across the region in 2008. Also, the region continues to be plagued by low levels of education and income. In 2008 the median household income in the Lower Rio Grande Valley, for example, was about $29,000 per year. That same year, the median household incomes in Texas and in the larger United States were $48,078 and $52,175, respectively. About 50 percent to 60 percent of adults twenty-five years of age or older had completed high school, compared to an average of roughly 80 percent of adults nationwide. Finally, the poor income levels in South Texas bear a direct relationship to the percentage of local society that is foreign-born. In the larger United States, where income levels are higher, about 12.5 percent of society in 2008 was foreign-born. The percentage of foreign-born people in South Texas was about twice that in most counties of the state, hovering around 25 percent of the population. Statistics like these make it easy to conclude that a number of the Latin American–born population continue to work in the low-income jobs that ethnic Mexicans found themselves in when the farming revolution took shape nearly a century ago.[4]

One other phenomenon that has made life in South Texas unique is the persistence of informal and underground economic networks. Michael J. Pisani and Chad Richardson, in their fascinating book *The Informal and Underground Economy of the South Texas Border,* argue that such economic exchange has been a fact of life in South Texas since the drawing of the international borderline. These activities range from the illegal—for example, nineteenth-century activities such as horse theft and modern activities such as transborder drug or weapons smuggling—to informal economic activities, which means private citizens avoiding government regulation but not necessarily breaking major laws. Statistics such as these in part indicate that extralegal economic exchange will always be part of life along any modern international border. Part of this, for whites and ethnic Mexicans alike, is driven by the desire for competitive economic advantage. But, given the persistence of poverty in South Texas over the course of the twentieth century, informal and illegal economic activities are also driven by need, which for more than a century has been felt by the region's impoverished ethnic Mexicans.[5]

Organizers seem to have realized that striking at the heart of agricultural South Texas—its racialized labor caste—is a losing battle. Therefore, since the 1970s many of the traditional farmworker unions have changed their focuses. Although the smaller Texas Farm Workers Union no longer exists, the United Farm Workers founded an organization in South Texas after its aborted efforts in the 1967 Starr County melon strike discussed in chapter 6. The organization, which is called *La Union del Pueblo Entero* (LUPE), is a "non-profit organization that focuses on community-based organizing, self-development, and civic engagement of members." Indeed, the frustration felt within the ranks of the UFW at the failed attempt at taking on the growers—due to the growers' ability to manipulate the porous border as an unending supply of cheap labor—no doubt led to the exploration of other options. LUPE, then, by focusing its efforts on assistance to the region's poor instead of making certain gains for farmworkers, can improve the lives of the region's people without being as direct a threat to the region's growers and agribusinesses.[6]

What, then, does all this mean? South Texas's colonization by white Americans had a specific point: farmers came down to the border because they, allegedly, could lead fulfilling and independent lives as commercial growers on Mexico's doorstep in what was, essentially, a foreign space. As this book has shown, the whole system's underpinning rested on racialized labor. Without it, there would have been no reason for commercial farmers to come to the region at all, as the farming project likely would not have been profitable. Subsequently, without the arrival of the commercial farmers, ethnic Mexican communities might never have faced the damning consequences of Anglo colonization in the South Texas borderlands. Late-twentieth-century organizers fully understood that growers—really, the entire economic system of South Texas commercial farming—stood to lose too much by relaxing their collective iron grip on impoverished ethnic Mexican workers. Instead, then, the organizers turned their attention toward what were in reality the nastiest by-products of local colonialism: segregation, discrimination, and, in general, the racial oppression that permeated the region.

Perhaps the saddest part of the story is that South Texas remains a place that can most aptly be characterized as an internal colony of the larger United States. Agriculture, once the dominant economic sector in the region, faded in importance through the second half of the twentieth century. Sociologist Robert Lee Maril noted in 1989 that 10 percent of all jobs in the Lower Rio Grande Valley were devoted to agriculture. This number had dropped from about 33 percent in 1960. Naturally, this decrease took place primarily because of modern economic development in the region. Nevertheless, given the fact that crippling poverty persists throughout South Texas, it is apparent that the system of vastly underpaying the wage labor force has persisted in the industries that have arrived in the region since the 1960s. By the late 1980s, Maril continued, the Valley was still very much a colonized space: "The Lower Rio Grande is very rich in resources even as its people are among the poorest in the United States. In part this is because the regional economy is premised upon poverty. It is poverty which shapes and drives the Valley's economy. Agriculture, manufacturing, tourism, each new industrial sector has been grafted on the existing economic arrangements between rich and poor and helped to strengthen those superior-subordinate relationships. In many ways, the Valley resembles an internal economic colony. The majority of the Valley's resources are exported out of the Valley and to the interior of this country."[7]

As Maril astutely points out, colonialism itself persists in the Valley beyond simply leaving some kind of historical legacy after the rise of social justice movements in the 1960s and '70s. Aside from Maril's observations, it is worth adding that this phenomenon is not limited to the Valley. The large-scale movement of *maquiladoras* as well as other manufacturing firms seeking to take advantage of cheap labor in the larger Texas-Mexico borderlands bespeaks a region-wide borderlands phenomenon not limited to one part of South Texas (or even to the northern banks of the Rio Grande).

Regional factors aside, macro-level factors must also be taken into account when considering the persistence of colonialism in South Texas. As this study has shown, the primary reason that South Texas commercial farming has had any success at all is because of its propinquity to the nearby border. Industrial development in the United States since the late nineteenth century compared to the patchy economic modernization of northern Mexico does much to explain why the problems in South Texas still exist. An international power discrepancy is at play along the US-Mexico border. As at the micro-level, statistics bear out this problem. At the end of the century the percentage of families living in poverty in South Texas totaled 23.2 percent, compared to the next poorest region (the Mississippi Delta) at 18.4 percent and the national average of 9.2 percent. Colonization and racial marginalization alone cannot fully account for this; conversely, Anglo commercial farmers in the early twentieth century knew full well that they could take advantage of a region inside of the nation's borders that had, essentially, the problems of a third-world country: poverty and want. Fortunately for some white Americans, the international border had been drawn over part of a region that historically, culturally, and politically belonged to Mexico.[8]

One might ask: How can it be said that colonialism persists in South Texas when younger generations enjoy better opportunities and more upward mobility than before? Although this is, of course, a reality, the historical trajectory of internally colonized spaces like South Texas differs markedly from the standard (and, in many cases, erroneous), straight-line trajectory of assimilation of latter-generation immigrants. If younger generations of ethnic Mexicans are enjoying greater mobility than their parents and grandparents, taxable income from upwardly mobile South Texas is certainly not to be given credit. The average revenue available to educate public school students as recently as 1998 was a paltry $4,341 per student, compared to school districts elsewhere in the state that average two or three times that amount. Statistics like this might also indicate a relative brain drain of educated and upwardly mobile South Texans leaving the region once a certain amount of success is achieved.[9]

The sheer will and ingenuity of the region's people is the direct cause of upward mobility. Part of this can be seen in the way that many people in South Texas earn their incomes. If necessity is the mother of invention, then South Texans have responded en masse. Chad Richardson and Michael J. Pisani recognize that South Texas is an area of the United States where economic informality—meaning the unreported exchange of legal goods, services, and wage work—alongside the underground economy is a significant factor in the regional economy. Part of this, as the authors note, stems from the prevalence of informality in Mexican society. Basic living situations in South Texas show that informality may even be more extensive now than ever before. Thousands of ethnic Mexicans in South Texas live in *colonias*, which are off-the-grid, informal communities that often lack basic amenities such as electricity, paved roads, and running water. One could easily take the owners of said plots to task for renting inadequate housing to poor people and immigrants, but without such informality in housing some of these same people might face homelessness. Informality in housing again speaks to the ingenuity of people living in a society with a structural bias toward keeping a large portion of society impoverished (much like Anglo South Texans kept ethnic Mexicans impoverished in the 1910s and '20s).[10]

Although colonialism persists in South Texas, life in the region is better now in two respects: first, racism is less vicious than it was earlier in the twentieth century, and second, the region's people enjoy much better opportunities than before. Richardson and Pisani recount the story of a man named Juan

José Flores, who crossed the border illegally as a farmworker some fifty years ago and later became a US citizen. In the course of his labor, Flores became subject to what some might consider typical anti-Mexican racist insults: being paid only eighty cents per hour after having been promised a dollar per hour, being called "a spic," "a dirty wetback," and other names that were apparently too offensive for him to repeat. The people hurling these insults at Flores were more often than not his bosses. Notably, Richardson and Pisani completed a number of other interviews with undocumented workers in their 2012 study, and most of their subjects reported having experienced less abuse than Flores did. Richardson and Pisani also rightly note that while Flores's treatment is reprehensible, it is not nearly as bad as the experiences of ethnic Mexicans in South Texas fifty or one hundred years previously, who could be beaten, tortured, or shot simply because of the color of their skin.[11]

Finally, the small chunk of South Texas covered in this story is at the heart of what geographer Daniel D. Arreola describes as the "Texas Mexican Homeland," an area stretching from Del Rio to Brownsville that contains one of the most concentrated populations of Mexican Americans and ethnic Mexicans in the US Southwest. Also, Arreola would note, the area is a place that is culturally distinct from other parts of the country with high Mexican American populations. Historically, white Americans from outside the region have treated this stretch of US territory as if it were a foreign space, colonizing it and taking advantage of it in the same way that many imperially minded white Americans sought to do overseas in the early twentieth century when the United States became a world power. As such, places like the Lower Rio Grande Valley and the Winter Garden District of South Texas will always seem foreign to many white Americans who are not from the region. The struggle to define place, citizenship, and belonging—such a long one in South Texas—continues for many. These issues have marked the Texas Mexican experience since the mid-nineteenth century. Colonialism has long reigned supreme throughout all aspects of what might be termed the broader narrative of South Texas borderlands history since 1848.[12]

As border fences, surveillance technology, and armed Border Patrol guards today continue to invade South Texas, it becomes quite clear that the US government's continued militarization of this borderlands space emphasizes the government's self-perceived inability to exert strong control over this stretch of territory. Despite the continued improvements in economic well-being and opportunities for South Texas Mexicans (as well as the above-mentioned improvements in race relations throughout the region), it is evident that the federal government, with the backing of many Americans, still views this region as dangerous and hostile territory. The current bipartisan clamoring about securing the border is sad evidence of the fact that most Americans fail to see the many problems that South Texans face on a daily basis, all of which can be boiled down to the persistence of abject poverty in this long marginalized and exploited space. For many Americans, South Texas remains a foreign space, one to be controlled by fences, armed men, and border patrols. For them, these are the solutions that the problems in borderlands spaces such as South Texas present to the nation on a daily basis.

NOTES

Introduction

1. Leroy P. Graf, "The Economic History of the Lower Rio Grande Valley, 1820–1875" (PhD diss., Harvard University, 1942), 436.

2. Carrol Norquest, *Rio Grande Wetbacks: Mexican Migrant Workers*, 107–8.

3. Ibid., 108. Norquest actually referred to the two men as Border Patrol agents, which is probably inaccurate. Norquest arrived in the Valley in 1922, but the US government did not establish the Border Patrol until May of 1924. For more information, see Kelly Lytle Hernández, *Migra! A History of the US Border Patrol*, 2.

4. For a lengthier discussion on the book's theoretical underpinnings, see Timothy Paul Bowman, "Negotiating Conquest: Internal Colonialism and Shared Histories in the South Texas Borderlands," *Western Historical Quarterly* 46 (Autumn 2015): 335–53.

5. Anthony Smith quoted in Tatiana Zhurzhenko, "Borders and Memory," in *The Ashgate Research Companion to Border Studies*, ed. Doris Wastl-Walter, 72; Alexander Diener, "The Borderland Existence of the Mongolian Kazakhs," in *Ashgate Research Companion*, 375; Anssi Passi, "A Border Theory: An Unattainable Dream or a Realistic Aim for Border Scholars?" in *Ashgate Research Companion*, 14. For more on Chicano views of the greater North American Southwest, see John Chávez, *The Lost Land: The Chicano Image of the Southwest*.

6. Daniel D. Arreola, *Tejano South Texas: A Mexican Cultural Province*, 58–62; Alicia Dewey, *Pesos and Dollars: Entrepreneurs in the Texas-Mexico Borderlands, 1880–1940*, 29; and Cynthia E. Orozco, *No Mexicans, Women, or Dogs Allowed: The Rise of the Mexican American Civil Rights Movement*, 38.

7. Quote from John R. Chávez, "Aliens in Their Native Lands: The Persistence of Internal Colonial Theory," *Journal of World History* 22, no. 4 (December 2011): 785–809. See also John R. Chávez, *Beyond Nations: Evolving Homelands in the North Atlantic World, 1400–2000*, 10n14; Matthew Frye Jacobson, *Barbarian Virtues: The United States Encounters Foreign Peoples at Home and Abroad, 1876–1917*, 221–65; Bill Belich, *Replenishing the Earth: The Settler Revolution and the Rise of the Angloworld*.

8. Robert J. Hind, "The Internal Colonial Concept," *Comparative Studies in Society and History* 26, no. 3 (July 1984): 564; Steven Sabol, "Comparing American and Russian Internal Colonization: The 'Touch of Civilisation' on the Sioux and Kazakhs," *Western Historical Quarterly* 43, no. 1 (Spring 2012): 29–51.

9. Chávez, *Beyond Nations*, 163, 164–65, 166; John R. Chávez, "When Borders Cross People: The Internal Colonial Challenge to Borderlands Theory," *Journal of Borderlands Studies* 28, no. 1 (June 2013): 33–46.

10. Gilbert González, *Culture of Empire: American Writers, Mexico, and Mexican Immigrants, 1880–1930*, 15–16, 19, 67–69.

Historian John Chávez coined the term *colonial paradigm*. Concerning internal colonialism's place in the paradigm, Chávez writes, "Internal colonialism is the domestic subset of a larger colonial (or imperial) paradigm," which includes "formal colonialism, neocolonialism, postcolonialism, borderlands theory, and postnationalism." Chávez also argues that the larger colonial paradigm can be used to explain "broader relationships of ethnic inequality across history and geography." For more information, see Chávez, "Aliens in Their Native Lands." My application of internal colonialism to South Texas highlights the important role that international borders play in creating internal colonies.

11. For more more on these critiques, see Hind, "Internal Colonial Concept," 553. For more on colonialism and Chicano history, see Fred A. Cervantes, "Chicanos as a Postcolonial Minority: Some Questions Concerning the Adequacy of the Paradigm of Internal Colonialism," in *Latino/a Thought: Culture, Politics, and Society*, ed. Francisco H. Vázquez and Rodolfo D. Torres, 331–42.

12. The four stages in the Texas-Mexico borderlands' colonization are not static, nor do they include the entirety of the Texas side of the border. Certain aspects of demographic, economic, or military colonization might overlap with other phenomena in Anglo Americans' drive to colonize South Texas.

13. I am not the first historian to apply the larger concept of colonialism to twentieth-century South Texas. Historian Trinidad Gonzales briefly describes the region as still undergoing colonization between 1900 and 1930. For more, see Trinidad Gonzales, "The Mexican Revolution, *Revolución de Texas*, and *Matanza de 1915*," in *War along the Border: The Mexican Revolution and Tejano Communities*, ed. Arnoldo de León, 110, 126. Gonzales does not specifically advocate, however, for the internal colonial model. Historian Linda Gordon makes a compelling case for the applicability of the internal colonial model to the Arizona mining community of Clifton-Morenci in the early twentieth century. She argues that parallels between Anglo-Mexican relations in that town and foreign colonial societies in India, Cuba, South Africa, and Algeria are apparent. For more information, see Linda Gordon, *The Great Arizona Orphan Abduction*, 178–85.

14. Growers in other parts of the United States, however, did not always follow the model of South Texas labor relations. Historian Jim Norris argues that farmers in the Red River Valley of Minnesota and North Dakota consciously treated their workers better than South Texas growers treated migrants, although the relationship was still paternalistic. Many workers fled to the Red River Valley to escape the harsh conditions on South Texas farms. For more information, see Jim Norris, *North for the Harvest: Mexican Workers, Growers, and the Sugar Beet Industry*, 87–111.

15. See, for example, Lawrence Herzog, *Where North Meets South: Cities, Space, and Politics on the US-Mexico Border*.

16. D. W. Meinig, *Imperial Texas: An Interpretive Essay in Cultural Geography*, 100. Historian Cynthia E. Orozco argues that all inhabitants of the region since the time of the US-Mexico War self-identified as Mexicans, with very few taking any pride in or claiming an American part of their identities. For more information, see Orozco, *No Mexicans*, 19. Thus, it was easy for new Anglo arrivals to ascribe to local Mexicans a "native" status in the region.

17. Terry H. Anderson, *The Movement and the Sixties: Protest in America from Greensboro to Wounded Knee*, 301.

18. Rodolfo A. Acuña, *Occupied America: A History of Chicanos*, 5th ed., 61; Arnoldo de León, *They Called Them Greasers: Anglo Attitudes toward Mexicans in Texas, 1821–1900*; Arnoldo De León, *The Tejano Community*. For examples of Anglocentric works, see Dorothy Lee Pope, *Rainbow Era of the Rio Grande*; Lee J. Stambaugh and Lillian J. Stambaugh, *The Lower Rio Grande Valley of Texas*; and William Ransom Hogan, *The Texas Republic: A Social and Economic History*.

19. David Montejano, *Anglos and Mexicans in the Making of Texas, 1836–1986*, 3. For an excellent study of racial identity in other parts of the state, see Neil Foley, *The White Scourge: Mexicans, Blacks, and Poor Whites in the Texas Cotton Culture*.

20. James Sandos, *Rebellion in the Borderlands: Anarchism and the Plan of San Diego, 1904–1923*; Benjamin H. Johnson, *Revolution in Texas: How a Forgotten Rebellion and Its Bloody Suppression Turned Mexicans into Americans*. See also Elliot Young, *Catarino Garza's Revolution on the Texas-Mexico Border*, and Jerry D. Thompson, *Cortina: Defending the Mexican Name in Texas*.

Numerous scholars have examined various aspects of life in the South Texas borderlands for ethnic Mexicans—such as Mexican culture, poverty, or ranch life—while other scholars have examined particular aspects of Mexican and Mexican Americans as migratory farm workers and wage-earners in the region. See, for example, Robert Lee Maril, *Poorest of Americans: The Mexican-Americans of the Lower Rio Grande Valley of Texas*; Arreola, *Tejano South Texas*; Armando C. Alonzo, *Tejano Legacy: Rancheros and Settlers in South Texas*; and Andrés Tijerina, *Tejano Empire: Life on the South Texas Ranchos*. For works that touch on the Lower Rio Grande Valley, see Juan Gómez-Quiñones, *Mexican-American Labor, 1790–1990*; Emilio Zamora, "Mexican Labor Activity in South Texas" (PhD diss., University of Texas at Austin, 1983); Emilio Zamora, *The World of the Mexican Worker in Texas*; John Mason Hart, ed., *Border Crossings: Mexican and Mexican-American Workers*; Miguel Antonio Levario, *Militarizing the Border: When Mexicans Became the Enemy*; and Omar S. Valerio-Jiménez, *River of Hope: Forging Identity and Nation in the Rio Grande Borderlands*.

21. For recent works on California citrus, see Douglas C. Sackman, *Orange Empire: California and the Fruits of Eden*; Matt Garcia, *A World of Its Own: Race, Labor, and Citrus in the Making of Greater Los Angeles, 1900–1970*; José Alamillo, "Bitter-Sweet Communities: Mexican Workers and Citrus Growers on the California Landscape" (PhD diss., University of California, Irvine, 2000); Gilbert González, *Labor and Community: Mexican Citrus Worker Villages in a Southern California County, 1900–1950*; Anthea Hartig, "'In a World He Has Created:' Class Collectivity and the Growers' Landscape of the

Southern California Citrus Industry, 1890–1940," *California History* 74, no. 2 (Summer 1995): 100–111; Anthea Hartig and Margo McBane, "Oranges on the Plains of Id: The Influences of the Citrus Industry on San Gabriel Valley Communities," *California Politics and Policy*, 1998, 9–17; Vincent Moses, "The Flying Wedge of Cooperation: G. Harold Powell, California Orange Growers, and the Corporate Reconstruction of American Agriculture" (PhD diss., University of California, Riverside, 1994).

Chapter 1

1. Luis Alberto Urrea, *Nobody's Son: Notes from an American Life*, 16 (emphasis in the original).

2. David M. Vigness and Mark Ordintz, "Rio Grande Valley," Handbook of Texas Online, https://tshaonline.org/handbook/online/articles/ryro1, published by the Texas State Historical Association; Jeremy Adelman and Stephen Aron, "From Borderlands to Borders: Empires, Nation-States, and the Peoples In Between in North American History," *American Historical Review* 104, no. 3 (June 1999): 814–41.

3. Andrés Reséndez, *A Land So Strange: The Epic Journey of Cabeza de Vaca*, 179.

4. Ibid., 181–82; Edwin J. Foscue, "Agricultural Geography of the Lower Rio Grande Valley of Texas" (PhD diss., Clark University, 1931), 9.

5. See, for example, David J. Weber, *The Spanish Frontier in North America*, 194–95, and Pekka Hämäläinen, *The Comanche Empire*, 353–54. For more information on Indian-Spanish interaction in eighteenth-century Texas, see Juliana Barr, *Peace Came in the Form of a Woman: Indians and Spaniards in the Texas Borderlands*.

6. Mary Margaret McAllen-Amberson, James A. McAllen, and Margaret H. McAllen, *I Would Rather Sleep in Texas: A History of the Lower Rio Grande Valley and the People of the Santa Anita Land Grant*, 28; McAllen-Amberson, McAllen, and McAllen, *I Would Rather Sleep in Texas*, 30; Weber, *Spanish Frontier*, 194; Graf, "Economic History," 107.

Unlike McAllen-Amberson, geographer Edwin J. Foscue reports much violence between Indians and Spaniards in the years preceding the colony's founding. The Spaniards' movement into the region represented a clear expansion of settler colonialism, as families of colonists planted firmer roots there than in Texas, which maintained the character of a defensive military outpost. Still, part of the reason for settling Nuevo Santander was similar to the establishment of the mission system and presidios in Texas: to fortify the region against expansion from other European imperial powers. For more information, see Foscue, "Agricultural Geography," 10–21. For more information on Escandón and Nuevo Santander's establishment in general, see Patricia Osante, *Origenes del Nuevo Santander, 1748–1772*, and Jovita González, *Life Along the Border: A Landmark Tejana Thesis*, ed. María Eugenia Cotera, 48.

7. Gregg Cantrell, *Stephen F. Austin: Empresario of Texas*, 299.

8. Andrés Reséndez, *Changing National Identities at the Frontier: Texas and New Mexico, 1800–1850*, 37–45; David J. Weber, *The Mexican Frontier, 1821–1846: The American Southwest Under Mexico*, 245–51.

9. Raúl Ramos, *Beyond the Alamo: Forging Mexican Ethnicity in San Antonio, 1821–1861*, 168–204; James Crisp, *Sleuthing the Alamo: Davy Crockett's Last Stand and Other Mysteries of the Texas Revolution*, 43; William D. Carrigan, *The Making of a Lynching Culture: Violence and Vigilantism in Central Texas, 1836–1916*, 24–29.

10. Graf, "Economic History," 136–139; Hämäläinen, *Comanche Empire*.

11. Historian Brian DeLay writes that scholars who have argued that the rebellion's ultimate goal was to establish a Republic of the Rio Grande have based their assumptions on various Texan sources that mistakenly spoke of the republic as if it were on the verge of becoming a reality. DeLay argues that the rebellion's leaders had never hoped to establish an independent republic. For more information, see Brian DeLay, *War of a Thousand Deserts: Indian Raids and the US-Mexican War*, 383n57. For more information on this often overlooked rebellion, see David M. Vigness, "The Republic of the Rio Grande: An Example of Separatism in Northern Mexico" (PhD diss., University of Texas, 1951); Joseph Milton Nance, *After San Jacinto: The Texas-Mexican Frontier, 1836–1841*, 252–315; Josefina Zoraida Vázquez, "La Supuesta República del Río Grande," *Historia Mexicana* 36 (1986): 49–80; Vito Alessio Robles, *Coahuila y Texas: Desde la consumación de la independencia hasta el tratado de paz de Guadalupe Hidalgo*; and Joseph B. Ridout, "An Anti-National Disorder: Antonio Canales and Northeastern Mexico, 1836–1852" (master's thesis, University of Texas at Austin, 1994).

12. Johnson, *Revolution in Texas*, 13; David J. Weber, ed., *Foreigners in Their Native Land: Historical Roots of the Mexican Americans*. For some interesting examinations of manifest destiny and its many meanings, see Sam W. Haynes and Christopher Morris, eds., *Manifest Destiny and Empire: American Antebellum Expansionism*, and Amy S. Greenberg, *Manifest Manhood and the Antebellum American Empire*.

13. Mario Barrera, *Race and Class in the Southwest: A Theory of Racial Inequality*, 82. For an explanation of the deep-rooted links between people on both sides of the border that persisted despite the establishment of the modern borderline, see, Meinig, *Imperial Texas*, 100.

14. González, *Culture of Empire*, 15–45. González ignores the Treaty of Guadalupe Hidalgo in 1848, which helped open Mexico to American interests.

15. Montejano, *Anglos and Mexicans*, 31. This source does not differentiate between ethnic Mexicans and Mexican Americans in the region.

16. Alonzo, *Tejano Legacy*, 162; Montejano, *Anglos and Mexicans*, 37; Johnson, *Revolution in Texas*, 13. This level of cross-cultural interaction and cooperation dissipated sharply after the coming of the commercial farmers in the early twentieth century. For more information, see González, *Life Along the Border*, 8–9.

17. Maril, *Poorest of Americans*, 33; Katherine Benton-Cohen, *Borderline Americans: Racial Division and Labor War in the Arizona Borderlands*, 21, 36–37, 169; Richard White, *The Middle Ground: Indians, Empires, and Republics in the Great Lakes Region, 1650–1815*, x.

18. Frederick Law Olmstead, *A Journey through Texas: or, A Saddle-Trip on the Southwestern Frontier*, ed. Randolph B. Campbell, 107.

19. De León, *They Called Them Greasers*, ix, 5–6. For a good recent summary of

Anglo mistreatment of Mexicans in Texas from 1848 into the twentieth century, see William D. Carrigan and Clive Webb, *Forgotten Dead: Mob Violence against Mexicans in the United States, 1848–1928*, 44–50.

20. Daniel Baker and William M. Baker, *The Life and Labours of the Rev. Daniel Baker, D.D.: Pastor and Evangelist*, 401–2, 405.

21. Melinda Rankin, *Twenty Years among the Mexicans: A Narrative of Missionary Labor*, ed. Miguel Ángel González-Quiroga and Timothy Paul Bowman, 25–26, 29.

22. Saúl Tijerina González, *Huellas imborrables: Historia de la Iglesia Nacional Presbiteriana*, 22–23; Tomás Martin Westrup, *Principios: Relato de la introducción del Evangelio en México*, ed. Enrique Tomás Westrup, 1–37; Mary Martina Rakow, "Melinda Rankin and Magdalen Hayden: Evangelical and Catholic Forms of Nineteenth Century Christian Spirituality" (PhD diss., Boston College, 1982), 197; Rankin, *Twenty Years among the Mexicans*, 125; William Butler, *Mexico in Transition from the Power of Political Romanism to Civil and Religious Liberty*, 301. For more information on repatriation and Mexico's attempt to secure its northern border, see José Ángel Hernández, *Mexican American Colonization during the Nineteenth Century: A History of the US-Mexico Borderlands*.

23. Johnson, *Revolution in Texas*, 23–25; Thompson, *Cortina*; Graf, "Economic History," 378; Valerio-Jiménez, *River of Hope*, 222–74.

24. De León, *They Called Them Greasers*, 88; Andrew Graybill, *Policing the Great Plains: Rangers, Mounties, and the North American Frontier, 1875–1910*, 61, 63.

25. *Informes que en cumplimiento del decreto de 2 de Octubre de 1872 rinde al ejecutivo de la unión la Comisión Pesquisidora de la Frontera del Norte, sobre el desempeño de sus trabajos.*, 12, published in English translation as *Reports of the Committee of Investigation Sent in 1873 by the Mexican Government to the Frontier of Texas* (New York: Baker & Godwin, 1875).

26. Young, *Catarino Garza's Revolution*; Johnson, *Revolution in Texas*, 25–26; Rob Johnson, *The Lost Years of William S. Burroughs: Beats in South Texas*, 125–26.

27. J. L. Allhands, *Gringo Builders*, 268–69.

28. Frank C. Pierce, *A Brief History of the Lower Rio Grande Valley*, preface, 107–15.

29. Montejano, *Anglos and Mexicans*, 82; Foscue, "Agricultural Geography," 37–38; Robert H. Wiebe, *The Search for Order, 1877–1920*, 1–43.

30. Montejano, *Anglos and Mexicans*, 107, 170; Johnson, *Revolution in Texas*, 27. See also Mark Wyman, *Hoboes: Bindlestiffs, Fruit Tramps, and the Harvesting of the West*, 9. Boosters in the US West often portrayed railroads' arrivals in various towns and cities as epoch-changing events. For example, historian Karl Jacoby writes that boosters in Tucson, Arizona, commented extensively on the significance of the transcontinental railroad's arrival in that town in 1880. For more information, see Karl Jacoby, *Shadows at Dawn: A Borderlands Massacre and the Violence of History*, 232–33, and David M. Wrobel, *Promised Lands: Promotion, Memory, and the Creation of the American West*. For more on the general history of the railroad in the US West, see Richard White, *Railroaded: The Transcontinentals and the Making of Modern America*.

31. Allhands, *Gringo Builders*, 11–12; J. L. Allhands, "Lott, Uriah," Handbook of Texas

Online, https://tshaonline.org/handbook/online/articles/fl024, and Mary M. Oroz-co-Vallejo, "Yoakum, Benjamin Franklin," Handbook of Texas Online, https://tshaon line.org/handbook/online/articles/fyo01, Crystal Sasse Ragsdale, "Kleberg, Robert Justice," Handbook of Texas Online, https://tshaonline.org/handbook/online/arti cles/fk106; Frank Wagner, "Driscoll, Robert, Jr.," Handbook of Texas Online, https:// tshaonline.org/handbook/online/articles/fdro5; Cynthia E. Orozco, "Kenedy, Petra Vela de Vidal," Handbook of Texas Online, https://tshaonline.org/handbook/online/ articles/fkerl; Evan Anders, "Wells, James Babbage, Jr.," Handbook of Texas Online, https://tshaonline.org/handbook/online/articles/fwe22; and John A. Cypher Jr., "Kle berg, Caesar," Handbook of Texas Online, https://tshaonline.org/handbook/online/ articles/fk116, all published by the Texas State Historical Association ; Allhands, *Gringo Builders*, 12.

32. Johnson, *Revolution in Texas*, 27–28.

33. Ibid., 86; Van Chandler, "A School . . . Is Born," *Kingsville Record*, October 6, 1954, 7D, box 42, Newspaper Collection, South Texas Archives, Texas A&M Univer-sity–Kingsville. Kingsville is north of the Valley.

King's school mirrored the hopes of Anglo Americans in "Americanizing" or "lift-ing up" Mexicans in South Texas as well as south of the border. Historian Gilbert G. González argues that many Anglos held similar designs for Americanizing Mexicans on both sides of the border. For more information, see González, *Culture of Empire*, 10. Americanizing Mexican children through education had a long history in South Texas prior to the establishment of King's school. The famous Mexican American activist J. T. Canales recalled learning from Mrs. Pennybacker's Texas history school-book in the 1880s that, while Anglo Americans were the heroes of Texas independen-dence, Mexicans "were painted as traitors, bandits, and an altogether inferior race. . . . [Pennybacker] never mentioned any single good quality on the Mexican character." Anglos, thus, expected ethnic Mexican students to take on the alleged superior quali-ties of the Anglo-American character. See J. T. Canales to Clarence R. Wharton, June 12, 1935, Law Papers 435.3, box 435, J. T. Canales Papers, Jernigan Library, Texas A&M University–Kingsville.

34. Allhands, Gringo Builders, 12.

35. Quoted in ibid., 165.

36. Pierce, *Brief History*, 128–32. Although technically north of the Valley, Kings-ville served as an important gateway into the Valley and Deep South Texas and is thus included in this table. The uncertainty about the date of the founding of Edinburg and La Feria stems from Pierce's original text, although other sources confirm that both towns were founded in 1908. Edinburg is not to be confused with the Hidalgo County town of Edinburgh, which was founded earlier and later changed its name to Hidalgo. For more, see McAllen-Amberson, McAllen, and McAllen, *I Would Rather Sleep in Texas*, 112, 439, 441.

37. David J. Schmidly, *Texas Natural History: A Century of Change*, 386, 390.

38. Ibid., 389; Sandos, *Rebellion in the Borderlands*, 69.

39. Benjamin Johnson, "The Plan de San Diego Uprising and the Making of the Modern Texas-Mexican Borderlands," in *Continental Crossroads: Remapping US-Mexico Borderlands History*, ed. Samuel Truett and Elliott Young, 276–77. For more on the land and town-founding boom in the Valley, see Zamora, *World of the Mexican Worker*, 30–40; Montejano, *Anglos and Mexicans*, 106–28; and Evan Anders, *Boss Rule in South Texas: The Progressive Era*, 139–70.

40. Emilio Zamora, "Labor Formation, Community and Politics: The Mexican Working Class in Texas, 1900–1945," in *Border Crossings: Mexican and Mexican-American Workers*, ed. John Mason Hart, 144; José Pastrano, "Industrial Agriculture in the Peripheral South: State, Race, and the Politics of Migrant Labor in Texas, 1890–1930" (PhD diss., University of California, Santa Barbara, 2006), 10, 72–82, 103.

41. Allhands, *Gringo Builders*, 165–66. As late as 1960, fruit pickers in the region were still among the poorest, least educated, and most disease-stricken people in the United States. In 1967 the average wage for Mexican and Mexican American workers in the melon industry in Starr County was only about $1.16 per hour, which translated to about $1,400 per year, presuming, perhaps mistakenly, continuous employment year-round. For more, see Timothy Paul Bowman, "What About Texas? The Forgotten Cause of Antonio Orendain and the Rio Grande Valley Farm Workers, 1966–1982" (master's thesis, University of Texas at Arlington, 2005), 14–15.

42. G. C. Parrish, "A History of the Rio Grande Valley Citrus Industry" (master's thesis, Texas College of Arts and Industries, 1940), 24; Johnson, *Revolution in Texas*, 119–20. Such a situation, in which the railroad's arrival augured the end of a period of relative good relations between Anglos and ethnic Mexicans in the US Southwest, was not rare. For example, historical sociologist David Montejano argues that the arrival of the railroad in Laredo, further west on the border, in 1881 ended the relative peace between white Americans and ethnic Mexicans in that city. As in the Lower Rio Grande Valley, the result was segregated Anglo and "Mexican" societies in the city. For more information, see Montejano, *Anglos and Mexicans*, 84–95.

43. Richard White, *"It's Your Misfortune and None of My Own": A New History of the American West*, 435–36, 438. For more information on Anglo–Mexican relations in Colorado and New Mexico, see Sarah Deutsch, *No Separate Refuge: Culture, Class, and Gender on an Anglo-Hispanic Frontier in the American Southwest, 1880–1940*. On land dispossession in other areas, see María E. Montoya, *Translating Property: The Maxwell Land Grant and the Conflict over Land in the American West, 1840–1900*, 118–19.

44. Montoya, *Translating Property*, 142; Walter Nugent, *Into the West: The Story of Its People*, 131.

45. Nugent, *Into the West*, 131–32.

46. Montejano, *Anglos and Mexicans*, 109–10; Orozco, *No Mexicans*, 21.

47. Mae M. Ngai, *Impossible Subjects: Illegal Aliens and the Making of Modern America*, 56–90; Acuña, *Occupied America*, 210–11; Johnson, *Revolution in Texas*, 59.

48. Mrs. Goldsby Goza, "American Rio Grande Land and Irrigation Company," Handbook of Texas Online, https://tshaonline.org/handbook/online/articles/gza01,

published by the Texas State Historical Association; "Declaration by the American Rio Grande Land and Irrigation Company to Irrigate from Its Ditches or Canals Approximately Two Hundred and Fifty Thousand (250,000) Acres of Land," manuscript, folder 13, American Rio Grande Land and Irrigation Company (unprocessed collection), Special Collections, University of Texas–Pan American Archives (hereafter cited as UTPA-ARGLIC); Orozco-Vallejo, "Yoakum, Benjamin Franklin."

49. "Deed from Benjamin F. Yoakum of the Llano Grande Land and Irrigation Company to the American Rio Grande Land and Irrigation Company, Dec. 5, 1905, of the Southwest Corner of the Llano Grande Tract," folder 3, UTPA-ARGLIC; "Skeleton Abstract to Title of All of Farm Tract One Hundred Thirty-Eight (138) of the West Tract Subdivision, in the Llano Grande, in Hidalgo County, Texas," folder 2, UTPA-ARGLIC; "Abstract of Title of the North 19.47 Acres, More or Less, of Farm Tract Number One Hundred Forty Six (146) of the West Tract Subdivision, in the Llano Land Grant, in Hidalgo County, Texas," n.d., folder 3, UTPA-ARGLIC; "Contract between the American Rio Grande Land and Irrigation Company and John T. Beamer of Kansas City, Missouri," January 1, 1914, folder 17, UTPA-ARGLIC; "Filing Made by W. T. Adams of the Llano Grande, Texas, for the Appropriation of Water from the Rio Grande for Irrigation Purposes," n.d., folder 13, UTPA-ARGLIC. Adams later became a land developer himself.

50. "Filing Made by W. T. Adams;" "Declaration of Water Rights and Rights of Way for Canals and Plat, American Rio Grande Land and Irrigation Company," May 25, 1906, folder 35, UTPA-ARGLIC; Smith and Gibson to O. O. Norwood, Austin, Texas, March 18, 1929, folder 32, UTPA-ARGLIC.

51. Joe Kilgore speech on John H. Shary History, n.d., tape recording, Special Collections, University of Texas–Pan American, Edinburg.

52. Ibid.

53. S. Zulema Silva-Bewley, *The Legacy of John H. Shary: Promotion and Land Development*, 92–93; Johnson, *Revolution in Texas*, 177.

54. Memorandum of Agreement between John H. Shary and the International Land and Investment Company of Omaha, 1913, folder 20, box D6D1, History of John H. Shary, John H. Shary Papers, University of Texas–Pan American (hereafter cited as JHSP-UTPA).

55. "Omaha Land Men Buy Mission Canals, Texas," *Omaha Evening World-Herald*, January 4, 1916, clipping in John H. Shary Scrapbook, vol. 11, JHSP-UTPA.

56. Statement, Farming Lot #414, Joseph Ebbers, Joseph Ebbers Clearing 2479–2, box 8 (Other—Irrigation), JHSP-UTPA.

57. Joseph Ebbers to John H. Shary, February 15, 1917; GFD to J. C. Elliott, October 25, 1922; John H. Shary to Unknown in Mission, Texas, January 24, 1927, all in Joseph Ebbers Tree Account 2479, box 8 (Other—Irrigation), JHSP-UTPA.

58. Gilbert G. González, *Guest Workers or Colonized Labor? Mexican Labor Migration to the United States*, 1–2; Luis G. Gómez, *Crossing the Rio Grande: An Immigrant's Life in the 1880s*, 25, 69–70.

59. L. L. Foster, *Forgotten Texas Census: First Annual Report of the Agricultural Bureau of the Department of Agriculture, Insurance, Statistics, and History, 1887–88*, introduction by Barbara J. Rozek, 30–31, 104–5, 206–7. Although it is difficult to establish the number of hours worked on a monthly basis or the average hourly pay for workers during this time period, there are reports of some Mexican and Mexican American workers making an average of $1.25 per day in Texas in the mid-1880s, while some special work projects could pay upwards of $2.50 per day. For more information, see Gómez, *Crossing the Rio Grande*, 72, 74. One historian, however, argues that most farmworkers could only expect to make about fifty cents per day. See Maril, *Poorest of Americans*, 38. Given such seemingly contradictory statistics regarding wages for Hispanic workers, it may be impossible to generalize normative wage statistics for workers in the region during this early period.

60. Foster, *Forgotten Texas Census*, 209.

61. "Hill Sees No End of Valley Possibilities," *Corpus Christi Caller*, April 23, 1955, clipping in folder 1989–6.8, box 426B, Lon C. Hill Papers, South Texas Archives, Texas A&M University–Kingsville; Johnson Bros. Bill of Lading to the Saint Louis, Brownsville, and Mexico Railway Co., July 1904, "For expense incurred in getting incompleted track in shape for operation of trains in July 1904," sheets 1 and 2, folder 2, box 34A; and H. E. Ensminger to J. L. Allhands, August 26, 1926, folder 5, box 34A, both in J. L. Allhands Papers, South Texas Archives, Texas A&M University–Kingsville.

62. Gómez-Quiñones, *Mexican-American Labor*, 66.

63. F. G. Jonah, "Notes on the Construction of St. Louis, Brownsville, and Mexico Railway," folder 9, box 34B, J. L. Allhands Papers, South Texas Archives, Texas A&M University–Kingsville.

64. Ibid.

65. Ibid. Such attitudes were not solely the domain of Anglo Americans toward Mexicans, but were also common between dominant and subordinate groups in colonial relationships the world over. Mexicans also exhibited such paternalistic attitudes toward Indian groups on Mexican soil. For example, in 1835 the comandante general in Chihuahua asked the secretary of war if Apaches and other rebellious tribes should be considered Mexican citizens or driven beyond the nation's boundaries. President Antonio López de Santa Anna responded to the inquiry himself, saying that the tribes "'are Mexicans, because they were born and live in the Republic. . . . The state of barbarity in which they are raised prevents them from knowing their universal obligations, and those that belong to them as Mexicans.' The President preferred that 'kindness and consideration' be used to bring these 'unfortunates' to live peacefully in settlements under legal authorities." Quoted from Weber, *Mexican Frontier*, 103.

66. Foster, *Forgotten Texas Census*, 104.

67. Camilo Amado Martínez Jr., "The Mexican and Mexican-American Laborers in the Lower Rio Grande Valley of Texas, 1870–1930" (PhD diss., Texas A&M University, 1987), 32–33. This phenomenon of the spread of the use of cheap labor is an example of Mario Barrera's reserve labor pool. For more information, see Barrera, *Race and Class in the Southwest*, 80–82.

68. Statistics compiled from Account Ledger Books, September 11–15, 20, October 2, November 1, 1915, Correspondence 2486-n001–n005, all in box 8, JHSP-UTPA. These wages, particularly the wage of one dollar per hour paid to unskilled laborers, appear to have been substantially lower than the average wages paid to daily harvest laborers in other parts of the US West during the early 1900s. According to historian Mark Wyman, daily harvest laborers received an average of about two dollars per hour in most western states as early as 1910. The one dollar per hour wage is also significantly lower than the wages paid to farm workers in other regions of the United States during this time period. For more information, see Wyman, *Hoboes*, 50.

69. Account Ledger Book, October 9–15, 1915, Correspondence 2486-n006, box 8, JHSP-UTPA; Carpenters' Bard Weekly Time Book, 2486-n008p8, box 8, JHSP-UTPA.

70. Texas had actually become the nation's leading state in cotton production in 1890, indicating the importance of the crop for farmers throughout the state, including those in the Lower Rio Grande Valley. For more information, see Pastrano, "Industrial Agriculture in the Peripheral South," 26–40.

71. Pierre Laszlo, *Citrus: A History*, 17; Robert Max Hutchings, "From Oranges to Orange Juice: A History of Florida's Indian River Growing Region" (master's thesis, North Dakota State University, 2008), 1–2.

72. John McPhee, *Oranges*, 6; Hutchings, "From Oranges to Orange Juice," 3–4; Laszlo, *Citrus*, 10, 13.

73. Hutchings, "From Oranges to Orange Juice," 2–4, 6–7; McPhee, *Oranges*, 22, 90; Laszlo, *Citrus*, 54, 96.

74. Sackman, *Orange Empire*, 7–19; Laszlo, *Citrus*, 20, 52, 56.

75. "United States Largest Producer of Oranges," *California Citrograph* 16, no. 10 (August 1931): 457. For an interesting explanation of how Spain kept pace with the more modernized US citrus industry, see Samuel Garrido, "Oranges or 'Lemons'? Family Farming and Product Quality in the Spanish Orange Industry, 1870–1960," *Agricultural History* 84, no. 2 (Spring 2010): 224–43.

76. Laszlo, *Citrus*, 43, 51–52; Sackman, *Orange Empire*, 66–83; McPhee, *Oranges*, 27; Marie Jones, "W. Clifford Scott: He Aided Growth of the Citrus Industry," in *Rio Grande Roundup: A Story of Texas Tropical Borderland*, 280–84; "California Cooperation Is Example for Others," *California Citrograph* 16, no. 10 (August 1931): 455, 457.

77. "John H. Shary Seventy-Second Birthday Anniversary, March 2, 1944," commemorative program, author's personal collection; Kevin Starr, *Inventing the Dream: California through the Progressive Era*, 163.

78. Silva-Bewley, *Legacy of John H. Shary*, 11.

79. James Edwin Hill Jr., "The Texas Citrus Industry" (PhD diss., University of Tennessee, 1963), 9; Virgil N. Lott, "First Valley Orange Trees Said in Brownsville," *Texas Farming and Citriculture*, September 1954, 2; "Texas Raised Lemons and Oranges in 1864," *Fort Worth Press*, May 7, 1936, clipping in Vertical Files, Dolph Briscoe Center for American History, University of Texas at Austin.

80. Parrish, "History of the Rio Grande Valley Citrus Industry," 31–32; J. L. Allhands

to C. S. Morton, June 24, 1927, folder 6, box 34A, J. L. Allhands Papers, South Texas Archives, Texas A&M University–Kingsville; Hill, "Texas Citrus Industry," 9–10, 12; William Kenneth Matthews, "A History of Irrigation in the Lower Rio Grande Valley" (master's thesis, University of Texas at Austin, 1938), 36–37; Camilo A. Martínez, "Labor in the Valley: The Development of Texas' Citrus Industry," *Journal of South Texas* 7, no. 1 (1994): 3.

81. Martinez, "Labor in the Valley," 2; William L. Watson, "Oblates of Mary Immaculate," Handbook of Texas Online, https://tshaonline.org/handbook/online/articles/ix001, published by the Texas State Historical Association; Hill, "Texas Citrus Industry," 10, 12; *The Golden Story of Sharyland: Where Nature Produces the World's Sweetest Citrus Fruits* (n.p.: ca. 1941), pamphlet, folder 39, box 2, Publications, JHSP-UTPA.

82. Parrish, "History of the Rio Grande Valley Citrus Industry," 25, 29.

83. Lott, "First Valley Orange Trees Said in Brownsville," 2, 48.

Chapter 2

1. "With San Antonio's Trade Excursionists in Southwest Texas," *Austin Times*, n.d. (ca. 1920), also in John H. Shary Scrapbook, vol. 7, JHSP-UTPA.

2. David Vaught, *Cultivating California: Growers, Specialty Crops, and Labor, 1875–1920*, 1–10. For a discussion of the problems inherent in empirical and imaginative histories in the retelling of borderlands history, see James F. Brooks, "Served Well by Plunder: La Gran Ladronería and Producers of History Astride the Río Grande," *American Quarterly* 52, no. 1 (March 2000): 23–58.

3. White, *"It's Your Misfortune,"* 417–18.

4. Wrobel, *Promised Lands*, 2.

5. Nugent, *Into the West*, 150.

6. Ibid.

7. Sackman, *Orange Empire*, 29, 34, 89.

8. Terry G. Jordan, "Perceptual Regions in Texas," *Geographical Review* 68, no. 3 (July 1978): 297, 300.

9. For more information on literary images of French Algeria, see Benjamin Claude Brower, *A Desert Named Peace: The Violence of France's Empire in the Algerian Sahara, 1844–1902*, 207–8.

10. Graf, "Economic History," 208, 209, 256. In fact, President James K. Polk had hoped to obtain a much larger chunk of territory from Mexico at the end of the US-Mexico War. Polk would have extended the territory acquired to include Baja California, a large portion of northern Mexico as far south as Tampico, and also the tip of the Yucatán Peninsula. Because of a number of issues related to the treaty negotiation, however, Polk was forced to settle for less. For more information, see David Walker Howe, *What Hath God Wrought: The Transformation of America, 1815–1848*, 800–811.

11. *The Missionite*, 1, no. 10 (December 3, 1909), Mission, Texas, also in folder 17, box 2, shelf 334, JHSP-UTPA.

12. *The Lower Rio Grande Valley: Without a Rival* (Brownsville, Texas: Lower Rio Grande Valley Commercial Club, 1909), pamphlet, B 2356, unmarked box, Ephemera Collection, DeGolyer Library, Southern Methodist University (hereafter cited as EC-SMU).

13. Ibid. See also, for example, Sackman, *Orange Empire*, 17–116. By comparing the Valley to California, this booster hoped to show the Valley's natural advantages over the sunny climes of southern California, which, through aggressive advertising campaigns, had already established itself as an Edenic paradise in the minds of consumers and land seekers throughout the country. There is also some evidence to suggest that people did find the Valley's climate to be relatively mild during the early part of the twentieth century; for more information, see Foster, *Forgotten Texas Census*, 30.

14. *Lower Rio Grande Valley.*

15. Ibid. Aside from booster literature, westerners commented and wrote widely on irrigation's ability to transform arid spaces into agricultural gardens. For more information, see Mark Fiege, *Irrigated Eden: The Making of an Agricultural Landscape in the American West*, 171–202.

16. *Lower Rio Grande Valley.* Readers will note that these figures are significantly lower than the one dollar per day wage noted for ethnic Mexican workers in the Valley in 1915, as noted in the first chapter. Workers benefited somewhat as the agricultural sector became rapidly developed in the early 1910s.

17. Ibid.

18. Lawrence Culver, *The Frontier of Leisure: Southern California and the Shaping of Modern America*, 1–14.

19. *Lower Rio Grande Valley.*

20. C. S. Fowler and Brother, *Facts About the Marvelous Country of South Texas, Compiled by "One Who Knows," A Brief Treatise of the Subject, Giving a Description of the General Conditions; Climate and Soil; Crops Statistics; and Other Valuable Information; Season of 1910* (Alice, Texas: 1910), pamphlet, box 17, Texas A–L, EC-SMU. See also promotion for Orangedale, Texas, in *A Satsuma Orange Grove in the Mid-Coast Country of Texas Produces Immense Returns: Insures Independence: Facts and Figures Tell the Story* (Bay City, Texas: Matagorda County Orchard Development Company, Home Office, ca. 1910), pamphlet, Special Collections, University of Texas at Arlington.

21. *Texas: An Agricultural Empire* (Katy, Texas: June 1910), pamphlet, A 2464, unmarked box, EC-SMU.

22. *Facts Worth Knowing about the Lower Rio Grande Valley of Texas* (Kansas City, Mo.: Rio Grande Land Corporation, 1913), pamphlet, box 17, Texas A–L, EC-SMU.

23. Ibid. The price of eight dollars to sixteen dollars per acre appears consistent with what Sharyland colonists paid for their land, as described in the previous chapter.

24. For more on the development of anti-Mexican sentiment among white Texans in the years immediately following the Texas Revolution, see Ramos, *Beyond the Alamo*, 168–204; Crisp, *Sleuthing the Alamo*, 43; and Carrigan, *Making of a Lynching Culture*, 24–29.

25. Michael Phillips, *White Metropolis: Race, Ethnicity, and Religion in Dallas, 1841–2001*, 20; Enrique Krauze, *Mexico: Biography of Power*, 131. Although direct linkages between the patrón-style system in the Valley and Mexican hacienda-style agriculture are difficult to establish, the similarities between the two systems are too obvious to ignore, given the Valley's propinquity to actual Mexican haciendas. A colonial labor system as described by Barrera, in which indigenous peons became indebted to farm owners or *hacendados*, existed in both cases. At least one historian has shown how European "padrones" and laborers both migrated to North American during the Progressive Era and shaped wage-labor relations. For more information, see Gunther Peck, *Reinventing Free Labor: Padrones and Immigrant Workers in the North American West, 1880–1930*.

One element common to colonizing powers throughout modern world history is their propensity to use racialized labor forces in plantation settings. British sugar planters in Jamaica panicked at their inability to keep former slaves employed on their farms after the British Parliament banned slavery throughout its empire in 1833. Planters imported workers from Canada, Germany, and the United States for a short time. "More satisfactory and long term replacements were found," according to historian Denis Judd, "in the form of Indian and Chinese coolie labourers, many thousands of whom were brought to the Caribbean and indentured to work in the sugar plantations." Denis Judd, *Empire: The British Imperial Experience from 1765 to the Present*, 85. Although numerous differences between the nature of racialized labor of South Texas and imperial Jamaica existed, such as the lack of formal indentured servitude in South Texas, the structure of the relationship between a landowning ruling Anglo minority and landless non-Anglo impoverished majority remain similar.

26. *The Famous Rio Grande Valley* (Des Moines, Iowa: La Feria Land Syndicate, 1914), pamphlet, C 100 C1, EC-SMU.

27. Ibid.

28. Group of Excursionists to Southwestern Land Company (mid-1910s), folder 4, box D6D1, History of John H. Shary, JHSP-UTPA. Although this letter does not appear to have been published, excursionists often did publish positive impressions of the Valley in numerous newspapers. See, for example, "Enjoyed Trip to Rio Grande," *Marion Daily Republican*, July 22, 1922. Land promoters also often published positive reviews of excursion visits to the Valley. For more information, see "Land Excursion Here," *Mission Times*, July 7, 1922, and "Land Sales Good," *Mission Times*, August 1, 1922. All three articles are in John H. Shary Scrapbook, vol. 10, JHSP-UTPA. Another group of excursionists sent a similar letter to Shary and the Southwestern Land Company, this one notarized to emphasize that the letter had "been prepared by us unsolicited by either Mr. Shary or the Southwestern Land Company." See "Sworn Resolution of a Group of Excursionists Hosted by Mr. Shary," John H. Shary Scrapbook, vol. 11, JHSP-UTPA.

29. *What Do You Know about Texas?* (n.p.: n.d.), pamphlet, folder 9, box 2, shelf 334, JHSP-UTPA.

30. *The Treasure of the Lower Rio Grande: Where Nature's Smiles are Brightest* (n.p.: ca. 1913–15), pamphlet, folder 36, box 2, shelf 334, JHSP-UTPA.

31. Ibid.

32. *Be Your Own Master! Let a Small Farm Work for You!* (n.p.: n.d.), pamphlet, uncataloged, DeGolyer Library, Southern Methodist University, Dallas, Texas.

33. See, for example, "Canaan Land Pool no. 3, Request for Participation, Class A and B Units," 1926, box 17, Texas A-L, EC-SMU. Some boosters simply called for investors for land buying schemes instead of permanent residents.

34. William T. Chambers, "Lower Rio Grande Valley of Texas," *Economic Geography* 6, no. 4 (October 1930): 369; Foscue, "Agricultural Geography," 144–53.

35. Julia Cameron Montgomery, "The Citrus Tree: Facts and Potentials of the Lower Rio Grande Valley's Great Industry," *Monty's Monthly Magazine*, supplement, 1922, also in A13 A1184, EC-SMU.

36. Ibid.

37. Ibid.

38. Julia Cameron Montgomery, *A Little Journey through the Lower Valley of the Rio Grande: The Magic Valley of Texas*, also in unmarked box, EC-SMU.

39. Ibid.; Montgomery, "The Citrus Tree."

40. *The American Rio Grande Land and Irrigation Company: Irrigated Lands in the Lower Rio Grande Valley, Mercedes, Texas* (Mercedes, Texas: American Rio Grande Land and Irrigation Company, ca. 1923), pamphlet, folder 42, box 2, Publications, JHSP-UTPA.

41. "San Perlita, Texas, 'The Pearl of the Valley,'" ca. 1925, pre-development poster advertisement, uncataloged, EC-SMU.

42. *Brownsville: In Texas on the Lower Rio Grande, "Where Uncle Sam Meets Mexico"* (n.p.: ca. 1925), pamphlet, C 920 C 2, EC-SMU. For other pamphlets that include idealized images of "Old Mexico," see H. A. Manley Company, *The Semi-Tropical Land in the Southmost Tip of Texas: The Lower Valley of the Rio Grande* (n.p.: ca. 1930), and *The Tour Alluring to the Lower Valley of the Rio Grande: The Magic Valley of Texas* (n.p.: 1929), both in box 18, Texas M-S, EC-SMU.

43. Ngai, *Impossible Subjects*, 52. For a detailed analysis of the Mexican Revolution, see Alan Knight, *The Mexican Revolution*, 2 vols.

44. George J. Sánchez, *Becoming Mexican American: Ethnicity, Culture, and Identity in Chicano Los Angeles, 1900–1945*, 70–71; John Nieto Phillips, *Language of Blood: The Making of Spanish-American Identity in New Mexico, 1880s-1930s*, 107–8, 147. Historian William Deverell has also examined Anglo elites' attitudes toward and whitewashing of the Mexican past of Los Angeles. For more information, see William Deverell, *Whitewashed Adobe: The Rise of Los Angeles and the Remaking of Its Mexican Past*. See also Phoebe S. Kropp, *California Vieja: Culture and Memory in a Modern American Place*.

American writers in the early twentieth century commented widely on the perceived slothfulness of Mexican *peones*, as well as Mexico's allegedly backwards society and culture. Many Americans considered Mexico a "society not yet ready for democracy or for economic development styled along the lines of the United States." Hence, in their minds it remained mired in oldness. For more information, see González, *Culture of Empire*, 80–93.

45. Benjamin H. Johnson, *Bordertown: The Odyssey of an American Place*, 24.

46. J. J. Morton, "The Tomorrow of the Rio Grande Valley and the Great Southwest," July 21, 1922, *Mission Times*, also in John H. Shary Scrapbook, vol. 10, JHSP-UTPA.]

47. *Harlingen in the Lower Rio Grande Valley of Texas: The City That Citrus Built* (n.p.: ca. early 1930s), pamphlet, folder 5, box 2, Publications, JHSP-UTPA. Golconda was a kingdom in India founded during the sixteenth century. It was renowned by British colonists in the seventeenth and eighteenth centuries for its diamonds. The British considered Golconda diamonds a sign of great status and wealth. The comparison of Harlingen with Golconda, then, evoked wealth in an exotic, foreign land. For more information, see Roderick Cavaliero, *Strangers in the Land: The Rise and Decline of the British Indian Empire*, 6, 23.

48. *Sharyland Orchards: Citrus Fruit* (n.p.: ca. 1925), pamphlet, folder 41, box 1, Publications, shelf 333, JHSP-UTPA.

49. Francis Miller, "Our Valley Assumes Natural Importance to the Outside World," *Rio Grande Valley Sun*, Pharr, Texas, June 10, 1927, also in John H. Shary Scrapbook, vol. 7, oversized box B3, Shary Scrapbooks, JHSP-UTPA.

50. Jacobson, *Barbarian Virtues*, 223–24. Jacobson also draws a direct correlation between the closing of the US frontier in the 1890s to the origins of overseas expansionism during the early part of the twentieth century.

51. *Monty's Monthly: Digest of Lower Rio Grande Valley Activities* 10, no. 1 (January 1928), also in B 2017, unmarked box, EC-SMU. See also, for example, *Willacy County, Texas* (Raymondville, Texas: Chamber of Commerce; Lyford, Texas: Commercial Club; and Sebastian, Texas: Commercial Club, ca. 1927), pamphlet, unmarked box and folder, EC-SMU.

52. *Monty's Monthly* 10, no. 1.

53. Robert S. McElvaine, *The Great Depression: America, 1929–1941*, 2nd ed., 16; Julia Cameron Montgomery, "A Camera Journey through the Lower Valley of the Rio Grande, the Garden of Golden Grapefruit," *Monty's Monthly*, December 1929, also in unmarked folder and box, EC-SMU; *Golden Groves: Lower Rio Grande Valley* (n.p.: ca. late 1929), pamphlet, unmarked folder and box, EC-SMU.

54. F. W. Parker, *Kingsville, Texas, Kleberg County* (n.p.: ca. late 1920s), pamphlet, B 2325, unmarked box, EC-SMU; *Welcome to Mission, Home of the Grapefruit* (n.p.: ca. early 1930s), pamphlet, folder 8, box 1, Publications, JHSP-UTPA. Emphasis on Mission's lack of either poverty or business failures spoke directly to issues that would have been common across midwestern towns and cities during the early years of the Depression.

55. *The Famous Fertile El Jardin and Los Fresnos Farms* (n.p.: ca. 1929), pamphlet, unmarked folder and box, EC-SMU.

56. "Sharyland—A Place to Live," ca. late 1920s, typed draft, folder 13, box 2, Publications, JHSP-UTPA.

57. Charles F. C. Ladd, *Adams Gardens: In the Heart of the Lower Rio Grande Valley* (n.p.: ca. 1931), pamphlet, folder 24, box 2, Publications, JHSP-UTPA.

58. *Harlingen in the Lower Rio Grande Valley of Texas: The City That Citrus Built*, (n.p.: 1931), pamphlet folder 5, box 2, Publications, JHSP-UTPA.

59. *Facts about the Lower Rio Grande Valley of Texas* (n.p.: 1930), pamphlet, unmarked box and folder, EC-SMU; "Valley Facts," *The Lower Rio Grande Valley Tourist: "Where Uncle Sam Meets Mexico"* 1, no. 1 (January 1930): 13, also in B 159 B 1, EC-SMU.

Although exact numbers of carloads of crops shipped from the Valley are somewhat difficult to establish for any given harvest season, it appears that the number of carloads shipped from the Valley only began to approach the 30,000 mark during the 1944–45 harvest season, when groves had been becoming larger and increasingly fewer small growers were participating in the citrus industry. Reports from the Missouri Pacific and Southern Pacific Railroads indicate that the total number of citrus fruits shipped by rail, boat, and "express" that season was approximately 29,301, which constituted about half of all agricultural products shipped from the Valley that season. For more information, see *Third Annual Meeting of the Texas Citrus and Vegetable Growers and Shippers, Gran Hotel Ancira, Monterrey, Mexico, October 1, 2, 3, 1945*, 155, yearbook, South Texas Archives, Jernigan Library, Texas A&M University–Kingsville.

60. Cleo Dawson, *She Came to the Valley*, 2nd ed., 28, 63.

61. Ibid., 65.

62. Norquest, *Rio Grande Wetbacks*, ix.

63. Ibid. Much like formal colonialism, neocolonialism involved a certain amount of risk taking on the part of the colonists, although the risks were not usually as dire. For an example of the riskiness involved in a formal colonial enterprise, see James Horn, "The Conquest of Eden: Possession and Dominion in Early Virginia," in *Envisioning an English Empire: Jamestown and the Making of the North Atlantic World*, ed. Robert Applebaum and John Wood Sweet, 25–48.

64. Norquest, *Rio Grande Wetbacks*, ix

65. "Promoters Swore Crops Hiked Rainfall in Valley," April 6, 1952, clipping, folder 1989–6.8, box 426B, Lon C. Hill Papers, South Texas Archives, Texas A&M University–Kingsville. Although such a patently unscientific claim appears at first glance to be a completely dishonest sales tactic, the notion that agriculture created a rainier climate was a common argument made in arid parts of the US West during the nineteenth century. It appears, however, that this theory might have fallen somewhat out of fashion by the early twentieth century. Land agents who made this argument might have believed it to be true, or they simply might have hoped that uneducated midwestern farmers to whom they wanted to sell land would believe it. For more information on the history of this idea, see Henry Nash Smith, "Rain Follows the Plow: The Notion of Increased Rainfall for the Great Plains, 1844–1880," *Huntington Library Quarterly* 10, no. 2 (February 1947): 169–93.

On the origins of the recruits, see, for example, "Land Buying De Luxe," January 29, 1915, clipping, folder 2, box D6D1, History of John H. Shary, JHSP-UTPA.

Songs sung on the trains included hymns, songs about patriotism, as well as numerous songs about the alleged many wonderful qualities of the Lower Rio Grande Valley.

For a typical songbook from an excursion trip, see "Sharyland Songbook," folder 38, box 2, Publications, JHSP-UTPA. See also Maril, *Poorest of Americans*, 36.

66. Dawson, *She Came to the Valley*, 106–7.

67. Ibid., 114.

68. Stambaugh and Stambaugh, *Lower Rio Grande Valley*, 231–32. It should be noted that Stambaugh and Stambaugh were likely whitewashing the true intent of the land developers, who, instead of losing sales, likely wanted to avoid the recruits' having any contact with dissatisfied growers with whom they might have incidentally come into contact.

69. Handwritten notes on how agents sold land to prospective buyers, ca. 1920, folder 12, box 2, Publications, JHSP-UTPA; *Houston Chronicle*, n.d., clipping, folder 2, box D6D1, History of John H. Shary, JHSP-UTPA; *Southwestern Land Company: Dallas and Mission, Texas* (n.p.: n.d.), pamphlet, folder 37, box 2, Publications, JHSP-UTPA.

70. "Mrs. McLaughlin Writes Letter from the 'Magic Valley,'" November 19, 1926, clipping, John H. Shary Scrapbook, vol. 10, JHSP-UTPA.

71. Bruce S. Meador, "Wetback Labor in the Lower Rio Grande Valley" (undergraduate thesis, University of Texas at Austin, 1951), 14–17.

72. Maril, *Poorest of Americans*, 37.

Chapter 3

1. Laszlo, *Citrus*, 200.

2. *Houston Chronicle*, July 7, 1917, clipping, folder 2, box D6D1, History of John H. Shary, JHSP-UTPA.

3. Parrish, "A History of the Rio Grande Valley Citrus Industry," 39, 41–42; Shary to E. G. Paschal, November 29, 1918, folder 1, shelf 16, United Irrigation Company, JHSP-UTPA.

4. Mission Canal Company Receiver to G. Weiske, July 31, 1915, folder 3, shelf 16, United Irrigation Company, JHSP-UTPA, and UIC to J. W. Hoit, November 22, 1922, folder 1, shelf 16, United Irrigation Company, JHSP-UTPA.

5. John A. Levenhagen to Shary, January 16, 1915; Shary to J. A. Mahoney, January 5, 1915; and Levenhagen to Shary, December 29, 1914, all in 2469, box 8, JHSP-UTPA.

6. Henry Mette to Shary, January 18, 1915, 2471, box 8, JHSP-UTPA.

7. Shary to Anonymous, August 29, 1916; Mette to Shary, December 5, 1916; Shary to Mette, December 7, 1916; and J. A. Grosscup to Shary, 1917, all in 2471, box 8, JHSP-UTPA.

8. Shary to J. C. Elliott, July 19, 1922; GFD to J. C. Elliott, October 25, 1922; and Anonymous to Shary, January 24, 1927, all in 2479, box 8, JHSP-UTPA.

9. Eunice R. Askew to Shary, March 9, 1917, Askew folder, box 10, JHSP-UTPA; EWS to Askew, March 14, 1917, Askew folder, box 10, JHSP-UTPA.

10. Shary to Joe Mills, March 15, 1915, 2528, box 10, JHSP-UTPA.

11. Shary to Gustav Gradert, November 29, 1915, 2483, box 8, JHSP-UTPA.

12. For example of the marketing involved in formal colonialism, see Michael G. Moran, *Inventing Virginia: Sir Walter Raleigh and the Rhetoric of Colonization, 1584–1590*, 17–21.

13. David B. Danbom, *Born in the Country: A History of Rural America*, 161–67.

14. Matthews, "History of Irrigation," 30–31; D. W. Glasscock to Shary, July 23, 1917, folder 1, shelf 16, JHSP-UTPA; Montejano, *Anglos and Mexicans*, 109–10.

15. "Shary Portrays Lower Rio Grande Valley History," *South Texan*, June 1940, 5, 9, clipping, folder 58, box 2, Publications, JHSP-UTPA; "Pioneer in Citrus," *Texas Farming and Citriculture*, March 1956, 14; Chan Connolly, "Yield, Price, and On-Tree Income Distributions for Texas Citrus, 1971–1972," Technical Report Number 73–4, Texas Agricultural Experiment Station, Weslaco, Texas, 7, and "Report on the Rio Grande Valley Citrus Industry," Texas Agricultural Extension Service and the Texas Agricultural Experiment Station, Texas A&M University System, n.d., 3, both in Special Collections, University of Texas–Pan American, Edinburg; Martínez, "Labor in the Valley," 3. See also L. Charles Ross, untitled article, *Houston Chronicle*, August 13, 1922, also in John H. Shary Scrapbook, vol. 10, JHSP-UTPA.

16. "Citrus Fruit is Great Industry," April 1922, clipping, John H. Shary Scrapbook, vol. 10, JHSP-UTPA; Victor H. Schofelmayer, "Citrus Industry Gaining Rapidly," *Dallas Morning News*, March 26, 1922, 8, also in John H. Shary Scrapbook, vol. 10, JHSP-UTPA.

17. J. M. Delcurto, E. W. Halstead, and H. F. Halstead, *The Citrus Industry of the Lower Rio Grande Valley of Texas*, Texas State Department of Agriculture Bulletin no. 75, 2nd ed., preface.

18. Ibid., 28–29, 34, 35, 46–47, 70–71, 74.

19. "Mexican Citrus Trees Inspected by Two Well Known Experts," clipping; and "Citrus Experts Back from Survey of Mexican Lands," clipping, both in John H. Shary Scrapbook, vol. 13, JHSP-UTPA.

20. Monocrop agricultural economies tend to coalesce around both formal and internal colonial ventures. Sugarcane, for example, spread quickly throughout the Caribbean islands in the sixteenth and seventeenth centuries to the point that European colonies in the Caribbean became known as "the sugar islands." Sugar became a driving force in slave-based Caribbean colonial economies for several centuries and remains a viable industry in Guyana, the Dominican Republic, and Cuba in particular. For more information, see Elizabeth Abbott, *Sugar: A Bittersweet History*, 37, 377.

21. "$5,000 an Acre for Rio Grande Valley Orchard," San Benito, Texas, March 14, 1924, clipping, John H. Shary Scrapbook, vol. 9, JHSP-UTPA.

22. "First Bale of 1924 Crop Brings $1405," clipping, John H. Shary Scrapbook, vol. 5, JHSP-UTPA. The "John A. Cherry" may actually have been John H. Shary, who was a close associate of the Bentsen family.

23. "Hidalgo's Area is Richest in U.S.," ca. 1926, clipping, John H. Shary Scrapbook, vol. 10, JHSP-UTPA.

24. Fifteenth Census of the United States, 1930, Population, vol. 1, 1058, 1060, and

Agriculture, Texas, Statistics by Counties, First Series, 8, 14, 25, entries for Cameron, Hidalgo, and Willacy Counties; Foscue, "Agricultural Geography," 245. The 50 percent Anglo population in the Valley by 1925 constituted a class of people that can only be described as settler colonists. Nevertheless, there were still many absentee owners of Valley citrus lands. Thus, the Valley's colonization consisted of both settler colonialism and absenteeism. For an example of absenteeism's role in a traditional colonial setting, see Abbott, *Sugar*, 157–66.

25. "Valley Society to Protect Citrus," *McAllen Monitor*, September 5, 1924, clipping, John H. Shary Scrapbook, vol. 13, JHSP-UTPA.

26. Shary to John H. Shapter, January 19, 1923; I. L. Martin to Shary, July 13, 1926; and "Shary Makes Courteous Reply to Sid," *Rio Grande Valley Sun*, July 13, 1926, 1, all in folder 2, C5D1#2, JHSP-UTPA.

27. "Texas Optimistic on Citrus Outlook," *California Citrograph* 14, no. 11 (September 1929): 457; "Valley Passes 25,000 Carloads in Shipments," *Port Isabel Pilot*, April 27, 1932, 1, and "8,200 Citrus Cars Move During Season," *Rio Grande Valley Digest* 3, no. 2 (April 1932): 3, both also in fourth unmarked folder, Public Work Advisory CI2192, JHSP-UTPA. See also "The Mission Times Third Annual Citrus Number," *Rio Grande Valley Digest* 3, no. 7 (September 1932): 4, also in unmarked folder, Public Work Advisory CI2192, JHSP-UTPA.

28. Fifteenth Census of the United States, 1930 Agriculture, Texas, Statistics by Counties, Third Series, Type of Farm, 12, 31.

29. Stambaugh and Stambaugh, *Lower Rio Grande Valley*, 239.

30. "Texas Grapefruit History," TexaSweet Citrus Marketing, Inc., http://www.texasweet.com/texas-grapefruits-and-oranges/texas-grapefruit-history/.

31. Frank and Dorothy Anderson interview by Sandra Barrera, ca. 1986–87, tape recording, Special Collections, University of Texas–Pan American, Edinburg. Large planters and landowners in the Valley dominated local politics. Similar situations occurred in the early-nineteenth-century US South, where large planters and slaveholders reigned supreme. For a brief example of how this functioned in one state in the antebellum South, see Sean Wilentz, *The Rise of American Democracy: Jefferson to Lincoln*, 727.

32. Frank and Dorothy Anderson interview.

33. Worth noting is that the Andersons' disinclination to speak out against segregation might have been a byproduct of living in Starr County, where ethnic Mexicans retained political control and still owned large portions of land. Anti-Mexican segregation in Starr County, then, was much less common than in neighboring Hidalgo or Cameron Counties. Also, the land development and irrigation rush largely bypassed Starr County in the early part of the century, which meant that midwestern Anglos were far less interested in Starr County than they were in the Valley's other areas. For more information, see Montejano, *Anglos and Mexicans*, 139, 244–47.

34. Louva Myrtis Douglas, "The History of the Agricultural Fairs of Texas" (master's thesis, University of Texas at Austin, 1943), 1; *Mission, Texas: Home of the Grapefruit*

(n.p.: ca. late 1920s), pamphlet, folder 61, box 2, Publications, JHSP-UTPA; Douglas, "History of the Agricultural Fairs," 274–75.

35. "Citrus King and Queen Close Fair," *San Antonio Express*, November 19, no year, ca. mid–late 1920s, clipping, folder 1, box D6D1, History of John H. Shary, JHSP-UTPA.

36. "Mission's Citrus Fiesta Promises to be Gala Event," *Port Isabel Pilot*, December 7, 1932, 1, also in fourth unmarked folder, Public Work Advisory CI2192, JHSP-UTPA; "Fiesta to Honor Citrus," *Texas Farming and Citriculture*, January 1956, 57; Douglas, "History of the Agricultural Fairs," 275.

37. "Planning New Exchange for Valley Fruit," ca. 1922–23, clipping, John H. Shary Scrapbook, vol. 13, JHSP-UTPA.

38. Joe Kilgore speech on John H. Shary History, n.d., tape recording, Special Collections, University of Texas–Pan American, Edinburg; Kalbfleisch quote in "Rules to be Adopted at Meet Monday: Every Valley Farmer Invited to Attend Conference in Mercedes," ca. 1923, clipping, folder 2, box D6D1, History of John H. Shary, JHSP-UTPA; "Arguments Apply to California Too," *California Citrograph* 15, no. 4 (February 1930): 149, also in folder 4, box 2 publications, JHSP-UTPA.

39. Kilgore speech, UTPA; Sixth Annual Report of the Texas Citrus Fruit Growers Exchange, May 15, 1928–May 15, 1929, 2, 10, 22, Special Collections, University of Texas–Pan American, Edinburg.

40. Gonzales, "Mexican Revolution, *Revolución de Texas*, and *Matanza de 1915*," 126.

Chapter 4

1. Wyman, *Hoboes*, 135.

2. Johnson, *Revolution in Texas*, 149; Barbara Tuchman, *The Zimmerman Telegram: America Faces the War, 1917–1918*.

3. Johnson, *Revolution in Texas*, 148–54; Montejano, *Anglos and Mexicans*, 182, 186; Marshall Roderick, "The 'Box Bill': Public Policy, Ethnicity, and Economic Exploitation in Texas" (master's thesis, Texas State University, 2011), 2, 5, 21 Anne W. Hooker, "Box, John Calvin," Handbook of Texas Online, https://www.tshaonline.org/handbook/online/articles/fb054, published by the Texas State Historical Association. Quotation from Roderick, "'Box Bill,'" 5.

4. Chávez, *Beyond Nations*, 163, 164–65, 166. For perhaps the best analysis of Jim Crow South Texas, see Montejano, *Anglos and Mexicans*, 157–256.

5. W. H. Friend, "Citrus Fruit Culture," Handbook of Texas Online, https://tshaonline.org/handbook/online/articles/afc01, published by the Texas State Historical Association.

6. Paul S. Taylor, *An American-Mexican Frontier: Nueces County, Texas*, 298–99. For more information on Taylor, see Richard Steven Street, "The Economist as Humanist: The Career of Paul S. Taylor," *California History* 58, no. 4 (Winter 1979–80): 350–61.

7. Wyman, *Hoboes*, 134–35, quote on 135. For more on the bifurcation of whiteness during this time period in Texas, see Foley, *White Scourge*.

8. Taylor, *American-Mexican Frontier*, 303–13.

9. Douglas E. Foley et al., *From Peones to Politicos: Ethnic Relations in a South Texas Town, 1900–1977*, 43.

10. Untitled notes, not dictated—Brownsville, Matamoros, and Nuevo Laredo, 12:10, Carton 12, BANC MSS 84/38 c, Paul Taylor Papers, Bancroft Library, Berkeley, California (hereafter cited as PTP-BANC).

11. "Nuevo Laredo—Nov. 6, 1928, Cost of Documents Required for a U.S. Visa," not dictated—Brownsville, Matamoros, and Nuevo Laredo, 12:10, PTP-BANC.

12. "Henry Allsmeyer," Land Agent, Cameron County, 1912, "Detailed Field Notes, Brownsville, Texas–San Antonio–Tucson–Phoenix," 12:10, PTP-BANC. For more on poverty in South Texas, particularly the Lower Rio Grande Valley, during the middle part of the twentieth century, see Anderson, *The Movement and the Sixties*, 301.

13. Felix Wirick, Rancher, North of Eagle Pass, Field Notes—Del Rio to Brownsville, Texas, December 10, 1928, 12:13, PTP-BANC.

14. Ibid.

15. "Farmer—6 mi west of Carrizo Springs–Wintergarden, Texas, Nov. 30, 1928," and quote in "Mr. Baylor—70 yr old cattleman and farmer 1 mile east of Carrizo Springs–November 30, 1928," both in Field Notes—Del Rio to Brownsville, Texas, December 10, 1928, 12:13, PTP-BANC. Carrizo Springs is in South Texas's Winter Garden district, north and west of the Lower Rio Grande Valley.

16. "W. Friend, Texas Agr. Experiment Station–Mercedes, TX, Dec. 10, 1928," Field Notes—Del Rio to Brownsville, Texas, December 10, 1928, 12:13, PTP-BANC.

17. "Pat Skutter [sp.?] Sept. 1929, Robstown, 12–15 years ago"; "John Magee—5 yrs ago"; and "Clifford Gaudy—3 yrs ago," all in Texas—Nueces County, Field Notes, September 1929, 12:25, PTP-BANC. For more on this system of labor controls, see Montejano, *Anglos and Mexicans*, 197–219.

18. For more information on the origins of debt peonage in colonial-era Mexican haciendas, see François Chevalier, *Land and Society in Colonial Mexico: The Great Hacienda*, 263–307.

19. Taylor, *American-Mexican Frontier*, 328. The pass system that these growers used resembled a similar pass system that Southern whites used to restrict slaves' movement in the pre–Civil War U.S. South. Slaves often faced severe punishment at the hands of citizen or law enforcement patrols if they failed to produce a credible pass that justified their physical movement between places. For more information, see Leon F. Litwack, *Been in the Storm so Long: The Aftermath of Slavery*, 27–30. For more on the Raymondville peonage case, see Taylor, *American-Mexican Frontier*, 325–29, and Montejano, *Anglos and Mexicans*, 205–6.

20. "Stokes Holmes, Bishop, Texas, August 29, 1929," Texas Field Notes, August 1929, 12:23 PTP-BANC.

21. "'Bill,' foreman for a farmer named Stubbs," Texas—Nueces County, Field Notes, September 1929, 12:24, PTP-BANC.

22. "Pat Skutter [sp.?] Sept. 1929, Robstown, 12–15 years ago"; "Clifford Gaudy—

3 years ago"; and "Galbreath—City Marshal, Robstown, Texas, Sept. 12, 1929," all in Texas—Nueces County, Field Notes, September 1929, 12:25, PTP-BANC.

23. "A. O. Stubbs, President Chamber of Commerce, Robstown, Texas," n.d. (ca. August 1929), Texas Field Notes, August 1929, 12:23 PTP-BANC.

24. "Mr. Bloodinorth, County Clerk, Kingsville, Kleberg County, Texas," 12:10, PTP-BANC. The name Bloodinorth might be a misspelling of the man's name in Taylor's handwritten field notes.

25. Ibid. For more on racial division in borderlands settings, see James N. Leiker, *Racial Borders: Black Soldiers along the Rio Grande.*

26. "Mr. Baylor—70 yr old cattleman and farmer 1 mile east of Carrizo Springs—November 30, 1928," Field Notes—Del Rio to Brownsville, Texas, December 10, 1928, 12:13, PTP-BANC.

27. "W. Friend, Texas Agr. Experiment Station—Mercedes, TX, Dec. 10, 1928," Field Notes—Del Rio to Brownsville, Texas, December 10, 1928, 12:13, PTP-BANC; Hernández, *Migra!* 2.

28. "John Stone, onion grower, Carrizo Springs, Texas, April 8, 1929," Texas, Field Notes—"S," April 1929, 12:14, PTP-BANC.

29. For more, see Hernández, *Migra!* 178.

30. "[Illegible] Peet, Onion buyer at Carrizo Springs, Texas," April 16, 1929, Texas, Field Notes, April 16, 1929, PTP-BANC.

31. "Mr. Miller, farmer near Carrizo Springs," no envelope, Texas, field notes, April 9, 1929, 12:19, PTP-BANC.

32. "Mrs. Russell and Mrs. Price—Near Carrizo Springs, April 9, 1929," 12:19, PTP-BANC.

33. Ibid.

34. "City Drug Store—Carrizo Springs, April 9, 1929," 12:19, PTP-BANC.

35. "Luis Perales, Valley Wells, April 24, 1929," Texas Field Notes, April 18–24, 1929, 12:22 PTP-BANC.

36. "Louis Bailey, farmer near Agua Dulce," Texas Field Notes, August 1929, 12:23 PTP-BANC; "Catterly, Supt. of Schools, Santa Cruz, Sept. 7," Texas—Nueces County, Field Notes, September 1929, 12:25, PTP-BANC.

37. "Mr. Miller, Corpus Christi National Bank, Corpus Christi, Texas," Texas Field Notes, August 1929, 12:23 PTP-BANC.

38. Norquest, *Rio Grande Wetbacks*, xiii.

39. Ibid., 4–5.

40. Ibid., 21–23, 91–93.

41. Ibid., 27, 28.

42. Ibid., 29. Throughout the book all of Norquest's ethnic Mexican workers refer to him as Carlos instead of his given first name, Carrol.

43. Ibid., 33, 41.

44. Ibid.

45. Ibid., 55, 56.

46. Ibid., 96–97, 98.

47. Ibid., 100–101. In fairness to Norquest, it is worth noting that pages 101–3 of the book do outline an Anglo grower who once cheated a group of undocumented immigrants out of their promised pay.

48. Ibid., 104.

49. Ibid., 107–34.

Chapter 5

1. Américo Paredes, *George Washington Gómez: A Mexicotexan Novel*, 195.

2. McElvaine, *Great Depression*, 21.

3. J. Gilberto Quezada, *Border Boss: Manuel B. Bravo and Zapata County*, 18, 22; Laura Caldwell, "Baker, Anderson Yancy," Handbook of Texas Online, https://tsha online.org/handbook/online/articles/fba19, published by the Texas State Historical Association. For more, see Anders, *Boss Rule in South Texas*.

4. Caldwell, "Baker, Anderson Yancy"; Quezada, *Border Boss*, 23. Boss rule refers to the Democratic machine-style politics that dominated the Valley in the late nineteenth and early twentieth centuries. South Texas political bosses resembled machine-style politicians in the urban Northeast in that they indulged in graft but also served a number of constructive functions, such as providing social benefits for the poor (whom they sometimes intimidated but often pandered to for votes), special privileges for businesses, and certain channels of upward mobility for the downtrodden. For more, see Anders, *Boss Rule in South Texas*, vii–viii.

5. Cynthia E. Orozco, "Hidalgo County Rebellion," Handbook of Texas Online, https://www.tshaonline.org/handbook/online/articles/pqhks, published by the Texas State Historical Association. For more information on LULAC, see Orozco, *No Mexicans*, and Johnson, *Revolution in Texas*, 185, 188.

6. "Editorial," *Texas Citriculture* 7, no. 6 (December 1930): 5; *Adams Gardens: In the Heart of the Lower Rio Grande Valley* (n.p.: n.d.), pamphlet, folder 24, box 2, Publications, shelf 334, JHSP-UTPA; "Texas Optimistic on Citrus Outlook," *California Citrograph* 14, no. 11 (September 1929): 457; *Harlingen in the Lower Rio Grande Valley of Texas: The City That Citrus Built* (n.p.: ca. 1931), pamphlet, folder 5, publications, box 2, shelf 334, JHSP-UTPA; "United States Largest Producer of Oranges," *California Citrograph* 14, no. 11 (September 1929): 457.

7. W. D. Toland to L. N. Olmsted, September 10, 1932, folder 9, box D5D2, JHSP-UTPA.

8. B. N. Moore to SWLC, September 8, 1932, folder 9, box D5D2, JHSP-UTPA.

9. L. E. Rosser to L. N. Olmsted, September 9, 1932, Genevieve Gowin to L. N. Olmsted, September 7, 1932, and Walter B. Ellis to SWLC, September 12, 1932, all in folder 9, box D5D2, JHSP-UTPA.

10. A. E. Bonnell to L. E. Olmsted, September 6, 1932, E. E. Russell to L. E. Olmsted, September 8, 1932, and J. Sherman Fox to SWLC, n.d., all in folder 9, box D5D2, JHSP-UTPA.

11. Charles Richardson to L. N. Olmsted, September 10, 1932, folder 9, box D5D2, JHSP-UTPA.

12. C. A. Weego to SWLC, September 1932, and Dave Burgess to SWLC, September 12, 1932, both in folder 9, box D5D2, JHSP-UTPA. Bullfights were clearly an exotic part of the Valley's landscape for Burgess, much like images of Mexicans and Mexico itself that boosters presented to Anglo midwesterners as exotic during the 1910s and 1920s.

13. "Valley Area Given Unusual Prominence in December Issue of Fortune Magazine," *Mission Times*, December 1, 1939, also in John H. Shary Scrapbook, vol. 1, oversized box B1, JHSP-UTPA; "Valley Wars Unfavorable Citrus Matter," *Mission Times*, July 18, 1930, also in folder 13, box D5D2, JHSP-UTPA.

14. John H. Shary to Carl Roetelle, July 17, 1930, and Roetelle to R. B. Shary, July 15, 1930, both in "Carl Roetelle, 76 W," box C7D4 #1, JHSP-UTPA.

15. "Valley Shipments Still Exceed Last Year's Record," *Port Isabel Pilot*, December 23, 1931, 1; "County Taxes $912,452.66 Less This Year," *Hidalgo County Independent*, December 4, 1931, 1, also in jumbo scrapbook, Public Work Advisory CI2192, JHSP-UTPA.

16. "Shipper Sees Bright Future for Valley Citrus Industry," and "Optimism Seizes Valley as a Result of Rising Prices," *Rio Grande Valley Digest* 3, no. 7 (September 1932): 3, also in unmarked folder, Public Work Advisory CI2192, JHSP-UTPA.

17. "'Live on Your Farm' Says Successful Valley Farmer," ibid.: "Oklahoma Judge is Pleased at Growth of Grove," *Rio Grande Valley Digest* 3, no. 9 (November 1932); and "Depression Pooh," *Rio Grande Valley Digest* 3, no. 7 (September 1932): 4, all also in unmarked folder, Public Work Advisory CI2192, JHSP-UTPA.

18. "Citrus Exchange Makes Economy in Marketing Its Fruit This Year," *Rio Grande Valley Digest* 3, no. 9 (November 1932): 4; "Citrus Authority Predicts Brilliant Future for Valley," *Rio Grande Valley Digest* 3, no. 1 (March 1932): 2; and "Valley Outlook Good, Belief of Martin Insull," *Rio Grande Valley Digest* 3, no. 1 (March 1932), 4, all also in unmarked folder, Public Work Advisory CI2192, JHSP-UTPA.

19. "Million Dollars Here in Week as 1,308 Cars Moved," *Valley Morning Star*, March 19, 1932, 1; "Valley Produces 25,000 Carloads in Shipments, *Port Isabel Pilot*, April 27, 1932, 1; and "8,200 Cars Move During Season," *Rio Grande Valley Digest* 3, no. 2 (April 1932): 3, all also in unmarked folder, Public Work Advisory CI2192, JHSP-UTPA.

20. "Why Aren't Times as Good As Ever in the Valley," n.p., n.d., editorial clipping, unmarked folder, Public Work Advisory CI2192, JHSP-UTPA.

21. Ibid.

22. Johnson, *Lost Years*, 73; Lisa Belkin, "Lloyd Bentsen, Sr., 95, the Father of Texas Senator, Killed in Crash," Obituaries, *New York Times*, January 18, 1989, http://www.nytimes.com/1989/01/18/obituaries/lloyd-bentsen-sr-95-the-father-of-texas-senator-killed-in-crash.html?pagewanted=1; Howard Lackman, "Bentsen, Lloyd Millard, Sr.," Handbook of Texas Online, http://www.tshaonline.org/handbook/online/articles/fbebb), published by the Texas State Historical Association.

23. Johnson, *Lost Years*, 15.

24. "Why Aren't Times as Good as Ever in the Valley?" n.p., n.d., clipping, fourth unmarked folder, Public Work Advisory CI2192, JHSP-UTPA.

25. C. H. Swallow to M. R. Safford, August 30, 1932, Low Excursion Rates Valley Advisory Board Committee, Public Work Advisory Board Minutes, JHSP-UTPA.

26. "Report of the LRGV Land Men and Developers, and Other Business Interests, Held at Cortez Hotel, Weslaco, Weds., Sept. 28, 1932," and John H. Shary to J. F. Hennessey, late 1932, both in LER, JHSP-UTPA. Theorist Mario Barrera argues that there is a distinct connection between land loss and the downward mobility of colonized peoples, particularly in regards to Chicanos in the US Southwest. For more, see Barrera, *Race and Class in the Southwest*, 48–49.

27. Charles F. C. Ladd to C. H. Swallow, September 19, 1932, and John H. Shary to C. H. Swallow, September 20, 1932, both in LER, JHSP-UTPA.

28. David Hinshaw, "A Common Sense Editorial Which Should Appeal to Valley People," n.d., clipping, John H. Shary Scrapbook, vol. 7, JHSP-UTPA.

29. L. M. Olmsted, "Depression Often an Alibi," n.d., clipping, and Henry Ansley, "Why I Like the Depression," *West Texas Today*, n.d., clipping, both in unmarked folder, Public Work Advisory, CI2192, JHSP-UTPA.

30. E. R. Mills, "Immediate Aid Needed by Valley If It Is to Survive, Leaders Say," September 24, 1933, clipping, unmarked folder, Public Work Advisory, CI2192, JHSP-UTPA.

31. Ibid.

32. Such incidents of colonial powers being at loggerheads with their national governments occasionally do occur. An example of this in the history of formal colonialism is the British Parliament's outlawing of slavery in 1833, which certainly undermined the interests of many British colonists in the Caribbean. For more information, see Judd, *Empire*, 84. Generally speaking, colonial powers rely on home governments as a tool for instituting measures that benefit individual colonists. State and local governments in Texas, as well as the federal government in Washington, DC, tended to support measures that they perceived to be beneficial to commercial farming in the Valley and greater South Texas. Examples of this include the institution of the Bracero Program in 1942, which will be discussed at length in the next chapter, and a gravity irrigation project that sought to counter Mexican irrigation on the south side of the river, which will be discussed at the end of this chapter.

33. "Valley Farm Loans," ca. 1933, n.p., clipping, P.W. Clippings, Public Work Advisory, CI2192, JHSP-UTPA; McElvaine, *Great Depression*, 148.

34. Norman Rozeff, "LRGV Citrus History Excerpts," revised November 2010, http://www.cchc.us/Articles/LRGV%20Citrus%20History%20Excerpts.pdf.

35. John H. Shary, "1933 Plan for Social Stabilization," speech, January 23, 1933, tape recording, Special Collections, University of Texas–Pan American, Edinburg.

36. Ibid.

37. "Citrus Loans to be Opened," *San Juan Sentinel*, July 11, 1935, 4; "Citrus Loans Placed on 'If, As, When' List," *San Juan Sentinel*, July 18, 1935, 1; "Rio Valley Sets Crop Record for Season," *San Juan Sentinel*, March 5 1936, n.p.; "Fruit Season Ends April 2 Says Hoidale," *Valley Morning Star*, March 24, 1935, 1, 4, all also in folder 3, box D6D1, History of John H. Shary, JHSP-UTPA.

38. Laszlo, *Citrus*, 51–52, 54–55.

39. Elizabeth K. Briody, *Household Labor Patterns among Mexican Americans in South Texas: Buscando Trabajo Seguro*, 47–49; Sixteenth Census of the United States, 1940, Agriculture, Texas, First Series, Uses of Land and Classes of Livestock with Statistics for Counties, 13, 19.

40. Hill, "Texas Citrus Industry," 66; Ralph Bray, "Cows and Sows Figure in New Hidalgo Vote Farce: Czar Sets New Record to Put Bonds Over," *McAllen Daily Monitor*, March 24, 1935.

41. Bray, "Cows and Sows."

42. "Hidalgo No. 7 PWA Probe Ordered," March 23, 1935, n.p., clipping, C5D1, JHSP-UTPA; Shary to Frank Andrews, April 16, 1935, folder 4, box C5D1#2, JHSP-UTPA.

43. HLS to Shary, May 2, 1935, folder 10, C5D1#2, JHSP-UTPA. There is also some indication that Bray himself may have been a somewhat unsavory character. For more information see "Antecedents of Ralph G. Bray," August 6, 1934, and Richard Elam to Shary, August 1, 1934, both in unmarked folders, C5D1#2, JHSP-UTPA.

44. Charles Postel, *The Populist Vision*, 5.

45. "Arguments Apply to California Too," *California Citrograph* 14, no. 4 (February 1930): 149.

46. Ralph Bray, "Citrus Marketing," *McAllen Daily Monitor*, June 17, 1934; and Carl C. Magee, "Turning on the Light," *Valley Evening Monitor*, June 15, 1938, 4, both also in folder 3, box D6D1, History of John H. Shary, JHSP-UTPA.

47. Quotation from Bray, "Citrus Marketing;" see also Magee, "Turning on the Light."

48. Ralph Bray, "An Open Letter to John H. Shary," *McAllen Daily Monitor*, June 28, 1934, also in unmarked folder, C5D1, JHSP-UTPA.

49. Ibid.

50. Ibid.

51. W. W. Jones to Ralph Bray, June 30, 1934, C5D1#2, JHSP-UTPA.

52. "Reconstruction Finance Corporation, Chief Auditor's Report on John H. Shary, Sole Proprietor, Mission, Texas, and Controlled Companies, at the Close of Business, April 30, 1940," unmarked folder, Shary C5D4, Loans, RFC, American National Reserve Loan Company—Colven Loan Deal, JHSP-UTPA. This situation is somewhat similar to the experiences of colonists in early British North America, who sometimes literally lived or died based on the finances of British joint stock companies. In the early seventeenth century the Virginia Company, for example, often left the Jamestown colonists to their own devices when the company faced economic calamity. For more information, see Benjamin Woolley, *Savage Kingdom: The True Story of Jamestown, 1607, and the Settlement of America*, 395–96.

53. Untitled, *California Citrograph* 16, no. 10 (August 1931); 460, also in folder 4, box 2, Publications, JHSP-UTPA; Ralph Bray, "Divergent Interests," *McAllen Monitor*, May 31, 1934, 4, also in C5D1, JHSP-UTPA.

54. "Overestimating the Situation," *Texas Citriculture* 5 (December 1929).

55. Joe Kilgore speech on John H. Shary History, n.d., tape recording, Special

Collections, University of Texas–Pan American, Edinburg; W. W. Jones to Ralph Bray, June 30, 1934, C5D1#2, JHSP-UTPA.

56. Floyd Clay Everhard interview by Robert E. Norton, January 4, 1991, Pharr, Texas, tape recording, Special Collections, University of Texas–Pan American, Edinburg; Eugene Walthall to UIC, December 26, 1931; UIC to Walthall Brothers, June 9, 1932; UIC to T. J. Walthall, June 21, 1932; T. M. Mulden to John H. Shary, December 5, 1936; John H. Shary to T. J. Walthall, December 8, 1936; T. J. Walthall to T. M. Mulden, December 12, 1936; UIC to T. J. Walthall, January 16, 1937, all in folder 2, United Irrigation Company, JHSP-UTPA.

57. Progreso, Texas, "Cities of Texas, M–Z," box 36A, J. L. Allhands Papers, South Texas Archives, Texas A&M University–Kingsville.

58. J. H. Welch, "Mose Hill: A Valley Product," draft for *Texas Farming and Citriculture*, June 1940, folder 1989–6.5, box 426B, Lon C. Hill Papers, South Texas Archives, Texas A&M University–Kingsville.

59. "Louis H. Cullen, Buying Broker and Shipper, Fruits and Vegetables, Harlingen, Texas," Financial Statements for June 5, 1933; June 1, 1935; June 1, 1936; October 1, 1937, all in folder 1, Cullen and Thompson Packers and Shippers Collection, University of Texas–Pan American Archives.

60. "Cullen and Thompson Balance Sheet," October 1, 1942, ibid. On the success of Elrod Ginco, see, for example, "1937 United States Partnership Return of Income, Elrod Ginco," folder 1, ibid.

61. "The Citrus Problem," *San Juan Sentinel*, December 3, 1936), 2.

62. Francisco E. Balderama and Raymond Rodríguez, *Decade of Betrayal: Mexican Repatriation in the 1930s*, 120. Historian Rodolfo Acuña argues that the repatriation campaign of Mexicans from Texas was harsh and that most of these repatriates came from the Lower Rio Grande Valley. See Acuña, *Occupied America*, 210–11.

63. Meador, "Wetback Labor," 15.

64. Juan Castillo interview by Corina Castillo, 1987, tape recording, University of Texas–Pan American, Edinburg.

65. Ibid.

66. Jose Infante interview by Corina Castillo, n.d., Special Collections, University of Texas–Pan American, Edinburg.

67. Acuña, *Occupied America*, 221; Johnson, *Revolution in Texas*, 201–2.

68. For more information, see Johnson, *Revolution in Texas*, 201–2.

69. Pauline Dunham interview by Larry W. Clubb, ca. 1987, Special Collections, University of Texas–Pan American, Edinburg.

70. Ibid. What Dunham failed to realize was that only a few ethnic Mexicans in the Valley made it far enough in their education to attend high school.

71. Ibid.

72. Studs Terkel, *Hard Times: An Oral History of the Great Depression*, 2nd ed., 49.

73. Albert Q. Maisel, "The Mexicans Among Us," *Reader's Digest*, March 1956, 182, A1990–34.7, box 430A, J. T. Canales Papers, Jernigan Library, Texas A&M University–Kingsville.

Chapter 6

1. José Ángel Gutiérrez, "La Raza and Revolution: A Study of Four South Texas Counties," 1968, unpublished manuscript, folder "Literary Productions—La Raza and Revolution," box 104, José Ángel Gutiérrez Papers, Nettie Lee Benson Latin American Collection, University of Texas at Austin (hereafter cited as JAG-BLAC).

2. Diener, "Borderland Existence of the Mongolian Kazakhs," 375; Zhurzhenko, "Borders and Memory," 72.

3. Chan Connolly, *Yield, Price, and On-Tree Income Distributions for Texas Citrus, 1971–1972*, Technical Report no. 73–4, in Special Collections, University of Texas–Pan American Library.

4. Hill, "Texas Citrus Industry," 15–16.

5. Ted R. Wylie, "Expert Says Small Farms Doomed by Big Operations," April 8, 1958, clipping, and L. S. Ellis, "Changing Agriculture in the United States," Presentation to the 55th Annual Southern Agricultural Workers in Little Rock, Arkansas, February 3, 1958, both in folder 5, Cullen and Thompson Packers and Shippers Collection, University of Texas–Pan American Archives. Historian Mary Neth argues that "most of the patterns that would characterize post–World War II agriculture—drastic declines in farms and farm population, decreased tenancy, and increased farm size—had just begun to appear by 1940." For more information, see Mary Neth, *Preserving the Family Farm: Women, Community, and the Foundations of Agribusiness in the Midwest, 1900–1940*, 10. For numbers of farmers in the Valley, see Fifteenth Census of the United States, 1930, Agriculture, Texas, Statistics by County, first series, 28, 34, 45; Sixteenth Census of the United States, 1940, Agriculture, Uses of Land, Principal Crops and Classes of Livestock with Statistics for Counties, first series, 59, 65, 77; United States Census of Agriculture, 1945, Texas, Statistics by Counties, Agriculture, Texas, first series, vol. 1, part 26, 75, 88, 110; Briody, *Household Labor Patterns*, 47–49.

6. Acuña, *Occupied America*, 266–69. For two excellent book-length treatments of the Bracero Program, see Kitty Calavita, *Inside the State: The Bracero Program, Immigration, and the I.N.S.*, and Deborah Cohen, *Braceros: Migrant Citizens and Transnational Subjects in the Postwar United States and Mexico.*

7. Acuña, *Occupied America*, 266–67. For more information on Stevenson's resolution and the Good Neighbor Commission, see Thomas A. Guglielmo, "Fighting for Caucasian Rights: Mexicans, Mexican Americans, and the Transnational Struggle for Civil Rights in World War II Texas," *Journal of American History* 92, no. 4 (March 2006): 1212–37, and George Norris Green, *The Establishment in Texas Politics: The Primitive Years, 1938–1957*, 80–81.

8. Acuña, *Occupied America*, 267, 269.

9. Carrol Norquest Jr. interview by Homero S. Vera, April 3, 2003, Edinburg, Texas, Item no. 97, Bracero History Archive (hereafter cited as BHA), http://braceroarchive .org/items/show/97.

10. Ibid.

11. Ibid. For a somewhat more recent examination of the *repartimiento* in one part

of New Spain, see Jeremy Baskes, *Indians, Merchants, and Markets: A Reinterpretation of the Repartimiento and Spanish-Indian Economic Relations in Colonial Oaxaca, 1750–1821.*

12. Norquest interview by Vera; Jesse Treviño interview by Homero S. Vera, May 7, 2003, location unknown, Item no. 100; and Tula Bareda Sánchez interview by Homero S. Vera, May 1, 2003, location unknown, Item no. 98, all in BHA, http://bracearchive .org/items/show/98.

13. "Alien Labor Debate Bitter," 2B, *San Antonio Light,* June 6, 1952, clipping; "Fisher Blocks Portal Funds," *San Antonio Light,* n.d., clipping; and "Shivers Uses Illegal Aliens," n.d., clipping, all in folder "Correspondence—American Council of Spanish-Speaking People A1990–34.23," box 436B, Canales-A&M.

14. "Shivers Accused of Using Cheap Workers," n.d., clipping; "Wetback Charge a Smear: Shivers," n.d., clipping; "Tobin Blasts Wetback Adherents," *Civil Liberties Newsletter no. 4 of the American Council of Spanish-Speaking People,* March 17, 1952, 1, all in folder "Correspondence—American Council of Spanish-Speaking People A1990–34.23," box 436B, Canales-A&M.

15. Ngai, *Impossible Subjects,* 153–56.

16. Anderson, *The Movement and the Sixties,* 300–301, 304. For an excellent discussion of early Mexican labor organizing in Texas, see Zamora, *World of the Mexican Worker.* Despite common grounds, recent scholarship has shown that Mexican Americans and African Americans failed to find any common ground with each other in their quests for civil rights in the middle of the twentieth century. For more, see Neil Foley, *Quest for Equality: The Failed Promise of Black-Brown Solidarity.*

17. Bowman, "What About Texas?" 8, 10–11.

18. "Valley Farm Union Pushed," *Corpus Christi Caller,* May 23, 1966, clipping, and "Mission-Based Drive Opens to Organize Farm Workers," *Valley Evening Monitor,* May 23, 1966, clipping, both in folder 5, box 3, AR-46, Mexican-American Farm Workers Movement Collection, Special Collections, University of Texas at Arlington (hereafter cited as MAFWM-UTA).

19. IWA Newsletter no. 2, folder 8, box 8, MAFWM-UTA; "Packers Picketing Valley Melon Men," *San Angelo Standard Times,* June 2, 1966; "Melon Pickers Back in the Fields," *Dallas Times-Herald,* June 3, 1966; "Nazi-Like Deed in Valley Charged," *San Antonio Express-News,* June 11, 1966; and Bill Durham, "Farmhands on Brink of Revolt," *Houston Post,* June 12, 1966, all also in folder 5, box 3, MAFWM-UTA. For several examples of characterization of unions as radicals, see, Bowman, "What About Texas?" 14–53.

20. Charles Carr Winn, "Mexican Americans in the Texas Labor Movement" (PhD diss., Texas Christian University, 1972), 97, 103.

21. Bowman, "What About Texas?" 17, 19–20.

22. Antonio Orendain interview by Charles Carr Winn, July 20, 1971, transcript, Special Collections, University of Texas at Arlington.

23. Ibid.

24. Ibid.

25. Ibid.

26. Ibid.; "Farm Union Pickets are Arrested at Roma for Halting Bridge Traffic," *Valley Morning Star*, October 25, 1966, 1, 3, also in folder 4, box 4, MAFWM-UTA.

27. Gary Garrison, "Valley Rail Trestle Destroyed by Fire," *Corpus Christi Caller*, November 11, 1966, 1, 14, also in folder 4, box 4, MAFWM-UTA; Orendain interview by Carr Winn.

28. "Rail Service Still Halted," *San Antonio Express*, November 6, 1966, and "Rio Grande City Terrorism Charged," *San Antonio Express*, November 8, 1966, 1-C, both also in folder 4, box 4, MAFWM-UTA.

29. Orendain interview by Carr Winn, OHP-UTA; "Jailed Union Men Urging Hunger Strike," *Valley Evening Monitor*, November 18, 1966; "10 Valley Organizers Released on Bond," *Houston Chronicle*, November 16, 1966; and "Hunger Strike Ends after Bond Posted for 10 Jailed Union Men," November 1966, no further information, in folder 4, box 4, MAFWM-UTA. See also "Summons for Francisco Medrano to Appear in the Missouri Pacific Railroad Company vs. UFWOC on June 8, 1967 at the Courthouse in Rio Grande City," folder 15, box 8, MAFWM-UTA.

30. "Orendain Jailed for 'Locking a Gate,'" *El Malcriado*, no. 51, also in Newspaper Collection, University Library Special Collections, University of Texas at Arlington. For more on the Plan de San Diego rebellion, see Johnson, *Revolution in Texas*.

31. "The Impact of Alien Commuters upon the Economy of US Towns on the Mexican Border," US Department of Labor, October 1967, folder 4, box 1, AR 278 series 11, Texas AFL-CIO, Mexican-American Affairs Committee, Special Collections, University of Texas at Arlington.

32. Armando Navarro, *Mexican-American Youth Organization: Avant-Garde of the Chicano Movement in Texas*, 33; Orendain interview by Carr Winn; Doug Adair, "Texas Strike," *Liberation*, August 1967, 6–9.

33. "Farm Union Plans Boycott," *San Antonio Express*, February 1, 1967, 1-C, also in folder 5, box 4, MAFWM-UTA. For general information on the poverty and poor conditions of ethnic Mexicans in the Valley, see Anderson, *The Movement and the Sixties*, 301.

34. John Staples Shockley, *Chicano Revolt in a Texas Town*, 1–4, 16.

35. Ibid., 4–17, quote on 13.

36. Ibid., 14, 16–17.

37. Ibid., 24.

38. Harley L. Browning and S. Dale McLemore, "A Statistical Profile of the Spanish-Surname Population of Texas," Bureau of Business Research, University of Texas at Austin, 1964, no folder, box 131, JAG-BLAC. For a recounting of the events leading up to the election, see ibid., 24–41; for more on PASSO, see, Acuña, *Occupied America*, 303.

39. Shockley, *Chicano Revolt*, 42–79; José Ángel Gutiérrez, "Toward a Chicano Mental Health Program," no other information, folder Lit. Prod. by JAG—Various Writings, box 103, JAG-BLAC.

40. Acuña, *Occupied America*, 316; Shockley, *Chicano Revolt*, 114. For more on

MAYO, see Navarro, *Mexican American Youth Organization.*

41. "MAYO Gets Valley Foothold," *McAllen Monitor*, November 24, 1968, clipping in folder MAYO 1968, box 53, JAG-BLAC.

42. Ibid.

43. Ibid.

44. "School Told to Readmit Boycotters," *San Antonio Express*, November 26, 1968; "Valley Students List Demands," November 15, 1968, no other information, clipping, folder "MAYO 1968," box 53, JAG-BLAC. See also Norma R. Cuellar, "The Edcouch-Elsa Walkout," undergraduate essay, University of Texas–Pan American, June 29, 1984, www.aaperales.com/school/files/walkout/eewalkout.doc.

45. "Edcouch-Elsa Trustees to Head Off 'Outside Agitators,'" *Valley Evening Monitor*, November 6, 1968, also in folder "MAYO 1968," box 53, JAG-BLAC.

46. José Ángel Gutiérrez, "A Study Into the Feasibility of Organizing Civil Rights Committees in Texas," November 1, 1969, folder "Lit. Prod. by JAG—Various Writings," box 103; "Report on Distribution of Shoes by the Border Project," no other information, folder "U.S.-Mexico Border Economic Development Project Correspondence-In, 1970–1972," box 76; and Gutiérrez, "Toward a Chicano Mental Health Program," all in JAG-BLAC.

47. United States Commission on Civil Rights, "Issue Presentation for Education Conference," Crystal City, Texas, March 7, 1970, folder "Walkout, 1969–1970," box 78, JAG-BLAC.

48. "Pupils Claim Victory," *San Antonio Light*, January 6, 1970, also in folder "Walkout, 1969–1970", and "The Walkout 1969: A Diary of Events," folder "The Walkout 1969: A Diary of Events," both in box 78, JAG-BLAC; "Crystal City School Election Looms as Political Showdown," *Beaumont Journal*, April 3, 1970, also in folder "Elections, 1970," box 35, JAG-BLAC.

49. "Boycott: 'A Lifetime Thing,'" *Houston Post*, December 21, 1969, also in folder "Walkout, 1969–1970," box 78, JAG-BLAC.

50. "U.S. to Investigate High School Boycott in Texas," *New York Times* December 19, 1969, also in folder "Elections '70 Clippings," box 35, JAG-BLAC; "Pupils Claim Victory," *San Antonio Light*, January 6, 1970, also in folder "Walkout, 1969–1970," box 78, JAG-BLAC.

51. "The Walkout 1969: A Diary of Events;" "Pupils Claim Victory," *San Antonio Light*, January 6, 1970, also in folder "Walkout, 1969–1970," both in box 78, JAG-BLAC.

52. Bill Combs to José Ángel Gutiérrez, December 21, 1969; "MAYO Members Meet in Mission," January 1, 1970, no other information, clipping, both in folder "MAYO, 1969," box 53, JAG-BLAC.

53. Bill Porterfield, "Chicanos: Ferment in the Valley," *Chicago Daily News*, December 22, 1969, 3–4, also in folder "MAYO, 1969," box 53, JAG-BLAC.

54. Ibid.

55. Gutiérrez, "Toward a Model Chicano Mental Health Program," JAG-BLAC.

56. "Crystal City School Board Election Looms as Political Showdown," JAG-BLAC.

57. "Candidate in Crystal City Asks for Federal Observers," *Corpus Christi Caller-*

Times, March 22, 1970, and "'Youth Ticket' Wins Crystal City," *Corpus Christi Caller-Times*, April 5, 1970, both also in folder "Elections, 1970," box 35, JAG-BLAC.

58. Untitled note, no other information, folder "Elections, 1970," box 35, JAG-BLAC.

59. "'Youth Ticket Wins Crystal City," JAG-BLAC.

60. "Raza Unida Party," no other information, and "La Raza Gets Second Victory," *San Antonio Light*, April 8, 1970, both clippings in folder "Elections '70 Clippings," box 35, JAG-BLAC.

61. Nelson Wolff to José Ángel Gutiérrez, May 11, 1970, folder "Correspondence 1970," box 19, JAG-BLAC.

62. Ibid.

63. Gutiérrez, "Toward a Model Chicano Mental Health Program," JAG-BLAC.

64. Gutiérrez, "La Raza and Revolution," JAG-BLAC.

65. Ibid.

66. Juan Morán González, *Border Renaissance: The Texas Centennial and the Emergence of Mexican American Literature*, 6.

67. Ibid.

68. José Ángel Gutiérrez, "The Hopelessness of Non Violence: The Dilemma for Chicanos," no other information, folder "Lit. Prod. by JAG—Various Writings," box 103, and José Ángel Gutiérrez, handwritten notes, folder "Correspondence 1969," box 19, both in JAG-BLAC.

69. Gutiérrez, "Hopelessness of Non Violence."

70. Gutiérrez to César Chávez, February 9, 1972, folder "Correspondence, 1972" (2), box 19, JAG-BLAC.

71. Ibid.

72. Ibid.

73. For more information, see, Bowman, "What About Texas?" 74–121.

74. José O. Mata interview by José Ángel Gutiérrez, Crystal City, Texas, February 2, 1998, Tejano Voices Project, Center for Mexican-American Studies, Special Collections, University of Texas at Arlington Library (hereafter cited as TV-CMAS).

75. Ibid.

76. Ofelia Santos interview by José Ángel Gutiérrez, Edinburg, Texas, June 18, 1998, TV-CMAS

77. Rudy Espinosa interview by José Ángel Gutiérrez, Crystal City, Texas, October 16, 1998, TV-CMAS.

78. Ibid.

79. Severita Lara interview by José Ángel Gutiérrez, Crystal City, Texas, July 18, 1996, TV-CMAS.

80. Ibid.

81. Ibid.

82. Ibid. For the sake of brevity I have shortened Lara's original quotation and given the English translation of several things that she originally expressed in Spanish.

83. Ibid.

84. Alma Canales interview by José Ángel Gutiérrez, October 23, 1997, TV-CMAS.

85. Ibid.

86. Ibid.

87. Ibid.

88. Judith N. McArthur and Harold L. Smith, *Texas through Women's Eyes: The Twentieth-Century Experience*, 225.

89. Leo Montalvo interview by José Ángel Gutiérrez, McAllen, Texas, December 20, 1997, TV-CMAS.

90. Ibid.

91. Ibid.

92. Antonio Bill interview by José Ángel Gutiérrez, Alice, Texas, June 16, 1998, TV-CMAS.

93. Ibid.

94. Arreola, *Tejano South Texas*.

Conclusion

1. Acuña, *Occupied America*, xv.

2. W. H. Friend, "Citrus Fruit Culture," Handbook of Texas Online http://www.tshaonline.org/handbook/online/articles/afc01, published by the Texas State Historical Association.

3. Chávez, *Beyond Nations*, 168; Maril, *Poorest of Americans*, 3, 4, 5–10, 11, 12–18.

4. Chad Richardson and Michael J. Pisani, *The Informal and Underground Economy of the South Texas Border*, 9–11.

5. Ibid., 1–7.

6. *The United Farm Workers, AFL-CIO, in Texas* (n.p.: n.d.), pamphlet, folder 13, box 1, MFWC-UTA; James C. Harington, "From La Casita to LUPE," *Texas Observer*, December 3, 2004.

7. Maril, *Poorest of Americans*, 55, 58, 90.

8. Richardson and Pisani, *Informal and Underground Economy*, 31.

9. Ibid.

10. Ibid., 32, 168–96.

11. Ibid., 256.

12. For more, see Arreola, *Tejano South Texas*.

BIBLIOGRAPHY

Archival Sources

Bancroft Library, University of California, Berkeley
Paul Taylor Papers
DeGolyer Library, Southern Methodist University, Dallas, Texas
Ephemera Collection
Dolph Briscoe Center for American History, University of Texas at Austin, Vertical
    Files
Citrus Fruit
Cleo Dawson
Frank Cushman Pierce
Hart Stilwell
Nettie Lee Benson Latin American Collection, University of Texas at Austin
José Ángel Gutiérrez Papers
South Texas Archives, Texas A&M University–Kingsville
J. L. Allhands Papers
J. T. Canales Papers
Lon C. Hill Papers
Newspaper Collection
Special Collections, University of Texas at Arlington
Mexican-American Farm Workers Movement Collection
Newspaper Collection
Texas AFL-CIO, Mexican-American Affairs Committee
Special Collections, University of Texas–Pan American, Edinburg
American Rio Grande Land and Irrigation Company
Cullen and Thompson Packers and Shippers Collection
John H. Shary Papers

Government Documents

Connolly, Chan. *Yield, Price, and On-Tree Income Distributions for Texas Citrus, 1971–*
    1972. Technical Report no. 73–4. Weslaco, Texas: Texas Agricultural Experiment
    Station, 1973.

Delcurto, J. M.; E. W. Halstead; and H. F. Halstead. *The Citrus Industry of the Lower Rio Grande Valley of Texas*. Bulletin no. 79 (March–April 1923). 2nd ed. Austin: Texas State Department of Agriculture, 1925.

"Report on the Rio Grande Valley Citrus Industry." College Station: Texas Agricultural Extension Service and Texas Agricultural Experiment Station, Texas A&M University System, n. d. In Special Collections, University of Texas–Pan American, Edinburg.

United States Census. Census of Agriculture, 1945, Texas, Statistics by Counties, First Series, Vol. 1, Part 26.

———. Fifteenth Census of the United States, 1930, Agriculture, Texas, Statistics by Counties, First Series.

———. Fifteenth Census of the United States 1930, Agriculture, Texas, Statistics by Counties, Third Series, Type of Farm.

———. Fifteenth Census of the United States, 1930, Population, Vol. 1.

———. Sixteenth Census of the United States, 1940, Agriculture, Texas, Uses of Land and Classes of Livestock with Statistics for Counties, First Series.

Books and Articles

Abbot, Elizabeth. *Sugar: A Bittersweet History*. London: Duckworth Overlook, 2009.

Acuña, Rodolfo A. *Occupied America: A History of Chicanos*. 5th ed. New York: Pearson/Longman, 2004.

Adelman, Jeremy, and Stephen Aron. "From Borderlands to Borders: Empires, Nation-States, and the Peoples In Between in North American History." *American Historical Review* 104, no. 3 (June 1999): 814–41.

Alanis Enciso, Fernando Saul. *Valle Bajo del Río Bravo, Tamaulipas, en la década de 1930: El desarollo regional en la posrevolución a partir de la irrigación, la migración interna y los repatriados de estados unidos*. Ciudad Victoria: El Colegio de Tamaulipas/El Colegio de San Luis, 2003.

Allen, John Houghton. *Southwest*. Philadelphia and New York: J. B. Lippincott Company, 1952.

Allhands, J. L. *Gringo Builders*. Joplin and Dallas, privately published, 1931.

Alonzo, Armando C. *Tejano Legacy: Rancheros and Settlers in South Texas*. Albuquerque: University of New Mexico Press, 1998.

Anders, Evan. *Boss Rule in South Texas: The Progressive Era*. Austin: University of Texas Press, 1982.

Anderson, Terry H. *The Movement and the Sixties: Protest in America from Greensboro to Wounded Knee*. Oxford: Oxford University Press, 1995.

Applebaum, Robert, and John Wood Sweet, eds. *Envisioning an English Empire: Jamestown and the Making of the North Atlantic World*. Philadelphia: University of Pennsylvania Press, 2005.

Appleby, Joyce; Lynn Hunt; and Margaret Jacob. *Telling the Truth about History*. New York: W. W. Norton & Company, 1994.

Arreola, Daniel D. *Tejano South Texas: A Mexican Cultural Province.* Austin: University of Texas Press, 2002.

Baker, Daniel, and William M. Baker. *The Life and Labours of the Rev. Daniel Baker, D.D.: Pastor and Evangelist.* Philadelphia: William S. & Alfred Martien, 1858.

Balderama, Francisco E., and Raymond Rodríguez, *Decade of Betrayal: Mexican Repatriation in the 1930s.* Albuquerque: University of New Mexico Press, 1995.

Barr, Juliana. *Peace Came in the Form of a Woman: Indians and Spaniards in the Texas Borderlands.* Chapel Hill: University of North Carolina Press, 2007.

Barrera, Mario. *Race and Class in the Southwest: A Theory of Racial Inequality.* Notre Dame: University of Notre Dame Press, 1979.

Baskes, Jeremy. *Indians, Merchants, and Markets: A Reinterpretation of the Repartimiento and Spanish-Indian Economic Relations in Colonial Oaxaca, 1750–1821.* Stanford: Stanford University Press, 2000.

Basson, Lauren L. *White Enough to be American? Race Mixing, Indigenous People, and the Boundaries of State and Nation.* Chapel Hill: The University of North Carolina Press, 2008.

Belich, Bill. *Replenishing the Earth: The Settler Revolution and the Rise of the Angloworld.* Oxford: Oxford University Press, 2011.

Bender, Thomas. *A Nation among Nations: America's Place in World History.* New York: Hill and Wang, 2006.

Bennett, Lerone, Jr. "System: Internal Colonialism Structures Black, White Relations in America." *Ebony,* April 1972, 33–42.

Benton-Cohen, Katherine. *Borderline Americans: Racial Division and Labor War in the Arizona Borderlands.* Cambridge: Harvard University Press, 2009.

Blackhawk, Ned. *Violence over the Land: Indians and Empires in the Early American West.* Cambridge: Harvard University Press, 2006.

Bowman, Tim. "Negotiating Conquest: Internal Colonialism and Shared Histories of the South Texas Borderlands." *Western Historical Quarterly* 46 (Autumn 2015): 335–53.

Briody, Elizabeth K. *Household Labor Patterns among Mexican Americans in South Texas: Buscando Trabajo Seguro.* New York: AMS Press, 1986.

Brooks, James F. "Served Well by Plunder: La Gran Ladronería and Producers of History Astride the Río Grande." *American Quarterly* 52, no. 1 (March 2000): 23–58.

Brower, Benjamin Claude. *A Desert Named Peace: The Violence of France's Empire in the Algerian Sahara, 1844–1902.* New York: Columbia University Press, 2009.

Butler, William. *Mexico in Transition from the Power of Political Romanism to Civil and Religious Liberty.* New York: Hunt and Eaton, 1892.

Calavita, Kitty. *Inside the State: The Bracero Program, Immigration, and the I.N.S.* New York: Routledge, 1992.

Cantrell, Gregg. *Stephen F. Austin: Empresario of Texas.* New Haven: Yale University Press, 1999.

Carrigan, William D. *The Making of a Lynching Culture: Violence and Vigilantism in Central Texas, 1836–1916.* Champaign: University of Illinois Press, 2006.

————, and Clive Webb. *Forgotten Dead: Mob Violence against Mexicans in the United States, 1848–1928*. Oxford: Oxford University Press, 2013.

Cavaliero, Roderick. *Strangers in the Land: The Rise and Decline of the British Indian Empire*. London: I. B. Tauris Publishers, 2002.

Cervantes, Fred A. "Chicanos as a Postcolonial Minority: Some Questions Concerning the Adequacy of the Paradigm of Internal Colonialism." In *Latino/a Thought: Culture, Politics, and Society*. Edited by Francisco H. Vázquez and Rodolfo D. Torres. Lanham, MD.: Rowman and Littlefield Publishers, 2003.

Chambers, William T. "Lower Rio Grande Valley of Texas." *Economic Geography* 6, no. 4 (October 1930): 364–73.

Chang, Kornel. *Pacific Connections: The Making of the U.S.-Canadian Borderlands*. Berkeley: University of California Press, 2012.

Chávez, John R. *Beyond Nations: Evolving Homelands in the North Atlantic World, 1400–2000*. Cambridge: Cambridge University Press, 2009.

————. *The Lost Land: The Chicano Image of the Southwest*. Albuquerque: University of New Mexico Press, 1984.

————. "Aliens in Their Native Lands: The Persistence of Internal Colonial Theory." *Journal of World History* 22, no. 4 (December 2011): 785–809.

————. "When Borders Cross People: The Internal Colonial Challenge to Borderlands Theory." *Journal of Borderlands Studies* 28, no. 1 (June 2013): 33–46.

Chevalier, François. *Land and Society in Colonial Mexico: The Great Hacienda*. Berkeley: University of California Press, 1970.

Cohen, Deborah. *Braceros: Migrant Citizens and Transnational Subjects in the Postwar United States and Mexico*. Chapel Hill: University of North Carolina Press, 2011.

Crisp, James. *Sleuthing the Alamo: Davy Crockett's Last Stand and Other Mysteries of the Texas Revolution*. Oxford: Oxford University Press, 2005.

Culver, Lawrence. *The Frontier of Leisure: Southern California and the Shaping of Modern America*. Oxford: Oxford University Press, 2010.

Danbom, David B. *Born in the Country: A History of Rural America*. Baltimore: The Johns Hopkins University Press, 1995.

Davis, Steven L. *J. Frank Dobie: A Liberated Mind*. Austin: University of Texas Press, 2009.

Dawson, Cleo. *She Came to the Valley*. 2nd ed. Austin: Jenkins Publishing Company, San Felipe Press, 1972.

DeLay, Brian. *War of a Thousand Deserts: Indian Raids and the U.S.-Mexican War*. New Haven: Yale University Press, 2008.

————, ed. *North American Borderlands: Rewriting Histories*. New York: Routledge, 2013.

De León, Arnoldo. *They Called Them Greasers: Anglo Attitudes toward Mexicans in Texas, 1821–1900*. Austin: University of Texas Press, 1983.

————. *The Tejano Community*. Albuquerque: University of New Mexico Press, 1982.

————, ed. *War along the Border: The Mexican Revolution and Tejano Communities*. College Station: Texas A&M University Press, 2012.

Deutsch, Sarah. *No Separate Refuge: Culture, Class, and Gender on an Anglo-Hispanic Frontier in the American Southwest, 1880–1940*. New York: Oxford University Press, 1987.

Deverell, William. *Whitewashed Adobe: The Rise of Los Angeles and the Remaking of its Mexican Past*. Berkeley: University of California Press, 2004.

Dewey, Alicia. *Pesos and Dollars: Entrepreneurs in the Texas-Mexico Borderlands, 1880–1940*. College Station: Texas A&M University Press, 2014.

Diener, Alexander. "The Borderland Existence of the Mongolian Kazakhs." In *The Ashgate Research Companion to Border Studies*. Edited by Doris Wastl-Walter. Surrey, England: Ashgate Publishing, 2011.

Evans, Sterling. *Bound in Twine: The History and Ecology of the Henequen-Wheat Complex for Mexico and the American and Canadian Plains, 1880–1950*. College Station: Texas A&M University Press, 2007.

Fiege, Mark. *Irrigated Eden: The Making of an Agricultural Landscape in the American West*. Seattle: University of Washington Press, 1999.

Foley, Douglas, et al. *From Peones to Politicos: Ethnic Relations in a South Texas Town, 1900–1977*. Austin: Center for Mexican-American Studies, University of Texas at Austin, 1977.

Foley, Neil. *The White Scourge: Mexicans, Blacks, and Poor Whites in the Texas Cotton Culture*. Berkeley: University of California Press, 1997.

————. *Quest for Equality: The Failed Promise of Black-Brown Solidarity*. Cambridge: Harvard University Press, 2010.

Foster, L. L. *Forgotten Texas Census: First Annual Report of the Agricultural Bureau of the Department of Agriculture, Insurance, Statistics, and History, 1887–88*. Introduction by Barbara J. Rozek. Austin: Texas State Historical Association, 2001.

Garcia, Matt. *A World of Its Own: Race, Labor, and Citrus in the Making of Greater Los Angeles, 1900–1970*. Chapel Hill: University of North Carolina Press, 2001.

Garner, Claud. *Wetback*. New York: Coward-McCann, 1947.

Garrido, Samuel. "Oranges or 'Lemons'? Family Farming and Product Quality in the Spanish Orange Industry, 1870–1960." *Agricultural History* 84, no. 2 (Spring 2010): 224–43.

Gómez, Luis G. *Crossing the Rio Grande: An Immigrant's Life in the 1880s*. College Station: Texas A&M University Press, 2006.

Gómez-Quiñones, Juan. *Mexican-American Labor, 1790–1990*. Albuquerque: University of New Mexico Press, 1994.

Gonzales, Trinidad. "The Mexican Revolution, *Revolución de Texas*, and *Matanza de 1915*." In *War along the Border: The Mexican Revolution and Tejano Communities*. Edited by Arnoldo de León. College Station: Texas A&M University Press, 2012.

González, Gilbert. *Labor and Community: Mexican Citrus Worker Villages in a Southern California County, 1900–1950*. Urbana: University of Illinois Press, 1994.

———. *Culture of Empire: American Writers, Mexico, and Mexican Immigrants, 1880–1930*. Austin: University of Texas Press, 2004.

———. *Guest Workers or Colonized Labor? Mexican Labor Migration to the United States*. Boulder: Paradigm Publishers, 2006.

González, Jovita. *Life Along the Border: A Landmark Tejana Thesis*. Edited by María Eugenia Cotera. College Station: Texas A&M University Press, 2006.

González, Juan Morán. *Border Renaissance: The Texas Centennial and the Emergence of Mexican American Literature*. Austin: University of Texas Press, 2009.

González, Saúl Tijerina. *Huellas imborrables: Historia de la Iglesia Nacional Presbiteriana*. Monterrey: Publicaciones El Faro, 1984.

Gordon, Linda. *The Great Arizona Orphan Abduction*. Cambridge: Harvard University Press, 1999.

Graybill, Andrew. *Policing the Great Plains: Rangers, Mounties, and the North American Frontier, 1875–1910*. Lincoln: University of Nebraska Press, 2007.

Green, George Norris. *The Establishment in Texas Politics: The Primitive Years, 1938–1957*. Norman: University of Oklahoma Press, 1979.

Greenberg, Amy S. *Manifest Manhood and the Antebellum American Empire*. Cambridge: Cambridge University Press, 2005.

Guglielmo, Thomas A. "Fighting for Caucasian Rights: Mexicans, Mexican Americans, and the Transnational Struggle for Civil Rights in World War II Texas." *Journal of American History* 92, no. 4 (March 2006): 1212–37.

Hämäläinen, Pekka. *The Comanche Empire*. New Haven: Yale University Press, 2008.

Hammerback, John C., and Richard J. Jensen. *The Rhetorical Career of Cesar Chavez*. College Station: Texas A&M University Press, 1998.

Hart, John Mason, ed. *Border Crossings: Mexican and Mexican-American Workers*. Wilmington: Scholarly Resource Books, 1998.

Hartig, Anthea. "'In a World He Has Created:' Class Collectivity and the Growers' Landscape of the Southern California Citrus Industry, 1890–1940." *California History* 74, no. 2 (Summer 1995): 100–111.

———, and Margo McBane. "Oranges on the Plains of Id: The Influences of the Citrus Industry on San Gabriel Valley Communities." *California Politics and Policy*, 1998, 9–17.

Haynes, Sam W., and Christopher Morris, eds. *Manifest Destiny and Empire: American Antebellum Expansionism*. College Station: Texas A&M University Press, 1997.

Hechter, Michael. *Internal Colonialism: The Celtic Fringe in British National Development, 1536–1966*. Berkeley: University of California Press, 1971.

Hentz, Caroline Lee. *The Planter's Northern Bride*, vol. 1. Philadelphia: A. Hart, Carey and Hart, 1854.

Hernández, José Ángel. *Mexican American Colonization during the Nineteenth Century: A History of the U.S.-Mexico Borderlands*. Cambridge: Cambridge University Press, 2012.

Hernández, Kelly Lytle. *Migra! A History of the US Border Patrol.* Berkeley: University of California Press, 2010.

Herzog, Lawrence. *Where North Meets South: Cities, Space, and Politics on the U.S.-Mexico Border.* Austin: Center for Mexican-American Studies at the University of Texas at Austin, 1990.

Hind, Robert J. "The Internal Colonial Concept." *Comparative Studies in Society and History* 26, no. 3 (July 1984): 543–68.

Hogan, William Ransom. *The Texas Republic: A Social and Economic History.* Norman: University of Oklahoma Press, 1946.

Hollinger, David. "Amalgamation and Hypodescent: The Question of Ethnoracial Mixture in the United States." *American Historical Review* 108, no. 5 (December 2003): 1363–90.

Horn, James. "The Conquest of Eden: Possession and Dominion in Early Virginia." In *Envisioning an English Empire: Jamestown and the Making of the North Atlantic World.* Edited by Robert Applebaum and John Wood Sweet. Philadelphia: University of Pennsylvania Press, 2005.

Horne, Gerald. *Black and Brown: African Americans and the Mexican Revolution, 1910–1920.* New York: New York University Press, 2005.

Howe, David Walker. *What Hath God Wrought: The Transformation of America, 1815–1848.* Oxford: Oxford University Press, 2007.

Informes que en cumplimiento del decreto de 2 de Octubre de 1872 rinde al ejecutivo de la unión la Comisión Pesquisidora de la Frontera del Norte, sobre el desempeño de sus trabajos. México, DF: Díaz de León y White, 1874.

Jacobson, Matthew Frye. *Barbarian Virtues: The United States Encounters Foreign Peoples at Home and Abroad, 1876–1917.* New York: Hill and Wang, 2000.

Jacoby, Karl. *Shadows at Dawn: A Borderlands Massacre and the Violence of History.* New York: The Penguin Press, 2008.

Johnson, Benjamin H. *Bordertown: The Odyssey of an American Place.* New Haven: Yale University Press, 2008.

————. "The Plan de San Diego Uprising and the Making of the Modern Texas-Mexican Borderlands." In *Continental Crossroads: Remapping US-Mexico Borderlands History.* Edited by Samuel Truett and Elliott Young. Durham, NC: Duke University Press, 2004.

————. *Revolution in Texas: How a Forgotten Rebellion and Its Bloody Suppression Turned Mexicans into Americans.* New Haven: Yale University Press, 2003.

————, and Andrew R. Graybill, eds. *Bridging National Borders in North America: Transnational and Comparative Histories.* Durham: Duke University Press, 2010.

Johnson, Rob. *The Lost Years of William S. Burroughs: Beats in South Texas.* College Station: Texas A&M University Press, 2006.

Jones, Marie. "W. Clifford Scott: He Aided Growth of the Citrus Industry." In *Rio Grande Roundup: A Story of Texas Tropical Borderland.* Mission, TX: Border Kingdom Press, 1980.

Jordan, Terry G. "Perceptual Regions in Texas." *Geographical Review* 68, no. 3 (July 1978): 293–307.

Judd, Denis. *Empire: The British Imperial Experience from 1765 to the Present.* London: Phoenix Press, 1996.

Knight, Alan. *The Mexican Revolution.* 2 vols. Lincoln: University of Nebraska Press, 1986.

Krauze, Enrique. *Mexico: Biography of Power.* New York: Harper Perennial, 1998.

Kropp, Phoebe S. *California Vieja: Culture and Memory in a Modern American Place.* Berkeley: University of California Press, 2006.

Laszlo, Pierre. *Citrus: A History.* Chicago: University of Chicago Press, 2007.

Leiker, James N. *Racial Borders: Black Soldiers along the Rio Grande.* College Station: Texas A&M University Press, 2010.

Levario, Miguel Antonio. *Militarizing the Border: When Mexicans Became the Enemy.* College Station: Texas A&M University Press, 2012.

Levy, Jacques A. *Cesar Chavez: Autobiography of La Causa.* New York: W. W. Norton and Company, 1966.

Litwack, Leon F. *Been in the Storm so Long: The Aftermath of Slavery.* New York: Vintage Books, 1980.

Maril, Robert Lee. *Poorest of Americans: The Mexican-Americans of the Lower Rio Grande Valley of Texas.* Notre Dame: University of Notre Dame Press, 1989.

Martínez, Camilo A. "Labor in the Valley: The Development of Texas' Citrus Industry." *Journal of South Texas* 7, no. 1 (1994): 1–27.

McAllen-Amberson, Mary Margaret; James A. McAllen; and Margaret H. McAllen. *I Would Rather Sleep in Texas: A History of the Lower Rio Grande Valley and the People of the Santa Anita Land Grant.* Austin: Texas State Historical Association, 2003.

McArthur, Judith N., and Harold L. Smith. *Texas through Women's Eyes: The Twentieth-Century Experience.* Austin: University of Texas Press, 2010.

McElvaine, Robert S. *The Great Depression: America, 1929–1941.* 2nd ed. New York: Three Rivers Press, 1993.

McPhee, John. *Oranges.* New York: Farrar, Straus, and Giroux, 1967.

Meeks, Eric V. *Border Citizens: The Making of Indians, Mexicans, and Anglos in Arizona.* Austin: University of Texas Press, 2007.

Meer, Sarah. *Uncle Tom Mania: Slavery, Minstrelsy, and Transatlantic Culture in the 1850s.* Athens: University of Georgia Press, 2005.

Meinig, D. W. *Imperial Texas: An Interpretive Essay in Cultural Geography.* Austin: University of Texas Press, 1969.

Menchaca, Martha. *Recovering History, Constructing Race: The Indian, Black, and White Roots of Mexican Americans.* Austin: University of Texas Press, 2001.

Mignolo, Walter D. *Local Histories/Global Designs: Coloniality, Subaltern Knowledges, and Border Thinking.* Princeton: Princeton University Press, 2000.

Montejano, David. *Anglos and Mexicans in the Making of Texas, 1836–1986.* Austin: University of Texas Press, 1986.

Montgomery, Julia Cameron. *A Little Journey through the Lower Valley of the Rio Grande: The Magic Valley of Texas*. Houston: Southern Pacific, 1929.

Montoya, María E. *Translating Property: The Maxwell Land Grant and the Conflict over Land in the American West, 1840–1900*. Berkeley: University of California Press, 2002.

Moran, Michael G. *Inventing Virginia: Sir Walter Raleigh and the Rhetoric of Colonization, 1584–1590*. New York: Peter Land Publishing, 2007.

Nance, Joseph Milton. *After San Jacinto: The Texas-Mexican Frontier, 1836–1841*. Austin: University of Texas Press, 1963.

Navarro, Armando. *Mexican-American Youth Organization: Avant-Garde of the Chicano Movement in Texas*. Austin: University of Texas Press, 1995.

Neth, Mary. *Preserving the Family Farm: Women, Community, and the Foundations of Agribusiness in the Midwest, 1900–1940*. Baltimore: The Johns Hopkins University Press, 1995.

Ngai, Mae M. *Impossible Subjects: Illegal Aliens and the Making of Modern America*. Princeton: Princeton University Press, 2004.

Norquest, Carrol. *Rio Grande Wetbacks: Mexican Migrant Workers*. Albuquerque: University of New Mexico Press, 1972.

Norris, Jim. *North for the Harvest: Mexican Workers, Growers, and the Sugar Beet Industry*. Saint Paul: Minnesota Historical Society Press, 2009.

Nugent, Walter. *Into the West: The Story of Its People*. New York: Alfred A. Knopf, 1999.

Olmstead, Frederick Law. *A Journey through Texas: or, A Saddle-Trip on the Southwestern Frontier*. Edited by Randolph B. Campbell. Dallas: William P. Clements Center for Southwest Studies, 2004.

Orozco, Cynthia E. *No Mexicans, Women, or Dogs Allowed: The Rise of the Mexican American Civil Rights Movement*. Austin: University of Texas Press, 2009.

Osante, Patricia. *Origenes del Nuevo Santander, 1748–1772*. Ciudad Victoria: Instituto de Investigaciones Históricas, Universidad Autónoma de México, 1997.

Paredes, Américo. *George Washington Gómez: A Mexicotexan Novel*. Houston: Arte Público Press, 1990.

Passi, Anssi. "A Border Theory: An Unattainable Dream or a Realistic Aim for Border Scholars?" In *The Ashgate Research Companion to Border Studies*. Edited by Doris Wastl-Walter. Surrey, England: Ashgate Publishing, 2011.

Peck, Gunther. *Reinventing Free Labor: Padrones and Immigrant Workers in the North American West, 1880–1930*. Cambridge: Cambridge University Press, 2000.

Phillips, John Nieto. *Language of Blood: The Making of Spanish-American Identity in New Mexico, 1880s-1930s*. Albuquerque: University of New Mexico Press, 2004.

Phillips, Michael. *White Metropolis: Race, Ethnicity, and Religion in Dallas, 1841–2001*. Austin: University of Texas Press, 2006.

Pierce, Frank C. *A Brief History of the Lower Rio Grande Valley*. Menasha, TX: George Banta Publishing Company, 1917.

Pope, Dorothy Lee. *Rainbow Era of the Rio Grande*. Brownsville, TX: Springman-King Company, 1971.

Postel, Charles. *The Populist Vision*. New York: Oxford University Press, 2007.

Quezada, J. Gilberto. *Border Boss: Manuel B. Bravo and Zapata County*. College Station: Texas A&M University Press, 1999.

Ramos, Raúl. *Beyond the Alamo: Forging Mexican Ethnicity in San Antonio, 1821–1861*. Chapel Hill: University of North Carolina Press, 2008.

Rankin, Melinda. *Twenty Years among the Mexicans: A Narrative of Missionary Labor*. Edited by Miguel Ángel González-Quiroga and Timothy Paul Bowman. Dallas: Clements Center for Southwest Studies, 2008.

Reséndez, Andrés. *A Land So Strange: The Epic Journey of Cabeza de Vaca*. New York: Basic Books, 2007.

———. *Changing National Identities at the Frontier: Texas and New Mexico, 1800–1850*. Cambridge: Cambridge University Press, 2005.

Richardson, Chad, and Michael J. Pisani. *The Informal and Underground Economy of the South Texas Border*. Austin: University of Texas Press, 2012.

Richmond, Douglas W. *The Mexican Nation: Historical Continuity and Modern Change*. Upper Saddle River, NJ: Prentice Hall, 2002.

Rio Grande Roundup: A Story of Texas Tropical Borderland. Mission, TX: Border Kingdom Press, 1980.

Robles, Vito Alessio. *Coahuila y Texas: Desde la consumación de la independencia hasta el tratado de paz de Guadalupe Hidalgo*. México, DF: Porrúa, 1946.

Roots by the River: A Story of Texas Tropical Borderland. Canyon: Staked Plains Press, 1978.

Sabol, Steven. "Comparing American and Russian Internal Colonization: The 'Touch of Civilisation' on the Sioux and Kazakhs." *Western Historical Quarterly* 43, no. 1 (Spring 2012): 29–51.

Sackman, Douglas C. *Orange Empire: California and the Fruits of Eden*. Berkeley: University of California Press, 2005.

Sánchez, George J. *Becoming Mexican American: Ethnicity, Culture, and Identity in Chicano Los Angeles, 1900–1945*. New York: Oxford University Press, 1993.

Sandos, James. *Rebellion in the Borderlands: Anarchism and the Plan of San Diego, 1904–1923*. Norman: University of Oklahoma Press, 1992.

Schmidly, David J. *Texas Natural History: A Century of Change*. Lubbock: Texas Tech University Press, 2002.

Shockley, John Staples. *Chicano Revolt in a Texas Town*. Notre Dame: University of Notre Dame Press, 1974.

Silva-Bewley, S. Zulema. *The Legacy of John H. Shary: Promotion and Land Development*. Edinburg: University of Texas–Pan American Press, 2001.

Smith, Henry Nash. "Rain Follows the Plow: The Notion of Increased Rainfall for the Great Plains, 1844–1880." *Huntington Library Quarterly* 10, no. 2 (February 1947): 169–93.

Stambaugh, Lee J., and Lillian J. Stambaugh. *The Lower Rio Grande Valley of Texas*. San Antonio: The Naylor Company, 1954.

Starr, Kevin. *Inventing the Dream: California through the Progressive Era.* New York: Oxford University Press, 1985.

Stilwell, Hart. *Border City.* Garden City, NJ: Doubleday, Doran and Company, 1945.

Street, Richard Steven. "The Economist as Humanist: The Career of Paul S. Taylor." *California History* 58, no. 4 (Winter 1979–80): 350–61.

Taylor, Paul S. *An American-Mexican Frontier: Nueces County, Texas.* Chapel Hill: University of North Carolina Press, 1934.

Terkel, Studs. *Hard Times: An Oral History of the Great Depression.* 2nd ed. New York: The New Press, 1986.

Thompson, Jerry D. *Cortina: Defending the Mexican Name in Texas.* College Station: Texas A&M University Press, 2007.

Tijerina, Andrés. *Tejano Empire: Life on the South Texas Ranchos.* College Station: Texas A&M University Press, 1998.

Truett, Samuel. *Fugitive Landscapes: The Forgotten History of the U.S.-Mexico Borderlands.* New Haven: Yale University Press, 2006.

———, and Elliott Young, eds. *Continental Crossroads: Remapping U.S.-Mexico Borderlands History.* Durham: Duke University Press, 2004.

Tuchman, Barbara. *The Zimmerman Telegram.* New York: Random House, 1985.

Urrea, Luis Alberto. *Nobody's Son: Notes from an American Life.* Tucson: University of Arizona Press, 2002.

Valerio-Jimenez, Omar S. *River of Hope: Forging Identity and Nation in the Rio Grande Borderlands.* Durham: Duke University Press, 2013.

Vargas, Zaragosa, ed. *Major Problems in Mexican-American History.* Boston: Houghton Mifflin Company, 1999.

Vaught, David. *Cultivating California: Growers, Specialty Crops, and Labor, 1875–1920.* Baltimore: The Johns Hopkins University Press, 1999.

Vázquez, Francisco H., and Rodolfo Torres, eds. *Latina/o Thought: Culture, Politics, and Society.* Lanham, MD.: Rowman and Littlefield Publishers, 2003.

Vázquez, Josefina Zoraida. "La Supuesta República del Río Grande." *Historia Mexicana* 36 (1986): 49–80.

Vila, Pablo. *Border Identifications: Narratives of Religion, Gender, and Class on the U.S.-Mexico Border.* Austin: University of Texas Press, 2005.

Wallace, Lucy H. "They Led the Way: Colonizers of the Delta." In *Gift of the Rio: Story of Texas' Tropical Borderland.* Mission, TX: Border Kingdom Press, 1975.

Walsh, Casey. *Building the Borderlands: A Transnational History of Irrigated Cotton along the Mexico-Texas Border.* College Station: Texas A&M University Press, 2008.

Wastl-Walter, Doris. *The Ashgate Research Companion to Border Studies.* Surrey, England: Ashgate, 2011.

Weber, David J. *The Spanish Frontier in North America.* New Haven: Yale University Press, 1992.

———. *The Mexican Frontier, 1821–1846: The American Southwest under Mexico.* Albuquerque: University of New Mexico Press, 1982.

———, ed. *Foreigners in Their Native Land: Historical Roots of the Mexican Americans.* Albuquerque: University of New Mexico Press, 1973.

Westrup, Tomás Martin. *Principios: Relato de la introducción del Evangelio en México,* ed. Enrique Tomás Westrup. Monterrey, Mexico, 1948.

White, Richard. *Railroaded: The Transcontinentals and the Making of Modern America.* New York: W. W. Norton and Company, 2011.

———. *The Middle Ground: Indians, Empires, and Republics in the Great Lakes Region, 1650–1815.* Cambridge: Cambridge University Press, 1991.

———. *"It's Your Misfortune and None of My Own": A New History of the American West.* Norman: University of Oklahoma Press, 1991.

Wiebe, Robert H. *The Search for Order, 1877–1920.* New York: Hill and Wang, 1967.

Wilentz, Sean. *The Rise of American Democracy: Jefferson to Lincoln.* New York: W. W. Norton and Company, 2005.

Woolley, Benjamin. *Savage Kingdom: The True Story of Jamestown, 1607, and the Settlement of America.* New York: HarperCollins, 2007.

Wrobel, David M. *Promised Lands: Promotion, Memory, and the Creation of the American West.* Lawrence: University Press of Kansas, 2002.

Wyman, Mark. *Hoboes: Bindlestiffs, Fruit Tramps, and the Harvesting of the West.* New York: Hill and Wang, 2010.

Young, Elliot. *Catarino Garza's Revolution on the Texas-Mexico Border.* Durham: Duke University Press, 2004.

Zamora, Emilio. "Labor Formation, Community and Politics: The Mexican Working Class in Texas, 1900–1945." In *Border Crossings: Mexican and Mexican-American Workers.* Edited by John Mason Hart. Wilmington: Scholarly Resource Books, 1998.

———. *The World of the Mexican Worker in Texas.* College Station: Texas A&M University Press, 1993.

Zhurzhenko, Tatiana. "Borders and Memory." In *The Ashgate Research Companion to Border Studies.* Edited by Doris Wastl-Walter. Surrey, England: Ashgate Publishing, 2011.

Theses and Dissertations

Alamillo, José. "Bitter-Sweet Communities: Mexican Workers and Citrus Growers on the California Landscape." PhD diss., University of California, Irvine, 2000.

Bowman, Timothy Paul. "What About Texas? The Forgotten Cause of Antonio Orendain and the Rio Grande Valley Farm Workers, 1966–1982." Master's thesis, University of Texas at Arlington, 2005.

Douglas, Louva Myrtis. "The History of the Agricultural Fairs of Texas." Master's thesis, University of Texas, 1943.

Foscue, Edwin J. "Agricultural Geography of the Lower Rio Grande Valley of Texas." PhD diss., Clark University, 1931.

Graf, Leroy P. "The Economic History of the Lower Rio Grande Valley, 1820–1875." PhD diss., Harvard University, 1942.

Hill, James Edwin, Jr. "The Texas Citrus Industry." PhD diss., University of Tennessee, 1963.

Hutchings, Robert Max. "From Oranges to Orange Juice: A History of Florida's Indian River Growing Region." Master's thesis, North Dakota State University, 2008.

Martínez, Camilo Amado, Jr. "The Mexican and Mexican-American Laborers in the Lower Rio Grande Valley of Texas, 1870–1930." PhD diss., Texas A&M University, 1987.

Matthews, William Kenneth. "A History of Irrigation in the Lower Rio Grande Valley." Master's thesis, University of Texas at Austin, 1938.

Meador, Bruce S. "Wetback Labor in the Lower Rio Grande Valley." Undergraduate thesis, University of Texas, 1951.

Moses, Vincent. "The Flying Wedge of Cooperation: G. Harold Powell, California Orange Growers, and the Corporate Reconstruction of American Agriculture." PhD diss., University of California, Riverside, 1994.

Parrish, G. C. "A History of the Rio Grande Valley Citrus Industry." Master's thesis, Texas College of Arts and Industries, 1940.

Pastrano, José. "Industrial Agriculture in the Peripheral South: State, Race, and the Politics of Migrant Labor in Texas, 1890–1930." PhD diss., University of California, Santa Barbara, 2006.

Rakow, Mary Martina. "Melinda Rankin and Magdalen Hayden: Evangelical and Catholic Forms of Nineteenth Century Christian Spirituality." PhD diss., Boston College, 1982.

Ridout, Joseph B. "An Anti-National Disorder: Antonio Canales and Northeastern Mexico, 1836–1852." Master's thesis, University of Texas at Austin, 1994.

Roderick, Marshall. "The 'Box Bill': Public Policy, Ethnicity, and Economic Exploitation in Texas." Master's thesis, Texas State University, 2011.

Vigness, David M. "The Republic of the Rio Grande: An Example of Separatism in Northern Mexico." PhD diss., University of Texas, 1951.

Winn, Charles Carr. "Mexican Americans in the Texas Labor Movement." PhD diss., Texas Christian University, 1972.

Zamora, Emilio. "Mexican Labor Activity in South Texas." PhD diss., University of Texas at Austin, 1983.

Online Sources

Bracero History Archive. http://braceroarchive.org/.

Cameron County Historical Commission. www.cchc.us/home.html.

Handbook of Texas Online. Texas State Historical Association. http://www.tsha online.org/handbook/online.

Internet Movie Database. http://www.imdb.com/.

Journal of the Life and Culture of San Antonio. http://www.uiw.edu/sanantonio/.

New York Times. http://www.nytimes.com/.

Portal to Texas History. University of North Texas. http://texashistory.unt.edu/.

Tejano Voices, University of Texas at Arlington Library. http://library.uta.edu/tejano voices/.

Texas Observer. http://www.texasobserver.org.

Periodicals

California Citrograph
Liberation
McAllen Daily Monitor
Port Isabel Pilot
San Juan Sentinel
Texas Citriculture
Texas Farming and Citriculture
Valley Evening Monitor

INDEX